Corpus Approaches to Discourse in Forensic and Legal Contexts

This book is the first of its kind to bridge the gap between corpus linguistics and forensic linguistics, illustrating the value of applying corpus linguistic data, tools, and methods in the analysis of language in the law, evidence, crime, and justice.

The volume begins by taking stock of the use of corpus linguistics in the field of forensic and legal linguistics over its roughly thirty-year history as a foundation for critically reflecting on the current state-of play within the discipline. Wright uses this discussion as a jumping-off point from which to demonstrate the opportunities and challenges of using corpora and corpus methods to analyse language in legal and forensic contexts and offers possible solutions to collecting and analysing types of data that are typically not in the public domain. The four analysis chapters that follow apply corpus methods to both established and emerging areas of forensic and legal linguistics, summarized in a concluding chapter which also looks ahead to future directions for the interface of the two fields.

This book will be key reading for graduate students and researchers in forensic linguistics and corpus linguistics methods as well as scholars working across disciplines interested in the intersection between language and the law.

David Wright is an Associate Professor in Linguistics at Nottingham Trent University in the United Kingdom.

Routledge Advances in Corpus Linguistics
Edited by Tony McEnery, Lancaster University, UK
Michael Hoey, Liverpool University, UK

24 The Religious Rhetoric of U.S. Presidential Candidates
A Corpus Linguistics Approach to the Rhetorical God Gap
Arnaud Vincent

25 Using Corpus Methods to Triangulate Linguistic Analysis
Edited by Jesse Egbert and Paul Baker

26 Overcoming Challenges in Corpus Construction
The Spoken British National Corpus 2014
Robbie Love

27 Corpora in ESP/EAP Writing Instruction
Preparation, Exploitation, Analysis
Edited by Maggie Charles and Ana Frankenberg-Garcia

28 The Register-Functional Approach to Grammatical Complexity
Theoretical Foundation, Descriptive Research Findings, Application
Douglas Biber, Bethany Gray, Shelley Staples, Jesse Egbert

29 Multifunctionality in English
Corpora, Language and Academic Literacy Pedagogy
Edited by Zihan Yin and Elaine Vine

30 Corpus Approaches to Language in Social Media
Matteo Di Cristofaro

31 Corpus Approaches to Discourse in Forensic and Legal Contexts
David Wright

For more information about this series, please visit: https://www.routledge.com/Routledge-Advances-in-Corpus-Linguistics/book-series/SE0593

Corpus Approaches to Discourse in Forensic and Legal Contexts

David Wright

Routledge
Taylor & Francis Group
NEW YORK AND LONDON

First published 2025
by Routledge
605 Third Avenue, New York, NY 10158

and by Routledge
4 Park Square, Milton Park, Abingdon, Oxon, OX14 4RN

Routledge is an imprint of the Taylor & Francis Group, an informa business

Library of Congress Cataloging-in-Publication Data
Names: Wright, David (Linguistics teacher) author.
Title: Corpus approaches to discourse in forensic and legal contexts / David Wright.
Description: Abingdon, Oxon [UK] ; New York, NY : Routledge, 2025. |
Series: Routledge advances in corpus linguistics |
Includes bibliographical references and index.
Identifiers: LCCN 2024043865 | ISBN 9780367819101 (hardback) |
ISBN 9781032974088 (paperback) | ISBN 9781003017301 (ebook)
Subjects: LCSH: Forensic linguistics. | Corpora (Linguistics) |
Law--Language. | Evidence, Expert. | Semantic (Law) | Grenfell Tower
(London, England)--Fire, 2017. | European Union--Great Britain.
Classification: LCC K2287.5 .W75 2025 | DDC 347/.067--dc23/eng/20241202
LC record available at https://lccn.loc.gov/2024043865

ISBN: 978-0-367-81910-1 (hbk)
ISBN: 978-1-032-97408-8 (pbk)
ISBN: 978-1-003-01730-1 (ebk)

DOI: 10.4324/9781003017301

Typeset in Sabon
by SPi Technologies India Pvt Ltd (Straive)

For my dad,
who asked me about this book every day
but never got to see it published.

Contents

Figures

Acknowledgements

I owe an enormous debt to my wife, my son and my parents for their unwavering patience and support as I worked on this book.

I would like to thank Linguistics students at Nottingham Trent University who, over the years, have seen and worked with various parts of the data used in this book, especially Roxanne Ablett, Elise Ewens, Natasha Jefferson, Selina Leung, Lena Maruhn, Ellie-Jayne Richardson and Holly Sampson, who helped me collect it. I would also like to thank Dr Ikechukwu E. Onyenwe, who collected the pick-up artist data in his role as a British Academy–funded Research Assistant. I am grateful to the School of Arts and Humanities at Nottingham Trent University for granting me a year-long sabbatical that gave me the time to write much of this book.

I would like to thank Elysse Preposi and Jasmine Erice-Harling from Routledge for their tireless help and guidance throughout the writing and publication of the book. I am very grateful to Professor Tony McEnery, Professor Michael Hoey and Dr Jesse Egbert for welcoming this book into their series *Routledge Advances in Corpus Linguistics*. I am thankful to the anonymous reviewers who provided their expert opinion on the proposal and manuscript for this book.

I am grateful to the audiences at conferences where I have presented various pieces of this work over the years, who have helped shape my thinking about the data. Finally, I would like to extend specific thanks to Dr Alison May, who introduced me to forensic linguistics as an undergraduate student in 2007. I am sure that almost every idea I have about forensic or legal linguistics has its origins somewhere in those early days at Leeds.

1 Introduction

Forensic, legal and corpus linguistics

This book sits at the intersection of corpus linguistics, forensic linguistics and legal linguistics. For that reason, perhaps the best place to start is with straightforward definitions of these fields, at least insofar as how they are characterised in this book. In this book, the use of *corpus linguistics* is line with Baker's (2023: 1) definition:

> it is about using *corpora* (large bodies of naturally occurring language data stored on computers) and corpus processes (computational procedures which manipulate this data in various ways) in order to uncover linguistic patterns which can enable us to make sense of the ways that language is used in the construction of discourses.

Corpus linguistics is therefore applied here as a methodology for studying 'language based on examples of real-life language use' (McEnery and Wilson 2001: 2). In this book, the language under examination is that which appears in legal and forensic contexts. This brings us to the fields of forensic linguistics and legal linguistics. *Forensic linguistics* refers to the analysis of language as evidence in criminal or civil cases and to work undertaken by linguists as expert witnesses for the police, security services and the courts, including research related to such work. *Legal linguistics*, by contrast, refers to the study of the language of the law and the language of the legal process. These two endeavours are often considered as two complementary parts within the overarching field of 'forensic linguistics', which serves as an umbrella term for all areas of work in language, law and evidence (e.g. Coulthard et al. 2017, 2021). Recently, there have been arguments in favour of separating these subdisciplines and reflecting this separation by using different names to refer to them (e.g. Guillén-Nieto and Stein 2022: 3). This book refers to both 'forensic linguistics' and 'legal linguistics' throughout, not to make a particularly impassioned contribution to this

DOI: 10.4324/9781003017301-1

emerging debate but rather because it is a convenient distinction to help describe the types of data analysed in its chapters (see Wright and Picornell [2024] for a more detailed discussion on this point).

Corpus linguistics played a central role in the origins of forensic linguistics. It was the methodology used by Svartvik (1968) in his analysis of statements allegedly given to the police by Timothy Evans in the U.K. (the so-called 'Evans Statements'), which is generally accepted as being the first published use of the term 'forensic linguistics'. Corpus methods were also applied by Malcom Coulthard in the analysis of the infamous case of Derek Bentley, who was wrongly convicted and executed on the basis of the content of a witness statement that he allegedly gave to police. Coulthard's (1994) report of this analysis was published in the first issue of the journal *Forensic Linguistics* (now called *The International Journal of Speech, Language and the Law*) and represents a watershed moment in the formalisation of forensic linguistics as a discipline. Now, some thirty years after Coulthard's seminal analysis, corpus linguistics is pervasive in forensic and legal linguistics. Given the complementary qualitative and quantitative perspectives they provide, corpus methods have become an integral part of the toolkit for those analysing language in legal and evidential contexts (Coulthard et al. 2017: 26).

Aims of this book

This book aims to make a significant contribution to the enhancement and advancement of corpus methods in forensic and legal linguistics. In doing so, it has four primary aims:

- To provide the most comprehensive survey to date of research in forensic and legal linguistics that has used corpus linguistics methods, identifying the main ways in which corpus linguistics has helped develop and expand the field.
- To reflect on the main considerations when building corpora for forensic or legal linguistic purposes, the challenges that working with forensic and legal corpora pose and proposing ways of addressing or circumnavigating those challenges.
- To apply methodologically transparent and theoretically underpinned corpus-assisted discourse analysis to provide brand-new insights into previously overlooked or under-researched forensic and legal genres and contexts, including opening statements, oral arguments in the most senior courts in the United Kingdom, an extreme misogynistic online community and the representation of law in the British press.
- To make tentative predictions about the future of corpus methods in forensic and legal linguistics.

Overview of the book

Chapter 2 provides details of the corpora and corpus linguistics methods employed in the analyses in the book. It gives an overview of the main challenges faced by forensic and legal linguists who wish to build their own specialised corpora. It then gives details of all of the corpora used in this book and how they can help overcome some of the major difficulties involved in compiling forensic and/or legal corpora: data scarcity and ethics and distressing data. It argues that the four corpora used in this book provide alternative sources or types of data for those working in forensic and legal linguistics and, in doing so, hopes to open new avenues of data collection for corpus-based work in the discipline. The chapter moves on to describe the corpus-assisted discourse studies (CADS) approach applied in the book. This starts by emphasising the core principles of CADS that have been followed and then discusses the technical aspects of the corpus techniques used.

Chapter 3 provides the most comprehensive survey to date of research and casework in forensic and legal linguistics that has used corpus linguistics methods. It begins by detailing the role that corpus methods played in the analysis of the Evans Statements (Svartvik 1968) and in the Derek Bentley case (Coulthard 1994). It then provides a timeline of sorts, reflecting the growing status of corpora in forensic and legal linguistics, represented by commentaries from within the field. The majority of the chapter is dedicated to discussing the ways in which corpora and corpus methods have developed and expanded the field(s) of forensic and legal linguistics, particularly in terms of providing new perspectives on familiar forensic/legal genres, providing new solutions to methodological challenges and providing brand-new avenues for research.

Chapter 4 analyses the opening statements given by Core Participants in Phase 1 of the Grenfell Tower Inquiry. The quasi-legal nature of this public inquiry provides an opportunity to analyse 22 opening statements, each providing a different version of the same event(s) and each from a different perspective. The chapter begins with a description of the events of the Grenfell Tower fire and an overview of the public inquiry and the corpus used. It describes the nature and role of opening statements and provides a background of the previous legal and linguistic research that has examined the language of opening statements. The analysis in this chapter combines corpus linguistic analysis of self-mention keywords with the discourse-analytic theory of positioning, particularly in relation to how the legal counsel for the Core Participants position their client in terms of responsibility. The chapter proposes a new four-part model for allocating and managing responsibility in opening statements, which can be applied to opening statements either in other public inquiries or in criminal trials.

Chapter 5 examines the marking of stance in the High Court and Supreme Court hearings in the so-called 'Brexit case' in the U.K. Some legal genres, such as judicial opinions and written judgements, have regularly been subjected to stance analysis. Much less often analysed in this way are the mechanics of the interaction between speakers in this context. Further still, this chapter analyses the interaction between advocates and judges in court, which has received very little attention in the literature. The chapter begins by providing a brief background to the Brexit case, before summarising some theoretical understandings of stance and the methodological challenges involved in analysing it. After providing a background of the research into stance in the courtroom, the analysis focuses on keywords and collocates as signposts of stance-marking, focusing on modal, mental and speaking verbs. The analysis compares and contrasts the stance-making strategies of advocates and judges and reveals the ways in which their relative status and institutional rules of engagement influence their different approaches to signalling stance, providing new insight into the nature of interaction between advocates and judges in this high-stakes legal context.

Chapter 6 explores ideologies around sexual consent and resistance in a corpus comprising data from an online pick-up artist (PUA) forum. The chapter starts by discussing the importance of consent and resistance in the criminal justice system, including in police interviews and cross-examination of complainants in rape cases. It then introduces the PUA community as self-styled seduction experts and, against the backdrop of existing literature from linguistics and beyond on PUAs, demonstrates why such a corpus provides a useful space for analysing (mis)perceptions around consent. The corpus is described, and then the salience of the community-specific term 'LMR' ('last-minute resistance') in the corpus is revealed. A collocate analysis of 'LMR' gives rise to four emerging discourse prosodies which reflect the prevailing beliefs in the PUA community around the significance, interpretation and treatment of women's resistance to sex. This chapter therefore provides a welcome forensic and legal linguistic perspective on PUA discourse, particularly in relation to implications for the safety of women and girls.

The fourth analysis chapter of the book, Chapter 7, examines the ways in which new legislation is discursively represented in the British national press in the twenty years between 2000 and 2020. It sets the scene by discussing the relationship between the media and law, drawing on literature from linguistics, law, politics, journalism and media that has demonstrated the bidirectional influence that media and legal discourses have on each other and the role that the media has in influencing public opinion in legal issues. The corpus used in the analysis is described, and it is emphasised that this analysis is focused not on the representation of one specific new law but on new laws generally over two decades. In doing so, a new method of identifying and analysing arguments using corpus-assisted methods is proposed, combining collocation analysis with an established model for analysing argument patterns. Overall, eight argument schemes are identified that have shaped the reporting of new laws in the British press over this period.

Chapter 8 concludes the book, offering thoughts on the past, present and future of corpus approaches to discourse in forensic and legal contexts, making some tentative predictions about future directions and the implications that these will have for the discipline(s) of forensic and legal linguistics.

References

Baker, P. (2023) *Using Corpora in Discourse Analysis* (2nd ed.). London: Bloomsbury.

Coulthard, M. (1994) On the use of corpora in the analysis of forensic texts. *The International Journal of Speech, Language and the Law* 1(1): 27–43. 10.1558/ijsll.v1i1.27

Coulthard, M., Johnson, A. and Wright, D. (2017) *An Introduction to Forensic Linguistics: Language in Evidence* (2nd ed.). London: Routledge.

Coulthard, M., May, A. and Sousa-Silva, R. (eds.) (2021) *The Routledge Handbook of Forensic Linguistics* (2nd ed.). London: Routledge.

Guillén-Nieto, V. and Stein, D. (2022) Introduction: Theory and practice in forensic linguistics. In V. Guillén-Nieto and D. Stein (eds.), *Language as Evidence: Doing Forensic Linguistics*. Cham: Springer, pp. 1–32.

McEnery, T. and Wilson, A. (2001) *Corpus Linguistics: An Introduction* (2nd ed.). Edinburgh: Edinburgh University Press.

Svartvik, J. (1968) *The Evans Statements: A Case for Forensic Linguistics*. Göteborg: University of Gothenburg Press.

Wright, D. and Picornell, I. (2024) Semiotic perspectives on forensic and legal linguistics: unifying approaches in the language of the legal process and language in evidence. *International Journal for the Semiotics of Law* 37(2): 293–304. 10.1007/s11196-023-10094-z

2 Tools for the trade

Data and methods

The title of this chapter, 'Tools for the trade', borrows the name of Woolls and Coulthard's (1998) and Woolls's (2003) articles in which they introduce and demonstrate the use of a series of computer programs that, though not developed specifically for that purpose, could be used to analyse forensic texts. 'Tools' in the context of this chapter comprises two elements: the corpora that were collected and analysed for this book and the corpus-assisted approach to discourse that was used to analyse them. The chapter begins by outlining some of the issues and considerations in building corpora for forensic and legal linguistic purposes, before providing details of the corpora used in this book and how they go some way in navigating these issues. Then attention turns to the brand of corpus-assisted discourse analysis that is adopted in this book, including the corpus techniques of keyword, collocation and concordance analysis as well as the relationship between quantitative corpus-oriented analyses and theoretically underpinned and methodologically rigorous discourse analysis.

Corpora for forensic and legal linguistics

Most corpus-based studies in forensic and legal linguistics will rely on purpose-built corpora. Besides studies that use large-scale general corpora in determining the 'ordinary meaning' of a word used in the law (see Chapter 3 for examples of such studies), corpus linguistic research in forensic and legal contexts will generally make use of corpora built specifically to answer particular research question(s). Such corpora need to be built 'ad hoc' (Partington et al. 2013: 12), from scratch by the researcher, because the types of texts, topics and communicative contexts that forensic and legal linguistics often are focused on do not feature at all (not to mention at any great scale) in existing general corpora. Corpora of this kind are known as 'specialised corpora' in that they contain 'texts of one particular type so that the language relating to a particular topic, register or situation can be studied' (Hunston 2022: 21). Corpora can be specialised

DOI: 10.4324/9781003017301-2

along any number of parameters (Hunston 2022: 21). Flowerdew (2004: 21) identifies ways in which a corpus can be specialised, including the purpose for which it is collected, the context, setting, communicative purpose that it captures, the genre or discourse type of the texts it includes, or the subject matter covered. Forensic and legal linguistics, therefore, sees specialised corpora being built for purposes such as analysing authorship, capturing discourse in a particular legal setting (e.g. U.S. Supreme Court opinions), or analysing a particular type of illicit text (e.g. threats) or community (e.g. online sex offenders).

When designing and building specialised corpora in forensic and legal linguistics, researchers need to follow the basic guiding principles that are fundamental to building any corpus. There must be a match between the research questions and language being examined and the type of material being collected (Reppen 2022: 13), and because the corpus being used will influence the results obtained, it is imperative that sufficient time and attention be spent in planning and decision-making during corpus building (Egbert et al. 2020: 4). A key consideration is the authenticity of the data being collected. It is a core tenet of corpus linguistics that the language collected and analysed is 'real life' and 'naturally occurring' language, with minimal intervention by the researcher (McEnery and Wilson 2001: 19). Therefore, the texts included in a corpus for forensic or legal linguistics must be authentic samples of language used in the context under examination. Corpus builders also must take account of the representativeness of their corpus. That is, they must be sure of the extent to which the sample of data they collect includes and reflects the full range of variability within the space being sampled (Biber 1993: 244; McEnery and Hardie 2012: 8). Addressing questions of representativeness will also, as a consequence, dictate issues around the size and shape (or 'balance') of the corpus rather than these leading the decision-making themselves. Depending on the type of data being collected and the source from which it is collected, the processes of cleaning the corpus, stripping away material that is not needed for analysis, will need to factor into a researcher's planning. So too will the decision as to whether the analysis to be conducted will require the corpus to be marked up or annotated and the extent to which such annotation will be needed (e.g. for textual features such as headings and paragraphs or more fine-grained grammatical part-of-speech tagging). If the texts for inclusion in the corpus are not already digitised, then the researcher will need to consider the processes required for digitising texts ready to be processed by corpus tools and the issues that can arise in this process. For corpora with a spoken element, either entirely spoken or multimodal, the researcher will need to decide on the conventions and granularity of transcription required for the analysis and, if a transcript already exists in some form, its accuracy and appropriacy for (corpus) linguistic analysis will need to be evaluated.

Every researcher building a corpus will need to give some consideration to the permissions, ethics and copyright requirements and responsibilities involved. The ways in which these points were addressed in the building of the corpora for this book are outlined below and detailed in the relevant analysis chapters (see Hunston 2022: 30–46; Knight and Adolphs 2022; McEnery and Brookes 2022; Reppen 2022; Baker 2023: 55–80 for dedicated and detailed discussions of corpus design and building).

The use of specialised corpora has a number of benefits. Besides being necessary in many cases because the type of corpus needed to answer a research question simply does not exist (Baker 2023: 55), specialised corpora have the advantage of a 'much closer link between the corpus and the contexts in which the texts in the corpus were produced' (Koester 2022: 49). An understanding and appreciation of the context of the texts in a corpus will aid the researcher's interpretation of the data and make direct associations between the linguistic patterns identified and the social and cultural contexts from which the texts originated (Flowerdew 2008: 116). As emphasised by Brookes and Collins (2023: 40), the entire purpose of a corpus linguistic investigation is to find out something valuable about language and its users and the social contexts in which the language is being used. In forensic and legal linguistics, the motivation behind collecting and analysing a corpus is often to understand more fully the patterns that characterise language use in a particular setting. Maintaining a close relationship between texts and their contexts is therefore essential.

A full understanding of the contexts represented in a corpus is arguably most achievable when the researcher has compiled the corpus themselves. Using pre-existing specialised corpora which have been collected by someone else may put this close text/context relationship at risk. Recent years have seen a welcome and long-overdue increase in data sharing in forensic and legal linguistics. One notable example of this is the Forensic Linguistics Databank (FoLD; Petyko et al. 2022), an online repository, launched in 2021, created and hosted by the Aston Institute for Forensic Linguistics, which provides (controlled) access to forensic and forensically relevant texts and genres. Similarly, the Forensic Linguistics Data & Resources (ForensicLing.com) website maintained by Tammy Gales and Dakota Wing brings together links and signposts to a range of publicly available forensic and legal linguistics datasets, often from high-profile cases, providing access to data types such as ransom notes, threats, emergency calls and courtroom transcripts. In terms of more focused corpora, Davies (2018) has complied and made available a Corpus of U.S. Supreme Court Opinions. More recently still, Egbert and Wood (2023) have developed the Corpus of U.S. State Statutes (CorUSSS), making available the statutory code from all 50 U.S. states, some 1.7 million texts and 443 million words. All of these initiatives represent significant and valuable resources for forensic and legal linguists, particularly those with a corpus linguistic slant, and they provide access to datasets that will help sustain the application of corpus linguistics in the field. As is the case when using any pre-existing corpus, however (see Egbert et al. 2020: 15), it is essential that the researcher take the time to examine the texts, metadata and documentation to ensure that they are clear on what is contained in the corpus and that it is appropriate for their purposes.

Nevertheless, in the vast majority of cases, forensic and legal linguists need to design and build their own corpora. Oftentimes, owing to the types of text and context that are of interest to researchers in this area, this requires searching in 'dusty corners' of research (Marchi and Taylor 2018: 9–10), dealing with under-researched and overlooked topics and text types. This presents challenges to the forensic and legal corpus linguist that are not faced by most other corpus-based discourse analysts. McEnery et al. (2005: 71) refer to specialised corpora built by researchers 'going solo' as 'DIY corpora', or 'do-it-yourself' corpora. However, it can be very difficult for those working with forensic or legal corpora to go solo, not least due to the limited accessibility of the types of data that they are concerned with and the potentially distressing nature of the text themselves. These challenges are discussed in the next sections through the lens of the corpora used in this book.

The corpora used in this book

Each analysis chapter in this book (Chapters 4–7) uses a different corpus. The full details of the corpora are provided in the relevant chapter, but a general overview of the corpora is in Table 2.1. All four corpora are specialised corpora in that they all comprise specific but different text-types, they each contain data from a particular discourse community and they were all collected to help answer precise research questions and aims. Koester (2022: 50) notes that specialised corpora 'can vary considerably in size', and that is the case with those used here, which, incidentally, increase in size as the book progresses, from the Grenfell Tower Inquiry Opening Statement Corpus at just over 150,000 tokens to the New Laws in the News Corpus at over 59 million words. All of the corpora are publicly available, accessible through official websites in the case of the Grenfell Tower Inquiry and Brexit Hearings or as online and offline public discourses (albeit with very different 'publics' in mind) in the case of online forum posts and newspaper articles.

All of these corpora contain authentic, naturally occurring language used in context, with no intervention on my part. All of the texts in all of the corpora were available online, and no work was required to digitise them in preparation for corpus analysis. With regard to representativeness,

Table 2.1 An overview of the corpora used in this book

Chapter	*Corpus name*	*Size*	*Description*
Chapter 4	The Grenfell Tower Inquiry Opening Statement Corpus	22 texts 105,307 tokens	A corpus containing all of the opening statements from the Core Participants in Phase 1 of the Grenfell Tower Inquiry
Chapter 5	The Brexit Hearings Corpus	35 texts 298,297 tokens	A corpus containing all of the oral arguments submitted by both sides of the Brexit hearings in the High Court and Supreme Court of the U.K., as well as all of the interventions by judges.
Chapter 6	The Seduction Forum Corpus	25,788 texts 26,527,412 tokens	A corpus comprising posts from an online Pick-Up Artist Forum
Chapter 7	New Laws in the News Corpus	74,977 texts 59,221,058 tokens	A corpus comprising all articles from British national newspapers that mention 'new law(s)' or 'new legislation' between 2000 and 2020.

I set out with these corpora to be comprehensive. I collected all of the opening statements delivered by Core Participants in the Grenfell Tower Inquiry Phase 1; I included all of the transcripts for every day of the High Court and Supreme Court Brexit Hearings; I collected all of the threads and posts from the Seduction Forum Corpus (SFC); and I collected all of the news articles that mentioned 'new law(s)' or 'new legislation' in the British national press between 2000 and 2020. No generalisations are made about a population, discourse or particular contextual settings beyond those which are supported by the samples collected. For example, although the corpus of opening statements includes all of those delivered during the oral hearings of Phase 1, there is no claim that this corpus represents all opening statements in public inquiries or criminal or civil trials. Similarly, although the Brexit Hearings Corpus represents all of the data for those hearings, there are no claims that the linguistic patterns found are common to all High Court or Supreme Court Hearings.

In terms of annotation, only minimal annotation was added/retained and that was limited to contextual information required to interpret the data in the analysis phase. For the Grenfell Tower Inquiry Opening Statement Corpus, each opening statement was made by a single speaker, and so each was designated its own file and no mark-up was needed. With the Brexit Hearing Corpus, the transcript for each day of the High Court and Supreme Court hearings was saved in a different file, and in each, simple mark-up was retained showing the name of the speaker (i.e. the name of the judge or advocate). Both the opening statements and the Brexit hearings corpus were official transcripts provided to the public. However, transcripts of proceedings cannot necessarily be relied upon to be verbatim accounts of the talk (Tkačuková 2015: 151), so in the case of the opening statements and the Supreme Court transcripts, they were checked against the video recordings of the original speech on the official YouTube channel for the Inquiry and on the U.K. Supreme Court website respectively.

In terms of cleaning, the boilerplate metadata that is downloaded with each news article from Nexis UK was removed from the New Laws in the News Corpus, leaving only the headline and body of the article, and they were downloaded and organised in folders by newspaper and by year. The data for the SFC was collected from the forum using GNU wget web-scraping scripts, by Dr Ikechukwu Onyenwe, a research assistant on the British Academy–funded project for which this data was initially collected. The posts and threads themselves were downloaded with all of their accompanying metadata, including thread name and ID, so that posts from the same thread could be followed. The cleaning of the data also involved removing all of the web-associated HTML tags and removing duplicate text in instances where a reply had 'quoted' chunks of the original or another post. The usernames and 'reputation' levels of the posters were retained, but the usernames are not reproduced here.

Data scarcity in forensic and legal linguistics

It is widely acknowledged that there are difficulties involved in sourcing the types of texts and genres that forensic and legal linguists are traditionally interested in analysing. In legal contexts, while some types of data, such as publicly available legislative texts or judicial opinions, are available in abundance, others, such as police interview or courtroom trial data, are far more difficult to access, for reasons of confidentiality or cost. Similarly, in a forensic context, again for reasons related to the protection of those involved, forensic linguists are often prohibited from publishing the data that they have analysed in cases. Therefore, there is undoubtedly a data scarcity issue in forensic and legal linguistics, and those new to the discipline (and some of those not so new to it) may quickly discover that they are not able to collect large amounts of the type of data that they wish to. As Heydon (2019: 139) states, 'one of the first problems encountered by linguists embarking on a research career in forensic applications of language analysis is the difficulty of obtaining data'.

The scarcity of data is well reported in the literature. In describing the amount of data typically made available to the linguist working on a case, Cotterill (2010: 578) laments, '[u]nfortunately, and frustratingly for the forensic linguist, any old collection of texts is precisely what is provided by either the police or solicitors'. In Wright (2021: 611), I make the sweeping assertion that 'the types of data that forensic linguists work with are often not in abundance' (Wright 2021: 611). Nini (2021) agrees, albeit with more nuance, that the 'problem' of dealing with the type of texts involved in investigative forensic linguistics 'is their rarity and sensitivity, which makes the collection of large and balanced corpora nearly impossible'. Likewise, Gillings (2022: 598) notes that given the highly sensitive nature of forensic and legal language data, 'accessing further data may be, at best, difficult or, at worst, unethical'. It is clear, therefore, that the construction of forensic and legal linguistic corpora is 'determined, influenced and *limited* by the data and resources available' (Larner 2015: 133, my emphasis). For Kredens and Coulthard (2012: 511), the difficulty in obtaining relevant data represents a 'cause for concern' in the otherwise rapid growth of corpus applications in forensic and legal contexts.

However, as the range of studies discussed in Chapter 3 shows, corpus approaches in forensic and legal linguistics are very common. Therefore, corpus approaches are being widely and fruitfully applied in forensic and legal linguistics, despite the challenges posed by data restrictions and inaccessibility. Data-sharing initiatives such as FoLD, ForensicLing.com and the corpora such as those compiled by Davies (2018) and Egbert and Wood (2023) mentioned above go some way in easing some of these pressures. As well as interventions such as these, the application of corpora and corpus linguistics can be accelerated by individual researchers, 'doing-it-themselves'. In some instances, for example, it has been possible for researchers to publish data and/or details from forensic cases, or the evidence in those cases may already be in the public domain (e.g. Grant 2017; MacLeod 2024). In other cases, notoriously expensive data, such as courtroom transcripts, can be obtained as part of large-scale funded projects (e.g. Jackson et al. 2024; Wright et al. 2025). Other times, corpus approaches to legal linguistics draws on legal discourse that is already in the public domain, such as (inter) national laws, judgements and other written legal genres (e.g. Biel 2015; Trklja and McAuliffe 2019; Cheng et al. 2021) or high-profile criminal proceedings (e.g. Cotterill 2003; Szczyrbak 2020). Elsewhere, forensic and legal linguists have benefitted from the availability of data that has been published for reasons that are not to do with linguistics but can be examined for linguistic purposes, ranging from small-scale 'raw' datasets (e.g. Chiang and Grant 2017; Wright 2017) to large-scale funded data digitisation projects (e.g. Johnson 2015, 2018). Nevertheless, in some cases, there is no alternative but for researchers starting from scratch to build the type of corpus that they need to answer their research questions (e.g. Nini 2017; Clarke 2019).

Overcoming data scarcity

The four corpora collected and analysed in this book navigate the usual issues of data scarcity and inaccessibility in different ways and hopefully show how such data has much to offer forensic and legal linguistic research.

Quasi-legal data: The Grenfell Tower Inquiry Opening Statement Corpus

As has been noted above and elsewhere, access to courtroom data is extremely limited because of its highly institutionalised and sensitive nature, strict confidentiality and data protection requirements and the very high costs of transcription services (Tkačuková 2015: 150; Petyko et al. 2022: 11). Public inquiries are part of the political rather than the legal process. They are inquisitorial rather than adversarial, there are no 'sides' or 'parties' and the inquiry's role is not to 'make a determination between the different viewpoints and positions of opposing parties' but instead is to 'investigate the evidence and to follow lines of inquiry where they lead' (Ireton 2023: 215). Moreover, 'they have no power to determine civil or criminal liability, nor can they impose sanctions on any individual or organisation' (Ireton 2023: 215). Having said that, public inquiries have been described as 'quasi-legal' in their format, with an 'adversarial climate' (Stark 2018: 50) and as 'quasi-judicial bodies' (Ireton 2018). Ireton (2018: 280) outlines a number of ways in which 'the powers and procedures of public inquiries resemble those of a court process': they analyse large quantities of evidence, they establish fact and determine accountability, many involve evidence being taken during oral hearings on oath, most are chaired by a judge, retired judge or senior member of the legal profession, with Counsel and a Solicitor to the Inquiry appointed, and some are even held in court buildings. These similarities 'blur the lines' between a political and legal process (Ireton 2023: 228), and it may be the case that if the public are to have confidence in the quasi-judicial process of inquiries, then they must be 'seen to be procedurally and substantively fair in the same way as for the civil and criminal court processes' (Ireton 2018: 280). One element of the processes for both public inquiries and legal proceedings is that of opening statements. In trials in England and Wales, the prosecution side are given the opportunity to provide a summary of the evidence in an opening statement. (In other jurisdictions, such as the United States, both the prosecution and defence give opening statements.) In the Grenfell Tower Inquiry, there were opening statements given by all 22 of the Core

Participants, including the Counsel to the Inquiry. Whereas a trial would include one such statement, here we have 22, all offering different versions and perspectives on the same event(s). And, unlike costly and inaccessible courtroom transcripts, the public inquiry provides publicly and freely accessible data to learn more about this (quasi-)legal discourse.

Opportunistic legal data: The Brexit Hearings Corpus

Unlike the Grenfell Tower Inquiry Opening Statement Corpus, the Brexit Hearings Corpus does not represent a quasi-legal genre. Rather, it captures discourse in two of the highest courts in the U.K.: the High Court of England and Wales (King's Bench Division, Administrative Court) and the United Kingdom Supreme Court (the final court in the U.K. system). Although in some ways these courts are more open and transparent to the public than 'lower' crown courts (see below for a discussion of the live streaming and recording of hearings), their process could arguably be considered more opaque and more mysterious to the public than typical criminal courts (e.g. very few televised legal dramas focus on the workings of these higher courts). Therefore, this corpus provides 'a valuable case study in the practice of advocacy' (Wright et al. 2022: 12). In a break from the norm and given the significance public and legal interest in the Brexit hearings, their transcripts were made freely accessible online. The proceedings of high-profile cases are commonly made available to the public in other jurisdictions such as the United States but rarely does this occur in the U.K. Therefore, the fact that this data is available for (corpus) linguistic analysis in this book is, simply, lucky. Partington et al. (2013: 9) write of 'serendipity' in corpus-assisted discourse analysis in that the observation of authentic data can lead to the 'chancing upon hitherto unforeseen phenomena'. The same might be said of data such as the Brexit hearing transcripts; the availability of data can be serendipitous, too. These transcripts therefore can be considered an 'opportunistic' corpus (McEnery and Hardie 2012: 11), not only in the sense that they 'represent nothing more nor less than the data that it was possible to gather' but also in the sense that it was only possible to gather the data at all as a result of external, timely and fortunate circumstances.

Potentially illicit data on the 'clear' web: The Seduction Forum Corpus

The 'clear' web, also known as the 'surface' web or 'clearnet', refers to the publicly accessible areas of the internet that can be accessed on any normal web browser and that are indexed by normal search engines. It can be contrasted with the 'dark web', which is a network of heavily encrypted websites, chatrooms and forums which requires special network-routing software (most popularly The Onion Router, or 'Tor') to access and which enables users to communicate and conduct transactions anonymously without revealing their location. Criminals exploit the increased levels of anonymisation on the dark web to commit serious criminal offences with new levels of protection against detection by law enforcement (Chiang et al. 2020; Davies 2020). There is a growing amount of (forensic) linguistic research that analyses data collected from the dark web (e.g. Chiang 2020, 2024; Chiang et al. 2020). However, there are many reasons why researchers may not want to work with dark web data, not least to protect themselves from particularly distressing or disturbing illegal material or, if they publish a paper exposing criminal activity, to avoid a potential risk of retaliation from criminals. More practically, university information technology (IT) policies and regulations may not facilitate research on the dark web and associated illegal content (e.g. University of Oxford 2021), and disciplinary guidelines as yet offer no specific direction on using software such as Tor (Franzke et al. 2019: 79). The manosphere, of which the pick-up artist community and the SFC are part, can be thought of as sitting in the 'murky space' where the line between the clear and dark web is blurred (Copland 2021: 719). The manosphere, as a sub-culture of interconnected misogynist online communities, is characterised by 'cyberhate' (Bacigalupo et al. 2022), in which men are radicalised to violent extremism (Kennedy-Kollar 2024) and the 'online sharing of beliefs cannot be easily removed from the potential for offline action' (Krendel 2021: 113). Previous work analysing the SFC, for example, has found potential instances of incitement of violence against women and girls (Wright 2024). Therefore, the use of the SFC in this book demonstrates that certain online spaces and communities on the clear web can allow the linguist to examine forensically relevant discourse without taking the added risks and/or overcoming logistical challenges of working in/on the dark web.

Language about the law: New Laws in the News Corpus

The corpus collected for the fourth and final analysis chapter comprises U.K. national news articles that mention 'new law(s)' or 'new legislation' over a twenty-year period, with a view to better understanding how legal changes are represented by the British press. This corpus is unlike the others in this book as it does not comprise (quasi-)legal or potentially forensically relevant discourse. In fact, one may question whether this is a 'forensic' or 'legal' corpus at all; it does not consist of written or spoken genres as part of the legal system, nor does it contain illegal or illicit texts. That is, it is neither language of the law and the legal process, nor is it language as evidence. Rather, it is language *about* the law. Previous research has shown the benefits of analysing language about the law, including media representations of the police and prison (e.g. Mayr and Machin 2011), the construction of offenders and victims in newspaper reports (Tabbert 2016; Bartley 2023), the representation of crime across fictional and non-fictional genres (e.g. Douthwaite and Tabbert 2022), and reader evaluations of sentencing in below-the-line comments (Wright forthcoming). News stories about crime and the law 'serve important social, cultural, political, economic and moral purposes' (Mayr and Machin 2011: 2) and act as a proxy for people's personal contact with the legal system (Gies 2007: 1–2). Grant and MacLeod (2020: 2) state that the aim of forensic linguistics is to improve the delivery of justice through the analysis of language. The analysis in Chapter 7 shows the ways in which the ideological representation of the law by the media can influence and obscure people's (mis)understanding of the law and the legal process and, in turn, argues that this serves as a barrier to justice. The broader point here is that corpora that do not necessarily fit the profile of 'forensic' or 'legal' data but instead focus on language about the law, can be used to make important contributions to the aims of the field.

Ethics and distressing data

As is the case with all specialised corpus building, those building corpora for forensic and legal linguistic purposes need to ensure that their corpus design and process take account of the ethical implications involved in their collection and publication of the data they are using. In terms of the corpora used in this book, they all draw on data that was in the public domain at the time of collection and therefore was not subject to any particularly prohibitive ethical or copyright conditions. Nevertheless, for all of the four corpora there were important considerations to be made around these issues.

The Grenfell Tower Inquiry Opening Statement Corpus (used in Chapter 4) contains opening statements that were made publicly available as part of the public inquiry into the Grenfell Tower fire in June 2017. The Grenfell Tower Inquiry and Opus 2 International Limited (the owner of the copyright in the public transcripts[1]) grant license for using the transcripts commercially and non-commercially. Generally speaking, public inquiry material is owned by the Crown and is made available for public use in the interests of openness and transparency. In addition to the transcripts I collected for my corpus, video recordings of the opening statements are available on the inquiry YouTube channel (https://www.youtube.com/c/GrenfellTowerInquiry/videos). However, public inquiries are subject to conflicting interests of those involved as survivors, bereaved and family members, the Government, the media, legal representatives and academics, many of whom can be seen to influence the scope and running of the inquiry, the role and function of inquiries and shaping expectations of what they can and cannot deliver (Ireton 2023). To avoid any possibility that the research here intended to make any such politicised intervention, only the opening statements from Phase 1 of the Inquiry were collected and analysed here. Phase 1 concluded in December 2018 and the final Phase 1 report was published in October 2019, before the work started on this chapter. Phase 2 was ongoing at the time, but that concluded in June 2022, and the report was published in September 2024.

The Brexit Hearings Corpus (Chapter 5) benefits from the same public availability in the interests of procedural transparency as the Grenfell Tower Inquiry data. This corpus comprises two sub-corpora: one from hearings in the High Court (Administrative Court) of England and Wales and one from hearings in the U.K. Supreme Court. Sittings in the Supreme Court are live-streamed, recorded and made available on the Supreme Court website 'for the sole purpose of the fair and accurate reporting of the judicial proceedings of the Supreme Court' (https://www.supremecourt.uk/). The Administrative Court, a specialist court within the King's Bench Division of the High Court of Justice, does not stream or record proceedings for the public. Neither court routinely makes transcripts of hearings publicly available. However, given the public interest in *R v Secretary of State for Exiting the European Union* (the so-called 'Brexit case'), the decision was made to publish transcripts. This decision helped overcome the general inaccessibility of courtroom data.

The New Laws in the News Corpus (Chapter 7) is compiled of news articles downloaded from the database Nexis UK. Given their political and societal influence, and the relative ease with which they can be collected, news articles have typically featured heavily in corpus-assisted discourse studies (CADS) (Gillings et al. 2023: 11). Nexis UK is a popular subscription-based resource which allows for the download of digitised international news articles (Baker 2023: 63). At the time of writing, Nexis UK allows for the download of 500 news articles at a time, which means a significant number of articles can be downloaded in a relatively short amount of time.

The SFC (Chapter 6) is more complicated. At the time of collection, the forum was in the public domain on the clear web and did not require registration to view threads or posts. Nevertheless, the data presents additional ethical considerations in comparison with the other corpora in this book, particularly in relation to the privacy of the community members and forum posters. First, at the start of the data collection, institutional ethical approval was sought and granted by Nottingham Trent University's Joint Inter College Ethics Committee (JICEC). In addition, there are relevant disciplinary guidelines that offered direction in the collection and publication of this data. In its *Recommendations on Good Practice in Applied Linguistics*, the

British Association for Applied Linguistics (BAAL 2021: 9) note that, in online contexts, it is not always sufficient to base ethical decisions on what is 'public' and what is 'private'. At the same time, the guidelines acknowledge that although 'informed consent is often considered a cornerstone of ethical research' in some cases, again especially with online research, it may not be possible to be sure who informants *are* and how to contact them and, even if it were possible, it would not be appropriate to seek consent of those involved in producing the texts (BAAL 2021: 5). Further to this point, in its 'Ethics Guidelines for Internet-mediated Research', the British Psychological Society (BPS 2021) advocate an approach that takes into consideration whether or not there is an expectation of privacy on the part of the users of the online platform. The guidelines state that 'where it is reasonable to argue that there is likely no perception and/or expectation of privacy' then the 'use of research data without gaining valid consent may be justifiable' (BPS 2021: 9). The posts in the SFC were in the public domain and *deliberately* so; the forum operators could have implemented necessary registration or signing in to view posts if they wished the forum to be private in the typical sense. Additionally, one of the forum rules explicitly tells forum members to take steps to make sure that that they are completely anonymous, not using any names or contact information that could personally identify them or link them to another personal social media account. Therefore, given that posters to the forum have already taken steps to anonymise themselves and protect their privacy, it is clear that they expect their posts to be accessible to anyone. Nevertheless, following Rüdiger and Dayter's (2017) recommendations for dealing with pick-up artist online forums specifically, a series of steps have been taken to protect the identities of the forum posters. The forum is not named in this book, no distinguishing details of it are mentioned and no usernames are presented in extracts, despite their already being anonymised. Specifically in relation to extracts from the data, no searchable verbatim quotes will be presented, so that the original texts cannot be traced (BAAL 2021: 8). Such steps are intended to add an extra level of protection to forum posters; I am interested in the discourse of this context, not the posters. To borrow the distinction made by Page et al. (2014: 60), the object of this analysis is the *text* rather than the *people*.

Another issue associated with the SFC data specifically is its potentially distressing content. This is a challenge for forensic linguists more generally (Giménez et al. 2021; Petyko et al. 2022). Barber (2021: 138) provides a personal reflection on working with data from the manosphere (of which pick-up artists are part), emphasising that analysing extremist discourses online is confronting and can take its toll on researchers. Being exposed to the 'dark views offered from within the extremists world', Barber (2021: 138–9) notes, 'certainly tests emotional resilience', including experiencing vicarious trauma and feelings of guilt at reducing harrowing violence to merely data. Dealing with this data can mean that researchers have to implement strategies to manage not only their own well-being but also that of anyone who might read the same data either before or after publication. Again, the BAAL (2021: 15–6) guidelines provide some helpful directions for those working with distressing data. They recommend that researchers use resilience strategies such as taking breaks and limiting the amount of distressing data viewed each day as well as engaging in good work hygiene, having a clear separation between work with such data and home life. More broadly, they recommend that researchers work within a supportive team or environment, reaching out to others when needed as well as accessing institutional counselling services if necessary. In terms of responsibilities to others, researchers should protect colleagues in close proximity of their workspace by using privacy filters or setting up a workstation that prevents others from viewing their screen. When it comes to publishing data that is extreme or hateful, researchers should be mindful as to whether they are disseminating and reproducing extreme views (Barber 2021: 137). To mitigate this, researchers should provide appropriate content warnings before data is presented and consider whether it is necessary to present the most distressing content unredacted (BAAL 2021: 16). These final points were taken into consideration in the writing of Chapter 7.

Corpus-assisted discourse studies

The four analysis chapters in this book examine the four corpora described above using a CADS approach. This approach uses corpora and corpus linguistic methods 'to uncover linguistic patterns which can enable us to make sense of the ways that language is used in the construction of discourses' (Baker 2023: 1). The term *discourse* has 'fuzzy conceptual boundaries' (Mautner 2022: 251) and is defined and used in various ways in linguistics and beyond. In this book, 'discourse' is used in different places to mean different, but interconnected, things:

(i) Naturally occurring instances of language larger than single clauses and sentences (e.g. Stubbs 1983: 1; 2001: 158; Mautner 2022: 251).
(ii) Language embedded in multilayered social contexts, used by individuals and groups to perform social functions (Mautner 2016: 156; 2022: 251) and carry out the practices that shape their particular professional, institutional and social worlds (Hocking 2015: 192).
(iii) Recurring and conventional language use that forms a 'constellation of repeated meanings' (Stubbs 2001: 158) and that is 'habitually drawn upon to represent, frame or make sense of certain practices or objects', often 'regulating the way that a practice or object can be understood' (Hocking 2015: 192).

Within the chapters of this book, I make mention of, amongst other examples, *monologic* discourse, *courtroom* discourse, *appeal hearing* discourse and *online* discourse (type [i]), alongside *corporate*, *legal*, *media* and *news(paper)* discourse (type [ii]), and the discourse *of consent/resistance*, *pseudo-scientific* discourse and *discriminatory* discourse (type [iii]). In all cases, the CADS approach here is used to investigate 'the features of particular discourse types, integrating into the analysis, where appropriate, techniques and tools developed within corpus linguistics' (Partington 2010: 88).

The overarching general principles or 'essential characteristics' of the corpus approach are its empirical foundations – analysing large datasets of actual language collected in a principled way – and making use of computational techniques to support the analysis in such a way that quantitative and qualitative methods and results can be combined (cf. Biber et al. 1998: 4). The corpora collected and used in the analyses for this book have been described above, and the computational techniques of corpus methods used are described below. The precise nature of the relationship between quantitative and qualitative approaches facilitated by CADS has been written about extensively. For the CADS approach to be maximally valuable, the quantitative results semi-automatically produced by corpus tools must be combined with 'close reading approaches' (Egbert and Baker 2020: 8) and analysis must include 'qualitative, functional interpretations of quantitative patterns' (Biber et al. 1998: 4). A useful way of conceptualising the relative roles of corpus linguistic and discourse-analytic methods, at least as they are applied in this book, is that the quantitative insights generated by computational means help 'to unravel how particular discourses, rooted in particular socio-cultural contexts, construct reality, social identities and social relationships' (Hardt-Mautner 1995: 1). Likewise, the approach taken in this book follows Partington et al.'s (2013: 11) often-cited description of CADS:

> By combining the quantitative approach, that is, statistical overviews of large amounts of the discourse in question– more precisely, large numbers of tokens of the discourse type under study contained in a corpus – with the more qualitative approach typical of discourse analysis, that is, the close, detailed analysis of particular stretches of discourse – stretches whose particularly interesting nature may well have been identified by the initial overview – it may be possible to better understand the processes at play in the discourse type. It may be possible, in other words, to access such non-obvious meanings.

The benefits of CADS, including the combination of qualitative and quantitative analyses, are wide-ranging and well reported. Corpus assistance can add a degree of objectivity to discourse analysis because it offers a set of predictable analytical techniques and is based on a spirit of methodological transparency underpinned by two guiding principles: (i) no systematic bias in the selection of texts included in the corpus (i.e. do not exclude a text because it does not fit a pre-existing argument or theory) and (ii) total accountability (all data gathered must be accounted for) (Wright and Brookes 2019: 63). In turn, these principles enable discourse analysts to significantly broaden their empirical base, thus helping to mitigate researcher bias and prevent 'cherry-picking' while increasing representativeness and reproducibility (Mautner 2016: 156; Rheindorf 2019: 39–52; Baker 2023: 13). The CADS approach therefore allows the analyst to identify recurring patterns which are not immediately visible to the 'naked eye' (Jaworska 2016: 151) but which reveal prevalent and even dominant ways of speaking or writing in a given context and permit the analysis of far larger datasets than would be possible if only 'manual' methods were used (Mautner 2007: 55).

In the CADS applied in this book, the corpus results enable the analyst to observe and identify patterns in the data that 'are made visible and significant by their recurrence' (Marchi and Taylor 2009: 3), and the corpus techniques subsequently present texts (or sections of texts) to the analyst for qualitative interpretation of these patterns (Baker and Egbert 2016: 2). In this quantitative-then-qualitative sequence (Partington 2017: 344), corpus linguistics 'goes first', before the detailed textual analysis (Gillings et al. 2023: 7) as the analysis starts quantitative and gradually becomes more qualitative (Baker and McEnery 2015: 2). What is emphasised in the analyses in this book is the need for principled and systematic theoretically informed approaches to analysing, interpreting and understanding discourse. That is, a serious attempt is made in each chapter to put some methodological and theoretical flesh on the bones of the qualitative 'close reading'. In doing so, this reinforces the vital role of the human analyst in CADS in interpreting and 'bringing to life' the meaningful patterns of language use represented by quantitative findings (Egbert et al. 2020: 39). Although corpus tools are very good at processing large amounts of data, the results that they produce are not self-explanatory (Mautner 2022: 258), and it is up to the researcher to produce meaningful, contextualised analyses (Mautner 2016: 177). In the effective application of CADS, it is generally expected that the analyst will interpret the corpus results, texts or text extracts 'with reference to one or more theoretical frameworks' (Baker et al. 2008: 277). Here, (potential) researcher bias re-enters the fray. Results that have, up to this point, emerged in a relatively objective way need to be interpreted in a subjective way. Indeed, *interpretations* become *findings* (Baker 2023: 23). 'Subjectivity' here refers to the fact that researchers choose to interpret and examine corpus results in a particular way, which may differ from analyst to analyst, depending on their particular disciplinary backgrounds or methodological slant, and this in turn will produce different findings (see Marchi and Taylor 2009). Therefore, as Marchi and Taylor (2018: 7) point out, although the corpus processes that have identified features or patterns which warrant qualitative interpretation are reproducible, the qualitative interpretation itself is not replicable.

There is a risk that the relative subjectivity involved in the qualitative analysis of discourse within CADS comes hand-in-hand with analysis that is theoretically or methodologically lacking or is at least so opaque that it appears to be. It is sometimes the case in CADS that studies are 'less than explicit' about the discourse-analytic methods (Mautner 2019: 3) and 'often fall short of providing adequate accounts of the qualitative methods used' (Rheindorf 2019: 68). Without explication of the qualitative method involved, any reference to a 'qualitative analysis' or 'close reading' becomes a token statement, 'inviting criticism from all sides' (Rheindorf 2019: 32–3). One of the main appeals of CADS is that it is not a fixed 'theory-cum-method' package (Gillings et al. 2023: 8). Rather, it 'can be paired with any "brand" of discourse analysis, thus supporting a wide range of perspectives and methodologies' (Mautner 2022: 252). This flexibility of the 'corpus' element of CADS means that it is well suited to being used in combination with rigorous, systematic and theoretically sound methods of discourse analysis that are explicit and as transparent as possible.

The same can be said the other way around. Methods and frameworks of discourse analysis have 'quantitative potential', and they 'offer a highly structured set of resources for classifying and interpreting language features, which gain salience against a pattern of (un)usuality' (Marchi and Taylor 2018: 2). This is the spirit in which CADS is applied in this book. Efforts are made in every chapter to ensure that the 'discourse' elements of CADS explicitly follow a methodological and/or theoretical framework so that the corpus results are analysed, interpreted and understood in a principled and transparent way. In Chapter 4, analyses are based on positioning theory (Davies and Harré 1990); in Chapter 5, the data is interpreted using perspectives from stance (Hyland and Tse 2004; Hyland 2005); Chapter 6 identifies and unpacks discourse prosodies (Stubbs 1996, 2001) emerging from corpus data, and Chapter 7 embeds quantitative analysis within a model of argumentation (Toulmin (2003 [1958]). Each of these theoretical or methodological approaches is unpacked fully in their respective chapters rather than here. In using these approaches, I am attempting to provide 'a methodological specification of the qualitative methods to be used' (Rheindorf 2019: 74). In combination with quantitative corpus results, these qualitative approaches aim to explicate the relationships between micro- and macro-linguistic phenomena, thereby 'allowing access to data aggregates as well as close attention to detail' (Mautner 2007: 66).

The division of analytical labour between the 'corpus linguistic' and 'discourse analysis' methodologies is not the same in every chapter of this book, nor indeed is it clear-cut, with analyses often exploiting 'the fuzzy boundaries between "quantitative" and "qualitative" approaches' (Baker et al. 2008: 296). Hunston (2022: 225) explains that 'corpus techniques can form a major part of the research, or a much smaller part', and Mautner (2016: 175) describes that 'there is no hard-and-fast rule about where exactly in the analytical process corpus linguistic methods ought to be brought in, or how much space they should take up in the research design overall'. The four analysis chapters in this book are characterised by different levels of 'intensity' (Mautner 2022: 252) with which the synergies between the corpus and discourse approaches are combined. There is the well-known distinction, posited by Tognini-Bonelli (2001), between 'corpus-based' and 'corpus-driven' approaches. Corpus-based approaches 'use corpus evidence mainly as a repository of examples to expound, test or exemplify given theoretical statements' (Tognini-Bonelli 2001). In contrast, rather than starting with hypotheses, the corpus-driven approach 'builds up the theory step by step in the presence of the evidence', and theory and hypotheses emerge from the corpus itself. McEnery and Gabrielatos (2006: 36) and Baker (2023: 19) see these two approaches as theoretical end points on a scale, with most research falling somewhere in the middle of this continuum. This is certainly true of the CADS applied in this book. My analyses in each of the chapters is driven by what is (and is not) known about the particular discourses and discourse types under examination. For instance, there is good reason to suggest that positioning of social actors is an important discursive strategy in opening statements, and we know that the courtroom is a stance-rich environment. Similarly, the misogynistic pick-up artist online community seems an appropriate place to examine representations of resistance to sex, and given the persuasive aims of national newspapers (in the U.K. at least), it seems reasonable to think that argumentation plays a key role in how they report on new legislation. In each case, the corpus analysis was motivated by and conducted in line with these informal 'hypotheses' in mind. At the same time, in every case the quantitative analysis was both inductive (or 'bottom-up') and based on the corpora in their entirety (i.e. the principle of 'total accountability' [Baker et al. 2008: 275]). No *specific* evidence was sought in support of (or counter to) a *specific* theoretical statement or hypothesis. Rather, the patterns identified shaped subsequent analyses, with each step informing the next (Marchi and Taylor 2009: 4). In such a combinatory approach, it could be argued that the adoption of an explicit approach to or framework within discourse analysis, as advocated for in CADS, precludes an entirely corpus-driven approach. The approach to discourse being taken would quite possibly dictate that one has to start *somewhere*. Hardt-Mautner's (1995: 24) metaphor of the analyst 'roaming' their corpus is useful here. In each of these chapters, the analysis involved a 'roaming' of the corpus, with corpus results drawing attention 'to phenomenon that can be investigated with the help of [...] qualitative apparatus' (Hardt-Mautner 1995: 24). In the CADS applied in the following chapters, the qualitative apparatuses themselves helped to dictate the direction(s) in which I roamed.

Corpus linguistic tools

This section provides details of the corpus techniques that are used in this book and the procedures that were followed in applying them. All of the techniques described here were carried out using *Wordsmith Tools*, version 8 (Scott 2020).

Keyword analysis

Keyword analysis is used in the analysis of positioning in the Grenfell Tower Inquiry Opening Statements (Chapter 4) and in the analysis of stance in the Brexit Hearings Corpus (Chapter 5). Keywords are words 'whose frequency is unusually high in comparison with some norm' (Scott 2024). A list of keywords in a given corpus can provide a good indication as to the 'aboutness' of the texts within it – that is, 'of the main concepts, topics or attitudes' found in them (Gabrielatos 2018: 225). Therefore, keyword analysis is often used in CADS as a first step in probing large corpora and has been characterised as providing a 'point of entry' (Baker 2010: 133) and a 'way in' (Baker 2012: 248) to data, with keywords functioning as 'analytical signposts' (Gillings et al. 2023: 34) that are worth further examination.

In Chapter 4, keyword analysis is used to identify salient 'self-mentions' used in the opening statements, wherein the lawyer delivering the statement makes reference to the client that they are representing. These keywords then are integrated into the analysis by examining the strategies of positioning that occur around them. In Chapter 5, a keyword analysis reveals that the first-person pronoun *I* is the most key word in the Brexit hearings. The main focus of that chapter, however, is on the collocates of *I*, particularly those that serve explicit stance-taking functions. Therefore, keywords provide a useful 'way in' to the data in both of these chapters that focus on self-orienting and self-oriented discursive phenomena in positioning and stance.

Keyword analysis necessarily involves comparing word frequencies in a 'target' corpus (i.e. the corpus under analysis) and a relevant 'reference' corpus, and there are different statistical methods of calculating keyness (Gabrielatos 2018; Gillings et al. 2023: 34). In this book, keywords are calculated by comparing the word frequency lists from the opening statements (Chapter 4) and the Brexit hearings (Chapter 5) with the 11.5 million–word spoken component of the British National Corpus 2014 (Love et al. 2017). The calculation of keyword lists in this book is a two-stage process (see also Hunt and Brookes 2020: 77). First, keyness was calculated using the log-likelihood statistic. Log-likelihood assigns to each word in the corpus a score which reflects the probability that the word is key when the corpus is compared against Spoken BNC2014. The higher the log-likelihood score, the greater confidence the analyst can have that the difference in frequencies of that word between the target and reference corpus is not due to chance (Baker 2023: 165). In this book, the default log-likelihood threshold score of 3.84 was used, meaning that if a word appeared in the keyword list, I could be confident to a level of 95% that the difference in frequency was not due to chance. Second, Hardie's Log Ratio (Hardie 2014) was used to determine the *size* of this frequency difference. Although log-likelihood tells the analyst how much evidence they have for a difference between two corpora, it does not give any indication as to the size of that difference. The Log Ratio statistic, on the other hand, is an effect-size statistic and does represent how big the difference between two corpora is for a particular keyword. Keyword lists generated initially using log-likelihood were then ranked by Log Ratio, so that words with higher Log Ratio scores appear at the top of the list. This process produced the keyword results discussed in Chapters 5 and 6.

Collocation analysis

McEnery and Hardie (2012: 122–3) describe 'collocation' as

> The idea that important aspects of the meaning of a word (or another linguistic unit) are not contained within the word itself, considered in isolation, but rather subsist in the characteristic associations that the word participates in, alongside other words or structures with which it frequently co-occurs.

When the notion of collocation is operationalised in corpus linguistics, it is distilled to 'the frequent co-occurrence' of the node word being investigated and its 'collocates' (Stubbs 2001: 29) or, more specifically, the frequent co-occurrence of words 'more often than would otherwise be expected by chance alone' (Gillings et al. 2023: 27). For Stubbs (1996: 172), the characteristic collocations of words 'show the associations and connotations they have, and therefore the assumptions which they embody'. The collocates or 'word-material' (Firth 1957: 11) in which words are frequently embedded, or their 'collocational' and 'discursive' profile(s) (Mautner 2005, 2007), allow the analyst to better understand 'how a speaker or writer expresses their stance towards certain people and events, how the roles of social actors are framed discursively and how they construct their own identities' (Mautner 2022: 256).

In this book, collocation analysis is central to the analysis of stance in the Brexit hearings (Chapter 5), the discourse prosodies of the pick-up-artist term 'last-minute resistance' (LMR) (Chapter 6) and the argumentation patterns in the reporting of 'new law(s)' and 'new legislation' in the British national press (Chapter 7). In Chapter 5, the focus is on stance-marking collocates of the first-person pronoun *I* in the speech of advocates and judges in the High Court and Supreme Court. In Chapter 6, the collocational profile of 'LMR' is constructed and analysed to observe how members of this online community view women's resistance to sex. In Chapter 7, the collocates of *new law*, *new laws* and *new legislation* are identified and interpreted as lexical indicators of argumentation.

As is the case with keywords, there are many different statistical means by which the strength of association between words can be measured, and there are several papers dedicated to testing, comparing and evaluating them (e.g. Evert 2009; Gries 2013; Brezina et al. 2015; Gablasova et al. 2017; Su et al. 2024). It is up to the analyst which association measure they choose to use to determine what counts as a collocate in their corpus-assisted discourse analysis (Gillings et al. 2023: 29). In this book, the association measure used is MI^3 (Mutual Information cubed). Alternative association measures such as log-likelihood and t-scores prioritise frequency in their calculations (Hunston 2022: 97), whereas mutual information (MI) does more than 'just tell us that a relationship is frequent' but calculates the expected probability of two words occurring near each other based on their individual relative frequencies in the corpus *as a whole* and then compares that to the frequency with which they occur together (Baker 2023: 139). MI therefore 'emphasizes the *exclusivity* of the collocational relationship' and thus has a propensity to highlight strong but infrequent combinations (Brezina et al. 2015: 159, my emphasis). MI^3 borrows this promotion of more exclusive associations while giving more weight to observed frequencies than straightforward MI and thus gives high scores to collocations which occur relatively frequently in the corpus (Brezina et al. 2015: 160). Therefore, no matter how suggestive, an association which is not repeated enough will be less influential in MI^3 collocate rankings than an association that is more firmly established in the corpus (Brookes and Wright 2020: 119).

Each collocate analysis in this book involved a 'process of narrowing and funnelling' (Egbert and Baker 2016: 195) to arrive at an amount of collocates appropriate for the task at hand and such a process necessarily relied on researcher selectivity (Baker 2023: 14). This narrowing and funnelling influenced decisions on two parameters of collocation analysis: frequency and strength thresholds and the span of collocates either side of the node word. With regard to cut-off thresholds, in Chapter 5, the top 50 ranked collocates were included in the analysis, while in Chapter 6, it was the top 100. This difference was due to the size of the datasets and the number of collocates produced in the analysis, with Chapter 6 involving a much larger amount of data and so the net was cast more widely to include a larger number of collocates. In Chapter 7, by contrast, this analysis involved more data again and instead of using a rank-based threshold, all collocates with an MI^3 of 11 or higher were included (following Brezina et al. 2015), based on thresholds recommended for representing 'genuine' collocations which tend to be much lower at 3 (Hunston 2002) or 6 (Durrant and Doherty 2010). With regard to the span of collocates included in the analysis (i.e. how many words to the left and right of the node to include), this also varies from chapter to chapter given that the type and number of collocates and collocational relationships of interest are different in each case (see Gillings et al. 2023: 28). Because Chapter 5 focuses on stance-marking collocates that follow the pronoun *I*, the span was restricted to R1 collocates (words occupying the slot immediately after *I*). Chapter 6 examines the discursive prosodies (Stubbs 2001) associated with a particular community-specific term ('LMR') and this required capturing its discursive profile (Mautner 2007) more broadly and identifying words that occurred in close proximity to it, but not necessarily adjacently or in any fixed order (McEnery and Hardie 2012: 123). Finally, Chapter 7 was similar to Chapter 6 in that both were interested in capturing a broader range of collocates, but owing to the sheer number and frequency of collocates returned in Chapter 7, the span was limited to R1–L1.

The final step in the collocation analyses in this book was that the collocates returned were semantically grouped in a way that allowed thematic patterns to emerge (e.g. Baker et al. 2013). Such categorisation is a subjective and 'imperfect' process (Baker 2023: 143) and is 'far from mechanical' (Hunston 2022: 212). Nevertheless, the thematic categorisation of collocates is important because it helps the analyst identify patterns that appear only when collocates are grouped together, combining more dominant collocates with those that might be less frequent yet still contribute to important themes in the corpus. The semantic characterisation of collocates 'requires sensitivity to recurring meanings and their significance' (Hunston 2022: 212) and this, in turn, necessitates the scrutiny of concordance lines (Hunston 2022: 114). The final section of this chapter turns to concordance analysis as it was applied in the book.

Concordance analysis

A concordance list displays all instances of a search term, phrase/cluster or character string in a corpus in its immediate context, with the term appearing in the centre of the list and a fixed number of characters to the left and right. The instances are presented in an example-per-line format (so-called concordance *lines*, Baker 2023: 107), which is initially in the order in which the instances appear in the corpus, but can be re-sorted so that the words immediately to the right or left of the search term appear in alphabetical order, making it easier to spot patterns in the co-text (e.g. Figure 2.1) (see McEnery and Hardie 2012: 35; Hunston 2022: 47).

Concordance analysis is often identified as the stage of CADS in which the qualitative analysis 'overlaps' with quantitative analysis (Gabrielatos and Baker 2008: 15) and serves to 'bridge' or even 'dissolve' the divide between the two approaches (Mautner 2022: 258). Concordances present corpus data in such a way that patterns that are not observable from individual instances of language become apparent and allow the analyst to build up discursive profiles of their search terms (Hunston 2022: 79; Gillings et al. 2023: 22). Showing the search terms surrounded by their co-texts moves the analysis closer to the original texts and brings the corpus to life (Mautner 2022: 257). However, even then, concordance lines are only 'snippits' of the full picture (Hunston 2022: 47), and the output in concordances is necessarily 'decontextualised' and 'semiotically reduced' (Mautner 2016: 173), and the limit of context visible in a concordance line

heart transplant boy, 10 65. Major retailer demands	new law	banning under-16s from buying energy drinks 'becau
. Detectives continue to hunt for the other two men.A	new law	comes into force this month that potentially doubles t
Warning for motorcyclists as	new law	could land them with two year prison sentence or hef
bal economy works. Concretely, Labour proposes a	new law,	ensuring that all aid money must be spent fighting in
la Merkel on the question of immigration. Under the	new law,	entry to Germany will be made measurably easier fo
iomes must be a hate crime Campaigners demand	new law	for crimes against elderly people Elder abuse: 'Natio
as they're optional. Unless Ms Perry plans to write a	new law	forcing everyone to switch to a smart meter, she sho
ar. Labour MP Karen Buck, who has spearheaded a	new law	giving tenants more rights, said: "The number of fami
House of Commons on Friday. The campaign for the	new law	has already attracted cross-party support from music
vho is behind the formerly shadowy companies. The	new law	has been met with staunch opposition by the Caymar
of those means the government has to introduce a	new law	if it wants to keep the UK in a customs union. The fin
eatest level of grooming since the introduction of the	new law	in 2010. Lothian and Borders had the most cases at
charges were banned, an investigation has found. A	new law	introduced in January banned retailers from adding a
ld Wide Fund for Nature (WWF) heavily criticised the	new law	last month in a press release, expressing 'profound c
ient policymaking. When a government introduces a	new law,	like the sugar tax for example, it impacts everyone at
ember and, if successful, will present his case for a	new law	making it a requirement for all care homes to install r
the new Assaults on Emergency Workers Act 2018 •	New law	means attackers face maximum of 12 months behind
desperately waiting for a life-saving transplant. The	new law	on organ donation will be called "Max's law" after Max
charge consumers for credit card payments after a	new law	outlawing the practice came into effect on Saturday, i
vers offering less money for the roles women take. A	new law	requires UK companies with 250 or more staff to pub
roclaimed that 'the North is next'. They believe that a	new law	should be decided in Northern Ireland. DUP MP Ian P
yground". Four months on from the introduction of a	new law	targeting human rights abusers with visa bans and a
im through a dating app, it should be included in the	new law	that judges can, as a condition of sentence, order the
d new legislation to set energy tariff caps. Under the	new law	the regulator will be able to set a cap on energy tariffs
NG CUT OF TIPS THERESA May will today pledge a	new law	to ban restaurants from taking a cut of staff tips. A stri
ne secretary at the time of the act, had been told the	new law	was dangerous and would put the Windrush generat
e's quite a few doing the same." Scotland hopes the	new law	will reduce drink-related deaths by 400 in five years. E

Figure 2.1 A sample of concordance lines for *new law* as the search term with results sorted alphabetically by R1 collocate from the New Laws in the News Corpus (Chapter 7).

limits the extent to which we can 'trace how meaning unfolds over longer stretches of discourse, or how meaning is negotiated between interactants' (Mautner 2007: 65). As Anthony (2018: 209) and Gillings and Mautner (2024) point out, this poses significant limitations on concordances as a method of visualisation and as sites for interpretation in discourse analysis. Therefore, the analysis of concordances in this book required going beyond the concordance line. For Gillings et al. (2023: 23), 'going beyond the concordance line' means two things, both of which are followed here. On the one hand, it entails the practical step of expanding the analysis to larger stretches of text that appear before and after the snippet shown in a concordance line. This is easily achievable in *Wordsmith Tools* (and other corpus linguistic programs), which provides the analyst with recourse to the full text. On the other hand, going beyond the concordance line means 'relating it to the wider social context which shapes the corpus and is shaped by it' (Gillings et al. 2023: 23). This, in turn, requires a systematic discourse analysis of these longer stretches of text. It is fundamental to CADS that concordance lines and texts are interpreted with reference to theoretical frameworks (Baker et al. 2008: 277). As Rheindorf (2019: 64) notes, 'extended concordance line can open a window, but it does not do it automatically – opening it and, more importantly, moving past it, requires additional methodology'. In this book, the additional methodology is discourse analysis underpinned and informed by theories of positioning (Chapter 4), stance (Chapter 5), discourse prosody (Chapter 6) and argumentation (Chapter 7). In this book, much of the concordance analysis is conducted 'behind the scenes', to fulfil a dual function. First, it is to determine or verify the semantic categorisation of collocates. Second, it is used to identify examples from the data that are to be presented to the reader in the analysis as being representative of the wider patterns identified in the corpora.

Note

1 https://assets.grenfelltowerinquiry.org.uk/inline-files/Opus%202%20Grenfell%20Tower%20Inquiry%20Licence_2.docx.

References

Anthony, L. (2018) Visualization in corpus-based discourse studies. In C. Taylor and A. Marchi (eds.), *Corpus Approaches to Discourse: A Critical Review*. London, UK: Routledge, pp. 197–224.

BAAL (2021) *Recommendations on Good Practice in Applied Linguistics 2021* (4th ed.). British Association for Applied Linguistics. Available at: https://www.baal.org.uk/wp-content/uploads/2021/03/BAAL-Good-Practice-Guidelines-2021.pdf [Last accessed April 2024]

Bacigalupo, J., Borgeson, K. and Valeri, R. M. (eds.). (2022) *Cyberhate: The Far Right in the Digital Age*. Lanham, MD: Lexington Books.

Baker, P. (2010) *Sociolinguistics and Corpus Linguistics*. Edinburgh: Edinburgh University Press.

Baker, P. (2012) Acceptable bias? Using corpus linguistics methods with critical discourse analysis. *Critical Discourse Studies* 9(3): 247–256. https://doi.org/10.1080/17405904.2012.688297

Baker, P. (2023) *Using Corpora in Discourse Analysis* (2nd ed.). London: Bloomsbury.

Baker, P. and Egbert, J. (2016) Introduction. In P. Baker and J. Egbert (eds.), *Triangulating Methodological Approaches in Corpus Linguistic Research*. London: Routledge, pp. 1–19.

Baker, P. and McEnery, T. (2015) Introduction. In P. Baker and T. McEnery (eds.), *Corpora and Discourse Studies: Integrating Discourse and Corpora*. Basingstoke: Palgrave, pp. 1–19.

Baker, P., Gabrielatos, C., KhosraviNik, M., Krzyżanowski, M., McEnery, T. and Wodak, R. (2008) A useful methodological synergy? Combining critical discourse analysis and corpus linguistics to examine discourses of refugees and asylum seekers in the UK press. *Discourse & Society* 19(3): 273–306. https://doi.org/10.1177/0957926508088962

Baker, P., Gabrielatos, C. and McEnery, T. (2013) Sketching Muslims: A corpus driven analysis of representations around the word 'Muslim' in the British press 1998–2009. *Applied Linguistics* 34(3): 255–278. https://doi.org/10.1093/applin/ams048

Barber, K. (2021) From the outside looking in: The risks and challenges of analysing extremist discourses on far-right and manosphere websites. In C. Cunningham and C. J. Hall (eds)., *Vulnerabilities, Challenges and Risks in Applied Linguistics*. Bristol: Multilingual Matters, pp. 131–146.

Bartley, L. V. (2023) "The Jogger and the Wolfpack": An analysis of the transitivity patterns in the global media coverage of the 1989 Central Park Five case. *International Journal for the Semiotics of Law* 37(2): 573–594. https://doi.org/10.1007/s11196-023-10026-x

Biber, D. (1993) Representativeness in corpus design. *Literary and Linguistic Computing* 8(4): 243–257. https://doi.org/10.1093/llc/8.4.243

Biber, D., Conrad, S. and Reppen, R. (1998) *Corpus Linguistics: Investigating Language Structure and Use*. Cambridge, UK: Cambridge University Press.

Biel, Ł. (2015) Phraseological profiles of legislative genres: Complex prepositions as a special case of legal phrasemes in EU law and national law. *Fachsprache* 37(3–4): 139–160. https://doi.org/10.24989/fs.v37i3-4.1286

BPS (2021) *Ethics Guidelines for Internet-Mediated Research*. British Psychological Society. https://doi.org/10.53841/bpsrep.2021.rep155

Brezina, V., McEnery, T. and Wattam, S. (2015) Collocations in context: A new perspective on collocation networks. *International Journal of Corpus Linguistics* 20(2): 139–173. https://doi.org/10.1075/ijcl.20.2.01bre

Brookes, G. and Collins, L. (2023) *Corpus Linguistics for Health Communication: A Guide for Research*. London: Routledge.

Brookes, G. and Wright, D. (2020) The shifting discourse of integration in the 'Speak English' debate: A corpus-assisted study of the UK press. In P. Rautionaho, A. Nurmi and J. Klemola (eds.), *Corpora and the Changing Society: Studies in the Evolution of English*. Amsterdam/Philadelphia: Benjamins, pp. 113–140.

Cheng, Le, Liu, Y., Zhao, Y. (2021) Exploring the U.S. institutional discourse about critical information infrastructure protection (CIIP): A corpus-based analysis. *International Journal of Legal Discourse* 6(2): 323–347. https://doi.org/10.1515/ijld-2021-2058

Chiang, E. (2020) 'Send Me Some Pics': Performing the offender identity in online undercover child abuse investigations. *Policing* 15(2): 1173–1187. https://doi.org/10.1093/police/paaa065

Chiang, E. (2024) "I read the rules and know what is expected of me": The performance of competence and expertise in 'newbie' offenders' membership requests to dark web child abuse communities. *Discourse, Context & Media* 57: 1–9. https://doi.org/10.1016/j.dcm.2023.100744

Chiang, E. and Grant, T. (2017) Online grooming: Moves and strategies. *Language and Law/Linguagem e Direito* 4(1): 103–141.

Chiang, E., Nguyen, D., Towler, A., Haas, M., and Grieve, J. (2020) Linguistic analysis of suspected child sexual offenders' interactions in a dark web image exchange chatroom. *International Journal of Speech, Language and the Law* 27(2): 129–161. https://doi.org/10.1558/ijsll.41446

Clarke, I. (2019) Functional linguistic variation in twitter trolling. *International Journal of Speech, Language and the Law* 26(1): 57–84. https://doi.org/10.1558/ijsll.34803

Copland (2021) Dark, clear or brackish? Using Reddit to break down the binary of the dark and clear web. *Continuum* 35(5): 719–731. https://doi.org/10.1080/10304312.2021.1983255

Cotterill, J. (2003) *Language and Power in Court: A Linguistic Analysis of the O.J. Simpson Trial.* Basingstoke: Palgrave Macmillan.

Cotterill, J. (2010). How to use corpus linguistics in forensic linguistics. In A. O'Keeffe and M. McCarthy (eds.), *The Routledge Handbook of Corpus Linguistics* (1st ed.). London: Routledge, pp. 578–590.

Davies, B. and Harré, R. (1990) Positioning: The discursive production of selves. *Journal for the Theory of Social Behaviour* 20(1): 43–63. https://doi.org/10.1111/j.1468-5914.1990.tb00174.x

Davies, G. (2020) Shining a light on policing of the dark web: An analysis of UK investigatory powers. *The Journal of Criminal Law* 84(5): 407–426. https://doi.org/10.1177/0022018320952557

Davies, M. (2018) The Corpus of US Supreme Court Opinions: 130 million words, 1790s- present. https://www.english-corpora.org/scotus/

Douthwaite, J. and Tabbert, U. (eds.) (2022) *The Linguistics of Crime.* Cambridge, UK: Cambridge University Press.

Durrant, P. and Doherty, A. (2010) Are high-frequency collocations psychologically real? Investigating the thesis of collocational priming. *Corpus Linguistics and Linguistic Theory* 6(2): 125–155. https://doi.org/10.1515/cllt.2010.006

Egbert, J. and Baker, P. (2016) Research synthesis. In P. Baker and J. Egbert (eds.), *Triangulating Methodological Approaches in Corpus Linguistic Research.* London: Routledge, pp. 183–208.

Egbert, J. and Baker, P. (2020) Introduction. In J. Egbert and P. Baker (eds.), *Using Corpus Methods to Triangulate Linguistic Analysis.* London: Routledge, pp. 1–21.

Egbert, J. and Wood, M. (2023) The corpus of United States state statutes—design, construction and use. *Applied Corpus Linguistics* 3(2): 1–5. https://doi.org/10.1016/j.acorp.2023.100047

Egbert, J., Larsson, T. and Biber, D. (2020) *Doing Linguistics with a Corpus: Methodological Considerations for the Everyday User*. Cambridge, UK: Cambridge University Press.

Evert, S. (2009) Corpora and collocations. In A. Lüdeling and M. Kytö (eds.), *Corpus Linguistics: An International Handbook*. Berlin, de Gruyter, pp. 1212–1248.

Firth, J. R. (1957) A synopsis of linguistic theory 1930–1955. In F. R. Palmer (ed.), *Selected Papers of J.R. Firth 1952–1959*. London: Longman, pp. 168–205.

Flowerdew, J. (2004) The argument for using English specialized corpora to understand academic and professional language. In U. Connor and T. A. Upton (eds.), *Discourse in the Professions: Perspectives from Corpus Linguistics*. Amsterdam/Philadelphia: John Benjamins, pp. 11–33.

Flowerdew, L. (2008) Corpora and context in professional writing. In V. K. Bhatia, J. Flowerdew and R. H. Jones (eds.), *Advances in Discourse Studies*. London: Routledge, pp. 115–131.

Franzke, A. S., Bechmann, A., Zimmer, M., Ess, C. and The Association of Internet Researchers. (2019) *Internet Research: Ethical Guidelines 3.0*. Available at https://aoir.org/reports/ethics3.pdf [Last accessed April 2024].

Gablasova, D., Brezina, V. and McEnery, T. (2017) Collocations in corpus-based language learning research: Identifying, comparing and interpreting the evidence. *Language Learning* 67(Suppl. 1): 155–179. https://doi.org/10.1111/lang.12225

Gabrielatos, C. (2018) Keyness analysis: Nature, metrics and techniques. In C. Taylor and A. Marchi (eds.), *Corpus Approaches to Discourse: A Critical Review*. London: Routledge, pp. 225–258.

Gabrielatos, C. and Baker, P. (2008) Fleeing, sneaking, flooding: A corpus analysis of discursive constructions of refugees and asylum seekers in the UK press, 1996-2005. *Journal of English Linguistics* 36(1): 5–38. https://doi.org/10.1177/0075424207311247

Gies, L. (2007) *Law and the Media: The Future of an Uneasy Relationship*. London: Routledge.

Gillings, M. (2022) How to use corpus linguistics in forensic linguistics. In A. O'Keeffe and M. McCarthy (eds.), *The Routledge Handbook of Corpus Linguistics* (2nd ed.). London: Routledge, pp. 589–601.

Gillings, M. and Mautner, G. (2024) Concordancing for CADS: Practical challenges and theoretical implications. *International Journal of Corpus Linguistics* 29(1): 34–58. https://doi.org/10.1075/ijcl.21168.gil

Gillings, M., Mautner, G. and Baker, P. (2023) *Corpus-Assisted Discourse Studies*. Cambridge, UK: Cambridge University Press.

Giménez, R., Elstein, S., and Queralt, S. (2021) The pandemic and the forensic linguistics caseworker's wellbeing: Effects and recommendations. *International Journal of Speech, Language and the Law* 27(2): 233–254. https://doi.org/10.1558/ijsll.19548

Grant, T. (2017) Duppying yoots in a dog eat dog world, kmt: Determining the senses of slang terms for the courts. *Semiotica* 216: 87–106. https://doi.org/10.1515/sem-2015-0082

Grant, T. and MacLeod, N. (2020) *Language and Online Identities: The Undercover Policing of Internet Sexual Crime*. Cambridge, UK: Cambridge University Press.

Gries, S. T. (2013) 50-something years of work on collocations: What is or should be next. *International Journal of Corpus Linguistics* 18(1): 137–166. https://doi.org/10.1075/ijcl.18.1.09gri

Hardie, A. (2014) Log Ratio – an Informal Introduction. 28 April 2014. ESRC Centre for Corpus Approaches to Social Science (CASS). (online). Available from: https://cass.lancs.ac.uk/log-ratio-an-informal-introduction/ [Last accessed April 2024].

Hardt-Mautner, G. (1995) Only connect: Critical discourse analysis and corpus linguistics. *UCREL Technical Papers* 6: 1–31. Available at https://ucrel.lancaster.ac.uk/papers/techpaper/vol6.pdf [Last accessed April 2024].

Heydon, G. (2019) *Researching Forensic Linguistics: Approaches and Applications*. London: Routledge.

Hocking, D. (2015) The use of corpus analysis in a multi-perspectival study of creative practice. In P. Baker and T. McEnery (eds.), *Corpora and Discourse Studies: Integrating Discourse and Corpora*. Basingstoke: Palgrave, pp. 192–219.

Hunston, S. (2002) *Corpora in Applied Linguistics* (1st ed.). Cambridge, UK: Cambridge University Press.

Hunston, S. (2022) *Corpora in Applied Linguistics* (2nd ed.). Cambridge, UK: Cambridge University Press.

Hunt D. and Brookes G. (2020) *Corpus, Discourse and Mental Health*. London: Bloomsbury.

Hyland, K. (2005) Stance and engagement: A model of interaction in academic discourse. *Discourse Studies* 7(2): 173–192. https://doi.org/10.1177/1461445605050365

Hyland, K. and Tse, P. (2004) Metadiscourse in academic writing reappraisal. *Applied Linguistics* 25(2): 156–177. https://doi.org/10.1093/applin/25.2.156

Ireton, E. (2018) How public is a public inquiry? *Public Law* 30(April): 277–298.

Ireton, E. (2023) Public inquiries: Irreconcilable interests and the importance of managing expectations. *Journal of Social Welfare and Family Law* 45(3): 212–233. https://doi.org/10.1080/09649069.2023.2243137

Jackson, J., Doak, J., Saunders, C., Wright, D. and Cooper, D. (2024) *Mapping the Changing Face of Cross-Examination in Criminal Trials. Report for the Nuffield Foundation*. https://doi.org/10.17631/rd-2024-0001-drep

Jaworska, S. (2016) Using a corpus-assisted discourse studies (CADS) approach to investigate constructions of identities in media reporting surrounding mega sports events: The case of the London Olympics 2012. In I. R. Lamond and L. Platt (eds.), *Critical Events Studies: Approaches to Research. Leisure Studies in a Global Era*. Basingstoke: Palgrave, pp. 149–174.

Johnson, A. (2015) Haunting evidence: Quoting the prisoner in 19th century old bailey trial discourse. The defences of Cooper (1842) and McNaughten (1843). In J. Arendholz, W. Bublitz and M. Kirner-Ludwig (eds.) *The Pragmatics of Quoting Now and Then*. Berlin: De Gruyter, pp. 369–400.

Johnson, A. (2018) "How came you not to cry out?" Pragmatic effects of negative questioning in child rape trials in the Old Bailey Proceedings 1730–1798. In D. Kurzon and B. Kryk-Kastovsky (eds.), *Legal Pragmatics*. Amsterdam/Philadelphia: Benjamins, pp. 41–64.

Kennedy-Kollar, D. (2024) *Extremism and Radicalization in the Manosphere: Beta Uprising*. London: Routledge.

Knight, D. and Adolphs, S. (2022) Building a spoken corpus: What are the basics? In A. O'Keeffe and M. McCarthy (eds.), *The Routledge Handbook of Corpus Linguistics* (2nd ed.). London: Routledge, pp. 21–34.

Koester, A. (2022) Building small specialised corpora. In A. O'Keeffe and M. McCarthy (eds.), *The Routledge Handbook of Corpus Linguistics* (2nd ed.), London: Routledge, pp. 48–61.

Kredens, K. and Coulthard, M. (2012) Corpus linguistics in authorship identification. In P. M. Tiersma and L. M. Solan (eds.), *The Oxford Handbook of Language and Law*. Oxford: Oxford University Press, pp. 504–516.

Krendel, A. (2021) From sexism to misogyny: Can online echo chambers stay quarantined? In I. Zempi and J. Smith (eds.), *Misogyny as Hate Crime*. London: Routledge, pp. 99–118.

Larner, S. (2015) From intellectual challenges to established corpus techniques: Introduction to the special issue on forensic linguistics. *Corpora* 10(2): 131–143. https://doi.org/10.3366/cor.2015.0071

Love, R., Dembry, C., Hardie, A., Brezina, V., McEnery, T. (2017) The Spoken BNC2014: Designing and building a spoken corpus of everyday conversations. *International Journal of Corpus Linguistics* 22(3): 319–344. https://doi.org/10.1075/ijcl.22.3.02lov

MacLeod, N. (2024) 'Encouraging or assisting others to commit an offence': The anatomy of a language crime. *The International Journal for the Semiotics of Law* 37(2): 677–694. https://doi.org/10.1007/s11196-023-10031-0

Marchi, A. and Taylor, C. (2009) 'If on a winter night two researchers': A challenge to assumptions of soundness of interpretation. *Critical Approaches to Discourse Analysis across Disciplines* 3(1): 1–20.

Marchi, A. and Taylor, C. (2018) Introduction: Partiality and reflexivity. In C. Taylor and A. Marchi (eds.), *Corpus Approaches to Discourse: A Critical Review*. London: Routledge, pp. 1–15.

Mautner, G. (2005) The entrepreneurial university. A discursive profile of a higher education buzzword. *Critical Discourse Studies* 2(2): 95–120. https://doi.org/10.1080/17405900500283540

Mautner, G. (2007) Mining large corpora for social information: The case of elderly. *Language in Society* 36(1): 51–72. https://doi.org/10.1017/S0047404507070030

Mautner, G. (2016) Checks and balances: How corpus linguistics can contribute to CDA. In R. Wodak and M. Meyer (eds.), *Methods of Critical Discourse Analysis* (3rd ed.). London: Sage, pp. 154–179.

Mautner, G. (2019) A research note on corpora and discourse: Points to ponder in research design. *Journal of Corpora and Discourse Studies* 2: 2–13. https://doi.org/10.18573/jcads.32

Mautner, G. (2022) What can a corpus tell us about discourse? In A. O'Keeffe and M. McCarthy (eds.), *The Routledge Handbook of Corpus Linguistics* (2nd ed.). London: Routledge, pp. 250–262.

Mayr, A. and Machin, D. (2011) *The Language of Crime and Deviance: An Introduction to Critical Linguistic Analysis in Media and Popular Culture*. London: Bloomsbury.

McEnery, T. and Brookes, G. (2022) Building a written corpus: What are the basics? In A. O'Keeffe and M. McCarthy (eds.), *The Routledge Handbook of Corpus Linguistics* (2nd ed.). London: Routledge, pp. 35–47.

McEnery, T. and Gabrielatos, C. (2006) English corpus linguistics. In B. Aarts and A. M. S. McMahon (eds.), *The Handbook of English Linguistics*. Oxford: Blackwell. pp. 33–71.

McEnery, T. and Hardie, A. (2012) *Corpus Linguistics: Method, Theory and Practice*. Cambridge, UK: Cambridge University Press.

McEnery, T. and Wilson, A. (2001) *Corpus Linguistics: An Introduction*. Edinburgh: Edinburgh University Press.

McEnery, T., Xiao, R., and Tono, Y. (2005) *Corpus-Based Language Studies: An Advanced Resource Book*. London: Routledge.
Nini, A. (2017) Register variation in malicious forensic texts. *International Journal of Speech, Language and the Law* 24(1): 99–126. https://doi.org/10.1558/ijsll.30173
Nini, A. (2021) Corpus analysis in forensic linguistics. In C. A. Chapelle, (ed), *The Concise Encyclopedia of Applied Linguistics*, Hoboken: Wiley-Blackwell, pp. 313–320. https://doi.org/10.1002/9781405198431.wbeal0238.pub2
Page, R., Barton, D., Unger, J. and Zappavigna, M. (2014) *Researching the Language of Social Media*. London: Routledge.
Partington, A. (2010) Modern Diachronic Corpus-Assisted Discourse Studies (MD-CADS) on UK newspapers: An overview of the project. *Corpora* 5(2): 83–108. https://doi.org/10.3366/cor.2010.0101
Partington, A. (2017) Varieties of non-obvious meaning in CL and CADS: From 'hindsight post-dictability' to sweet serendipity. *Corpora* 12(3): 339–367. https://doi.org/10.3366/cor.2017.0124
Partington, A., Duguid, A. and Taylor, C. (2013) *Patterns and Meanings in Discourse: Theory and Practice in Corpus-Assisted Discourse Studies (CADS)*. Amsterdam/Philadelphia: John Benjamins.
Petyko, M., Busso, L. Grant, T., and Atkins, S. (2022) The Aston forensic linguistic databank (FoLD). *Language and Law/Linguagem e Direito* 9(1): 9–24. https://doi.org/10.21747/21833745/lanlaw/9_1a1
Reppen, R. (2022) Building a corpus: What are key considerations? In: A. O'Keeffe and M. McCarthy (eds.), *The Routledge Handbook of Corpus Linguistics* (2nd ed.). London: Routledge, pp. 13–20.
Rheindorf, M. (2019) *Revisiting the Toolbox of Discourse Studies: New Trajectories in Methodology, Open Data, and Visualization*. Basingstoke: Palgrave.
Rüdiger, S. and Dayter, D. (2017) The ethics of researching unlikable subjects. *Applied Linguistics Review* 8(2–3): 251–269. https://doi.org/10.1515/applirev-2016-1038
Scott, M. (2020) *WordSmith Tools version 8*. Stroud: Lexical Analysis Software.
Scott, M. (2024) *WordSmith Tools Help*. Stroud: Lexical Analysis Software.
Stark, A. (2018) *Public Inquiries, Policy Learning, and the Threat of Future Crises*. Oxford: Oxford University Press.
Stubbs, M. (1983) *Discourse Analysis: The Sociolinguistic Analysis of Natural Language*. Chicago: University of Chicago Press.
Stubbs, M. (1996) *Text and Corpus Analysis: Computer-Assisted Studies of Language and Culture*. London: Blackwell.
Stubbs, M. (2001) *Words and Phrases: Corpus Studies of Lexical Semantics*. London: Blackwell.
Su, Q., Gu, C. and Liu, P. (2024) Association measures for collocation extraction: Automatic evaluation on a large-scale corpus. *International Journal of Corpus Linguistics* 29(1): 59–86. https://doi.org/10.1075/ijcl.21056.su
Szczyrbak, M. (2020) Verb patterns in trial discourse: The case of 'I think'. *Discourse and Interaction* 13(2): 119–135. https://doi.org/10.5817/DI2020-2-119
Tabbert, U. (2016) *Language and Crime – Constructing Offenders and Victims in Newspaper Reports*. Basingstoke: Palgrave Macmillan.
Tkačuková, T. (2015) A corpus-assisted study of the discourse marker well as an indicator of judges' institutional roles in court cases with litigants in person. *Corpora* 10(2): 145–170. https://doi.org/10.3366/cor.2015.0072

Tognini-Bonelli, E. (2001) *Corpus Linguistics at Work*. Amsterdam/Philadelphia: John Benjamins.

Toulmin, S. E. (2003) *The Uses of Argument*. Cambridge, UK: Cambridge University Press. (1st ed. 1958).

Trklja, A. and McAuliffe, K. (2019) Formulaic metadiscursive signalling devices in judgments of the Court of Justice of the European Union: A new corpus-based model for studying discourse relations of texts. *International Journal of Speech, Language and the Law* 26(1): 21–55. https://doi.org/10.1558/ijsll.36920

University of Oxford. (2021) *Internet-mediated Research*. Central University Research Ethics Committee (CUREC). Best Practice Guidance 06_Version 7. Available at: https://researchsupport.web.ox.ac.uk/files/bpg-06-internet-based-research-ibr [Last accessed April 2024].

Woolls, D. (2003) Better tools for the trade and how to use them. *International Journal of Speech, Language and the Law* 10(1): 102–112. https://doi.org/10.1558/sll.2003.10.1.102

Woolls, D. and Coulthard, M. (1998) Tools for the trade. *International Journal of Speech, Language and the Law* 5(1): 33–57. https://doi.org/10.1558/sll.1998.5.1.33

Wright, D. (2017) Using word n-grams to identify authors and idiolects: A corpus approach to a forensic linguistic problem. *International Journal of Corpus Linguistics* 22(2): 212–241. https://doi.org/10.1075/ijcl.22.2.03wri

Wright, D. (2021) Corpus approaches to forensic linguistics. In M. Coulthard, A. May and R. Sousa-Silva (eds.), *The Routledge Handbook of Forensic Linguistics* (2nd ed.). London: Routledge, pp. 611–627.

Wright, D. (2024) The importance of context in analysing the incitement of violence: A case study of an online community. In S. Rüdiger and D. Dayter (eds.), *Manipulation, Influence and Deception: The Changing Landscape of Persuasive Language*. Cambridge, UK: Cambridge University Press, pp. 157–176.

Wright, D. (forthcoming) Forensic linguistics. In M. Mahlberg and G. Brookes (eds.), *The Bloomsbury Handbook of Corpus Linguistics*. London: Bloomsbury.

Wright, D. and Brookes, G. (2019) 'This is England, speak English!': A corpus-assisted critical study of language ideologies in the right-leaning British press. *Critical Discourse Studies* 16(1): 56–83. https://doi.org/10.1080/17405904.2018.1511439

Wright, D., Robson, J., Murray-Edwards, H. and Braber, N. (2022) The pragmatic functions of 'respect' in lawyers' courtroom discourse: A case study of Brexit *hearings. Journal of Pragmatics* 187: 1–12. https://doi.org/10.1016/j.pragma.2021.10.028

Wright, D., Jackson, J., Doak, J., Saunders, C. and Cooper, D. (2025) Signposting topics in the cross-examination of vulnerable witnesses. In T. Grieshofer and K. Haworth (eds.), *Communication and Legal Practice: Language, Procedure, Process*. Cambridge, UK: Cambridge University Press.

3 Thirty years of corpora in forensic and legal linguistics

Corpora at the birth of forensic linguistics

On Wednesday, 30 November 1949, Timothy Evans entered the Central Police Station in Merthyr Tydfil, Wales, and said 'I want to give myself up. I have disposed of my wife'. When asked what he meant by a constable at the station, Evans responded, 'I put her down the drain'. Evans then offered to make a statement to the police, despite admitting 'I am not very well educated and cannot read or write' (Brabin 1966: 7). Two hours later, Evans had given the first of four statements that he would eventually give to two different police forces and that marked the beginning of 'a series of events that will be forever remembered in criminal history' (Svartvik 1968: 7). The four statements that Evans gave varied dramatically in their content. In the first two, both given to Merthyr Tydfil police force on 30 November 1949, Evans alleges that his wife Beryl had died during failed attempts to abort their second unborn baby. First, Evans reported that this was a result of ingesting an unknown substance from a bottle that he had been given by a stranger, before he changed his story and told police that she had died during an abortion attempt by John Christie, the couple's co-tenant at their home at 10 Rillington Place in Notting Hill, London. In both of these statements, Evans told police that he had arranged to have their 14-month-old daughter Geraldine looked after, before getting the train to Wales. In the second two statements, both given to Notting Hill police force on 2 December 1949, Evans confessed to killing his wife in a fit of anger and then later killing Geraldine. The next day, Evans was charged with the murder of both his wife and daughter. Evans was found guilty of the murder of his daughter Geraldine and was hanged at Pentonville prison, London on 9 March 1950.[1]

In 1953, the bodies of six women, including that of John Christie's wife, were found in the kitchen, under the floorboards and in the garden of Christie's flat at 10 Rillington Place. On 25 June 1953, John Christie was convicted of the murder of his wife and was hanged in Pentonville prison,

DOI: 10.4324/9781003017301-3

the same place that Evans was hanged only three years earlier. In 1965, a Public Inquiry led by Hon. Mr Justice Brabin was launched to examine the evidence in the cases against both Evans and Christie relating to the deaths of Beryl and Geraldine Evans and in particular to help determine whether Evans was indeed responsible for their deaths. The inquiry concluded that it was more probable than not that Evans killed Beryl but that it was probably Christie who killed Geraldine, the murder for which Evans had hanged. In October 1966, sixteen years after his hanging, Timothy Evans was granted a royal pardon, and in 2004, the High Court of England and Wales concluded that Evans was not responsible for the killing of either his wife or his daughter, formally exonerating him of both murders. His execution is considered one of the most significant miscarriages of justice in the U.K. (Carradice 2012).

Throughout the case and the subsequent inquiry, a great deal of attention was paid to the two statements that Evans allegedly gave to Notting Hill police – the first of which was just over 100 words long and the second of which was much longer, totalling almost 2000 words – in which he confessed to murdering both his wife and child. In particular, there are two paragraphs in the middle section of the longer statement which contain the confessions themselves. The Brabin report details that Evans claimed that he made a false confession because he was shocked and upset to find out that his daughter had died, that he did not care what happened to him, and that he was afraid the police officers would beat him up (Brabin 1966: 102). It also outlines the opinions of medical professionals who offered theories as to why Evans would confess, including guilt, tension, emotional shock or that he was particularly susceptible to suggestion and brainwashing (Brabin 1966: 140–8), though Brabin himself was inclined to think that Christie had somehow persuaded Evans to implicate himself in his daughter's murder (Brabin 1966: 156). In any case, there was reason to believe that the specific parts of the final statement that Evans gave to the police were in some way different or divergent from not only the other statements that he gave but in fact the other parts of that same statement. Jan Svartvik set out to conduct a linguistic analysis of the statements to 'find out whether the intuitively based observations' about the statement(s) 'have any support from a more rigid, objective linguistic scrutiny' (Svartvik 1968: 19). Svartvik used a corpus linguistic approach to combine quantitative and qualitative analyses of the 4,861-word dataset, and found a number of 'stylistic discrepancies' in the statements, relating to the use of double negatives, non-standard verb forms and relative pronouns, and found a set of lexico-grammatical features in the second confessional statement 'which appear to be uncharacteristic' of Evans's idiolect as exhibited in the other statements, such as *incurring*, *in his presence* and *in a fit of temper* (Svartvik 1968: 24).

One of the key findings of Svartvik's analysis related to the distribution of certain types of finite clauses within and across the four statements. He found that there was a statistically significant difference in the frequency distributions of these six clause types in the two sections of the final statement in which he admitted killing his wife and daughter when compared with the rest of that statement. In particular, the two incriminating sections have much higher frequencies of two types of finite clause: (i) clauses with a mobile relator, namely *then* (e.g. *I then made my baby some food and fed it, then I saw with the baby by the fire*), and (ii) clauses with elliptic subject linkage – those which have no overt subject since they share it with a previous clause (e.g. *I then put the baby back in the cot and sat down in the kitchen*). No such variation was found in any of the other statements that Evans gave, serving to rule out, at least to some extent, that this was a possible register effect. Not only that, but there were 23 instances of subject + relator constructions (i.e. *I then*, as opposed to *then I*), 21 of which occurred in the confessional parts of the statement. Although Svartvik (1968: 46) acknowledges that his analysis cannot be the basis of firm conclusions, he argues that the differences in the two most significant parts of Evans's final statement 'appear to be too remarkable' to be explained by the small corpus size and the process of statement taking. Whatever the reasons for the distinctive nature of the most important, indeed *fatal*, parts of this statement, Svartvik claims, 'the results of this study corroborate Evans's standpoint' that these sections of the statement are different to the rest, whether they be false confessions or otherwise. In his preface to this corpus analysis, Svartvik (1968: i) notes that

> This sally into the relatively uncultivated field of 'forensic linguistics' has been interesting for a number of reasons, but two in particular. Firstly, it has provided the linguist with one of those rare opportunities of making a contribution that might be directly useful to society.

This quotation contains what is widely regarded as the first published mention of 'forensic linguistics' and so, in that way, corpus linguistics – or at least a corpus-based approach of quantitatively and qualitatively analysing text – was present at the 'birth' of forensic linguistics.

Twenty-six years later, in the inaugural issue of *Forensic Linguistics: The International Journal of Speech, Language and Law*,[2] Malcolm Coulthard published an article entitled 'On the use of corpora in the analysis of forensic texts', the aim of which was 'to discuss a major new resource for the forensic linguist, the rapidly growing discipline of *corpus linguistics*' (Coulthard 1994: 27, original emphasis). In the article, Coulthard uses real cases to demonstrate the utility of corpora in forensic linguistic analysis. This includes a discussion of the ways in which John Sinclair used a 5 million-word newspaper corpus and the Birmingham Corpus of English Text to give an opinion to the court on the 'ordinary' meaning of the word *visa*. He also advocates for the courts to permit forensic linguist expert witnesses to present concordance lines to demonstrate language patterns rather than through the usual and rigid courtroom practice of question-and-answer witnesses examination. But the headline-grabbing case in this article, and the case with which the article is synonymous, is Coulthard's report on how he used a corpus approach in his analysis of the now infamous police statement allegedly given by Derek Bentley.

In 1953, 19-year-old Derek Bentley was convicted and hanged for the murder of a police officer after his friend, Chris Craig, fatally shot the officer while Bentley was under arrest. Bentley's conviction relied entirely on the statement that he gave to the police and the reliability and honesty of the testimony given by the officers on the scene. In the trial, the prosecution needed to demonstrate that Bentley could be guilty of murder despite being under arrest when the murder was committed. The evidence used by the prosecution to do this was two-fold. First, in his statement, Bentley had allegedly said 'I did not know he was going to use the gun'. The trial judge emphasised to the jury that the use of '<u>the</u> gun' rather than '<u>a</u> gun' showed that Bentley knew his friend had a gun before it was used. Second, in their statements and evidence given in court, the arresting officers testified that Bentley had said 'let him have it, Chris', immediately before the fatal shots were fired, which they interpreted as incitement. During the initial trial, Bentley contested the statement and claimed that, rather than the statement being a product of a monologue by Bentley, the police had 'helped' him with it, a claim that the officers denied under oath, asserting that it was a verbatim account of what Bentley had said (Coulthard 1994: 32).

Malcolm Coulthard was commissioned to produce a report for an appeal against Bentley's conviction in 1993, after which Bentley was granted a limited posthumous pardon. Part of Coulthard's analysis took a corpus-assisted analysis of the register of statements given to police. In brief, one of the most marked features of Bentley's 588-word statement was the use of the word *then*, appearing eleven times – a frequency which, when compared with other witness statements, suggested at that this may be an intrusion of a specific feature of the professional police register. To test this hypothesis, Coulthard used corpora in two ways. First, he built two small corpora for comparison, one made up of three ordinary witness statements totalling 930 words and another made up of statements written by police officers, two of whom were involved in the Bentley case, comprising 2270 words. Coulthard found that *then* appeared only once in the ordinary witness statements but 29 times in those written by police, an average of once every 78 words. Coulthard's second-stage corpus analysis involved turning to the general reference Corpus of Spoken English, a subset of the COBUILD Birmingham Collection of English Text, which at the time held 1.5 million words of naturally occurring speech. There were only 3,164 instances of *then* in the reference corpus, or once every 500 words. This provided support for the hypothesis that Bentley's frequent use of *then* was closer to that of the police statements than of other ordinary witnesses statements and spoken English generally. This evidence was strengthened further when close attention was paid to the positioning of *then*, and in particular Bentley's frequent use of subject + *then* (e.g. *Chris then jumped*), which accounted for seven of his eleven uses. In particular, Bentley's short statement contains three instances of *I then*, about one occurrence in every 190 words. In contrast, the *I then* structure appears only nine times in the 1.5 million–word spoken reference corpus and not at all in the corpus of ordinary witness statements. However, *I then* appeared as many as nine times in *one* of the police statements alone that was part of the police comparison corpus – as many as were found in the whole 1.5 million–word spoken corpus. Coulthard made the point that this appears to be a feature of the police's written register and its embedding, along with other features, provided support for the claim that Bentley's statement was not a product of Bentley alone but was a jointly authored document. This undermined the incriminating force of the mention of *the gun* in the statement as well as the reliability of the officers who allegedly heard Bentley incite Craig to *let him have it*. For a fuller, detailed account of the case and the analysis, see Coulthard (1994) and Coulthard et al. (2017: 163). The Court of Appeal eventually quashed Derek Bentley's conviction in 1998, 45 years after he was executed.

Svartvik's and Coulthard's analyses of the Evans and Bentley statements respectively share many similarities. Coulthard (1994: 33) himself notes that the use of *then* post-positioned after the subject was a telling feature in both statements. Besides that, both cases focus on 'verballing in disputed confessions' (Grant 2022: 12), both Bentley and Evans had low levels of literacy, and both are now considered to be among the most significant miscarriages of justice the U.K. has seen. However, the most important similarity as far as this book is concerned is that they both used a combination of qualitative and quantitative analyses facilitated by a corpus approach to forensic texts. This puts corpora at not only at the site at which 'forensic linguistics' was coined by Svartvik but also the analysis of Bentley's statement by Coulthard in 1994 which proved to be the catalyst for the establishment and rapid expansion of contemporary forensic and legal linguistics.

The growing status of corpora in forensic and legal linguistics

Although both Svartvik (1968) and Coulthard (1994) both used corpus-based approaches to analysing language in forensic contexts, Coulthard was far more explicit in his promotion of corpus methods. In the introduction to his article, Coulthard (1994: 27) states that corpus linguistics 'provides not only a new kind of data but also new ways of analysing those data on which forensic linguists have traditionally concentrated.' Later, in concluding the article, he predicts that the future of forensic linguistics 'must lie in the creation of a better, standardized and more widely used methodology' and that 'any improved methodology must depend, to a large extent, on the setting up and analysing of corpora' (Coulthard 1994: 40). The thirty years since this prediction has seen the widespread uptake of corpora and corpus methods in studies of forensic and legal linguistics. Although it is possible that Coulthard was primarily referring to the use of corpora in forensic linguistic casework, dealing with language in evidence, corpora have permeated all corners of the field and have contributed in a significant way to the field's development and expansion. The aims of this chapter are to provide an overview of this work and account for the ways in which corpora and corpus methods have been utilised in forensic and legal contexts in the thirty years since Coulthard (1994).

Since Coulthard's call to action in 1994, there has been a series of chapters published which provide an outline of the ways in which corpus linguistics has featured in forensic linguistic research and casework. One of the earliest reflective discussions of corpus approaches in forensic linguistics appeared in Hunston's (2002) monograph on the role of corpora in applied linguistics. Here, forensic linguistics is considered a sub-discipline of applied linguistics in which corpora can be used. Hunston focuses primarily on two applications of corpus linguistics in this context, both of which hinge on the comparison of texts and corpora. She first outlines Coulthard's (1994) use of corpora in the Derek Bentley case before summarising the use of lexical frequencies and shared vocabulary across sets of texts in the analysis of plagiarism in studies such as Johnson (1997). Seven years later, Blackwell (2009) published a chapter with a title that echoed Coulthard's sentiment fifteen years earlier: 'why forensic linguistics needs corpus linguistics'. Like Coulthard, Blackwell advocates for the use of corpora to answer forensic linguistic questions, particularly questions of authorship, drawing on two case studies involving a disputed witness statement and a suspected falsified suicide note. Interestingly, Blackwell notes the different opportunities afforded by general reference corpora and more specialised corpora, and makes the case for a 'purpose-built corpus for research in language and law' (Blackwell 2009: 16). Olsson's (2009) chapter 'Some aspects of the use of corpora in forensic linguistics' opens with the assessment that 'it is arguable that corpus linguistics has had some of its greatest successes in the field of forensic linguistics' (Olsson 2009: 84), before describing the ways in which corpora have been used in cases of questioned authorship. Cotterill's (2010) chapter 'How to use corpus linguistics in forensic linguistics' focused on the comparison of texts and corpora in cases of authorship analysis, including the comparison of author-specific corpora in Svartvik (1968) and Eagleson (1994), the use of general reference corpora in Fox (1993) and Coulthard (1994) and the use of the web-as-corpus in the Unabomber case in 1995 (a technique problematised twenty years later by Larner (2014a)). Up until this point, then, it would appear that the use of corpus linguistics in forensic linguistics had been restricted to questions of authorship, or at least this was considered the *main* area in which corpora could benefit forensic linguists.

That may have been the case until Kredens and Coulthard's (2012) chapter 'corpus linguistics in authorship identification'. The chapter reiterates, with examples, the utility of corpora in text comparison for purposes of authorship or plagiarism analysis. However, the scope of the chapter extends beyond the specificity of its title, as Kredens and Coulthard go on to demonstrate and discuss the ways in which corpora and corpus linguistic techniques can be used in many other areas of forensic and legal linguistics, namely in the determination of meaning in corporate litigation, statutory interpretation, the analysis of the variability of legal language across genres, the analysis of police interviews and trial discourse and the use of the web-as-corpus for accessing patterns of usage and meaning underrepresented in traditional corpora. In addition, Kredens and Coulthard (2012) discuss a range of corpora of different text-types that had been or were being complied contemporaneously to their chapter that could be valuable for forensic purposes, such as datasets of suicide notes (e.g. Shapero 2011), SMS text messages (e.g. Tagg 2009) and threatening letters (e.g. Gales 2010). In the conclusion to their chapter, Kredens and Coulthard (2012: 516) state their hope that they 'have given a sufficiently wide range of examples to indicate the value of language corpora and corpus techniques across the whole spectrum of forensic linguistics'. Indeed, they did, and for the first time this chapter brought together work from across the field that had hitherto not been represented in overviews of corpus linguistics in forensic linguistics. This chapter was followed shortly after by another overview of corpus analysis in forensic linguistics by Cotterill (2012). Although Cotterill (2012: 1249) makes the point that 'corpus linguistics can prove extremely useful in exploring linguistic characteristics of legal genres', she again focuses her attention on the use of corpora in comparative text analyses in cases of authorship (as in her 2010 chapter), either using specialised text-type specific corpora (e.g. SMS text messages) or the web-as-corpus, detailing at length the methodology employed in the Unabomber case. Sousa-Silva (2018) considers corpus approaches to forensic linguistics as being part of a larger field which he terms 'computational forensic linguistics'. The point is made that computational forensic linguistics can be heavily computational to the extent that it involves little to no human intervention or can be 'computer-assisted' where computational tools and techniques are used to aid manual analysis (Sousa-Silva 2018: 120) and has a broad range of applications across authorship analysis, plagiarism detection, fake news analysis and predictive policing. In discussing corpus approaches specifically, Sousa-Silva (2018: 123) draws attention to Finegan's (2010) use of corpus methods in the analysis of adverbials in U.S. Supreme Court opinions and Johnson and Wright's (2014) corpus approach to analysing idiolectal style and authorship, as well as outlining the respective affordances of general reference corpora and 'DIY corpora' to forensic linguistics. The range of corpus linguistic approaches to forensic linguistics is also represented by Nini (2021). Like Cotterill (2012), Nini focuses on the 'investigative' element of forensic linguistics but discusses a wider variety of investigative challenges that corpus linguistics can help with. First, Nini discusses ways in which more recent work in comparative authorship analysis has built on the methodological foundations laid by Coulthard (1994) in both research (e.g. Johnson and Wright 2014; Larner 2016) and casework (e.g. Grant 2013) contexts. Nini goes further, however, to detail the benefits of corpus approaches in authorship profiling, an area not captured by previous overviews (e.g. Nini 2015; Perkins and Grant 2018). In addition, Nini's chapter details the way in which corpora and corpus methods have been employed in trademark disputes (e.g. Kilgariff 2015) and the determination of meaning of both legal terms (e.g. Solan and Gales 2016) and of slang terms (e.g. Grant 2017). Following his overview, Nini (2021) argues that corpus linguistics is 'not only is a promising method but has the potential to become the most important way to analyse linguistic evidence in the future'. Goźdź-Roszkowski (2021) is a departure from the norm in terms of overviews of corpus and forensic linguistics, as the focus in this article is corpus approaches to legal discourse (rather than 'investigative' applications). The article reviews a wide range of corpus applications in the analysis of the lexico-grammar of legal discourse, including phraseology, collocation and co-selection in legislative text and judicial argumentation, legal translation, variation, genre and register perspectives on legal texts and evaluative language in legal contexts, demonstrating how 'corpus studies of legal discourse have revealed patterns of use and distribution that are not visible when examining individual texts or even many texts individually' (Goźdź-Roszkowski 2021: 1533). Although relevant criticisms of the corpus approach are outlined, it is argued that they have 'brought greater scientific rigour thanks to systematic explorations of reliable, representative and balanced corpora, superseding anecdotal illustrations based on scant and random textual evidence' (Goźdź-Roszkowski 2021: 1533). Most recently, Gillings (2022), in the same way as most overviews of the area, focuses primarily on uses of corpora and corpus linguistics in investigative forensic linguistics (though there is a mention of courtroom and legal discourse). Gillings (2022: 589) notes that despite predicting the widespread uptake of corpora in forensic linguistics, Coulthard (1994) could not have predicted 'the wide range of applications that corpus linguistics has had' and dedicates the chapter to, at least in part, provide detail of how corpus approaches have been used in emerging areas of forensic linguistics. Gillings starts by discussing the way(s) in which corpus approaches can be used to combine quantitative and qualitative analyses in comparative authorship attribution, before broadening out to describing corpus approaches to the determination of meaning in statutory interpretation, deception detection and disinformation, the inclusion of the latter two areas reflecting the increasing amount of work in these emerging areas (e.g. Archer and Lansley 2015; Larner 2019a; Dance 2019).

Perhaps the most balanced treatment of corpora in forensic and legal linguistics is given by Larner (2015), in the introduction to his special issue on forensic linguistics in the journal *Corpora*. The issue itself includes four articles which together demonstrate the use of corpora across a wide range of forensic and legal texts and/or purposes, including judges' courtroom discourse (Tkačuková 2015), threats (Gales 2015a), online trolling (Hardaker 2015) and deception detection (Archer & Lansley 2015). In the introduction, Larner (2015: 132) argues that 'corpus techniques and approaches are now accepted and widely used by forensic linguists' and sets out to 'bring together a disparate array of forensic linguistics research which uses corpora and corpus techniques'. To do that, Larner provides a 52-entry annotated bibliography of studies that use corpora or corpus methods in some way as a means by which to show the 'development of corpus linguistics in forensic linguistics', as well as the 'multitude of ways in which corpora have been developed and used in a variety of different applications' (Larner 2015: 133). Even though Larner makes clear that, for reasons of space, the list 'should not be treated as exhaustive' (Larner 2015: 134), it was the broadest and most representative account of the ways in which corpora have been used in forensic or forensically relevant ways. Furthermore, in compiling and presenting the bibliography, Larner follows Johnson and Coulthard's (2010: 7) three-part classification of forensic linguistic work; in the list of 52 items, 16 were categorised as 'written language of the law', 13 as 'interaction in the legal process' and 24 as 'linguists acting as an expert witness'. The last of these three areas of forensic linguistics corresponds to the investigative forensic linguistics that has been at the heart of most overviews of corpus and forensic linguistics. However, as these numbers show, there is far more work in legal linguistics than has traditionally been accounted for in discussions of corpora in forensic linguistics; 29 of the 52 items saw corpora being applied in the analysis of written or spoken language in the legal process. Larner's bibliography reflects the fact that corpora and corpus approaches have been, and are being, employed regularly in forensic linguistics far beyond authorship problems.

The overviews of corpus methods in forensic and legal linguistics discussed here can also be used to track the gradually increasing prevalence of corpora and corpus methods in forensic such (Table 3.1). In 1994, Coulthard introduced corpus methods as a new development in the field and demonstrated their potential applications and importance. By 2010, Cotterill noted that corpus methods were 'becoming increasingly commonplace' in forensic linguistics. By the time Larner was writing in 2015, the view was that corpus approaches not only were becoming more common but were being 'accepted and widely used'. Fast-forwarding another six years to 2021, Nini initiated that, at least for some forensic questions, corpus linguistics was 'the main methodological approach'. Finally, in 2022, Gillings echoes Cotterill some twelve years earlier, emphasising that corpus approaches are no longer *becoming* commonplace, but are now established in the field. These quotations reflect the changing status of corpora and corpus methods in forensic and legal linguistics, from being a new and promising approach to the field in 1994 to being accepted, common and widely used by 2022.

Corpora and the development of forensic linguistics

Most discussions of corpora in forensic and legal linguistics have taken what might be considered a 'topical' approach, in which details are given about the different areas in which corpus methods have been applied to good effect. This chapter takes a slightly different, more functional, approach, insofar as it is structured in terms of the developments that corpus linguistics have facilitated in forensic and legal linguistics. That is, it aims to answer the question: what have corpora *allowed* analysts to do, and how has this served in developing and expanding the field? In order to do this, we can revisit the three potential benefits of corpus linguistics indicated by Coulthard:

- 'New ways of analysing those data on which forensic linguists have traditionally concentrated' (1994: 27)
- Offering a new 'improved methodology' for forensic linguistic analysis (1994: 40)
- Providing 'a new kind of data' (1994: 27).

Inspired by these three points, the discussion below aims to outline the role that corpus approaches have had in the development of forensic and legal linguistics in terms of offering (i) new perspectives on familiar genres, (ii) possible solutions to methodological challenges and (iii) new avenues for research. The aim of this survey of work is not to provide a comprehensive

Table 3.1 Quotations reflecting the growing centrality of corpora and corpus methods in forensic and legal linguistics (my emphasis)

Citation	*Relevant quotation*
Coulthard (1994: 27):	'[corpus linguistics] provides not only a *new kind of data*, but also *new ways of analysing those data* on which forensic linguists have traditionally concentrated'
Cotterill (2010: 578):	'In an age of computerisation, the use of corpora in many types of forensic linguistic analysis *is becoming increasingly commonplace*'.
Larner (2015: 132):	'Despite the fact that there is still much more work to be done [...] corpus techniques and approaches are *now accepted and widely used* by forensic linguists.'
Nini (2021: 313):	'[C]orpus analysis is therefore gradually establishing itself as the norm for solving certain forensic problems and how it is *becoming the main methodological approach* for forensic linguistics.'
Gillings (2022: 590):	'What we will find, therefore, is that rather than the use of corpora *becoming* increasingly commonplace, *it is now commonplace*.'

overview of all of the research that exists which combines corpus and forensic/legal linguistics but to represent the scope and nature of this work.

New perspectives on familiar genres

The collection and analysis of large datasets have provided new insights and into discourse types that have long been at the heart of forensic linguistics; in Coulthard's (1994: 27) terms, they have provided 'new ways of analysing those data on which forensic linguists have traditionally concentrated'. Much of this work falls in three broad areas: written legal genres, the language of the courtroom and the language of judicial opinions. This work, and research in related extensions of these areas, is outlined here.

Written legal genres

The nature of legal language (or more accurately legal *English*) has long been the focus of analysis for both linguists and lawyers, with early seminal studies such as those by Mellinkoff (1963), Crystal and Davy (1969), Bhatia (1993) and Tiersma (1999) forming the foundations of much of this work. The addition of corpus techniques to the analyst's toolbox has facilitated the quantitative examination of the linguistic features of the law and legal language(s), which has provided a broader evidence base for the distinctive nature of legal register(s). (See Chapter 3 of Coulthard et al. 2017 for a straightforward demonstration of the benefits of a quantitative approach.) Not only has corpus linguistics provided new approaches to analysing written legal language, but it has also seen the examination of a much wider range of international legal languages and jurisdictions, often facilitating a comparative analysis across languages and contexts. Such are the processes and procedures of corpus analysis that they are well positioned to aid in the systematic and rigorous analysis of the prevalence, use and function of specific linguistic features in specific legal contexts, thereby enhancing our understanding of discourse and participant roles within these contexts. Goźdź-Roszkowski and Pontrandolfo (2018) provide a collection of studies which take a corpus-based and interdisciplinary approach to analysing phraseology in legal settings, with contributing chapters investigating lexical bundles, phrasal units, binomial expressions, word n-grams and formulaic sequences in monolingual, multilingual and translated legislative and judicial discourses. Goźdź-Roszkowski and Pontrandolfo (2018: 2) argue that the analyses contained with their collection 'confirm that it is hardly possible to study legal phrasemes manually' and 'provides fresh and compelling evidence that corpora and corpus linguistics techniques remain the driving force being much of the current research into legal phraseology'. Similarly, Fanego and Rodríguez-Puente (2019) bring together a collection of studies that apply corpus linguistic in the analysis of various types of legal discourse, including contracts, written legislation, law reports and the criminal trial. The collection represents work on historical as well as contemporary data and includes English, French, Spanish and Italian language corpora. Across the book, the chapters use the well-established corpus techniques of (word) frequencies, collocation, lexical bundles/clusters and concordance analysis to investigate a wide range of linguistic phenomena including relativization, nominalization, binomials, modality, conditionals, tense and aspect, phrase and clause structure, social actor representation and rhetorical moves. Fanego and Rodríguez-Puente (2019: 17) note 'the utility of corpora as data pools to be analysed through ever more sophisticated computational tools' for analysing legal discourses of past and present.

Multilingual corpora of European Union (EU) law have often been the target of corpus analysis. Biel (2015) uses a corpus-based comparative approach in analysing the frequency and use of complex prepositions in Polish, U.K. and multilingual EU law, comparing not only the distribution and function of complex prepositions in legislative registers with that in 'general language' (represented by British and Polish reference corpora) but also across languages and legal systems. The results from the corpus analysis lead to the findings that 'the phraseological profiles of legislative instruments are marked by the high frequency and resulting cognitive salience of complex prepositions' (Biel 2015: 158). In a later study, Biel et al. (2018) identify and examine key terms and their collocates in a 1.5 million–word corpus of

EU Competition Law in English, with their results identifying features that 'attest to the impact of the EU's constitutive languages and cultures and the resulting hybridity of EU English' (Biel et al. 2018: 205). Staying with EU Competition Law, Dobrić Basaneže (2018) and Sosoni (2018) compare multilingual and translated EU legislation using parallel corpora. Dobrić Basaneže (2018) takes a corpus approach to investigating binomial expressions two parallel corpora of EU Competition Law – English and Croatian – producing results suggesting that binomials are more idiomatic in some languages than others. Bajčić and Dobrić Basaneže (2021) extend the English/Croatian comparison, identifying strategies of 'foreignization' and 'domestication' in the translation of legal terminology. Meanwhile, Sosoni (2018) compares the use and translation of EU Competition Law concepts and terms in English, Greek, Italian and Spanish, highlighting 'the demanding role of lawmakers, translators and all those involved in interpreting and implementing EU legislation' (Sosoni 2018: 149).

It is not only European law and/or languages that have been subject to corpus attention. Wang and Yin (2020) focus on the lexical and semantic character of Chinese legislation by performing a keyword analysis of a corpus Chinese legislative texts by comparing it with a 1.7 billion–word Chinese Web 2011. Through the semantic categorisation of the top 50 keywords, Wang and Yin (2020: 651) conclude that 'legislative Chinese is biased towards Politics and Economy', with a focus on living things and quantity and driven by the requirement for accuracy and precision. Combining corpus linguistics, Critical Discourse Analysis and Conceptual Metaphor Theory, Chiu and Chiang (2011) examine FIGHT metaphors in a corpus of 134,141 Taiwan legal statutes and judgements. They focused in particular on the LITIGATION IS A FIGHT metaphor, revealing 'the relationship among concepts, ideologies, and linguistic configurations in legal discourse' and arguing that legal professionals and the individuals involved in litigation should 'reconsider how FIGHT metaphors affect the legal culture and, by extension, individuals' lives as part of society' (Chiu and Chiang 2011: 908). Li et al. (2016) focus on features of modality and negation in Chinese legislation in Hong Kong, Macau, Taiwan and Mainland China. Their analysis relied on frequency profiles and concordances of a range of modal verbs and their negated forms in legislative texts and found an important interaction between the two, with the authors arguing that 'negation helps us to investigate the distribution of deontic modality in Hong Kong legislation and therefore revisit the legal framework in Hong Kong' (Li et al. 2016: 338). Sun and Cheng (2017) conduct a multidimensional analysis (MDA) on a Chinese legislative corpus, the corresponding English translation corpus and an American legislative corpus, identifying and comparing the general characteristics, tendencies and preferences identified in the three types of legislative texts. For the authors, the use of a corpus approach makes the examination of legislative language 'more meaningful' by virtue of the size of the dataset and this, they argue, has 'implications for future studies in both the systematic and functional descriptions of lexico-grammatical patterns exploring linguistic variation in legal language' (Sun and Cheng 2017: 418). Cheng and Wang (2017) and Gong et al. (2020) use corpus methods to analyse modality in Chinese civil laws, with Gong et al. (2020: 337) arguing that a corpus-driven approach not only helps to examine the legislative use of modality over time but also contributes to an understanding of 'modality mechanisms by providing both empirical evidence and theoretical insights'. Pei and Cheng (2020) explore the relationship between terminology and ideology in U.S. and E.U data protection legislation. Based on collocation analyses of the two most frequent lexical words in the corpora, *data* and *information*, Pei and Cheng (2020: 179) argue that variation in legal terminology is ideologically underpinned, and that 'the birth, evolution and death of legal terms may be put down to the ideological divide over values regarding online data protection' including 'different ideological philosophies of individual jurisdictions and distinct partisan ideologies'. Leung (2015) also takes a critical approach to multilingual law, combing the corpus analysis of bilingual English and Chinese sexual offence legislation and the enactment of that legislation in interpreted trial discourse. The analysis revealed the various stages of mediation, translation and interpretation a witness narrative undergoes and the power asymmetries involved. The use of the corpus approach, Leung (2015: 481) argues, has 'provided evidence to argue for better organised interpreting services and a more functional approach towards the translation of the legislation' in relation to rape trials in Hong Kong.

Corpus techniques have also been drawn on as offering new perspectives on the challenges and solutions to issues in the translation of legal documents. Goźdź-Roszkowski (2013), for example, applies a corpus-based collocation approach to discriminate between near-synonymous, semantically related terms across a range of American legal genres which often prove troublesome when translating legal texts. Pontrandolfo (2019) provides a detailed overview of the benefits and challenges of corpus methods in legal translation studies, reviewing the range of corpora available, the major trends in translation research using legal corpora and methodological approaches used as part of the empirical and 'technological turn' in legal translation studies. At the same time, Monzó Nebot (2008) demonstrates the role that corpus resources and corpus-driven activities can play in the training of legal translators. A training agenda using specialised legal corpora, Monzó Nebot (2008: 246) argues, can improve the proficiency of legal translators by revealing to them how genre-specific features are used in practice, how relevant conventions should be replicated and retained and how legal texts are presented and are read. Giampieri (2018: 51) also advocates for the use of corpus-oriented tools for teaching legal translation, particularly the triangulation of the web-as-corpus, web concordancers and specialised corpora in helping L2 English scholars and translators with the painstaking task of learning the 'peculiarities and the formulaic, fixed terms of the language of the law'. This position is reinforced by Giampieri and Milani (2021: 48), who conclude that the embedding of online legal corpora and consultation of such corpora for concordance and collocation searches in training sessions with translators and lawyers can help the 'linguistic intricacies of the language of law'.

Corpora and corpus tools have also been applied in the analysis of other written legal genres, sometimes in combination or comparison with legislative texts. Bhatia et al. (2004) report two studies of legal language, one analysing a corpus of 105 judgements from common law countries with relevance to Hong Kong and one analysing a corpus of Hong Kong law students' answers to legal problem questions. Using word frequency and concordance analysis, Bhatia et al. (2004: 224) demonstrate the ways that corpus analysis can be used to identify important lexico-grammatical patterns in professional legal discourses, and argue that corpus linguistics is a tool that can be integrated with qualitative measures to help answer the question 'Why do legal professionals use the language the way they do?' Motivated by linguistic observations that legal English is characterised by the 'frequent use' of Latin and French terminology (e.g. Mellinkoff 1963), Yuan et al. (2018) examine the frequency and use of Latin and French words in a specialised corpus of law journal articles and legal textbooks. Their analysis finds that such terminology is still 'actively used' in legal English reference work but is not evenly distributed across genres, with journal articles containing far more technical Latin terms than legal textbooks. The authors argue that these corpus findings have implications for legal English teaching and the Plain English Movement (Yuan et al. 2018: 170). Breeze (2011, 2013) combines commercial legislative discourse with academic journal articles, case law (law reports, court opinions) and legal documents (contracts, agreements) in a 2 million–word corpus of professional legal discourse. Breeze (2011) compared the relative frequencies and associated n-grams and semantic preferences of six stance-denoting adjective/adverb pairs across the four corpora, and identified *reasonable/reasonably*, *correct/correctly*, *proper/properly* and *appropriate/appropriately* as 'being particularly prominent in particular areas of legal discourse' and as 'being likely to embody community-specific values that shape the disciplinary culture of law' (Breeze 2011: 110). Breeze (2013) analyses the same corpus for the frequency and use of lexical bundles of between four and eight words. The comparison across the four genre sub-corpora finds lexical bundles of all lengths being most common in legislation and legal documents, reflecting their repetitive and formulaic nature. Elsewhere, Breeze (2019) shifts from lexical bundles to part-of-speech patterns and reveals grammatical similarities and differences across four corpora of different legal genres: academic texts, case law, legal documents, and legislation). Findings in relation to patterns pertaining to possessives, cohesion, grammatical specificity and grammatical co-ordination provides evidence for the 'highly specific ways in which language functions in legal genres' (Breeze 2019: 100). Cheng et al. (2021) use corpus techniques in combination with the discourse-historical approach to critical discourse analysis to examine U.S. laws and policy and strategy documents that are directly related to critical information infrastructure protection which, they argue, helps to provide a 'better understanding the legal practices in U.S. cybersecurity'. Zozula (2019) compares syntactic features across Polish, English (USA) and Indonesian constitutions and civil codes, showcasing the benefits of corpus-comparative approaches 'which have the potential to further our understanding of linguistic universality' (Zozula 2019: 85). Vogel et al. (2018) outline the various aspects of what they call 'Computer-Assisted Legal Linguistics', in which they detail the way in which corpus analysis can contribute to legal studies and be applied in various legal and socio-legal contexts. This includes areas such as legal semantics and legal interpretation, legal education and training law students, citations analysis and the analysis of legislation. The authors also provide examples of existing international legal corpora comprising legislative texts, judgements, case law, legal-administrative texts, decisions and legal learning resources. Buendía Castro and Faber (2015) meanwhile focus on legal dictionaries, in particular examining the collocation profiles of *vista* (*trial/hearing* in Spanish) to present 'a comparative analysis of how phraseology is dealt with in some of the most representative English-Spanish legal dictionaries' (Buendía Castro and Faber 2015: 172). Corpus approaches have also been used to examine the lexico-grammar of legal-lay texts, including terms of conditions/terms of use, EU legislation summaries, bank contracts and utility company contracts in English and Italian (Busso 2022a, 2022b), life insurance contracts in English (Hlioui 2020), and Philippine consumer-finance, insurance, construction services, employment and investment contracts (Ballesteros-Lintao et al. 2016).

Corpus linguistics, therefore, has seen a rapid expansion and variation in the ways that written legal language(s) have been analysed and the ways in which they can be understood, in terms of not just legislative texts themselves but also case law, academic journal articles, legal education texts, law student answers and legal dictionaries.

Courtroom genres

The discourse(s) of the courtroom trial has been a traditional focus of analysis in forensic and legal linguistics for many years (e.g. Woodbury 1984; Harris 1984; Drew 1992; Matoesian 1993; Eades 2000; Gibbons 2003).

Again, corpus approaches have provided new ways of analysing courtroom data, augmenting the largely (though not exclusively) qualitative methodological norm with quantitative analyses. Stubbs (1996: 101), in his seminal book on corpus linguistics, demonstrated the benefits of a corpus approach in analysing a judge's summing-up in a case of actual bodily harm, in particular in examining the connotations of words used, the frequency and function of modal verbs and the presuppositions in the messages conveyed by the judge. The affordances of a corpus linguistic approach to analysing courtroom discourse were also clearly demonstrated in the work of Janet Cotterill. Cotterill (2001, 2003) used the COBUILD Bank of English as a reference corpus to determine the semantic prosody (Stubbs 1996; Louw 1993) of lexical items in the representation of marital violence in the opening statements in the criminal trial of O.J. Simpson. Using corpus evidence to determine the 'semantic profile' of strategically chosen words by the attorneys for the prosecution (e.g. *control*, *cycle* [*of violence*]) and defence (e.g. *incident, discussion, conversation*), Cotterill illustrated the value of using corpus techniques to investigate the ways in which opposing sides in the trial leveraged semantic prosody to construct different 'representations of reality' to the jury (Cotterill 2001: 311). Cotterill (2004) employed a similar approach to a 5 million–word corpus of rape, sexual assault and domestic violence trials held in the late 1990s in the U.K. Cotterill observed a process of 'lexical negotiation' during witnesses' testimony, through which the words used by witnesses to refer to events and people, were changed or reformulated by lawyers to words which had more favourable 'semantic profiles' (based on their use in the COBUILD Bank of English), for their narrative and client. More recently, Cotterill (2014) conducted a concordance analysis of explicit references to the jury during witness examination, through the strings *for the jury* and *show/tell/explain to the jury*. The nature of such strategic references which acknowledge the presence and importance of the jury was argued to provide 'a clear indication of the extent to which lawyer-witness interaction in court is at least partly a display exercise' (Cotterill 2014: 87). Around the same time as Cotterill's early corpus analyses of courtroom discourse, Heffer (2005) produced a seminal work on the corpus-aided analysis of jury trials in England and Wales. Heffer collected and analysed a large corpus U.K. trial data, comprising 100 complete witness examinations (containing both examination-in-chief and cross-examination), 100 judges' summing-ups and 100 judicial sentences as well as 16 opening addresses and 10 closing speeches. Heffer's quantitative and qualitative exploration 'mapped out the terrain' (Heffer 2005: 211) of the various sub-genres of the trial, bringing new insights to the understanding of courtroom discourse, including but extending beyond, the role of narrative in trial genres and the dynamics and complexities of legal–lay interaction.

Since the work of Cotterill and Heffer, corpus linguistic approaches have been widely applied in the analysis of many aspects of courtroom discourse. Krisda Chaemsaithong has taken a corpus approach to the quantitative and qualitative analysis of trial opening statements from a range of different perspectives by investigating a number of different linguistic features and rhetorical strategies, including pronouns and person markers (Chaemsaithong 2015a), naming strategies and social actor analysis (Chaemsaithong 2018, 2019a, 2021), transitivity patterns (Chaemsaithong 2019b) stance-taking and engagement (Chaemsaithong 2015b, 2017a) and reported speech (Chaemsaithong 2017b).[3] The witness examination stage of both criminal and civil trials has also been subject to corpus-assisted analysis in recent years. Magdalena Szczyrbak has been particularly active in this area, applying corpus linguistic techniques to the analysis of verb patterns and stance used and enacted by legal and lay speakers in witness examination in criminal cases such as the trial of Boston Marathon bomber Dzhokhar Tsarnaev (Szczyrbak 2020), civil cases, namely the David Irving vs Deborah Lipstadt/Penguin Books Ltd libel trial in the U.K. (Szczyrbak 2016, 2018a, 2018b, 2019a, 2021) and political-legal hearings (Szczyrbak 2019b).[4] Johnson and Clifford (2011) also take a corpus-based approach to the analysis of witness examination in the Irving trial, observing and interpreting the barrister's use of strategic (im)politeness in cross-examination as a form of attack, taking into account the frequency and nature of aspects of the interaction such as interruption, accusatory and damaging referential strategies, making requests and sarcasm. Wright et al. (2022) also take a corpus approach to analysing pragmatic strategies in the courtroom, in particular the use of the word *respect** by advocates and judges in the High Court of Justice in England and Supreme Court of the United Kingdom, emphasising the value of a corpus approach in identifying salient lexico-grammatical patterns in courtroom discourse and understanding the dynamics of interaction in these professional spaces (Wright et al. 2022: 11). In a similar way, Tkačuková (2015) focuses on judges' use of *well* as a discourse marker across seven civil and criminal trials, concluding that a corpus approach provides 'a firm methodological basis for socio-legal studies' (Tkačuková 2015: 167). Khafaga (2023) conducts a corpus-assisted critical discourse analysis former U.S. President Bill Clinton during his impeachment trial in 1998. Focusing on Clinton's use of 17 lexical items, across all content word classes, Khafaga (2023: 24) shows how within the context of courtroom testimony, lexemes are used strategically to achieve specific pragmatic functions in ways that are revealed by their 'collocational and connotational attributes in the discourse'. Recent work by Jackson et al. (2024) and Wright et al. (2025) has used a corpus linguistic approach in analysing the cross-examination of vulnerable witness in criminal trials in England and Wales. By using corpus-based and corpus-driven methods, these analyses have identified the differences in how vulnerable and non-vulnerable witnesses are questioned by barristers, highlighting examples of both good and bad practice.

Closing arguments have also been examined from a corpus perspective. Felton Rosulek (2015) collected and analysed a corpus of 17 closing arguments from the same state district court in the Midwestern United States across a range of different offence types, organising the corpus-based analysis around representations and construction of 'the most important people in the closing arguments: the defendants, victims, jurors, and lawyers' (Felton Rosulek 2015: 190). Bartley (2018) applied a corpus-assisted discourse-analytical approach to examining transitivity patterns in the closing arguments of both the prosecution and defence in a sexual assault case in the U.S. which ultimately saw the male defendant wrongly convicted. The quantitative and qualitative analyses of the representational patterns in the closing arguments demonstrated the ways in which strategic language choices can, in instances such as this, lead to miscarriages of justice. Chaemsaithong deploys some of the tools which they applied to the analysis of opening statements in examining closing arguments, such as self-reference pronouns as a means by which lawyers 'orchestrate as multiplicity of selves' in their final monologues (Chaemsaithong and Kim 2021: 587). Chaemsaithong (2022) uses corpus linguistics to develop and apply a lexico-grammatical model of moral legitimation (van Leeuwen 2008), demonstrating the ways in which prosecutors legitimize the death penalty for guilty defendants and distancing and differentiating capital punishment from the criminal violence enacted by the perpetrators. Chaemsaithong and Kim (2018) set out to compare opening statements and closing arguments in the same U.S. criminal trial in terms of the frequency and function of reported speech, finding that 'different patterns of intertextual practices [...] contribute to the realization of the lawyer's distinct communicative goals in each phase of the trial'. Similarly, Chaemsaithong and Kim (2020) combine social actor analysis (van Leeuwen 2008) and transitivity analysis in the comparison of representations of agency in opening and closing statements in a trial, revealing the 'prosecution's and the defence's polarized linguistic patterns in both genres' (Chaemsaithong and Kim 2020: 339).

As well as opening and closing statements and witness examination, corpus tools and techniques have been applied to the analysis of trial genres that have typically received somewhat less research attention. One example of such genre judges' summing-up. Driven by a keyword analysis indicating frequent and salient patterns of quotation (e.g. *told* and *said*), Johnson (2014) demonstrates the ways in which the judge, in their summing-up at the end of the Harold Shipman trial recapitulates Shipman's words and 'organises and synthesises the evidence for the jury', using the authority of quotation 'to make the jury question the contrasted material and to stimulate meaning-making and decision-making' (Johnson 2014: 53). Another generally overlooked trial genre, judges' sentencing remarks, is examined in a corpus analysis by Potts and Weare (2018). Potts and Ware identify the frequency and type of naming strategies used by judges when sentencing women convicted of murder in England, finding that women are represented in ways that 'systematically create dichotomous narratives of degraded victims or dehumanised monsters' (Potts and Weare 2018: 21) and set out a number of recommendations for the judiciary when writing sentencing remarks. Exploring a similarly overlooked courtroom genre, Abrams and Potts (2021) conduct a corpus-based discourse analysis of 148 Victim Impact Statements that were read during the sentencing of Larry Nassar, former doctor for the U.S. women's gymnastics team. Focusing on the ways in which victims describe Nassar, what he did and the harms they suffered, their analysis 'reveals the challenges that rape, sexual assault, and abuse survivors face in naming the crime and describing the harms' (Abrams and Potts 2021: 133), and the authors emphasise policy lessons that can be learned from their corpus data. Meanwhile, Boginskaya (2020) builds on earlier work on the comprehensibility of jury instructions in U.S. courts (e.g. Tiersma and Curtis 2008; Tiersma 2010) and develops a corpus-based exploration of explanatory strategies and patterns generally aimed to improve laypeople's understanding of jury instructions in California. Triangulating the corpus analysis with a reader comprehensibility experiment and survey the study contributes to the 'knowledge of the ways of accommodating professional discursive practices towards a lay audience' and 'draws attention to the issues of knowledge asymmetries' (Boginskaya 2020: 314). In the bilingual context of the Zimbabwean courtroom, Svongoro and Kufakunesu (2019) use corpus techniques to analyse the ways in which court interpreters (re)presented the lexical, grammatical and interactional features of courtroom speakers and found, amongst other things, that interpreters fluctuate between speaking on behalf of (first person) and about (third person) other court actors, and that through the process of interpretation, the pragmatic force of a question can be substantially altered.

Legal judgements and judicial opinions

The language of judges, judicial opinions and legal judgements have been of interest to forensic and legal linguists since Solan (1993: 1) noted that any judge who takes their position seriously struggles with the dual tasks of decision-making and the presentation of that decision. Research into discourses of this kind has proven to be very well placed to benefit from the building and availability of corpora and the application of corpus tools. Finegan (2010) provides an early example of such corpus work, focusing on a feature of legal language in a legal register that, at the time, had 'received relatively little attention from forensic linguists but which is crucially important in the training of attorneys in the United States' (Finegan 2010: 65) – adverbial expressions of attitude and emphasis in decisions rendered by the Supreme Court of the United States. In a later iteration of this analysis, Finegan and Lee (2021: 61) find that Supreme Court justices frequently express their feelings and interpretations of their fellow jurists, and this provides new, empirical evidence counter to the 'general understanding of supreme court justices as dispassionate appliers of law to a set of facts'. In fact (and perhaps for this reason), stance and evaluation in judicial opinions and judgements have very often been the subject of corpus-assisted discourse analysis. Stanisław Goźdź-Roszkowski, in particular, has written widely on this area, examining in depth the evaluative and stance-marking properties of phraseology and grammar patterns in U.S. Supreme Court opinions (Goźdź-Roszkowski 2016, 2018a, 2024), including comparing patterns of stance and evaluation between judicial opinions and other genres of legal writing (Goźdź-Roszkowski 2019a), as well as court judgements across languages, such as English, Polish and Italian (Goźdź-Roszkowski 2017, 2018b; Goźdź-Roszkowski and Pontrandolfo 2013; Pontrandolfo and Goźdź-Roszkowski 2014). Indeed, many others have used corpus linguistic tools to analyse stance and evaluation in the discourse(s) of judicial opinion. Some of this work also focuses on stance, such as Pontrandolfo (2018), who demonstrates the use of sentence adverbs to express evaluative stance in Italian, English and Spanish judicial argumentation. Marín Pérez (2019, 2022) also analyses the use of evaluative and affective lexis in Spanish and British judicial decisions finding that, despite 'the common assumption that legal texts should leave little room for subjectivity [...] a considerable amount of lexical items expressing appraisal' was found in the judgements, particularly in British judgements (Marín Perez 2019: 161). Similarly, Mazzi (2010: 374) focuses on the use of evaluative lexis as 'a prominent aspect in the construction of the judge's argumentative position' in U.S. Supreme Court judgements, identifying a diverse range of strategies used by judges 'to take stance as they organise their argumentative discourse in judgements' (Mazzi 2010: 383). Poole (2021) also provides a corpus analysis of stance adverbs in U.S. judicial opinions, in order to provide more evidence-based teaching of legal writing in English. Poole (2021: 126) concluded that the findings of his analysis of stance adverbs highlight the 'potential pedagogical value of corpus-aided instruction and/or corpus-informed materials that heightens awareness of these items and others in ELP [English for Legal Purposes] classrooms for novice legal writers'. It is not only evaluative stance that has been examined using corpus approaches to such discourses. Szczyrbak, for example, has demonstrated the ways which modal verbs of certainty are used to express epistemic stance in the Opinions of the Advocates General at the European Court of Justice and U.S. Supreme Court oral arguments and written opinions (Szczyrbak 2014, 2017). More recently, Szczyrbak (2022) has examined evidentiality in U.S. Supreme Court opinions from the perspective of reporting verbs *say* and *told* and their passive constructions. Cheng and Cheng (2014) examine how different types of epistemic modality are used in judicial practices in Hong Kong and Scotland. Their analyses find that epistemic modality is employed in adjudication 'wherein the judges decide the degree of probability' and that such modality is equally adopted between the two jurisdictions.

It is safe to say that corpus approaches have been used productively when analysing the language of court judgements and legal decisions, with a wide range of studies focusing on an equally wide range of linguistic features and discursive phenomena. As well as the substantial attention paid to stance, attitude, evaluation and evidentiality already discussed, research has subjected international legal judgements to an array of different analyses, bolstered and facilitated by corpus methods. Cheng et al. (2015), for example, collect and analyse a corpus of judgements from defamation cases in Hong Kong and by identifying the most frequent collocates of *defense* in the corpus; the authors build what they call a 'phraseological profile of defenses to defamation' in Hong Kong. They emphasise that their analysis demonstrates 'how a corpus-based study enables us to visit the fundamental issues in defamation cases in Hong Kong' (Cheng et al. 2015: 19). Mazzi (2011, 2014, 2018, 2022) also takes a phraseological perspective but uses a lexical bundle/word n-gram approach to analysing the ways in which phraseology in legal judgements from the Supreme Court of the Republic of Ireland can bring insights into judicial narrative and argumentation. In reflecting on the benefits of a corpus approach, Mazzi (2018: 200) argues that the study of the 'procedural matters and technicalities of jurisprudence is [...] profitably integrated by the application of quantitative and qualitative methods to the investigation of phraseology in judicial texts' and that corpus linguistics is 'a handy tool and a flexible instrument' to check and support the legal scholar's first-hand intuition. Similarly, Goźdź-Roszkowski (2018c, 2019b) examines strategies of legal argumentation in judicial opinions, using keyword analysis to identify salient terms and semantic domains relied upon by judges in their justifications in U.S. Supreme Court majority and dissenting opinions in relation to same-sex marriage. The identification of 'value-laden' words and their collocational profiles 'revealed important differences within the argumentative strategies employed by the judges' (Goźdź-Roszkowski 2019b: 89). Elsewhere, Trklja (2018) uses a corpus method in analysing formulaicity in judgements of the Court of Justice of the European Union (CJEU), concluding that the judgements are characterised by 'a high degree of formulaicity' and that they contain 'hybrid expressions which are created through translation' (Trklja 2018: 105). Trklja and McAuliffe (2019) also examine formulaicity in CJEU judgements, in combination and comparison with judgements from the U.K. Supreme Court, focusing specifically on paragraph-initial metadiscursive lexical items. Their analysis finds that these formulaic expressions signal discourse relations in judgements, contributing particularly to the development of argumentation. Ultimately, they argue that 'judgments are made up of almost wholly automised subcodes of grammar and syntax' and that judgements are created in a 'lego-building block' fashion (Trklja and McAuliffe 2019: 50).

Both formulaicity and metadiscourse in legal judgements have been examined by others. Pontrandolfo (2021), for example, compared the frequency and uses of complex prepositions in judgements from Spanish Supreme Court and by the CJEU. A comparison of the two corpora leads to Pontrandolfo (2021: 271) suggesting that 'EU language is more formulaic than national language' when it comes to legal judgements and that rather than having their own distinct formulaic sequences, EU judgements – which are the results of a complex translation and multilingual drafting procedure – contain 'formulaic profiles' that are affected by source-language interference. Cross-linguistic comparisons of CJEU opinions are also analysed by Mattioli and McAuliffe (2021), whose corpus analysis of a range of lexical characteristics of the texts finds that opinions have become more 'stylistically simpler and less "fluent"' since 2004, when the CJEU requested that opinions be drafted in one of five 'pivot languages' of the Court (French, English, German, Spanish and Italian). Goźdź-Roszkowski (2020) uses lexical bundles to identify the ways in which judges in both Poland and the U.S. rely on formulaic expressions to mark disagreement in dissenting opinions. This use of 'highly formulaic expressions' to express disagreement is particularly noteworthy as there are no 'clear guidelines that would prescribe precise ways in which their stance should be declared' (Goźdź-Roszkowski 2020: 398). In terms of metadiscourse, McKeown (2021) compares the amount and function of reflexive metadiscourse in majority and dissenting opinions of the U.S. Supreme Court. The results reveal that although majority and dissenting writers use a similar amount of reflexive metadiscourse overall, there are important differences beneath the surface. For instance, whereas majority opinions contained more 'enumerating devices' (e.g. organising the discourse through numerical tags such as *first, finally*), dissenting opinions used more 'communicating devices' (foregrounding the fact that something is being communicated, such as *we should speak to* and *the only thing to be said*). What's more, the comparison found that whereas majority writers relied on self-focused reflexive metadiscourse, dissenting writers used significantly more other-focused metadiscourse, orienting themselves in strong opposition to the majority. McKeown (2021: 234) emphasises the benefit of the corpus comparison approach in treating written legal data with more 'sensitivity' teasing out differences that are otherwise, and normally, overlooked. Relatedly, Ye and McKeown (2023) combined corpus techniques with appraisal theory in investigating the ways in which judges discursively construct targeted (dis)agreement on appeal court decisions in Hong Kong. Both metadiscourse and disagreement, or more accurately dissenting judicial opinions, are also the object analysis for Boginskaya (2022), who examines metadiscursive boosters in a corpus of 27 opinions from the Russian Constitutional Court in which judges challenge the majority opinion. The results of the analysis are summarised as revealing the vital role that boosters play in gaining ratification for judge's claims and views from peers and other legal professionals (Boginskaya 2022: 274). When it comes to the representation of different 'voices' or perspectives in judicial writing, Cheng (2012) examines the nature of attribution in court judgements in Hong Kong, Taiwan and Mainland China, showing that some judgements allow for a multiplicity of different voices and opinions (such as Hong Kong) while others 'tend to speak with one monolithic institutional voice' in which 'the contributions of the individual judge are backgrounded but the institutional power is brought into the foreground' (Cheng 2012: 46).

In summing up the value of corpus approaches to gaining insights into legal language, Goźdź-Roszkowski and Pontrandolfo (2015: 131) comment that '[I]t is the advent of Corpus Linguistics that has radically changed the landscape of contemporary legal phraseology resulting in an array of different approaches and perspectives'. It is clear on the basis of the breadth of literature cited here that this is an accurate characterization of the impact of corpus methods on forensic and legal linguistics. What has been shown in this section is that the advent, introduction and development of corpora and corpus techniques have pushed the boundaries of legal discourse analysis, in the analysis of legislative texts, courtroom genres and judicial opinions. This expansion has been seen across jurisdictions and languages and has examined an array of different linguistic features and discursive strategies from a range of different theoretical perspectives. In this way, corpus methods have provided new ways of analysing texts that have long been of interest to forensic and legal linguists, before corpora and associated tools became as widely available as they now are. Indeed, there are still analyses of the types of discourse discussed here that do not take a corpus approach. It is hoped, though, that this account provides some insight into the continuing role of corpus linguistics in bringing new insights to these familiar genres. The next two sections outline slightly different corpus contributions for forensic linguistics: potential solutions to methodological challenges and providing brand-new avenues for research.

Possible solutions to methodological challenges

Corpus linguistics has made significant contributions to the ways in which analysts can approach common forensic and legal linguistic problems. As will be detailed below, this primarily pertains to areas where a corpus linguistic approach can be beneficial to (forensic) linguists engaging in casework of and research in authorship analysis and in questions of statutory interpretation.

Authorship

Given the ways in which Svartvik (1968) and Coulthard (1994) demonstrated the utility of corpora and corpus-assisted methods in addressing questions of authorship, it is no surprise that authorship in forensic contexts has attracted a great deal of corpus linguistic attention. For the purposes of this section, it is important to distinguish between the different *kinds* of authorship problem that not only exist in forensic contexts but have seen a swell of corpus linguistic application. The different kinds of authorship problem that are discussed here are: comparative authorship analysis, sociolinguistic author profiling and native language identification. Broadly speaking, comparative authorship analysis is concerned with determining whether a set of texts, at least some of which are anonymous, disputed or 'questioned', share the same author. Sociolinguistic author profiling, meanwhile, is concerned with garnering as much information as reliably possible about the identity of an unknown author, in relation to social variables such as their age, gender, level of education and social class on the basis of the language exhibited in an anonymous text or set of texts. Other Language Identification (OLID) (alternatively referred to as Native Language Identification, or NLID) is different again and is focused specifically on identifying which languages, other than that in which a given text is written, might be influencing the language being used. Grant (2022: 18) provides a taxonomy and detailed explanation of these and other forensic authorship analysis tasks.

Of the three kinds of authorship task outlined here, comparative authorship analysis has attracted the most corpus attention, probably by virtue of having attracted the most research attention generally, given that is the most common type of authorship problem for which forensic linguists are asked to help with by investigating police and/or the courts. Methodologically speaking, corpus linguistics is well positioned to make meaningful contributions to the analyst's toolkit for comparative authorship analysis. Traditionally in the literature, there are two main approaches to comparative authorship analysis – the *stylometric* and the *stylistic* – which are used to compare 'known' writings of authors involved in a case with some 'disputed' or 'questioned' texts. Broadly speaking, these represent respectively *quantitative* (statistical, algorithmic) and *qualitative* (close textual analysis) means by which to compare the writing styles exhibited by different authors and across different texts. Each has their own strengths and weaknesses in terms of methodological transparency, reliability and replicability, and much has been written about these relative (dis)advantages (e.g. Solan 2013; Wright 2014). Over time, these approaches have been seen as being in 'competition' with one another (Grant 2008: 225), and the use of corpus methods to combine quantitative and qualitative analysis has gone some way to bridging the gap between these two divergent approaches and providing new methodological opportunities. The role of corpus linguistics in doing this has generally taken two forms: (i) the use of corpus methods to identify and linguistic features, or 'style markers' (McMenamin 2002, 2021), that might be useful in a given authorship comparison and compare authors and texts on the basis of these features, and (ii) the use of corpora as a means by which to measure the frequency, rarity and distinctiveness of particular style markers against some reference population, or both.

Shortly after Coulthard (1994), Winter (1996) presented an experimental case study of three short statements given by 'the accused'; Text 1 and 2 were statements given to the police and Text 3 was an uncompleted statement given to Malcolm Coulthard. The question of authorship here was similar to that seen in Svartvik and Coulthard and related to Text 2, the second statement allegedly given to the police, which the accused claimed was not given by him. Using *Vocalyse*, a computer programme developed by David Woolls and one of the first of its kind designed to automate and present comparisons between texts, Winter compared frequencies and concordance lines for shared and unique vocabulary and found that Text 2 was markedly divergent from the other texts, in terms of both the frequency of words and how these words were used in context. Kredens (2002) expanded the use of corpus linguistics in his experiment comparing small spoken corpora of two famous male English singers, Robert Smith and Steven Morrissey, in order to 'provide a better understanding of idiolectal variation' and contribute 'to the debate on the status of linguistic evidence in legal and forensic settings' (Kredens 2002: 412). Kredens is committed to a corpus approach in his analysis, emphasising that it is not sufficient for the analysis to involve 'automated data-processing' and pressing the need for 'the adoption of the methodology of corpus linguistics' in the robust, in-depth analysis of data (Kredens 2002: 406). Using frequency-based comparisons and qualitative examination of a range of lexical and grammatical features used by the two authors, such as average word length, adverbs, contracted forms, and discourse markers, Kredens is able to observe significant idiolectal variation between the two corpora. In his concluding remarks, Kredens

(2002: 443) argues that 'the use of a corpus-based methodology [...] may eventually lead to new ideas for forensic authorship attribution as a scientific technique'. Nini and Grant (2013) present two corpus-based experiments intended to demonstrate how theoretical notions from Systemic Functional Linguistics can bridge the gap between disparate methodologies. Across the two analyses, Nini and Grant draw on features from Systemic Function Linguistics, including patterns in mood, theme and transitivity and from Biber's (1988) MDA to combine the quantitative measurement of similarity and difference between authors and the qualitative examination of inter-author variation in action. In methodological terms, Nini and Grant (2013) propose that 'this kind of analysis provides forensic stylistics with methods that resolve potential biases in replication and scientific method'.

A number of studies have used corpus approaches to testing and evaluating the usefulness of specific linguistic features as style markers for distinguishing between authors and identifying possible authors of disputed texts. Many of these features have been lexically derived, such as Larner's (2014b, 2016, 2019b) investigation of formulaic sequences (see Wray 2002) as a marker of authorship, including both the number and frequency of formulaic sequences and specific sequences themselves. Across the different studies, Larner has ultimately found that while formulaic sequences are used distinctively by authors (i.e. 'individual authors use different formulaic sequences', Larner 2019b: 274), they have been less successful in attributing texts to their correct authors. Meanwhile, Wright (2021) follows Winter (1996) in emphasising that an examination of the collocational profiles of words commonly shared between authors and texts can reveal distinctive patterns of use. Using the Enron Email Corpus and drawing on one of the most frequent and widely used register-embedded content words in the corpus, *deal*, as an example, Wright argues that a pre-occupation with frequency differences between authors alone risks overlooking author-specific variation in how those words are used. The utility of grammatical style markers as a way to distinguish between authors' idiolects has also been examined using corpus methods. A recent example of this is in Fonteyn and Nini's (2020) investigation of variation in gerund alternation across the prose and letter writing of 19 authors from the Early Modern Multiloquent Authors (EMMA) corpus. Despite the 17th-century authors sharing the same level of education, social class and professions, the corpus study 'demonstrated that there can still be heterogeneity within such a centralized population' and that 'individuals seem to have different systems to condition the variation they observe' (Fonteyn and Nini 2020: 302). Emoji use has also been shown to discriminate between authors and attribute texts to their correct author. Marko (2020) found that the function, strings, compositions and position of emojis can indeed be valuable for authorship analysis in an analysis of a corpus of 60 individuals' Instagram use.

As well as corpus techniques being used to examine and compare style markers across texts and authors, corpora have been drawn upon in the assessment of how common, rare and distinctive particular features are of authors or texts in question. As Grant (2013: 471) notes, 'a good stylometric marker should demonstrate that, on that marker, an individual is distinctive against the background population from which it is drawn'. McMenamin (2004: 78), a major proponent of the stylistic method of authorship analysis, argues that one 'very promising' area of linguistic research is the use of large corpora to provide 'baseline data for determining the relative frequency of occurrence (i.e. identifying or discriminating potential) of specific style markers used in a given population of writers'. Such 'Base Rate Knowledge'

> implies the collection of data regarding the general usage of the linguistic parameters being considered by a relevant population or group of language users from the same linguistic community, with which the specific behavior of the speakers or writers under comparison can be compared.
>
> (Turell and Gavaldà 2013: 499)

It is widely acknowledged that a major methodological issue for forensic authorship analysts, especially those of the stylistic school, is the lack of availability of reliable reference data from which to make claims about population-level distinctiveness or 'base rate knowledge'. Coulthard (1994: 31) emphasised this challenge, stating that forensic linguists do not have access to corpora from which stylistic norms in a given population could be derived, which would add weight and reliability about the distinctiveness of a given writer's style. Nevertheless, his use of the Google search engine to demonstrate the rarity, and therefore author-distinctiveness, of short and apparently ordinary word strings such as *I picked something up like* and *I asked her if I could carry her bags* (Coulthard 2004: 441) underlined the discriminatory power that large-scale corpora can offer. Despite conceding that forensic linguists are unlikely to have going to have population statistics akin to those available to forensic speech scientists (e.g. about the average pitch of an adult male) (Coulthard 2013: 466), Coulthard (2021: 535) has recently been more optimistic, suggesting that the ongoing development of 'forensically useful and accessible corpora [...] will enable linguists to derive more reliable population statistics'.

There have been a number of corpus-based authorship studies have attempted to show how population level data, or general reference corpora, can be used effectively in forensic authorship analysis. Wright (2013), for example, attempts to address the challenge of determining what qualified as a 'relevant' population corpus for authorship analysis (see Kredens 2002; Grant 2013; Wright 2014). By comparing the email greetings and sign-offs used by four employees in the Enron email corpus,[5] the analysis demonstrates not only how such features discriminated between the four authors but how some forms used by these authors remained extremely distinctive when compared with the usage of the other 126 authors in the Enron corpus, with some forms, such as *hello*: being 555 times more likely to appear in an email written by the author in question than another writer in the Enron community. Wright argues that, used in this way, the Enron email corpus represents relevant population data for determining the distinctiveness of the writing style of the four-author sample, given that the genres, dates and community of practice are all constant. That is, it ensures that emails written by Enron employees are being compared with emails written by Enron employees (Wright 2013: 51). Johnson and Wright (2014) also use the Enron email corpus as a source of reference population data to investigate the author-distinctiveness of word n-grams, or 'n-gram textbites', strings of *n* words and their usefulness of style-markers. Drawing on a case study of one lawyer in the company – James Derrick – Johnson and Wright's analysis took two steps. The first, an authorship attribution experiment, found that word n-grams could be used to successfully attribute email samples as small as 55–145 tokens to their correct author, with success rates of 100% for larger samples of between 763 and 1018 tokens. The second part of the analysis aimed to explain these successful attributions by identifying which word n-grams in particular accounted for the correct attributions. By focusing on Derrick's two-, three-, four- and five-word n-grams and again using the rest of the Enron corpus as a relevant population set, they found a number of patterns that were unique to Derrick. Many of these features were routine, unremarkable strings, such as *please format and print* and *see the message below from*. This led Johnson and Wright (2014: 61) to argue that Derrick was remarkably formulaic in his use of politeness structures, and this accounted for the accuracy with which his emails could be attributed. Wright (2017) expanded this idea, and the use of word n-grams, to test their effectiveness in distinguishing between a larger set of twelve Enron employees. Again, results of an authorship experiment using word n-grams as style markers was successful, with accuracy reaching 95% for identifying the correct author of anonymised samples from a pool of 176 other Enron employee candidate authors. Then, again using a case study approach of a single author – this time Gerald Nemec – Wright isolated author-distinctive n-grams when compared with the rest of the Enron population data. Wright (2017: 238) found that Nemec's most distinctive n-grams are 'tied to recurrent and routine communicative situations that he encounters during his daily work' and that different employees in the Enron population performed the same communicative acts as Nemec, but in different ways. On this basis, Wright (2017: 234) draws on a usage-based perspective to cognitive grammar and argues that certain word n-grams become 'entrenched' (Schmid 2016) for particular authors and are habitually chosen when they encounter certain communicative situations. In terms of authorship, different n-grams become entrenched for different authors and as such become part of author's distinctive idiolectal style. Since Wright (2017), the effectiveness of word n-grams in authorship studies has been shown elsewhere, such as by Grieve et al. (2019), and the potential role of entrenchment and individuality has been further explored by Nini (2023).

In his authorship analysis of the Jack the Ripper letters, Nini (2018a) also relied on word n-grams and their syntactic composition to determine which, if any, of the over 200 letters that were received by the police and the press signed by Jack the Ripper in the wake of his murders in 1888–1896 were written by the Ripper himself. Nini used three contemporaneous reference corpora to measure the rarity and distinctiveness of particular n-grams that were found across different letters, and to assess the extent to which the presence of these n-grams indicated that these texts shared the same author: the Corpus of Historical American English (COHA), the Corpus of Late Modern English Texts 3 (CLMET3) and the Extended Old Bailey Corpus (EOBC). On the basis of 'the number and the distinctiveness of the linguistic similarities', Nini (2018a: 634) argued that the linguistic evidence presented 'supports the hypothesis that the two most iconic texts signed as "Jack the Ripper", the "Dear Boss" letter and the "Saucy Jacky" postcard, were written by the same person' as well as a third, previously overlooked letter. Meanwhile, Queralt (2018) uses a corpus approach to evaluate the applicability and usefulness of Base Rate Knowledge and likelihood ratio framework in an experimental authorship task of 47 authors of Peninsular Spanish texts. The method involved compiling a corpus of all of the authors, which was used to determine the Base Rate Knowledge, or 'population distribution' for a range of different linguistic variables and variants, before using those features with high discriminatory potential to attribute samples of text to the correct author. Grieve (2023) approaches the problem of authorship analysis from the perspective of register variation, using MDA in the comparison of two authors' writing. Grieve (2023: 72) argues that newspaper articles written by two different authors, for the same newspaper and over the same period of time, can be distinguished by the quantitative analysis of style because they write in subtly different registers and that the functional explanation for the differences observed between authors is that the 'authors chose to adopt slightly different rhetorical strategies to effectively express their specific opinions in this specific communicative context'. Recent corpus applications have seen researchers attempt cross-genre authorship analysis. That is, exploring whether authors can be identified when they are writing in different genres. Marko et al. (2022), for example, compare the writing of three authors across Instagram and Twitter, finding that while their use of some features (such as emojis) is platform-specific, others (such as patterns of punctuation and speech acts) remain stable in their writing across platforms. Elsewhere, in their corpus-based study, Mojedano Batel et al. (2023) find that epistemic modality constructions (i.e. markers expressing low commitment and indirectness) display 'idiolectal stability'. Their results find that five of their nine Spanish authors 'displayed a consistent and distinct production of epistemic modality constructions' across different types of written and spoken communication including WhatsApp messages, emails, interviews and work meetings (Mojedano Batel et al. 2023: 23). This corpus method and the results of the analysis, they conclude, contribute to a 'greater understanding of the linguistic elements that survive genre effects and are therefore potentially useful in both investigative and evidential forensic linguistic work' (Mojedano Batel et al. 2023: 24).

Corpora not only have been applied to authorship comparison in experimental contexts but also have played an important role in forensic casework. Grant (2013) presents a method for the forensic authorship analysis of SMS text messages by describing the linguistic analysis he carried out in the case of the murder of Amanda Birks. Grant extends the purely stylistic method he applied in the case and integrates a statistical procedure for measuring the consistency and distinctiveness of two authors' text messaging style in the case, Amanda Birks and her husband and prime suspect Christopher Birks. Grant's stylistic analysis used as a starting point a word frequency list, computed by *Wordsmith Tools* (Scott 1999) to identify all word forms, vocabulary choices and spelling variants exhibited in the writings of the two authors. This ultimately produced a set of 18 lexical features which not only discriminated between the writing styles of Amanda and Christopher Birks but also found that Christopher's style was closer to that in the disputed texts in the case than was Amanda's. Grant (2013: 491) argues that the corpus approach avoids 'an overreliance on subjective expertise and an apparent lack of method in the identification of features'. A similar method is reported by Grieve and Woodfield (2021) and Grant and Grieve (2022) in relation to another murder case, the murder of Jenny Starbuck by her husband Jamie Starbuck. This case involved 29 emails sent from Debbie's email account, apparently while overseas, about which her family were concerned as not being typical of her style. Grant and Grieve as the experts in the case compared the corpus of disputed texts with corpora of known emails for each of Debbie and Jamie. They combined stylistic and stylometric analyses, which 'allowed for a broad range of linguistic evidence to be considered, minimising the chance that important features were missed' (Grieve and Woodfield 2021: 666). Overall, the features attributed the majority of the questioned documents to Jamie Starbuck; that is, his writing style was far more consistent with that of the questioned documents than the writing style of Debbie. Grant and Grieve (2022: 24–5) emphasise that the identification of potential style markers in the known texts, *before* the disputed texts are analysed, avoids the bias inherent in 'retroactively considering new features not identified at first pass'.

Turell (2010) presents the analysis that was used by the defence in a forensic authorship case to provide evidence showing that the author of four non-disputed faxes could also be the author of four disputed emails, both written in Spanish. After identifying stylistic similarities between the disputed emails and non-disputed faxes, Turell isolated two variables that were shared across the faxes and emails and were considered marked as being unusual in general Spanish usage, and searched for their frequencies in the general reference Corpus de Referencia del Español Actual (CREA). With one of these features in particular, the compound relative pronoun, Turell (2010: 231) shows that while both the disputed and non-disputed texts in the case exhibited a high relative frequency for the compound pronoun (36%–43%), the frequency results from the CREA reference corpus showed an overwhelming preference for the simple pronoun, with the complex pronoun appearing with a relative frequency of only 1.1%. Therefore, not only was this feature shared by the texts in this case, but it was a very rare feature in the relevant population. Thus, the similarity between the texts under analysis, Turell (2010: 232) argues, 'lends weight to the conclusion that these sets may have not been produced independently and may have very likely been produced by the same author'. Similarly, Heydon (2019: 15–28) details a murder case in Australia which involved the authorship analysis of a letter written to and about a woman who had subsequently been murdered. The victim's boyfriend became the prime suspect in the case, and the investigating police force had reason to believe that he had written the letter. The style markers central to this case were misspelt words which, Heydon emphasises, are usually notoriously unreliable in distinguishing one particular author given the commonality of the same misspellings in the general population. After comparing the style markers in the questioned documents to 850 text messages known to have been written by the suspect, Heydon set about finding out how rare or common these (mis)spellings were in the general population by searching for their frequency in the 630 million–word Birmingham Blog Corpus. In presenting the analysis, Heydon (2019: 22–25) demonstrates how using a large general reference corpus to observe the frequency or rarity of a particular (set of) linguistic feature(s) can be a powerful tool in evaluating the evidential weight or diagnostic significance of a particular style marker.

Corpora can also play an important role in methodologies of author profiling – the task of analysing a linguistic sample to obtain information about the author's demographic background. This can be a very helpful stage in reducing the pool of candidate writers or in opening new lines of investigation (Queralt 2022: 44). Nini (2018b) presents an author profiling experiment based on the writings of 96 participants in three different registers of letter, elicited for the purpose of this study: a letter of complaint to a holiday agent, a letter of complaint to the Prime Minister and a letter to a fictitious abusive employer. Participants comprised writers identifying as male or female, from a range of social backgrounds, with different levels of formal education and were between 19 and 78 years of age. After demonstrating that writers can be distinguished in terms of their characteristics, Nini (2018b: 52) sets out a proposed procedure for forensic authorship profiling. Much like Base Rate Knowledge in author comparison, corpora play an important role in Nini's proposal as a means by which of establishing 'norms' for the use of linguistic features under examination in a particular register, by a stratified sample of the population. It is against this 'norm' that a disputed text would then be positioned in order to determine if the linguistic behaviour within that text patterned in predicable ways with regard to writer characteristics such as age, sex, level of education, and so on. Indeed, Donlan and Nini (2022) demonstrate this process as it was used in a casework context, in a case in Ayia Napa in which a 19-year-old British woman allegedly retracted a statement she had made to the Cypriot police that she was raped by a group of Israeli men. The so-called retraction statement explained that she had made a fake report of rape in the first instance because she was embarrassed. The men were released after having been arrested, and the woman herself was charged with public mischief for making a false rape statement. However, the woman testified that she had been raped and that she signed the retraction statement under duress, fearing for her life, having been held in a police station for hours with no lawyer. She alleged that the paragraph in the retraction statement in which she allegedly admitted to lying had been dictated to her by Cypriot police and she had written it down. Nini was appointed as an expert in the case to provide an opinion on whether the defendant herself had written that paragraph or whether it had been dictated by local officers. Because there were no known texts against which the statement could be compared, Nini approached this question from an author profiling perspective and worked to determine whether there was linguistic evidence to support the claim that the text was authored by an L1 speaker of English or whether evidence suggested that the style was more consistent with that of a speaker of English as another language. In an initial qualitative analysis of the paragraph, Nini identified five features of interest, including [Do [REPORT]] (as in *the report I did* in the retraction statement) and [DO [*sexual intercourse*]] as in *recording me doing sexual intercourse*). Then, using a range of large-scale English reference corpora including enTenTen 2015, Global Web-Based English Corpus and the British National Corpus (BNC), Nini investigated how common such features are in British English. The corpus results showed that, for the most part, these features were very rare in British English, which led to the opinion that the disputed paragraph was unlikely to have been written by a person with English as a first language and was more likely to have been composed by a non-native English speaker. As Donlan and Nini (2022: 32) argue, the use of appropriate large-scale corpora in this way makes it possible to determine 'how likely it is for someone of a particular socio-demographic profile to use a construction'; in this case, this was that certain features in the disputed text were not consistent with the overwhelming population preferences in British English.

In the case described by Donlan and Nini, the key issue at hand was the potential influence of an L2 on the English exhibited in the disputed text. This particular issue is the central concern of a sub-fields of author profiling known as NLID or OLID, which involves analysing an anonymous author's writing in an L2 to detect any influence from and L1 or another language and, where possible, determine what that other language(s) may be. Corpora can be used at various stages in such analyses (Perkins 2022: 68, 72), such as in determining the uniqueness of certain features (informed by the literature on common patterns in particular languages), to investigate calques or phrases borrowed through translation, and to check common or standard usage for a particular variable in a particular language. A number of studies have demonstrated the value of corpora and corpus methods in augmenting purely computational/statistical approaches to NLID with a more (socio)linguistically informed stage of qualitative linguistic analysis, particularly when the language of the disputed text is English (though see Malmasi and Dras 2015 for a large-scale NLID study using six different non-English languages). Perkins and Grant (2018) conduct an experimental analysis which set out to distinguish between blog posts written by L1 Persian speakers writing in English from those written by L1 English speakers. Their approach involved the qualitative identification of features of 'marked' language (by which they mean language that is unlikely to be used by an L1 English speaker in the given context) in the blog posts. Logistic regression was then run, using the features identified, which accurately classified each of the authors as being either L1 Persian or L1 English, as well as distinguishing blog posts written by L1 Persian speakers and those written by speakers of geographically and linguistically close languages Azeri and Pashto. Perkins and Grant (2018: 15) then provide a worked example of how their combinatory quantitative and qualitative method can accurately identify the author of a short simulated disputed text as being an L1 Persian speaker. Kredens et al. (2019) further advocate for an explanation-based approach to NLID and OLID, which focuses on the need for the linguistic to 'understand the implications of the presence or absence of features' (Kredens et al. 2019: 22) in an analysis, so that the features relied upon are explicable, be that on the basis of typographical, lexico-grammatical or sociolinguistic explanation(s). In making their case of this approach, Kredens et al. (2019) make a number of observations regarding the type of corpora that should be used in NLID/OLID research, such as ensuring that the data are not homogenous to the extent that features identified are tied too strongly to the register of the corpus and that the corpora being used are at least reflective of the modes of communication that are most forensically relevant, such as discourse in online contexts. Such explanation-based work, the authors argue, stands to 'deepen the utility' of purely computational approaches (Kredens et al. 2019: 22).

Corpora and corpus methods, therefore, serve an important role in the development and refinement of methods and approaches to authorship, including comparative authorship tasks and author profiling. This includes providing forensically appropriate data for experimental research, a quantitative and qualitative approach to feature identification and explanation, and the use of relevant and/or general reference corpora as a means by which to determine the frequency, rarity and therefore diagnostic strength of particular linguistic style markers in a given analysis.

Determination of word meaning

Corpora have offered a new and effective method by which (forensic) linguists working across a range of different types of case can ascertain the meaning of a word. Grant (2017), for example, shows how corpus techniques can provide insight into the meanings of slang terms used in a particular community of practice that can help in the investigation of language crimes such as conspiracy to murder. Similarly, MacLeod (2024) uses corpus techniques and the BNC to determine the semantic prosodies of otherwise innocuous words in the analysis of indirect incitement. The accessibility and useability of corpora have also proven useful in trademark litigation cases in which linguists are asked to determine the meaning of words and the likelihood of confusion between two trademarks or the strength of an existing mark. This has sometimes included the search of newspapers, magazines and the internet to observe 'third-party use' that the courts can find persuasive when deciding how generic or distinctive a particular piece of language is (Butters 2021: 375; also Shuy 2012). Kilgariff (2015) provides a discussion dedicated to the use of corpora in trademark cases as a means by which to analyse 'namehood' and to observe whether a term in a dispute tends to behave as a proper noun or a common noun. Kilgariff details the considerations that must be made in such cases, including which corpus to use and what to count. Taking a similar approach to relying on proper and common noun status as a means of assessing the genericization of trademarks that have become so strong and ubiquitous that they start being used to denote all similar products and brands, Vacalopoulou (2020) draws on corpora to help understand how such trademarks gain 'lemma status' in dictionaries.

The area of meaning determination that has gained by far the most traction and received by far the most attention as far as corpus methods are concerned is statutory interpretation (also called legal interpretation). So widespread is the emerging trend of using corpus methods in the interpretation of legal texts that Römer-Barron and Cunningham (2024: 1), in the introduction to a special issue on the topic, designate the practice its own (albeit possibly too broad) name: 'legal corpus linguistics'. In order for legislative and statutory texts to be applicable to 'real life' and to fulfil their functions, this 'presupposes that the meanings of these texts are (correctly and consistently) interpreted' by their readers and users, including laypeople and legal practitioners (Gries 2021: 628). This includes the interpretation of each and every word contained in those texts. In many cases, words that play a significant role in the application of a legislative text are given explicit definitions in that text. When such statutory definitions exist, they are relied upon in the use and interpretation of the law in question. However, when no legal definition exists, the aim is that the correct interpretation is that which the legislators *intended* when the texts were drafted, that is, the word's 'ordinary everyday meaning' (Scalia and Garner 2012: 69). However, determining the 'ordinary' or 'plain' meaning of a given word is not a straightforward task. As Solan (2010: 54) points out, 'it is not always easy to decide what makes ordinary meaning ordinary', and Hutton (2014: 44) goes as far as saying that 'ordinary meaning' or 'ordinary language' might be considered 'a convenient fiction' (Hutton 2014: 44). When issues arise in the interpretation or the ordinary meaning of a word in court, it is (usually) the responsibility of the judge to ascertain what that meaning is. Hutton (2014) provides an in-depth discussion of a number of cases of this kind across international jurisdictions which involved questions such as is a burrito a 'sandwich', is an airplane a 'vehicle' and is a bicycle a 'carriage'?

There are a number of ways that judges have typically sought to determine the ordinary meaning of a word and has usually involved one or a combination of judges' linguistic knowledge and intuition about ordinary meaning, using dictionaries, via etymological information and, occasionally, with the help of linguists. However, as Gries (2021: 629) points out, 'all of these practices are even more problematic than they are widespread'. Judges' intuitions about language, for example, are clearly subject to confirmation bias and personal experience and exposure to particular words and their context of use and are thus an unreliable and opaque means of determining meanings of words, let alone the commonness or 'ordinariness' of meanings. At the same time, although dictionaries are effective in identifying *potential* or *possible* meanings or a word, they do not give much of an indication of which of those meanings is the 'ordinary' one. This leaves room for judges (and lawyers) to choose the meaning that supports their intuition and ignore meaning(s) that contradict or undermine it. Even the choice of dictionary used is open to question, with different dictionaries giving different meanings and no clear objective sense as to which dictionary is 'best' in general or in any given case. In terms of etymology, it is impossible and nonsensical to rely on the original meaning of words and their constituent morphemes to determine the contemporary, not to mention *ordinary*, meanings of words given the phenomena of perpetual social and linguistic change. Gries (2021: 630) exemplifies this through the fact that *December*, with its Latin etymology of *decem* meaning *ten* to denote 'tenth month of the year', would now mean *October*. The pitfalls of these different approaches to ascertaining ordinary meanings in a legal context are considerable, and readers are encouraged to consult other work that provides a far more detailed discussion of these than is possible here (e.g. Mouritsen 2010; Hutton 2014; Solan and Gales 2016, 2017; Gries 2021).

Relatively recently, corpus linguistics has emerged as a tool to help in statutory interpretation and the determination of ordinary meaning, and a tool that can serve as an antidote to some of the issues with the other more traditional methods. Large-scale general reference corpora provide the courts with databases of language which can be queried for individual words, phrase and syntactic patterns. According to Mouritsen (2010: 1970), the corpus method 'removes the determination of ordinary meaning from the black box of the judge's mental impression' and therefore 'renders the discussion of ordinary meaning one of tangible and quantifiable reality'. This empirical investigation of word use and meaning is a more transparent, 'certain' and 'verifiable' approach to analysing ordinary meaning, which ultimately serves to 'improve the predictability and consistency of judicial decision making' (Mouritsen 2011: 205). The frequency-oriented approach at the heart of the corpus method also gives clear indications of how common (and therefore how *ordinary*) particular uses and meanings of a word are across a population in such a way that a judge's intuition and dictionary definitions are simply not able to reliably achieve (Mouritsen 2011: 190). At the same time, the naturally occurring nature of corpus data is a major advantage over the use of dictionaries to determine meanings, in that it is already one step removed from the interpretative processes of the lexicographer and is '"undigested" and therefore free from definitional reduction' (Hutton 2021: 86). Tobia et al. (2023) combine 'traditional tools' of statutory interpretation such as dictionaries and intuition with corpus linguistic analysis and survey experiments with members of the public on determining the meaning of *and*. They argue that the empirical data from corpora and surveys 'seems at least as relevant as these other traditional tools' (Tobia et al. 2023: 52). Ultimately, they argue in favour of 'triangulating ordinary meaning' in which corpus linguistics and survey data are used to complement more traditional approaches, given 'their ability to make interpretation more robust, reliable, verifiable, transparent, and objective' (Tobia et al. 2023: 54).

The corpus techniques that are central to ascertaining ordinary meaning are concordances and collocation, with the former being most important as concordance lines are annotated for senses and meanings of their node word (Gries 2021: 632). Such a method allows analysts and/or judges to make linguistic enquiries about word use and meaning 'systematically' and 'and to gain meaningful and quantifiable insight about the range of possible uses of a word and the frequency of its different senses' (Lee and Mouritsen 2018: 832). There are a number of cases of legal interpretation which appear recurrently across the literature. One early example of corpus-oriented evidence in such as case is Cunningham and Fillmore's (1995) collection and probing of purpose-built corpora of British and American newspaper data to determine the meaning of *use a firearm*. The purpose of this was to ascertain whether trading a MAC-10 machine gun in exchange for two ounces of cocaine, or having a gun stored in a location not on the person (e.g. in a bedroom closet or in glovebox of a car) while in possession of or dealing drugs, constituted 'using a firearm' in those offences. A more recent application is Goldfarb et al.'s (2010) brief produced to help the U.S. Supreme Court determine if the word *personal* in *personal privacy* included corporations, particularly U.S. telecommunications giant AT&T. The authors used three large general reference corpora to examine the most common use (and meaning) of *personal*: TIME Corpus of American English (100m words) the Corpus of Contemporary American English (COCA) (410m+ words, at the time) and the Corpus of Historical American English (COHA), (400m words). Identifying the most frequent R1 collocates of *personal* in these corpora, they found that *personal* is used overwhelmingly most often in reference to human beings. On the basis of this evidence, the report concluded that the results 'decisively' support the interpretation that '"personal" has developed a specialized meaning such that it is used with regard to human beings, not corporations' (Goldfarb et al. 2010: 16). Mouritsen (2010) retrospectively demonstrates the way in which a corpus linguistic approach would have provided more reliable and accurate results than a reliance on dictionaries in another U.S. Supreme Court decision. In this case, a man was given a ten- to sixteen-month sentence for selling marijuana from his car, which was extended to a mandatory five-year sentence for *carrying* a firearm. The firearm in question was a handgun locked in the glovebox of his car and remined there until his arrest. The question posed, then, was did having a handgun locked away in a glovebox of a car constitute 'carrying' the firearm? By running a query for the verb lemma *carry** in COCA and analysing a random sample of 500 concordance lines, Mouritsen (2010: 1965) found that 'in the overwhelming majority of cases, when *carry* is used in the context of a firearm, *carrying on one's person* is the intended meaning' and therefore this is the most obvious candidate for the word's 'ordinary meaning'. This analysis, according to Mouritsen (2010: 1919), shows how corpus methods offer 'intriguing possibilities for ambiguity resolution, while avoiding some of the pitfalls of [...] dictionary-based jurisprudence'. Other case studies have seen corpus approaches being used to determine the ordinary meanings of statutorily significant words such as *defraud* (Solan and Gales 2016), *discharge* (Solan and Gales 2017), *custody* (Mouritsen 2017), *interpreter* and *harbouring (an alien)* (Lee and Mouritsen 2018), *labor* (Gales and Solan 2020) and *income(s)* (Lee et al. 2023).

There are, however, challenges and common criticisms associated with corpus approaches to statutory interpretation. Some of these are more perennial considerations for corpus linguistics generally rather than being peculiar to corpus-assisted legal interpretation. For example, there are concerns over the representativeness of the corpora being used, be that in relation to the speech community in question, the time-appropriacy of the datasets available and the general finiteness of corpus data (Gries 2021: 637). As Mouritsen (2010: 1969) argues, 'given the infinite permutability of human language, the corpus can never capture every possible human utterance, even in a narrowly-defined speech community'. Furthermore, corpus methods do not entirely remove subjectivity or bias; 'the judicial interpreter must still read through the concordance lines and her biases may shape how she perceives the words in the data' (Mouritsen 2011: 202). There is also the argument that, even when used in the appropriate way, corpus results can still be indeterminate, not leading to clear-cut results, though this is still preferable to the obscurity and opacity of judge or lawyer intuition (Gries 2021: 638). There are also concerns over the practicalities of embedding the routine use of corpora in judicial interpretation. Although Mouritsen (2011: 203) argues that judges who are already familiar with the tools of statutory interpretation could be trained to use corpus methods, others are less optimistic and are of the opinion that corpus methods are 'not automatically intuitive' (Ehrett 2019: 68). Gries and Slocum (2017: 1471) argue that, on balance, it is 'highly doubtful that the cost-benefit analysis of acquiring the knowledge necessary to perform corpus linguistics competently favors widespread judicial adoption'. However, Lee and Mouritsen (2018: 865) address issues of proficiency, propriety and practicality of judges and lawyers using corpus methods in depth, concluding that 'lawyers are crafty, ingenious creatures with the capacity to learn and even master new tools, technologies, and methodologies' (Lee and Mouritsen 2018: 872). In any case, as Lee and Mouritsen (2018: 873) and Gries (2021: 639) emphasise, if the stakes are high enough and the issues at hand are complex enough, expert (corpus) linguistic testimony should be sought.

There have also been questions raised about the position of corpora in the criminal justice system, in relation to corpora threatening to displace or replace the judicial role in cases involving the determination of ordinary meaning but also threatening the foundations of legal interpretation. Solan and Gales (2016: 274), who found that intuition, dictionaries and corpora all led to same conclusion about the ordinary meaning of *defraud*, cautioned that although corpora provide detailed data about a word's use, they do not 'replace the legal analyst's obligation to ask the right questions in exploiting that data'. Similarly, Ehrett (2019: 70) warns that corpus linguistics does not 'obviate many of the critical questions of interpretation; it merely outsources them to corpus compilers or overlooks them entirely'. Hessick (2017: 1511) particularly emphasises the potential difficulties with frequency-oriented corpus results:

> the idea that the traditional ordinary meaning inquiry is somehow inferior to a frequency analysis because judges might rely on their intuition—that is, their professional judgment—rejects the very foundation of the judicial role.

Hessick (2017: 1508) identifies the problems with 'proponents of corpus linguistics', believing that the frequency with which words are used in a given corpus 'can tell us how a member of the public would understand those words when they appear in statutes'. This is a point that Gries (2021: 639) rebuts, noting that no corpus linguist would infer anything on the basis of frequency alone, a point also made by Lee and Mouritsen (2018: 875). Indeed, Gries (2021) presents counterpoints to most of the major and recurrent criticisms of corpus methods in statutory interpretation. Lee and Mouritsen (2021) dedicate a full paper to outlining common criticisms of corpus linguistics and systematically addresses them, offering refinements to the methods as used to-date. Ultimately, they argue in conclusion that most of the prevailing critiques actually do more to highlight the core contributions of corpus linguistics to the tasks, rather than its shortcomings, and further underscore the basic problems with the traditional approaches (Lee and Mouritsen 2021: 350). Solan and Gales (2017) identify four issues that should be addressed in order for corpus analysis to be 'maximally convincing' in legal interpretation: (i) the case must concern the distribution of language usage over a particular population, (ii) it is for the court to decide upon and adopt a clear notion of 'ordinary meaning', (iii) the right search must be conducted on the right corpus and (iv) caution must be exercised in drawing inferences from frequency results, particularly the *absence* of particular usages in the corpus/corpora being used. On this last point, Gales and Solan (2020: 500) highlight what they call the 'blue pitta problem', which relates to the fact that corpus approaches to determining meaning rely on there being attested referents in the corpus or corpora that are being used (i.e. just because the term 'blue pitta' does not appear in a corpus that does not mean it is not a bird). Recent research by Egbert and Lee (2024) and Gries et al. (2024) proposes corpus-based approaches embedding prototype theory into the analysis that can be used to determine conceptual (intensional) meaning rather than relying on attested referential (extensional) meaning and can help determine the meaning of words for which there may be no textual evidence.

It is clear that the legal-linguistic debate around the role and procedures for using corpora in determining the ordinary meaning of words in statues will continue, with methods being refined in response to criticisms. While the metaphorical jury may be out over whether the judicial adoption of interdisciplinary knowledge from (corpus) linguistics will 'serve to enhance both the theory and practice of legal interpretation (Gries and Slocum 2017: 1417), it is clear that corpus methods have opened up 'new ways of thinking about issues of [...] word meaning' offering 'new kinds of questions to ask, new modes of analysis, and new lines of argument for litigators to pursue' (Goldfarb 2017: 1416).

New avenues for research

Forensic and legal linguistic enquiry has expanded into new territory via the use of corpora for one of two reasons. Either (i) new corpora have been built and previously inaccessible genres have become available or (ii) interest in (or indeed existence of) new areas of research areas have developed contemporaneously with the general increased use and availability of corpora and corpus tools. This section surveys research across both of these camps.

Historical legal discourse

The building of specialised corpora has seen the emergence of a brand-new avenue for research in the language of the historical courtroom. Notably, the 1.2 million–word *Corpus of English Dialogues 1560–1760* (CED) (Kytö & Walker 2006) contained courtroom proceedings as one of its five text types. A number of subsequent studies used this resource to obtain previously impossible corpus-derived insights into historical courtroom discourse. For example, using an annotated sub-corpus of CED, Archer

(2005) investigates the discursive strategies in questions and answers by judges, lawyers, witnesses and defendants between 1640 and 1760. Archer's (2005: 282) analysis identifies a period of 'emerging and changing roles' in court during this time, as well as the emergence of the prosecution–defence adversarial system that exists in England and Wales today. In their account of the linguistic features across the speech-related written genres in the CED, Culpeper and Kytö (2010) identified common lexical bundles found in early modern English (EME) trials. These lexical bundles were subsequently compared with those used in the present-day O.J. Simpson trial by Reppen and Chen (2019), who argued that similarities in the use of bundles between EME and present-day English (PDE) trials 'reflect the similar goals and functions of the macro register of spoken courtroom language' (Reppen and Chen 2019: 119). A more narrowly focused approach to historical trial discourse in CED has involved isolating specific discourse markers and their sociopragmatic functions in this context, such as Lutzky's (2019) analysis of *but*. Much like Archer's (2005), Lutzky's (2019: 16) observations regarding the frequency and distribution of the contrastive marker reflect the changing nature of courtroom discourse at that time, particularly the emergence of new and different participant roles in the seventeenth century, most notably defence counsel.

The online publication of the *Old Bailey Proceedings* in 2012 (Hitchcock et al. 2023) and subsequent corpora extracted from the original database (e.g. Huber et al. 2016) revolutionised the study of the language of the English courtroom in the seventeenth to twentieth centuries. This has included new insights into particular trial sub-genres, such as Chaemsaithong's (2014) analysis of opening statements from over 50 trials in the eighteenth century which found evidence of lawyers using the same interactive and persuasive narrative features – such as character representations, attitudinal stance and reported discourse – as are now familiar in contemporary instances of the genre. In a similar way, Johnson's (2018) investigation of the use of negative questioning in the witness examination of children complainants in 36 child rape cases finds striking similarities in the contemporary cross-examination of rape victims. In particular, on the basis of aspects such as the lawyer's dominance in the reproduction of the rape story and the law's exploitation of cultural beliefs and ideologies about rape, Johnson (2018: 60) argues that 'in the historical data examined here we see the historical underpinnings of many of today's abuse stories'. Ronan's (2020) analysis of questioning strategies in trials at different periods covered by the *Proceedings* shows, like Lutzky (2019), how linguistic analysis reflects the changing nature and participant roles in the historical development of criminal trials, in particular the differing coercive skills of defendants and lawyers in examining prosecution witnesses. Other corpus-based studies have focused on different sociopragmatic elements of courtroom discourse and how they were used in historical trials, such as Archer's (2014) analysis of 'verbal aggression' in the courtroom space, and Johnson's (2015) examination of the 'selective power of quotation' in the defence of the prisoner by their legal counsel. Meanwhile, Claudia Claridge and colleagues have, in a range of works, examined the use and function of specific lexico-grammatical features in the historical courtroom, namely maximisers (Claridge et al. 2020), words denoting *drunk* (Claridge 2019), the pragmatic marker *now* (Claridge 2018) and the intensifier *little* (Claridge et al. 2021). This momentum in corpus-based research on the historical courtroom complements the diachronic corpus work that has been undertaken focusing on historical and contemporary legal texts, such as register analyses of British law reports over five centuries (Rodríguez-Puente 2020) change in the lexical bundles of Scottish legislation between the 1300s and 1500s (Kopaczyk 2013) and diachronic development of rhetorical moves British patents (Groom and Grieve 2019). These studies, along with the others cited here, demonstrate how the construction and publication of appropriate corpora and the application of corpus techniques not only have facilitated but have driven new areas of historical research in forensic and legal linguistics.

New access to forensic genres

Elsewhere, corpora have been collected of genres for which data had previously been scarce, at least in terms of sizeable corpora. Three such genres are threats, suicide notes, and grooming interactions. For reasons that may be obvious, until recently there had not been means by which texts of these kinds could be readily accessible and collectable at scale. The advent of corpus approaches, however, has changed this.

In terms of threats, Tammy Gales's work on threatening communications laid much of the groundwork for future research in this area. Some of Gales's early published work was from a qualitative perspective analysing a small number of threatening texts (e.g. Gales 2011), but her application of the corpus methodology broadened the insights to be gained by forensic linguists on this previously hidden genre. In this regard, Gales (2015a) is a key text, in which almost 400 authentic threats are examined, using corpus means, for the overt grammatical markers of stance that they exhibit. In particular, Gales's analysis focused on threats to stalk and found that, in terms of stance markers, stalking threats can be 'defined and delineated' from other types of threats, such as threats to defame and harass. Using a corpus approach, Gales (2015a: 196) argues that 'links between a stalker's language, his or her behaviour, and the professional assessment of such behaviour can be seen' when their distinctive stance functions identified in the analysis are compared with established typologies of stalkers. In turn, this contributes 'valuable insights that may help shape law-enforcement assessment protocols' (Gales 2015a: 196). Gales (2015b) again analyses threats from a stance perspective, this time to determine the difference in stance-taking between realised and non-realised threats. The analysis ultimately reveals stance functions and forms that are significant in either realised or non-realised threats, providing evidence that there can be linguistic clues to signal threatener intent. The analysis found two interpersonal sets of stance functions emerge from the corpora: those stance functions which strengthen the threatener's perceived level of commitment to the threatened action and those which weaken it (Gales 2015b: 18). Although, as Gales (2015a: 18–19) acknowledges, more corpus work is needed to examine and corroborate the results of this study, she also emphasises that empirical linguistic evidence of this sort, relating to the differences between realised and non-realised threats, should act as an antidote to ideological misconceptions and misunderstandings of writer intent which, if left unchecked, 'may result in dire consequences'. Hurt and Grant (2018) also examine the difference between realised and non-realised violent fantasies or 'pledges to harm' conducting a quantitative and qualitative appraisal analysis (Martin and White 2005), of a set of 14 short threatening texts. They too note the lack of empirical evidence in how violent intent is expressed linguistically and underline the counter-intuitive nature of some of their findings, such as that non-realised threats feature a higher ratio of violent to non-violent lexemes, and non-realised threats more commonly place the imagined violence in a grammatical future time (Hurt and Grant 2018: 168). Here, as with Gales (2015b), linguistic analysis and language-based evidence is offered as a bridge between threats of violence and intent to realize that harm. Meanwhile, Nini (2017) subjects a corpus of 104 authentic malicious forensic texts, comprising threats, abuse and texts spreading malicious information, to a register analysis based on Biber's (1988) features for MDA. Nini's (2017: 122) results find that malicious forensic texts are involved, persuasive and transactional in character and that different dimensions in the analysis can indicate the difference between a threatening and non-threatening text and the direction of harm. Analyses such as these, Nini (2017: 124) argues, contribute towards the development of 'a better working model that can predict and explain the language of malicious communication'. A diverse range of specific contexts and types of threatening language have also been tackled using corpus methods, including rape threats on Twitter (now 'X') (Hardaker and McGlashan 2016) and abusive letters (Busso et al. 2022). Elsewhere, the focus has been on terrorist texts, including corpus analysis of 'lone-wolf' terrorist manifestos (Mustafa 2022) and the analysis of violent jihadist discourse (Brookes and McEnery 2020; Baker et al. 2021). Meanwhile, Longhi (2021, 2022) outlines ways in which corpus linguistic methods can be used to help in terrorism investigations, either through identifying shared stylistic features between texts, thus suggesting possible shared authorship, or revealing themes running through online threats in the context of terrorism.

Along with threats, suicide notes have been subject to corpus linguistic analysis. Alongside qualitative analyses of suicide notes (e.g. Galasinski 2017), some corpus work has set out to use corpus methods to identify features of suicide notes as a genre, collecting and analysing sets of suicide notes written offline and online (e.g. Samraj and Gawron 2015; Jaafar and Jasim 2022). However, suicide notes are not in and of themselves a *forensic* genre. Rather, they can become of interest to the forensic linguist when there is a suspicion that the suicide may be fabricated, thus throwing into question the nature and manner of a person's death. The first large-scale forensically oriented corpus analysis of suicide notes was Shapero's (2011) doctoral dissertation, which initially set out to 'describe suicide notes in such a way that genuine ones could be distinguished from fake ones' (Shapero 2011: 1). However, given the difficulty of obtaining a substantial corpus of non-authentic suicide notes, Shapero's dissertation pivoted towards defining the typical suicide note and away from the 'real versus fake' issue (Shapero 2011: 2). That said, in addition to 286 genuine suicide notes collected from the Birmingham Coroner's Office in the U.K., Shapero's dataset included a corpus of 66 American suicide notes built by Edwin Shneidman (Shneidman and Farberow 1957), which contained 33 genuine and 33 'simulated' notes. Part of Shapero's analysis involved comparing the genuine and simulated notes for any observable linguistic differences between them, with the eventual conclusion being that it was not possible to determine a 'litmus test' for genuineness or fakeness, 'because there is probably no absolute means of distinguishing real from fake suicide notes' (Shapero 2011: 247). The aim of distinguishing between real and fake suicide notes was revisited by Grundlingh (2018), who combined Shneidman and Farberow's corpus of 33 simulated notes with 33 notes collected by Black (1993) to form one corpus and compared it against genuine suicide notes. Grundlingh performed an appraisal category analysis (Martin and Rose 2003) on each suicide note and a statistical measure of association to identify any significant differences between the genuine and fake corpora. Grundlingh (2018: 9) is more positive than Shapero in conclusion, determining that there are 'differences in the linguistic characteristics of the two corpora of suicide notes'. This assessment is based on the findings that three appraisal categories (trust, propriety and negative appreciation) are possible 'legitimacy markers', distinguishing authentic suicide notes from fake ones. This problem has most recently been tackled by Zaśko-Zielińska (2022) in the analysis of the Polish Corpus of Suicide Notes (PCSN; Marcińczuk et al. 2011), which consists of 614 genuine suicide notes, 79 simulated suicide notes and 117 suicide notes forged during an experiment. Zaśko-Zielińska

(2022: 380) argues that when forging a suicide note, the forger is paying so much attention to hiding their authorship of the note and assuming the linguistic identity of their victim that they are less attuned to the 'social context' of the note, particularly the intended recipient(s) of the note, whom the forger may know very little about. The comparative analysis is qualitative, comparing two genuine notes by the same person (to different addressees) and one forged one, in places drawing on larger generalisations about genuine notes from the PCSN. The study invites the reader to answer questions about the forged note and alludes to ways in which it might be distinctive from genuine notes in terms of spelling, punctuation, the communicative situation, time orientation, rhetorical moves and content. As these studies indicate, there is much to be learnt about any differences between real and faked suicide notes, and it is likely that corpora and corpus methods will be central to future attempts at addressing this issue.

The third type of forensic (con)text that corpus linguistics has had a key role in examining is online child grooming discourses. Chiang and colleagues have shown that move analysis (inspired by Swales 1981), which combines quantitative and qualitative analysis of the frequency and structures of rhetorical moves by interactants, is an important means by which to understand various different types of online child sexual offence discourses. This work began with Chiang and Grant (2017) conducting a move analysis on transcripts of online grooming interactions between volunteer decoys from a U.S. organization called Perverted Justice and would-be child groomers. Although the ultimate conclusion was that 'chatroom grooming interactions follow only a loose generic move structure' (Chiang and Grant 2017: 121), the analysis identified 14 rhetorical moves used in chatroom grooming, including *building rapport*, *assessing likelihood and extent of engagement*, *assessing and managing risk introducing sexual content* and *planning/arranging contact*. The application of this method to genuine online conversations between an actual offender and 20 victims found that moves used by offenders to index different identity positions when grooming children, such as 'engaged listener', 'friend', and 'sexual aggressor' (Chiang and Grant 2019: 695). Interestingly, this later work using genuine grooming interactions found important differences between real interactions and those involving decoys from Perverted Justice, casting doubt on whether such 'decoy' corpora are reliable proxies for understanding real grooming discourse (Chiang and Grant 2019: 696). This is a finding corroborated by Schneevogt et al. (2018), who strongly suggest that researchers across disciplines who want or need to analyse conversations involving the abuse of children must work with data that involves or includes genuine grooming interactions. Chiang's later work has focused on moves in offender–offender interactions on a dark web image exchange chatroom (Chiang et al. 2020) and has shown that undercover police officers posing as an offender in such chatrooms are able to convincingly adopt and accommodate to the rhetorical moves of actual offenders (Chiang 2020). Most recently, Chiang et al. (2023) turn attention back to self-styled 'paedophile-hunting' groups, with a corpus-assisted analysis of stance in 18 months of private Facebook group chat messages between members. The analysis finds that hunters position themselves as 'selfless knights who ride out to save their communities from an evil threat that formal institutions are unable, or unwilling, to manage' (Chiang et al. 2023: 21). Moreover, their analysis foregrounds the significance of social binding and community identity, not observed in previous studies, as well the suggestion that hunting is an 'entertaining as much as a moral pursuit' and that members have a generally negative view of the police (Chiang et al. 2023: 21).

Corpus-based methods have also been used to analyse grooming discourses by Lorenzo-Dus and colleagues. This work has used large-scale corpora of Perverted Justice chatlogs to model discourse-level communicative strategies of online groomers, including in comparison to offline groomers (Lorenzo-Dus et al. 2016), and has identified recurring collocation patterns and their use by offenders in realising grooming goals (Lorenzo-Dus et al. 2020). Lorenzo-Dus's work has also used corpus approaches to examine specific pragmatic strategies in grooming discourse, such as the highly formulaic nature of compliments by abusers to develop trust with victims (Lorenzo-Dus and Izura 2017) and how groomers use vague language in order to achieve their manipulative and abusive goals (Lorenzo-Dus and Kinzel 2021). In their methodologically reflective paper, Lorenzo-Dus and Kinzel (2019) use lexical dispersion, collocation and concordance analysis to emphasise the advantages of using a corpus method in favour of other software-assisted approaches to grooming data that focus only on lexis, namely Linguistic Inquiry and Word Count (LIWC). In comparison with analyses that remain at the lexical level, it is shown that methods from corpus-assisted discourse studies (CADS) have the benefit of being to 'reveal the complex and nuanced ways in which discourse features such as sexual explicitness/implicitness and interpersonal (in)directness operate' in groomers strategic use of language (Lorenzo-Dus and Kinzel 2019: 14). They conclude by arguing that

> Having established that CADS can make a positive contribution, future work on online grooming should continue to apply this approach to a range of pressing issues, including determining how extra-linguistic factors, such as duration of grooming, may reflect and shape different 'groomer' communicative profiles beyond compliment use. This line of work, geared towards developing a nuanced understanding of online groomers' communicative modus operandi, is crucial when it comes to working with law enforcement and other stakeholders (e.g. educationalists, social workers) on developing targeted interventions for preventing CSA online.
>
> (Lorenzo-Dus and Kinzel 2019: 31)

This is a position that Lorenzo-Dus et al. (2023) demonstrate in their use of CADS to analyse genuine grooming conversations between offenders and victims across social media platforms. Importantly, they explicate how corpus methods and results have been applied to inform and develop detection and prevention resources to in the fight against online grooming, and how corpus research 'can deliver "real-world" impact and help improve the safety of children online' (Lorenzo-Dus et al. 2023: 75).

New and emerging issues in language, law and evidence

In addition to the new avenues that corpus methods have opened up in terms of working with new types of data, new forensic and legal linguistic issues have emerged simultaneously alongside the increase in corpus approaches. One such issue is online trolling. Hardaker (2021: 697) outlines the impossibility of providing a specific definition of 'trolling' and instead characterises trolling as comprising two broad components: it 'involves deliberate antisocial online behaviour' and it 'is typically carried out for some form of gain'. Moreover, trolling sometimes, but far from always, constitutes a criminal offence and therefore not all forms of trolling are of interest to forensic linguists (Hardaker 2021: 697). According to Hardaker (2021: 704–5), corpus linguistics is 'excellent for providing us with access to potentially hundreds of cases of trolling'. However, this comes with a significant caveat:

> it is actually remarkably difficult to extract the trolls themselves because their behaviour varies so widely that no one search, or set of searches, will extract even a reasonable amount of them.

This difficulty is also emphasised by Clarke (2018: 153), who describes the challenges facing approaches which define the behaviours of trolling and then identify posts that exhibit such behaviour, given that trolling is such as disparate and non-uniform collage of linguistic features and behaviours. Instead, the path that both Hardaker and Clarke advocate in the corpus analysis of trolling is to identify accusations of trolling by participants in the data under analysis and working backwards from these accusations to the messages that prompted the accusations. Using this method 'involves using the perceptions of others' in the interaction (Clarke 2018: 154), is comparatively and relatively quick to conduct and can 'garner indications from the person making the accusation about the norms or rules that have been broken' (Hardaker 2021: 705). Using this method of identifying (perceived) trolling, Hardaker (2010) uses examples from a 172 million–word corpus of web forum data to classify the main conditions that appear to constitute trolling from the perspective of other users. These conditions

– aggression, deception, disruption and success – are then used as the basis for a working definition of 'trolling' (this definition is vastly different to that offered by Hardaker 2021, and reasons for that are explained in that later chapter). Hardaker (2013) identifies a range of trolling strategies from discussions and accusations of trolling from an eighty-six million–word corpus of web forum data, each of which sits on a cline between what Hardaker refers to as 'covert' and 'overt' strategies. Covert strategies are those which are as implicit as possible 'where the would-be troller can plausibly deny the ascribed intent', whereas overt strategies are 'more heavily characterised by aggression- and shock-based behaviours that are increasingly difficult for speakers to plausibly deny as trolling' (Hardaker 2013: 79). Meanwhile, Hardaker (2015) shifts focus to users' responses to perceived trolling themselves and shows how users react interactionally in a range of different ways to trolling, from engaging and responding sincerely, exposing, challenging or mocking the perceived troll, or ignoring them altogether. Hardaker (2015: 224) extends this analysis and uses these categories of response as a means by which to evaluate the outcomes of perceived trolling attempts as either successful, frustrated, thwarted or failed. In reflecting on the method, Hardaker argues that despite the apparent incompatibility of the two, corpus methods can facilitate pragmatic analysis in forensic contexts. Clarke (2018, 2019) also focuses on the multifunctional nature of trolling and uses MDA (Biber 1988) to describe the linguistic variation of perceived trolling in a corpus of tweets. The results of Clarke's (2018) MDA found that trolling tweets can be interactive (directly addressing or responding to people) or less interactive and informationally dense, they can be dismissive or mocking of others and they can be overtly argumentative. Clarke (2019) tentatively suggests that corpus-based MDA may be useful as a means by which forensically significant instances of trolling might be distinguished from non-forensically significant instances. The method, Clarke (2019: 77) argues, can be used to identify particularly hostile and provocative tweets against a backdrop of a larger population of trolling behaviour. Elsewhere, Petykó (2017) offers a different perspective on trolling, based on a corpus of comment threads of British political blogs. Also extracting instances of perceived trolling through responses to posts, Petykó identifies the motives ascribed to trolls by others and finds that users attribute trolling behaviour to emotional/mental health-related/social reasons, financial gain, political beliefs, being employed by a political body, and having some unspecified political affiliation. Although based on an explicitly political corpus, Petyko's findings offer new insights into how users account for others' trolling behaviour.

Like trolling, deception (and its detection) is not always a forensic or legal problem, and corpus approaches have been developed in the detecting of deception in a wide variety of 'non-forensic' contexts (e.g. Archer and Gillings 2020). The last decade, however, has seen an increased interested in deception detection from a forensic linguistic perspective and much of this research has drawn on corpus applications. Fitzpatrick and Bachenko (2010) describe the process of collecting, annotating and analysing corpora of criminal statements, police interrogations, and civil testimony in order to test the usefulness of linguistic cues associated with deception and outlines the issues and challenges involved in compiling forensic corpora of this kind. McQuaid et al. (2014) used wMatrix (Rayson 2009) to compare the language of deceptive and genuine pleaders who were pleading for the return of a missing loved one during televised press conferences. Their analysis revealed a number of lexical features which distinguished genuine pleaders from deceptive killers, including the frequency of the third-person plural *they*, singular indefinite pronouns, certain adverbs and temporal references. Similarly, Archer and Lansley (2015) explore the value that corpus methods can add in incorporating linguistic analysis in a (semi-)automatic investigation of potential deception across all communication channels. Also using wMatrix, their analysis identified keywords, key POS and key semantic fields in four televised clips relating to U.K. cases involving press appeals. They conclude that 'there appears to be much more mileage in CL techniques playing a useful role' in helping to determine 'the validity of language features previously identified as potential deception indicators' as well as playing an important role in linking linguistic features with visual and auditory cues encompassed in their multi-channel model for deception detection (Archer and Lansley 2015: 255). Larner (2019a) took a focused approach, isolating formulaic sequences as potential markers of deception in a corpus of deceptive and truthful online hotel reviews, finding that there are significant differences in the type of formulaicity exhibited in truthful and deceptive texts. Gillings (2024) combined the qualitative and quantitative affordances of corpus methods in exploring cues to deception in simulated police interviews and border control interviews. Using corpus methods of frequency, distribution, collocation and concordance analyses, found differences in the language of truth-tellers and liars. However, these differences interacted with social variables of speakers, such as gender, age, socioeconomic status, or region, and therefore argue for a more context-sensitive approach to deception detection (Gillings 2022: 597; 2024). Such corpus approaches have also been applied to deception detection in languages other than English, such as Almela's (2021) corpus-based study of linguistic deception in written Spanish, who ends their study with a call to arms:

> the use of corpus tools developed out of linguistic theory is of the utmost importance as is the adoption of reliable scientific methods. Researchers should keep on testing methods on real life data, deploying their

> knowledge of linguistics—theory, corpus linguistics, and computational linguistics—to improve both low-stakes and high-stakes deception detection.
>
> (Almela 2021: 14)

A final set of questions that corpus approaches have been used to address is that of disinformation and fake news. Like trolling and deception, the proliferation of disinformation and fake news is not always a forensic issue but becomes one when it 'poses a security threat by clouding decision-making at both individual and national levels' (Dance 2023: 16). Sousa-Silva (2022: 2421) agrees, arguing that 'disinformation meets all the criteria of language crimes' and that given the 'nature of fake news, mis- and disinformation and their potential embodiment of cybercriminal activities', a forensic linguistic analysis is 'able, not only to assist its investigation and detection but also to provide evidence in legal cases' (Sousa-Silva 2022: 2418). Sousa-Silva's analysis of English and Portuguese articles from outlets known to be sources of disinformation and fake news follows a methodological a procedure 'identical to the analyses done in forensic authorship scenarios […] to identify idiosyncratic features of fake and hyperpartisan news' (Sousa-Silva 2022: 2423). The results of the analysis find sets of linguistic features that are characteristic or 'typical' of disinformation and these are found across text-level elements such as paragraph, sentence and word length and punctuation, structural elements such as grammar and spelling mistakes and aspects of the discourse such as othering and attribution of agency. Ultimately, Sousa-Silva (2022: 2429) concludes

> The findings are promising and have a significant potential to contribute to scholarship, not only by enabling a streamlined development of computational detection systems, but more importantly by permitting the forensic linguistics expert to assist criminal investigations and give evidence in court.

In the same vein as Sousa-Silva, Moura et al. (2021) aim to take a forensic linguistic approach to detecting fake news in Portuguese. This study takes methods of text classification that are commonly used in stylometric (forensic) authorship analysis research and applies them to the automatic discrimination and identification of fake and genuine news. Using quantifiable linguistic features of texts, such as average paragraph and sentence length, frequencies of punctuation and part-of-speech tags, vocabulary richness and readability measures and word n-grams, Moura et al. run a series of experiments using different machine learning algorithms, and report accuracy rates as high as 97% in identifying fake news. They conclude, therefore, that 'a forensic linguistics-grounded approach for classifying fake news can be applied with great success' (Moura et al. 2021: 798). Grieve and Woodfield (2023) develop a framework for the linguistic analysis of fake news based on the MDA of register based on fake news articles written by Jayson Blair of *The New York Times*. Based on their quantitative corpus analysis of his use of forty-nine grammatical features, Grieve and Woodfield (2023: 66) found that the relative frequencies of twenty-eight of these features revealed 'substantial differences across twenty-eight real and thirty-six fake articles written by Blair over a six-month period'. The vast majority of these features (twenty-three of the twenty-eight), Grieve and Woodfield (2023: 47) continue, are associated with variation in information density when Blair is writing genuine as opposed to fake news articles. Essentially, these differences see Blair 'creating long and complex noun phrases to maximise the amount of information that can be packed into sentences' when writing genuine articles, whereas his fake news articles contain more features 'associated with an interactive and spontaneous style of discourse, including pronouns, verbs, and adverbs' (Grieve and Woodfield 2023: 47). Grieve and Woodfield propose explanations for these differences, arguing that they can be accounted for by the context in which Blair was writing the fake articles. They suggest that he wrote with lower levels of information density in his fake articles because he was trying to write many articles quickly over short periods of time, and because he knew he was communicating fabricated information, he inadvertently marked his fake news for uncertainty (Grieve and Woodfield 2023: 66–7). Their results provide 'clear evidence of variation in Blair's style of writing when he is telling the truth and when he is lying' (Grieve and Woodfield 2023: 38). Also considering people's motivations for sharing disinformation, this time on Twitter (now called 'X'), Dance (2019) uses the semantic tagging function in wMatrix (Rayson 2009) to identify key semantic domains in disinformation-sharing. He finds 'truth' to be a recurring theme in the corpus, 'whether this is social media users saying articles are *revealing* the truth or users accusing others of being *disingenuous* or *fake*' (Dance 2019: 22). Corpus approaches therefore have good potential for developing frameworks and methods in detecting and interpreting fake news and disinformation in forensic contexts and beyond. However, there is an issue of the availability of large-scale corpora of fake news (versus genuine news) that has been verified as fake by experts or fact-checking websites (Asr and Taboada 2019) and that, at the moment at least, international research on fake news across languages and cultures 'suffer from a lack of quality data [...] for linguistic analyses' (Põldvere et al. 2023: 164). It is very likely that, in time, as for many different types of corpora written about in this chapter, reliable datasets of fake news will become more readily available.

This chapter has provided an overview of corpus linguistic applications in forensic and legal linguistics that, though not exhaustive, provides the most representative account of the breadth of such work to date. It has been shown that corpora and corpus methods have played a significant role in the development and expansion of forensic and legal linguistics as (a) discipline(s). In some cases, they have provided access to previously inaccessible data, whereas in others, they have complemented areas of research that have typically been characterised by qualitative-only methods. The benefits of corpus linguistics have been felt in both research and casework contexts, as the techniques associated with corpus linguistics provide valuable additions to the toolkits of forensic and legal linguists.

Notes

1 At the time in England and Wales, because a guilty verdict would result in the death penalty, there was no issue of additional charges or sentences, and so defendants charged with murder were indicted only on a single count. In this case, although the charge for the murder of his wife still stood, Evans was tried and convicted of *only* the murder of his daughter.
2 In 2003, 'Forensic Linguistics' was dropped from the title, and since then the journal has been known as the *International Journal of Speech, Language and the Law*.
3 Chaemsaithong's work on opening statements is discussed in more detail in Chapter 4.
4 Szczyrbak's work on stance-taking in court is discussed in more detail in Chapter 5.
5 Enron is a former American energy company which filed for bankruptcy in late 2001 following a now infamous accounting scandal. In 2003, a database of 1.6 million Enron documents, including employees' emails, was released into the public domain by the Federal Energy Regulatory Commission.

References

Abrams, J. R. and Potts, A. (2021) The language of harm: What the Nassar victim impact statements reveal about abuse and accountability. *University of Pittsburgh Law Review* 82(1): 71–134. https://doi.org/10.5195/lawreview.2020.775
Almela, Á. (2021) Corpus-based study of linguistic deception in Spanish. *Applied Sciences* 11(19), 8817. https://doi.org/10.3390/app11198817
Archer, D. (2005) *Questions and Answers in the English Courtroom (1640–1760): A Sociopragmatic Analysis*. Amsterdam/Philadelphia: John Benjamins.
Archer, D. (2014) Exploring verbal aggression in English historical texts using USAS: The possibilities the problems and potential solutions. In I. Taavitsainen, A. Jucker and J. Tuominen (eds.), *Diachronic Corpus Pragmatics*. Amsterdam/Philadelphia: John Benjamins, pp. 277–301.
Archer, D. and Gillings, M. (2020) Depictions of deception: A corpus-based analysis of five Shakespearean characters. *Language and Literature* 29(3): 246–274. https://doi.org/10.1177/0963947020949439
Archer, D. and Lansley, C. (2015) Public appeals, news interviews and crocodile tears: An argument for a multi-channel annotation scheme. *Corpora* 10(2): 231–258. https://doi.org/10.3366/cor.2015.0075

Asr, F. T. and Taboada, M. (2019). Big Data and quality data for fake news and misinformation detection. *Big Data & Society* 6(1): 1–14. https://doi.org/10.3390/su142114365

Bajčić, M. and Dobrić Basaneže, K. (2021) Considering foreignization and domestication in EU legal translation: A corpus-based study. *Perspectives: Studies in Translation Theory and Practice* 29(5): 706–721. https://doi.org/10.1080/0907676X.2020.1794016

Baker, P. Vessey, R. and McEnery, T. (2021) *The Language of Violent Jihad*. Cambridge, UK: Cambridge University Press.

Ballesteros-Lintao, R., Arriero, M. R. P., Claustro, J. M. A. S., Dichoso, K. I. U., Leynes, S. A. S., Aranda, M. R. R. and Reintegrado-Celino, J. (2016) Deontic meanings in Philippine contracts. *International Journal of Legal Discourse* 1(2): 421–454. https://doi.org/10.1515/ijld-2016-0017

Bartley, L. (2018) "Justice demands that you find this man not guilty": A transitivity analysis of the closing arguments of a rape case that resulted in a wrongful conviction. *International Journal of Applied Linguistics* 28(3): 480–495. https://doi.org/10.1111/ijal.12227

Bhatia, V. K. (1993) *Analysing Genre: Language Use in Professional Settings*. London: Longman.

Bhatia, V. K., Langton, N. M. and Lung, J. (2004) Legal discourse: Opportunities and threats for corpus linguistics. In T. A. Upton and U. Connor (eds.), *Discourse in the Professions: Perspectives from Corpus Linguistics*. Amsterdam/Philadelphia: John Benjamins, pp. 203–227.

Biber, D. (1988) *Variation across Speech and Writing*. Cambridge, UK: Cambridge University Press.

Biel, Ł. (2015) Phraseological profiles of legislative genres: Complex prepositions as a special case of legal phrasemes in EU law and national law. *Fachsprache* 37(3–4): 139–160. https://doi.org/10.24989/fs.v37i3-4.1286

Biel, Ł., Biernacka, A. and Jopek-Bosiacka, A. (2018) Collocations of terms in EU Competition Law: A corpus analysis of EU English collocations. In S. Marino, Ł. Biel, M. Bajčić and V. Sosoni (eds.), *Language and Law: The Role of Language and Translation in EU Competition Law*. Cham: Springer, pp. 249–274.

Black, S. T. (1993). Comparing genuine and simulated suicide notes: A new perspective. *Journal of Consulting and Clinical Psychology* 61(4): 699–702. https://doi.org/10.1037//0022-006x.61.4.699

Blackwell, S. (2009) Why forensic linguistics needs corpus linguistics. *Comparative Legilinguistics. International Journal for Legal Communication* 1: 5–19.

Boginskaya, O. (2020) The simplification of jury instructions: Legal-lay interactions in jury trials. *ESP Today* 8(2): 297–318. https://doi.org/10.18485/esptoday.2020.8.2.6

Boginskaya, O. (2022) Dissenting with conviction: Boosting in challenging the majority opinion. *International Journal of Legal Discourse* 7(2): 257–279. https://doi.org/10.1515/ijld-2022-2073

Brabin, D. J. (1966) 'The case of Timothy John Evans'. Home Office report by Hon Mr Justice Brabin. Wellcome Collection (online). Available at: https://wellcomecollection.org/works/tx9cv447 [Last accessed 24 March 2022].

Breeze, R. (2011) Disciplinary values in legal discourse: A corpus study. *Iberica* 21: 93–116.

Breeze, R. (2013) Lexical bundles across four legal genres. *International Journal of Corpus Linguistics* 18(2): 229–253. https://doi.org/10.1075/ijcl.18.2.03bre

Breeze, R. (2019) Part-of-speech patterns in legal genres. Text-internal dynamics from a corpus-based perspective. In T. Fanego and P. Rodriguez-Puente (eds), *Corpus-based Research on Variation in English Legal Discourse*. Amsterdam/Philadelphia: John Benjamins, pp. 79–104.

Brookes, G. and McEnery, T. (2020) Correlation, collocation and cohesion: A corpus-based critical analysis of violent jihadist discourse. *Discourse and Society* 31(4): 351–373. https://doi.org/10.1177/0957926520903528

Buendía Castro, M. and Faber, P. (2015) Phraseological units in English-Spanish legal dictionaries: A comparative study. *Fachsprache* 37(3–4): 161–175. https://doi.org/10.24989/fs.v37i3-4.1288

Busso, L. (2022a) An investigation of the lexico-grammatical profile of English legal-lay language. *Language and Law/Linguagem e Direito* 9(1): 146–184. https://doi.org/10.21747/21833745/lanlaw/9_1a7

Busso, L. (2022b) Lexicon and grammar in legal-lay language: A quantitative corpus study on Italian. *Studi Italiani di Linguistica Teorica e Applicata (SILTA)* 51(1): 5–33.

Busso, L., Petyko, M., Atkins, S. and Grant, T. (2022). Operation Heron: Latent topic changes in an abusive letter series. *Corpora* 17(2): 225–258. https://doi.org/10.3366/cor.2022.0255

Butters, R. (2021) Trademark linguistics. Trademarks: Language that one owns. In M. Coulthard, A. May and R. Sousa-Silva (eds.), *The Routledge Handbook of Forensic Linguistics* (2nd ed.). London: Routledge, pp. 364–381.

Carradice, P. (2012) The execution of Timothy Evans. *BBC News (Online)* 12 January 2012. Available from: https://www.bbc.co.uk/blogs/wales/entries/cdc56160-91eb-366d-ae0e-5d9c5a676fe2 [Last accessed 4 July 2022].

Chaemsaithong, K. (2014) Interactive patterns of the opening statement in criminal trials: A historical perspective. *Discourse Studies* 16(3): 347–364. https://doi.org/10.1177/1461445613508900

Chaemsaithong, K. (2015a) Positioning self and others in the courtroom: Person markers in the opening statement. *Poznań Studies in Contemporary Linguistics* 51(1): 1–25. https://doi.org/10.1515/psicl-2015-0001

Chaemsaithong, K. (2015b) Communicating with silent addressees: Engagement features in legal opening statements. *Language and Communication* 43: 35–46. https://doi.org/10.1016/j.langcom.2015.04.004

Chaemsaithong, K. (2017a) Evaluative stancetaking in courtroom opening statements. *Folia Linguistica* 51(1): 103–132. https://doi.org/10.1515/flin-2017-0003

Chaemsaithong, K. (2017b) Speech reporting in courtroom opening statements. *Journal of Pragmatics* 119: 1–14. https://doi.org/10.1016/j.pragma.2017.08.003

Chaemsaithong, K. (2018) Referential practice and contested identities in legal narratives. *Lingua* 212: 44–59. https://doi.org/10.1016/j.lingua.2018.06.001

Chaemsaithong, K. (2019a) Deconstructing competing courtroom narratives: Representation of social actors. *Social Semiotics* 29(2): 240–260. https://doi.org/10.1080/10350330.2018.1434978

Chaemsaithong, K. (2019b) When grammar clashes: Negotiation of guilt and innocence in courtroom discourse. *Poznań Studies in Contemporary Linguistics* 55(1): 27–52. https://doi.org/10.1515/psicl-2019-0002

Chaemsaithong, K. (2021) Naming as doing: Identities, positioning, and ideologies in capital trials. *Poznan Studies in Contemporary Linguistics* 57(2): 195–220. https://doi.org/10.1515/psicl-2021-0009

Chaemsaithong, K. (2022) Moral legitimation in capital trials: The case of the prosecution's closing summation. *Text & Talk* 42(6): 849–870. https://doi.org/10.1515/text-2020-0129

Chaemsaithong, K. and Kim, Y. (2018) From narration to argumentation: Intertextuality in two courtroom genres. *Lingua* 203: 36–50.

Chaemsaithong, K. and Kim, Y. (2020) Actions, actors, and agency in the penalty phase of capital trials: A comparison of two genres. *Ibérica* 39: 319–344.

Chaemsaithong, K. and Kim, Y. (2021) "Let's kill him": Self-reference pronouns and speaking roles in capital trials. *Social Semiotics* 31(4): 585–603. https://doi.org/10.1080/10350330.2019.1661484

Cheng, L. (2012) Attribution and judicial control in Chinese court judgments: A corpus-based study. *International Journal of Speech, Language and the Law* 19(1): 27–49. https://doi.org/10.1558/ijsll.v19i1.27

Cheng, L and Wang, X. (2017) Modals and modality in legal discourse: A corpus-based sociosemiotic interpretation. *International Journal of Semiotics and Visual Rhetoric* 1(1): 19–29. https://doi.org/10.4018/IJSVR.2017010103

Cheng, L., Cheng, W. and Li, J. (2015) Defamation case law in Hong Kong: A corpus-based study. *Semiotica* 2016(208): 203–222. https://doi.org/10.1515/sem-2015-0114

Cheng, Le, Liu, Y., Zhao, Y. (2021) Exploring the U.S. institutional discourse about critical information infrastructure protection (CIIP): A corpus-based analysis. *International Journal of Legal Discourse* 6(2): 323–347. https://doi.org/10.1515/ijld-2021-2058

Cheng, W. and Cheng, L. (2014) Epistemic modality and court judgements: A corpus-driven comparison of civil cases in Hong Kong and Scotland. *English for Specific Purposes* 33(1), 15–26. https://doi.org/10.1016/j.esp.2013.07.006

Chiang, E. (2020). 'Send Me Some Pics': Performing the offender identity in online undercover child abuse investigations. *Policing* 15(2): 1173–1187. https://doi.org/10.1093/police/paaa065

Chiang, E. and Grant, T. (2017) Online grooming: Moves and strategies. *Language and Law/Linguagem e Direito* 4(1): 103–141.

Chiang, E. and Grant, T. (2019) Deceptive identity performance: Offender moves and multiple identities in online child abuse conversations. *Applied Linguistics* 40(4): 675–698. https://doi.org/10.1093/applin/amy007

Chiang, E., Nguyen, D., Towler, A., Haas, M., and Grieve, J. (2020) Linguistic analysis of suspected child sexual offenders' interactions in a dark web image exchange chatroom. *International Journal of Speech, Language and the Law* 27(2): 129–161. https://doi.org/10.1558/ijsll.41446

Chiang, E., De Rond, M. and Lok, J. (2023). Identity in a self-styled 'paedophile-hunting' group: A linguistic analysis of stance in Facebook group chats. *Applied Linguistics* amad034: 1–27. https://doi.org/10.1093/applin/amad034

Chiu, S. and Chiang, W. (2011) FIGHT metaphors in legal discourse: What is unsaid in the story? *Language and Linguistics* 12(4): 877–915.

Claridge, C. (2018). 'Now' in the historical courtroom: Users and functions. *Journal of Historical Pragmatics* 19(2): 223–242. https://doi.org/10.1075/jhp.00020.cla

Claridge, C. (2019) Drinking and crime. Negotiating intoxication in courtroom discourse, 1720 to 1913. In T. Fanego and P. Rodriguez-Puente (eds.), *Corpus-based Research on Variation in English Legal Discourse*. Amsterdam/Philadelphia: John Benjamins, pp. 261–286.

Claridge, C., Jonsson, E. and Kytö, M. (2020). 'Entirely innocent': A historical sociopragmatic analysis of maximizers in the Old Bailey Corpus. *English Language and Linguistics* 24(4): 855–874. https://doi.org/10.1017/S1360674319000388

Claridge, C., Jonsson, E. and Kytö, M. (2021). A 'little' something goes a long way: 'little' in the Old Bailey corpus. *Journal of English Linguistics* 49(1): 61–89. https://doi.org/10.1177/0075424220982063

Clarke, I. (2018) Stylistic variation in twitter trolling. In J. Golbeck (ed.), *Online Harassment: Human-Computer Interaction*. Cham: Springer, pp. 157–178.

Clarke, I. (2019). Functional linguistic variation in twitter trolling. *International Journal of Speech, Language and the Law* 26(1): 57–84. https://doi.org/10.1558/ijsll.34803

Cotterill, J. (2001) Domestic discord, rocky relationships: Semantic prosodies in representations of marital violence in the O.J. Simpson trial. *Discourse & Society* 12(3): 291–312. https://doi.org/10.1177/0957926501012003002

Cotterill, J. (2003) *Language and Power in Court: A Linguistic Analysis of the O.J. Simpson Trial*. Basingstoke: Palgrave Macmillan.

Cotterill, J. (2004) Collocation, connotation, and courtroom semantics: Lawyers' control of witness testimony through lexical negotiation. *Applied Linguistics* 25(4): 513–537. https://doi.org/10.1093/applin/25.4.513

Cotterill, J. (2010). How to use corpus linguistics in forensic linguistics. In A. O'Keeffe and M. J. McCarthy (eds.), *The Routledge Handbook of Corpus Linguistics* (1st ed.). London: Routledge, pp. 578–590.

Cotterill, J. (2012) Corpus analysis in forensic linguistics. In C. Chapelle (ed.), *The Encyclopedia of Applied Linguistics*. London: Wiley-Blackwell. https://doi.org/10.1002/9781405198431.wbeal0238

Cotterill, J. (2014) Discourse and discord in court: The role of context in the construction of witness examination in British criminal trial talk. In J. Flowerdew (ed.), *Discourse in Context: Contemporary Applied Linguistics* (Volume 3). London: Bloomsbury, pp. 71–89.

Coulthard, M. (1994) On the use of corpora in the analysis of forensic texts. *The International Journal of Speech, Language and the Law* 1(1): 27–43. https://doi.org/10.1558/ijsll.v1i1.27

Coulthard, M. (2004) Author identification, idiolect, and linguistic uniqueness. *Applied Linguistics* 24(4): 431–447. https://doi.org/10.1093/applin/25.4.431

Coulthard, M. (2013) On admissible linguistic evidence. *Journal of Law and Policy* 21(2): 441–466

Coulthard, M. (2021) Experts and opinions. In M. Coulthard, A. May and R. Sousa-Silva (eds.), *The Routledge Handbook of Forensic Linguistics* (2nd ed.). London: Routledge, pp. 523–538.

Coulthard, M., Johnson, A. and Wright, D. (2017). *An Introduction to Forensic Linguistics: Language in Evidence* (2nd ed.). London: Routledge.

Crystal, D. and Davy, D. (1969) *Investigating English Style*. Bloomington: Indiana University Press.

Culpeper, J. and Kytö, M. (2010) *Early Modern English Dialogues: Spoken Interaction as Writing*. Cambridge, UK: Cambridge University Press.

Cunningham, C. D. and Fillmore, C. J. (1995) Using common sense: A linguistic perspective on judicial interpretations of "use a firearm". *Washington University Law Quarterly* 73(3): 1159–1214.

Dance, W. (2019) Disinformation online: Social media user's motivations for sharing 'fake news'. *Science in Parliament* 75(3): 20–22.

Dance, W. (2023) Addressing algorithms in disinformation. *CREST Security Review* 17: 16–17. (online) Available from: https://crestresearch.ac.uk/download/4730/csr17_dance_16-17.pdf

Dobrić Basaneže, K. (2018) Binomials in EU competition law. In S. Marino, Ł. Biel, M. Bajčić and V. Sosoni (eds.), *Language and Law: The Role of Language and Translation in EU Competition Law*. Cham: Springer, pp. 225–248.

Donlan, L. and Nini, A. (2022) A forensic authorship analysis of the Ayia Napa rape statement. In I. Picornell, R. Perkins and M. Coulthard (eds.), *Methodologies and Challenges in Forensic Linguistic Casework*. Chichester: Wiley-Blackwell, pp. 29–43.

Drew, P. (1992) Contested evidence in courtroom cross-examination: The case of a trial for rape. In P. Drew and J. Heritage (eds.), *Talk at Work: Interaction in Institutional Settings*. Cambridge, UK: Cambridge University Press, pp. 470– 520.

Eades, D. (2000) "I don't think it's an answer to the question": Silencing aboriginal witnesses in court. *Language in Society* 29(2), 161–196. https://doi.org/10.1017/S0047404500002013

Eagleson, R. (1994. Forensic analysis of personal written texts: A case study. In J. Gibbons (ed.), *Language and the Law*. London: Routledge, pp. 362–373.

Egbert, J. and Lee, T. R. (2024) Prototype-by-component analysis: A corpus-based, intensional approach to ordinary meaning in statutory interpretation. *Applied Corpus Linguistics* 4(1): 1–9. https://doi.org/10.1016/j.acorp.2023.100078

Ehrett, J. S. (2019) Against corpus linguistics. *The Georgetown Law Journal* 108: 50–73.

Fanego, T. and Rodríguez-Puente, P. (2019). *Corpus-based Research on Variation in English Legal Discourse*. Amsterdam/Philadelphia: Benjamins.

Felton Rosulek, L. (2015) *Dueling Discourses: The Construction of Reality in Closing Arguments*. Oxford: Oxford University Press.

Finegan, E. (2010) Corpus linguistic approaches to 'legal language': Adverbial expression of attitude and emphasis in Supreme Court opinions. In M. Coulthard and A. Johnson (eds.), *The Routledge Handbook of Forensic Linguistics* (1st ed.). London: Routledge, pp. 65–77.

Finegan, E. and Lee, B. T. (2021) Legal writing: Attitude and emphasis. In M. Coulthard, A. May and R. Sousa-Silva (eds.), *The Routledge Handbook of Forensic Linguistics* (2nd ed.). London: Routledge, pp. 48–63.

Fitzpatrick, E. and Bachenko, J. (2010) Building a forensic corpus to test language-based indicators of deception. In S. T. Gries, S. Wulff and M. Davies (eds.), *Corpus-Linguistic Applications: Current Studies, New Directions*. Leiden: Brill, pp. 183–195.

Fonteyn, L. and Nini, A. (2020). Individuality in syntactic variation: An investigation of the 17th-century gerund alternation. *Cognitive Linguistics* 31(2): 279–308. https://doi.org/10.1515/cog-2019-0040

Fox, G. (1993). A comparison of 'policespeak' and 'normalspeak': A preliminary study. In G. Fox, M. Hoey and J. M. Sinclair. (eds.), *Techniques of Description: Spoken and Written Discourse. A festschrift for Malcolm Coulthard*. London: Routledge, pp. 183–195.

Galasinski, D. (2017) *Discourses of Men's Suicide Notes: A Qualitative Analysis*. London: Bloomsbury.

Gales, T. (2010) *Threat Level High: A Corpus-driven Approach to Authorial Intent in Threatening Communications*. Unpublished PhD dissertation. University of California, Davis.

Gales, T. (2011). Identifying interpersonal stance in threatening discourse: An appraisal analysis. *Discourse Studies* 13(1): 27–46. https://doi.org/10.1177/1461445610387735

Gales, T. (2015a) The stance of stalking: A corpus- based analysis of grammatical markers of stance in threatening communications. *Corpora* 10(2): 171–200. https://doi.org/10.3366/cor.2015.0073

Gales, T. (2015b). Threatening stances: A corpus analysis of realized vs. non-realized threats. *Language and Law/Linguagem e Direito* 2(2): 1–25.

Gales, T. and Solan, L. (2020) Revisiting a classic problem in statutory interpretation: Is a minister a laborer? *Georgia State University Law Review* 36: 491–534.

Giampieri, P. (2018) The web as corpus and online corpora for legal translations. *Comparative Legilinguistics* 33: 35–56. https://doi.org/10.14746/cl.2018.33.2

Giampieri, P. and Milani, G. (2021) Legal corpora: A trial lesson with translators and lawyers. *International Journal of Language Studies* 15(1): 47–66.

Gibbons, J. (2003) *Forensic Linguistics: An Introduction to Language in the Justice System*. Oxford: Blackwell.

Gillings, M. (2022) How to use corpus linguistics in forensic linguistics. In A. O'Keeffe and M. McCarthy (eds.), *The Routledge Handbook of Corpus Linguistics* (2nd ed.). London: Routledge, pp. 589–601.

Gillings, M. (2024) *Corpus Linguistic Approaches to Deception Detection*. London: Routledge.

Goldfarb, N. (2017) A lawyers' introduction to meaning the framework of corpus linguistics. *Brigham Young University Law Review* 2017(6): 1359–1417.

Goldfarb, N., Zaid, M. S., Amey, S., Chance, S. and Hitchcock, C. (2010) *Brief for the Project on Government Oversight: The Brechner Center for Freedom of Information, and Tax Analysts as Amici Curiae in Support of Petitioners*. Available from: https://www.fcc.gov/document/fcc-usa-v-att-inc-et-al-no-09-1279-supreme-court-10 [Accessed September 2022].

Gong, M., Cheng, W. and Cheng, L. (2020) Development of deontic modality in Chinese civil laws. A corpus study. *Pragmatics and Society* 11(3): 337–362. https://doi.org/10.1075/ps.16058.gon

Goźdź-Roszkowski, S. (2018c) Values and valuations in judicial discourse. A corpus-assisted study of (dis)respect in US Supreme Court decisions on same-sex marriage. *Studies in Logic, Grammar and Rhetoric* 53(1): 61–79. https://doi.org/10.2478/slgr-2018-0004

Goźdź-Roszkowski, S. (2013) Exploring near-synonymous terms in legal language. A corpus-based, phraseological perspective. *Linguistica Antverpiensia. New Series: Themes in Translation Studies* 12: 94–109. https://doi.org/10.52034/lanstts.v12i.236

Goźdź-Roszkowski, S. (2016) "Justice with an attitude?" – towards a corpus-based description of evaluative phraseology in judicial discourse. In P. Pęzik and J. Waliński (eds.), *Language, Corpora and Cognition*. Frankfurt am Main: Peter Lang, pp. 107–127.

Goźdź-Roszkowski, S. (2017) Signalling sites of contention in judicial discourse. An exploratory corpus-based analysis of selected stance nouns in US Supreme Court opinions and Poland's Constitutional Tribunal judgments. *Comparative Legilinguistics: International Journal for Legal Communication* 32: 91–115. https://doi.org/10.14746/cl.2017.32.4

Goźdź-Roszkowski, S. (2018a). Between corpus-based and corpus-driven approaches to textual recurrence: Exploring semantic sequences in judicial discourse. In

J. Kopaczyk and J. Tyrkko (eds.), *Applications of Pattern-driven Methods in Corpus Linguistics*. Amsterdam/Philadelphia: John Benjamins, pp. 131–158.

Goźdź-Roszkowski, S. (2018b). Facts in law: A comparative study of 'fact that' and its phraseologies in American and Polish judicial discourse. In S. Goźdź-Roszkowski and G. Pontrandolfo (eds.), *Phraseology in Legal and Institutional Settings. A Corpus-Based Interdisciplinary Perspective*. London: Routledge, pp. 143–159.

Goźdź-Roszkowski, S. (2019a) "It is not just a fact that the law requires this, but it is a reasonable fact": Using the Noun that-pattern to explore stance construction in legal writing. In T. Fanego and P. Rodriguez-Puente (eds), *Corpus-based Research on Variation in English Legal Discourse*. Amsterdam/Philadelphia: John Benjamins, pp. 123–146.

Goźdź-Roszkowski, S. (2019b) Marriage, liberty and constitution: A corpus-assisted study of value-laden words in legal argumentation. *Research in Language* 17(1): 71–91. https://doi.org/10.2478/rela-2019-0006

Goźdź-Roszkowski, S. (2020) Communicating dissent in judicial opinions: A comparative, genre-based analysis. *International Journal for the Semiotics of Law* 33: 381–401. https://doi.org/10.1007/s11196-020-09711-y

Goźdź-Roszkowski, S. (2021) Corpus linguistics in legal discourse. *International Journal for the Semiotics of Law* 34: 1515–1540. https://doi.org/10.1007/s11196-021-09860-8

Goźdź-Roszkowski, S. (2024) *Language and Legal Judgments: Evaluation and Argument in Judicial Discourse*. London: Routledge.

Goźdź-Roszkowski, S. and Pontrandolfo, G. (2013) Evaluative patterns in judicial discourse: A corpus-based phraseological perspective on American and Italian criminal judgments. *International Journal of Law, Language and Discourse* 3(2): 3–69.

Goźdź-Roszkowski, S. and Pontrandolfo, G. (2015) Legal phraseology today: Corpus-based applications across legal language and genres. *Fachsprache* 37(3–4): 130–139. https://doi.org/10.24989/fs.v37i3-4.1287

Goźdź-Roszkowski, S. and Pontrandolfo, G. (2018). *Phraseology in Legal and Institutional Settings: A Corpus-based Interdisciplinary Perspective*. London: Routledge.

Grant, T. (2008) Approaching questions in forensic authorship analysis. In J. Gibbons and M. T. Turell (eds.), *Dimensions of Forensic Linguistics*. Amsterdam/Philadelphia: John Benjamins, pp. 215–229.

Grant, T. (2013). TXT 4N6: Method, consistency, and distinctiveness in the analysis of SMS text messages. *Journal of Law and Policy* 21: 467–494.

Grant, T. (2017). Duppying yoots in a dog eat dog world, kmt: Determining the senses of slang terms for the courts. *Semiotica* 216: 87–106. https://doi.org/10.1515/sem-2015-0082

Grant, T. (2022) *The Idea of Progress in Forensic Authorship Analysis*. Cambridge, UK: Cambridge University Press.

Grant, T. and Grieve, J. (2022) The Starbuck Case: Methods for addressing confirmation bias in forensic authorship analysis. In I. Picornell, R. Perkins and M. Coulthard (eds.), *Methodologies and Challenges in Forensic Linguistic Casework*. Chichester: Wiley-Blackwell, pp. 13–28.

Gries, S. T. (2021) Corpus approaches to ordinary meaning in legal interpretation. In M. Coulthard, A. May and R. Sousa-Silva (eds.), *The Routledge Handbook of Forensic Linguistics* (2nd ed.). London: Routledge, pp. 628–643.

Gries, S. T. and Slocum, B. G. (2017) Ordinary meaning and corpus linguistics. *Brigham Young University Law Review* 2017(6): 1417–1472.

Gries, S. T., Slocum, B. G. and Tobia, K. (2024) Corpus-linguistic approaches to lexical statutory meaning: Extensionalist vs. intensionalist approaches. *Applied Corpus Linguistics* 4(1): 1–14. https://doi.org/10.1016/j.acorp.2023.100079

Grieve, J. (2023) Register variation explains stylometric authorship analysis. *Corpus Linguistics and Linguistic Theory* 19(1): 47–77. https://doi.org/10.1515/cllt-2022-0040

Grieve, J. and Woodfield, H. (2021). Investigative linguistics. In M. Coulthard, A. May and R. Sousa-Silva (eds.), *The Routledge Handbook of Forensic Linguistics* (2nd ed.). London: Routledge, pp. 660–674.

Grieve, J. and Woodfield, H. (2023) *The Language of Fake News*. Cambridge, UK: Cambridge University Press

Grieve, J., Chiang, E., Clarke, I., Gideon, H., Heini, A., Nini, A. and Waibel, E. (2019) Attributing the Bixby letter using n-gram tracing. *Digital Scholarship in the Humanities* 34(3): 493–512. https://doi.org/10.1093/llc/fqy042

Groom, N. and Grieve, J. (2019) The evolution of a legal genre: Rhetorical move in British patent specifications, 1711 to 1860. In T. Fanego and P. Rodriguez-Puente (eds.), *Corpus-based Research on Variation in Legal Discourse*. Amsterdam/Philadelphia: John Benjamins, 201–234.

Grundlingh, L. (2018) Exploring the possibility of using appraisal theory to determine the legitimacy of suicide notes. *Lingua* 218: 1–10. https://doi.org/10.1016/j.lingua.2018.07.004

Hardaker, C. (2010) Trolling in asynchronous computer-mediated communication: From user discussions to theoretical concepts. *Journal of Politeness Research* 6(2): 57–86. https://doi.org/10.1515/jplr.2010.011

Hardaker, C. (2013) "Uh.....not to be nitpicky,,,,,but…the past tense of drag is dragged, not drug.": An overview of trolling strategies. *Journal of Language Aggression and Conflict* 1(1): 58–86. https://doi.org/10.1075/jlac.1.1.04har

Hardaker, C. (2015) "I refuse to respond to this obvious troll": An overview of responses to (perceived) trolling. *Corpora* 10(2): 201–229. https://doi.org/10.3366/cor.2015.0074

Hardaker, C. (2021) Pranksters, provocateurs, propagandists: Using forensic corpus linguistics to identify and understand trolling. In M. Coulthard, A. May and R. Sousa-Silva (eds.), *The Routledge Handbook of Forensic Linguistics* (2nd ed.). London: Routledge, pp. 694–708.

Hardaker, C. and McGlashan, M. (2016) "Real men don't hate women": Twitter rape threats and group identity. *Journal of Pragmatics* 91: 80–93. https://doi.org/10.1016/j.pragma.2015.11.005

Harris, S. (1984) Questions as a mode of control in magistrates' courts. *International Journal of the Sociology of Language* 49: 5–27. https://doi.org/10.1515/ijsl.1984.49.5

Heffer, C. (2005) *The Language of Jury Trial: A Corpus-Aided Analysis of Legal-Lay Discourse*. Basingstoke: Palgrave Macmillan.

Hessick, C. B. (2017) Corpus linguistics and the criminal law. *Brigham Young University Law Review* 2017(6): 1503–1530.

Heydon, G. (2019) *Researching Forensic Linguistics: Approaches and Applications*. London: Routledge.

Hitchcock, T., Shoemaker, R., Emsley, C., Howard, S. and McLaughlin, J. et al. (2023) *The Old Bailey Proceedings Online, 1674-1913* (www.oldbaileyonline.org, version 9.0, Autumn 2023).

Hlioui, A. (2020) Generic instability in a frozen legal genre? *International Journal of Legal Discourse* 5(1): 57–82. https://doi.org/10.1515/ijld-2020-2028

Huber, M., Nissel, M. and Puga, K. (2016) *The Old Bailey Corpus 2.0*, 1720–1913. https://hdl.handle.net/11858/00-246C-0000-0023-8CFB-2

Hunston, S. (2002) *Corpora in Applied Linguistics* (1st ed.). Cambridge, UK: Cambridge University Press.

Hurt, M. and Grant, T. (2018) Pledging to harm: A linguistic appraisal analysis of judgment comparing realized and non-realized violent fantasies. *Discourse & Society* 30(2): 154–171. https://doi.org/10.1177/0957926518816195

Hutton, C. (2014) *Word Meaning and Legal Interpretation: An Introductory Guide*. Basingstoke: Palgrave MacMillan.

Hutton, C. (2021) Legal interpretation. The category of ordinary meaning and its role in legal interpretation. In M. Coulthard, A. May and R. Sousa-Silva (eds.), *The Routledge Handbook of Forensic Linguistics* (2nd ed.). London: Routledge, pp. 79–92.

Jaafar, E. A. and Jasim, H. A. (2022) A corpus-based stylistic analysis of online suicide notes retrieved from Reddit. *Cogent Arts & Humanities* 9(1): 2047434. https://doi.org/10.1080/23311983.2022.2047434

Jackson, J., Doak, J., Saunders, C., Wright, D. and Cooper, D. (2024) *Mapping the Changing Face of Cross-Examination in Criminal Trials*. Publicly available report for the Nuffield Foundation. https://doi.org/10.17631/rd-2024-0001-drep

Johnson, A. (1997) Textual kidnapping – a case of plagiarism among three student texts. *International Journal of Speech Language and the Law* 4(2): 210–225. https://doi.org/10.1558/ijsll.v4i2.210

Johnson, A. (2014) 'Dr Shipman told you that…' The organising and synthesising power of quotation in judicial summing-up. *Language & Communication* 36: 53–67. https://doi.org/10.1016/j.langcom.2013.12.005

Johnson, A. (2015) Haunting evidence: Quoting the prisoner in 19th century Old Bailey trial discourse. The defences of Cooper (1842) and McNaughten (1843). In J. Arendholz, W. Bublitz and M. Kirner-Ludwig (eds.), *The Pragmatics of Quoting Now and Then*. Berlin: De Gruyter, pp. 369–400.

Johnson, A. (2018). "How came you not to cry out?" Pragmatic effects of negative questioning in child rape trials in the Old Bailey proceedings 1730–1798. In D. Kurzon and B. Kryk-Kastovsky (eds.), *Legal Pragmatics*. Amsterdam/Philadelphia: Benjamins, pp. 41–64.

Johnson, A. and Clifford, R. (2011) Polite incivility in defensive attack: Strategic politeness and impoliteness in cross-examination in the David Irving vs. Penguin Books Ltd and Deborah Lipstadt trial. *Journal of Politeness Research* 7: 43–71. https://doi.org/10.1515/jplr.2011.003

Johnson, A. and Coulthard, M. (2010) Introduction: Current debates in Forensic Linguistics. In M. Coulthard and A. Johnson (eds.), *The Routledge Handbook of Forensic Linguistics*. London: Routledge, pp. 1–15.

Johnson, A. and Wright, D. (2014) Identifying idiolect in forensic authorship attribution: An n-gram textbite approach. *Language and Law/Linguagem e Direito* 1(1): 37–69.

Khafaga, A. (2023) Strategic lexicalization in courtroom discourse: A corpus-assisted critical discourse analysis. *Cogent Arts & Humanities* 10(1): 2217585 https://doi.org/10.1080/23311983.2023.2217585

Kilgariff, A. (2015). Corpus linguistics in trademark cases. *Dictionaries: Journal of the Dictionary Society of North America* 36(1): 100–114. https://doi.org/10.1353/dic.2015.0015

Kopaczyk, J. (2013) *The Legal Language of Scottish Burghs: Standardization and Lexical Bundles (1380-1560)*. Oxford: Oxford University Press.

Kredens, K. (2002) Towards a corpus-based methodology of forensic authorship attribution: A comparative study of two idiolects. In B. Lewandowska-Tomaszczyk (ed.), *PALC'01: Practical Applications in Language Corpora*. Frankfurt am Mein: Peter Lang, pp. 405–446.

Kredens, K. and Coulthard, M. (2012) Corpus linguistics in authorship identification. In P. M. Tiersma and L. M. Solan (eds.), *The Oxford Handbook of Language and Law*. Oxford: Oxford University Press, pp. 504–516.

Kredens, K., Perkins, R. and Grant, T. (2019) Developing a framework for the explanation of interlingual features for native and other language influence detection. *Language and Law/Linguagem e Direito* 6(2): 10–23. https://doi.org/10.21747/21833745/lanlaw/6_2a2

Kytö, M. and Walker, T. (2006) *Guide to a Corpus of English Dialogues 1560–1760* [Studia Anglistica Upsaliensia 130]. Uppsala: Acta Universitatis Upsaliensis

Larner, S. (2014a) *Forensic Authorship Analysis and the World Wide Web*. Basingstoke: Palgrave Macmillan.

Larner, S. (2014b) A preliminary investigation into the use of fixed formulaic sequences as a marker of authorship. *International Journal of Speech, Language and the Law* 21(1): 1–22. https://doi.org/10.1558/ijsll.v21i1.1

Larner, S. (2015) From intellectual challenges to established corpus techniques: Introduction to the special issue on forensic linguistics. *Corpora* 10(2): 131–143. https://doi.org/10.3366/cor.2015.0071

Larner, S. (2016) Using a core word to identify different forms of semantically related formulaic sequences and their potential as a marker of authorship. *Corpora* 11(3): 343–369. https://doi.org/10.3366/cor.2016.0099

Larner, S. (2019a) Formulaic sequences as a potential marker of deception: A preliminary investigation. In T. Docan-Morgan (ed.), *The Palgrave Handbook of Deceptive Communication*. Cham: Palgrave Macmillan, 327–346.

Larner, S. (2019b) Formulaic word n-grams as markers of forensic authorship attribution: Identification of recurrent n-grams in adult L1 English writers' short personal narratives. In S. Goźdź-Roszkowski and G. Pontrandolfo (eds.), *Phraseology in Legal and Institutional Settings. A Corpus-Based Interdisciplinary Perspective*. London: Routledge, pp. 258–277.

Lee, T. R. and Mouritsen, S. C. (2018) Judging ordinary meaning. *Yale Law Journal* 127(4): 788–879.

Lee, T. R. and Mouritsen, S. C. (2021) The corpus and the critics. *The University of Chicago Law Review* 88(2): 275–366.

Lee, T. R., Solum, L. B., Phillips, J. C. and Egbert, J. (2023). Corpus linguistics and the original public meaning of the Sixteenth Amendment. *Duke Law Journal Online* 73: 159–189. https://doi.org/10.2139/ssrn.4560166

van Leeuwen, T. (2008) *Discourse and Practice: New Tools for Critical Discourse Analysis*. Oxford: Oxford University Press.

Leung, E. S. M. (2015) What can a bilingual corpus tell us about the translation and interpretation of rape trial? *International Journal for the Semiotics of Law* 28: 469–483. https://doi.org/10.1007/s11196-014-9400-y

Li, J., Cheng, L. and Cheng, W.. (2016) Deontic meaning making in legislative discourse. *Semiotica* 209: 323–340. https://doi.org/10.1515/sem-2016-0002

Longhi, J. (2021) Using digital humanities and linguistics to help with terrorism investigations. *Forensic Science International* 318(110564): 1–13. https://doi.org/10.1016/j.forsciint.2020.110564

Longhi, J. (2022) Linguistic approaches to the analysis of online terrorist threats. In Guillén-Nieto, V. and Stein, D. (eds.), *Language as Evidence: Doing Forensic Linguistics*. Cham: Springer, pp. 439–459.

Lorenzo-Dus, N. and Izura, C. (2017) "cause ur special": Understanding trust and complimenting behaviour in online grooming discourse. *Journal of Pragmatics* 112: 68–82. https://doi.org/10.1016/j.pragma.2017.01.004

Lorenzo-Dus, N. and Kinzel, A. (2019) 'So is your mom as cute as you?': Examining patterns of language use by online sexual groomers. *Journal of Corpora and Discourse Studies* 2(1): 14–39. https://doi.org/10.18573/jcads.31

Lorenzo-Dus, N. and Kinzel, A. (2021) 'We'll watch TV and do other stuff': A corpus-assisted discourse study of vague language use in online child sexual grooming. In M. Fuster-Márquez, J. Santaemilia, C. Gregori-Signes and P. Rodríguez-Abruñeiras (eds.), *Exploring Discourse and Ideology Through Corpora*. Bern: Peter Lang, pp. 189–210.

Lorenzo-Dus, N., Izura, C. and Pérez-Tattam, R. (2016) Understanding grooming discourse in computer-mediated environments. *Discourse, Context & Media* 12: 40–50. https://doi.org/10.1016/j.dcm.2016.02.004

Lorenzo-Dus, N., Kinzel, A. and Di Cristofaro, M. (2020) The communicative modus operandi of online child sexual groomers: Recurring patterns in their language use. *Journal of Pragmatics* 155: 15–27. https://doi.org/10.1016/j.pragma.2019.09.010

Lorenzo-Dus, N., Evans, C. and Mullineux-Morgan, R. (2023) *Online Child Grooming Discourse*. Cambridge, UK: Cambridge University Press.

Louw, B. (1993) Irony in the text or insincerity in the writer? – The diagnostic potential of semantic prosodies. In M. Baker, G. Francis and E. Tognini-Bonelli (eds.), *Text and Technology: In Honour of John Sinclair*. Amsterdam/Philadelphia: John Benjamins, pp. 157–176.

Lutzky, U. (2019) "But it is not prov'd": A sociopragmatic study of the discourse marker 'but' in the Early Modern English courtroom. *Journal of Historical Pragmatics* 20 (1): 1–19. https://doi.org/10.1075/jhp.00026.lut

MacLeod, N. (2024) 'Encouraging or assisting others to commit an offence': The anatomy of a language crime. *The International Journal for the Semiotics of Law* 37(2): 677–694. https://doi.org/10.1007/s11196-023-10031-0

Malmasi, S. and Dras, M. (2015) Multilingual native language identification. *Natural Language Engineering* 23(2): 163–215. https://doi.org/10.1017/S1351324915000406

Marcińczuk, M., Zaśko-Zielińska, M. and Piasecki, M. (2011) Structure annotation in the Polish corpus of suicide notes. In I. Habernal and V. Matoušek (eds.), *Text, Speech and Dialogue*. Cham: Springer, pp. 419–426.

Marín Pérez, M. J. (2019) Exploring the unexpected in legal discourse: A corpus-based contrastive analysis of Spanish and British judgments on immigration. *ESP Today* 7(2): 148–164. https://doi.org/10.18485/esptoday.2019.7.2.2

Marín Pérez, M. J. (2022) A corpus-based comparative analysis of the evaluative lexicon found in judicial decisions on immigration. In S. Goźdź-Roszkowski, and G. Pontrandolfo (eds.), *Law, Language and the Courtroom. Legal Linguistics and the Discourse of Judges*. London: Routledge, pp. 126–143.

Marko, K. (2020) Exploring the distinctiveness of emoji use for digital authorship analysis. *Language and Law/Linguagem e Direito* 7(1–2): 36–55. https://doi.org/10.21747/21833745/lanlaw/7_1_2a9

Marko, K., Reitbauer, M. and Pickl, G. (2022) Same person, different platform: Challenges and implications for forensic authorship analysis. An exploratory study of Instagram and Twitter users. *Register Studies* 4(2): 202–231. https://doi.org/10.1075/rs.22006.mar

Martin, J. R. and Rose, D. (2003) *Working with Discourse: Meaning Beyond the Clause*. London: Continuum.

Martin J. R. and White P. R. (2005) *The Language of Evaluation*. Basingstoke: Palgrave Macmillan.

Matoesian, G. M. (1993) *Reproducing Rape: Domination through Talk in the Courtroom*. Cambridge, UK: Cambridge University Press.

Mattioli, V. and McAuliffe, K. (2021) A corpus-based study on opinions of advocates general of the court of justice of the European Union: Changes in language and style. *International Journal of Legal Discourse* 6(1): 87–111. https://doi.org/10.1515/ijld-2021-2047

Mazzi, D. (2010) "This argument fails for two reasons...": A linguistic analysis of judicial evaluation strategies in US Supreme Court judgments. *International Journal for the Semiotics of Law* 23: 373–385. https://doi.org/10.1007/s11196-010-9162-0

Mazzi, D. (2011) "In other words, ...": A corpus-based study of reformulation in judicial discourse. *Hermes – Journal of Language and Communication Studies* 46: 11–24. https://doi.org/10.7146/hjlcb.v24i46.97361

Mazzi, D. (2014) Phraseology, argumentation and identity in the Supreme Court of Ireland's judgments on language policy. *Journal of Applied Linguistics and Professional Practice* 11(3): 315–337. https://doi.org/10.1558/japl.32729

Mazzi, D. (2018) "By partially renouncing their sovereignty ..." On the discourse function(s) of lexical bundles in EU- related Irish judicial discourse. In S. Goźdź-Roszkowski and G. Pontrandolfo (eds.), *Phraseology in Legal and Institutional Settings: A Corpus-based Interdisciplinary Perspective*. London: Routledge, pp. 189–202.

Mazzi, D. (2022) "Without proof of negligence or a causative connection". On causal argumentation in the discourse of the Supreme Court of Ireland's judgments on data protection. In S. Goźdź-Roszkowski, and G. Pontrandolfo (eds.), *Law, Language and the Courtroom. Legal Linguistics and the Discourse of Judges*. London: Routledge, pp. 26–38.

McKeown, J. (2021) A corpus-based examination of reflexive metadiscourse in majority and dissent opinions of the U.S. Supreme Court. *Journal of Pragmatics* 186: 224–235. https://doi.org/10.1016/j.pragma.2021.10.019

McMenamin, G. R. (2002) *Forensic Linguistics: Advances in Forensic Stylistics*. Boca Raton, Florida: CRC Press.

McMenamin, G. R. 2004. Disputed authorship in US law. *International Journal of Speech, Language and the Law* 11(1), 74–82. https://doi.org/10.1558/sll.2004.11.1.73

McMenamin, G. R. (2021) Forensic stylistics. The theory and practice of forensic stylistics. In M. Coulthard, A. May and R. Sousa-Silva (eds.), *The Routledge Handbook of Forensic Linguistics* (2nd ed.). London: Routledge, pp. 539–557.

McQuaid, S. M., Woodworth, M., Hutton, E. L., Porter, S. and ten Brinke, L. (2014) Automated insights: Verbal cues to deception in real-life high-stakes lies. *Psychology, Crime and Law* 21(7): 617–631. https://doi.org/10.1080/1068316X.2015.1008477

Mellinkoff, D. (1963) *The Language of the Law*. Boston, MA: Little, Brown and Company.

Mojedano Batel, A., Soler Bonafont, A. and Kredens, K. (2023) Epistemic modality constructions as stable idiolectal features: A cross-genre study of Spanish.

International Journal for the Semiotics of Law, 1–27. https://doi.org/10.1007/s11196-023-10056-5

Monzó Nebot, E. (2008) Corpus-based activities in legal translator training. *The Interpreter and Translator Trainer* 2(2): 221–252. https://doi.org/10.1080/1750399X.2008.10798775

Moura, R., Sousa-Silva, R. and Lopes Cardoso, H. (2021) Automated fake news detection using computational forensic linguistics. In G. Marreiros, F. S. Melo, N. Lau, H. Lopes Cardoso and L. P. Reis (eds.), *Progress in Artificial Intelligence: 20th EPIA Conference on Artificial Intelligence, EPIA 2021 Virtual Event, September 7–9, 2021 Proceedings*. Cham: Springer, pp. 788–800.

Mouritsen, S. C. (2010) The dictionary is not a fortress: Definitional fallacies and a corpus-based approach to plain meaning. *Brigham Young University Law Review* 2010(5): 1915–1978.

Mouritsen, S. C. (2011) Hard cases and hard data: Assessing corpus linguistics as an empirical path to plain meaning. *Columbia Science and Technology Law Review* 13: 156–205.

Mouritsen, S. C. (2017) Corpus linguistics in legal interpretation – An evolving interpretative framework. *International Journal of Language and Law* 6: 67–89. https://doi.org/10.14762/jll.2017.067

Mustafa, M. (2022) Analysing stance in the Christchurch and El Paso manifestos. In Ralarala, M. K., Kaschula, R. H. and Heydon, G. (eds.), *Language and the Law: Global Perspectives in Forensic Linguistics from Africa and Beyond*. Stellenbosch: African Sun Media, pp. 339–358.

Nini, A. (2015). Authorship profiling in a forensic context (Unpublished doctoral dissertation). Aston University, UK. Available from: https://publications.aston.ac.uk/id/eprint/25337/1/Nini_Andrea_2015.pdf

Nini, A. (2017). Register variation in malicious forensic texts. *International Journal of Speech, Language and the Law* 24(1): 99–126. https://doi.org/10.1558/ijsll.30173

Nini, A. (2018a) An authorship analysis of the Jack the Ripper letters. *Digital Scholarship in the Humanities* 33(3): 621–636. https://doi.org/10.1093/llc/fqx065

Nini, A. (2018b) Developing forensic authorship profiling. *Language and Law/Linguagem e Direito* 5(2), 38–58.

Nini, A. (2021). Corpus analysis in forensic linguistics. In Chapelle, C. A. (ed), *The Concise Encyclopedia of Applied Linguistics*. London: Wiley-Blackwell. https://doi.org/10.1002/9781405198431.wbeal0238.pub2

Nini, A. (2023). *A Theory of Linguistic Individuality for Authorship Identification*. Cambridge, UK: Cambridge University Press.

Nini, A. and Grant, T. (2013) Bridging the gap between stylistic and cognitive approaches to authorship analysis using Systemic Functional Linguistics and multidimensional analysis. *International Journal of Speech, Language and the Law* 20(2): 173–202. https://doi.org/10.1558/ijsll.v20i2.173

Olsson, J, (2009) Some aspects of the use of corpora in forensic linguistics. In K. Hyland, M. H. Chau and M. Handford (eds.), *Corpus Applications in Applied Linguistics*. London: Bloomsbury, pp. 84–99.

Pei, J. and Cheng, L. (2020) Mapping terminological variation and ideology in data protection laws. *Terminology* 26(2): 159–183. https://doi.org/10.1075/term.00049.pei

Perkins, R. (2022) Other language influence detection: Profiling the native language of a dark web pedophile. In I. Picornell, R. Perkins and M. Coulthard (eds.), *Methodologies and Challenges in Forensic Linguistic Casework*. Chichester: Wiley-Blackwell, pp. 63–76.

Perkins, R. and Grant, T. (2018) Native language influence detection for forensic authorship analysis: Identifying L1 Persian bloggers. *International Journal of Speech, Language and the Law* 25(1): 1–20. https://doi.org/10.1558/ijsll.30844

Petykó, M. (2017) "You're trolling because…" – a corpus-based study of perceived trolling and motive attribution in the comment threads of three British political blogs. In E. W. Stemle and C. R. Wigham (eds.), *Proceedings of the 5th Conference on CMC and Social Media Corpora for the Humanities (cmccorpora17)*, pp. 56–60.

Põldvere, N., Kibisova, E. and Alvestad, S. S. (2023) Investigating the language of fake news across cultures. In S. Maci, M. Demata, P. Seargent and M. McGlashan (eds.), *The Routledge Handbook of Discourse and Disinformation* (pp. 153–165). London: Routledge.

Pontrandolfo, G. (2018) Sensibly and appropriately the judge considered… A corpus-based study of sentence adverbs in judicial language. *Linguistik Online* 92(5). https://doi.org/10.13092/lo.92.451

Pontrandolfo, G. (2019) Corpus methods in legal translation studies. In Ł. Biel, J. Engberg, R. Martín Ruano and V. Sosoni (eds.), *Research Methods in Legal Translation and Interpreting: Crossing Methodological Boundaries*. London: Routledge, pp. 13–28.

Pontrandolfo, G. (2021) National and EU judicial phraseology under the magnifying glass: A corpus-assisted analysis of complex prepositions in Spanish. *Perspectives: Studies in Translation Theory and Practice* 29(2): 260–277. https://doi.org/10.1080/0907676X.2020.1815816

Pontrandolfo, G. and Goźdź-Roszkowski, S. (2014) Exploring the local grammar of evaluation: The case of adjectival patterns in American and Italian judicial discourse. *Research in Language* 12(1): 71–91. https://doi.org/10.2478/rela-2014-0014

Poole, R. (2021). A corpus-aided study of stance adverbs in judicial opinions and the implications for English for legal purposes instruction. *English for Specific Purposes* 62: 117–127. https://doi.org/10.1016/j.esp.2021.01.002

Potts, A. and Weare, S. (2018) Mother, Monster, Mrs, I: A critical evaluation of gendered naming strategies in English sentencing remarks of women who kill. *International Journal for the Semiotics of Law* 31: 21–52. https://doi.org/10.1007/s11196-017-9523-z

Queralt, S. (2018) The creation of Base Rate Knowledge of linguistic variables and the implementation of likelihood ratios to authorship attribution in forensic text comparison. *Language and Law/Linguagem e Direito* 5(2): 59–76.

Queralt, S. (2022) Linguistic profiling: A Spanish case study. In I. Picornell, R. Perkins and M. Coulthard (eds.), *Methodologies and Challenges in Forensic Linguistic Casework*. Chichester: Wiley-Blackwell, pp. 44–62.

Rayson, P. (2009) Wmatrix: A web-based corpus processing environment, Computing Department, Lancaster University. https://ucrel.lancs.ac.uk/wmatrix/

Reppen, R. and Chen, M. (2019) A comparison of lexical bundles in spoken courtroom language across time, registers, and varieties. In T. Fanego and P. Rodriguez-Puente (eds), *Corpus-based Research on Variation in English Legal Discourse*. Amsterdam/Philadelphia: John Benjamins, pp. 105–122.

Rodríguez-Puente, P. (2020) Historical legal discourse: British law reports. In E. Friginal and J. A. Hardy (eds.), *The Routledge Handbook of Corpus Approaches to Discourse Analysis*. London: Routledge, pp. 499–517.

Römer-Barron, U. and Cunningham, C. D. (2024) Applied corpus linguistics and legal interpretation: A rapidly developing field of interdisciplinary scholarship. *Applied Corpus Linguistics* 4(1): 1–7. https://doi.org/10.1016/j.acorp.2023.100080

Ronan, P. (2020) Question strategies in the Old Bailey Corpus. In E. Jonsson and T. Larsson (eds.), *Voices Past and Present - Studies of Involved, Speech-related and Spoken Texts: In Honor of Merja Kytö*. Amsterdam/Philadelphia: John Benjamins, pp. 153–172.

Samraj, B. and Gawron, J. M. (2015) The suicide note as a genre: Implications for genre theory. *Journal of English for Academic Purposes* 19: 88–101. https://doi.org/10.7575/aiac.ijalel.v.9n.3p.1

Scalia, A. and Garner, B. (2012) *Reading Law: The Interpretation of Legal Texts*. St Paul, MN: Thompson/West.

Schmid, H.-J. (2016) A framework for understanding linguistic entrenchment and its psychological foundations. In H-J. Schmid (ed.), *Entrenchment and the Psychology of Language Learning: How We Reorganize and Adapt Linguistic Knowledge*. Berlin: De Gruyter Mouton, pp. 9–36.

Schneevogt, D. Chiang, E. and Grant, T. (2018) Do perverted justice chat logs contain examples of overt persuasion and sexual extortion? A research note responding to Chiang and Grant 2017 and 2018. *Language and Law/Linguagem e Direito* 5(1): 97–102.

Scott, M. (1999) *WordSmith Tools version 3*, Oxford: Oxford University Press.

Shapero, J. (2011) The Language of Suicide Notes. Unpublished PhD dissertation. The University of Birmingham. (Online) Available from: https://etheses.bham.ac.uk/1525/

Shneidman, E. S. and Farberow, N. L. (1957). Genuine and simulated suicide notes. In E. S. Shneidman and N. L. Farberow (eds.), *Clues to Suicide*. New York: McGraw-Hill, pp. 197–215.

Shuy, R. (2012) Using linguistics in trademark cases. In P. M. Tiersma and L. M. Solan (eds.), *The Oxford Handbook of Language and Law*. Oxford: Oxford University Press, pp. 449–462.

Solan, L. (2010) *The Language of Statutes: Laws and their Interpretation*. Chicago: University of Chicago Press.

Solan, L. and Gales, T. (2017) Corpus linguistics as a tool in legal interpretation. *Brigham Young University Law Review* 2017(6): 1311–1358.

Solan, L. M. (1993) *The Language of Judges*. Chicago: University of Chicago Press.

Solan, L. M. (2013) Intuition versus algorithm: The case for forensic authorship attribution. *Journal of Law and Policy* 21(2): 551–576.

Solan, L. M. and Gales, T. (2016) Finding ordinary meaning in law: The judge, the dictionary or the corpus? *International Journal of Legal Discourse* 1(2): 253–276. https://doi.org/10.1515/ijld-2016-0016

Sosoni, V. (2018) Language and translation in EU Competition Law: Insights from English, Greek, Italian and Spanish versions of legislative texts. In S. Marino, Ł. Biel, M. Bajčić and V. Sosoni (eds.), *Language and Law: The Role of Language and Translation in EU Competition Law*. Cham: Springer, pp. 179–205.

Sousa-Silva, R. (2018) Computational forensic linguistics: An overview. *Language and Law/Linguagem e Direito* 5(2): 118–143.

Sousa-Silva, R. (2022) Fighting the fake: A forensic linguistic analysis to fake news detection. *International Journal for the Semiotics of Law* 35: 2409–2433. https://doi.org/10.1007/s11196-022-09901-w

Stubbs, M. (1996) *Text and Corpus Analysis: Computer-Assisted Studies of Language and Culture*. Oxford: Blackwell.

Sun, Y. and Cheng, L. (2017) Linguistic variation and legal representation in legislative discourse: A corpus-based multi-dimensional study. *International Journal of Legal Discourse* 2(2): 397–421. https://doi.org/10.1515/ijld-2017-0017

Svartvik, J. (1968) *The Evans Statements: A case for Forensic Linguistics*. Göteborg: University of Gothenburg Press.

Svongoro, P. and Kufakunesu, P. (2019) Interpreters' renditions in Zimbabwean courtrooms: A corpus-based analysis from frequency profiles to key semantic domains. In M. K. Ralarala, R. H. Kaschula and G. Heydon (eds.), *New Frontiers in Forensic Linguistics: Themes and Perspectives in Language and Law in Africa and Beyond*. Stellenbosch: African Sun Media, pp. 211–237.

Swales, J. (1981) *Aspects of Article Introductions*. Ann Arbor, MI: University of Michigan Press.

Szczyrbak, M. (2014) *Of course*, *indeed* or *clearly*? The interactional potential of modal adverbs in legal genres. *SKASE Journal of Theoretical Linguistics* 11(2): 90–102.

Szczyrbak, M. (2016) Say and stancetaking in courtroom talk: A corpus-assisted study. *Corpora* 11(2): 143–168. https://doi.org/10.3366/cor.2016.0090

Szczyrbak, M. (2017) Modal adverbs of certainty in the rhetoric of Advocates General: A dialogic view. *Topics in Linguistics* 18(1): 48–58. https://doi.org/10.1515/topling 2017 0001

Szczyrbak, M. (2018a). Verba dicendi in courtroom interaction: Patterns with the progressive. In S. Goźdź-Roszkowski and G. Pontrandolfo (eds.), *Phraseology in Legal and Institutional Settings: A Corpus-based Interdisciplinary Perspective*. London: Routledge, pp. 240–257.

Szczyrbak, M. (2018b) Diminutivity and evaluation in courtroom interaction: Patterns with *little*. *Studia Linguistica Universitatis Iagellonicae Cracoviensis* 135: 59–68. https://doi.org/10.4467/20834624SL.18.005.8165

Szczyrbak, M. (2019a) But, you see, the problem is: Perception verbs in courtroom talk: Focus on 'you see'. *Topics in Linguistics* 20(1): 24–40. https://doi.org/10.2478/topling-2019-0002

Szczyrbak, M. (2019b) Epistemic stance in the Kavanaugh confirmation hearing: Focus on mental and communication verbs. *Discourse and Interaction* 12(2): 72–94. https://doi.org/10.5817/DI2019-2-72

Szczyrbak, M. (2020) Verb patterns in trial discourse: The case of 'I think'. *Discourse and Interaction* 13(2): 119–135. https://doi.org/10.5817/DI2020-2-119

Szczyrbak, M. (2021) I'm thinking and you're saying: Speaker stance and the progressive of mental verbs in courtroom interaction. *Text & Talk* 41(2): 239–260. https://doi.org/10.1515/text-2019-0145

Szczyrbak, M. (2022) Evidentiality in US Supreme Court opinions: Focus on passive structures with say and tell. In S. Goźdź-Roszkowski, and G. Pontrandolfo (eds.), *Law, Language and the Courtroom. Legal Linguistics and the Discourse of Judges*. London: Routledge, pp, 26–38.

Tagg, C. (2009). *A Corpus Linguistic Study of SMS Text Messaging*. Unpublished PhD dissertation. The University of Birmingham. (Online) Available from: https://etheses.bham.ac.uk/253/

Tiersma, P. (1999) *Legal Language*. Chicago: University of Chicago Press.

Tiersma, P. (2010) Redrafting California's jury instructions. In M. Coulthard and A. Johnson (eds.), *The Routledge Handbook of Forensic Linguistics* (1st ed.). London: Routledge, pp. 251–264.

Tiersma, P. and Curtis, M. (2008) Testing the comprehensibility of jury instructions: California's old and new instructions on circumstantial evidence. *Journal of Court Innovation* 1: 231–264.
Tkačuková, T. (2015) A corpus-assisted study of the discourse marker well as an indicator of judges' institutional roles in court cases with litigants in person. *Corpora* 10(2): 145–170. https://doi.org/10.3366/cor.2015.0072
Tobia, K. Egbert, J. and Lee, T. R. (2023). Triangulating ordinary meaning. *Georgetown Law Journal Online* 112: 23–54.
Trklja, A. (2018) A corpus investigation of formulaicity and hybridity in legal language: A case of EU case law texts. In S. Goźdź-Roszkowski and G. Pontrandolfo (eds.), *Phraseology in Legal and Institutional Settings: A Corpus-based Interdisciplinary Perspective*. London: Routledge, pp. 89–108.
Trklja, A. and McAuliffe, K. (2019) Formulaic metadiscursive signalling devices in judgments of the Court of Justice of the European Union: A new corpus-based model for studying discourse relations of texts. *International Journal of Speech, Language and the Law* 26(1): 21–55. https://doi.org/10.1558/ijsll.36920
Turell, M. T. (2010) The use of textual, grammatical and sociolinguistic evidence in forensic text comparison. *International Journal of Speech, Language and the Law* 17(2): 211–250. https://doi.org/10.1558/ijsll.v17i2.211
Turell, M. T. and Gavaldà, N. (2013) Towards an index of idiolectal similitude (or distance) in forensic authorship analysis. *Journal of Law and Policy* 21(2): 495–514.
Vacalopoulou, A. (2020) Exploring criteria for the inclusion of trademarks in general language dictionaries of Modern Greek. *Dictionaries: Journal of the Dictionary Society of North America* 41(1): 155–177. https://doi.org/10.1353/dic.2020.0009
Vogel, F., Hamann, H. and Gauer, I. (2018) Computer-assisted legal linguistics: Corpus analysis as a new tool for legal studies. *Law & Social Inquiry* 43(4): 1340–1363. https://doi.org/10.1111/lsi.12305
Wang, S. and Yin, J. (2020) A corpus-based study of keywords in legislative Chinese and General Chinese. In J.-F. Hong, Y. Zhang and P. Liu (eds.), *Chinese Lexical Semantics. 20th Workshop, CLSW 2019*. Cham: Springer, pp. 639–653.
Winter, E. (1996) The statistics of analysing very short texts in a criminal context. In H. Kniffka (ed.), *Recent Developments in Forensic Linguistics*. Frankfurt am Main: Peter Lang, pp. 141–179.
Woodbury, H. (1984) The strategic use of questions in court. *Semiotica* 48(3/4): 197– 228. https://doi.org/10.1515/semi.1984.48.3-4.197
Wray, A. (2002) *Formulaic Language and the Lexicon*. Cambridge, UK: Cambridge University Press.
Wright, D. (2013) Stylistic variation within genre conventions in the Enron email corpus: Developing a text-sensitive methodology for authorship research. *International Journal of Speech, Language and the Law* 20(1): 45–75. https://doi.org/10.1558/ijsll.v20i1.45
Wright, D. (2014) *Stylistics versus Statistics: A Corpus Linguistic Approach to Combining Techniques in Forensic Authorship Analysis Using Enron Emails*. (Unpublished doctoral dissertation). University of Leeds, UK. Available from: https://etheses.whiterose.ac.uk/8278/
Wright, D. (2017) Using word n-grams to identify authors and idiolects: A corpus approach to a forensic linguistic problem. *International Journal of Corpus Linguistics* 22(2): 212–241. https://doi.org/10.1075/ijcl.22.2.03wri

Wright, D. (2021) Corpus approaches to forensic linguistics. In M. Coulthard, A. May and R. Sousa-Silva (eds.), *The Routledge Handbook of Forensic Linguistics* (2nd ed.). London: Routledge, pp. 611–627.

Wright, D., Jackson, J., Doak, J., Saunders, C. and Cooper, D. (2025) Signposting topics in the cross-examination of vulnerable witnesses. In T. Grieshofer and K. Haworth (eds.), *Communication and Legal Practice: Language, Procedure, Process*. Cambridge, UK: Cambridge University Press.

Wright, D., Robson, J., Murray-Edwards, H. and Braber, N. (2022) The pragmatic functions of 'respect' in lawyers' courtroom discourse: A case study of Brexit hearings. *Journal of Pragmatics* 187: 1–12. https://doi.org/10.1016/j.pragma.2021.10.028

Ye, M. and Mckeown, J. (2023) Investigating the targeted use of (dis)agreement in leave to appeal decisions of the HKSAR appellate courts: A corpus-assisted discourse analysis. *International Journal of Legal Discourse* 8(2): 235–255. https://doi.org/10.1515/ijld-2023-2012

Yuan, C., Zhang, S. and He, Q. (2018) Popularity of Latin and law French in legal English: A corpus-based disciplinary study of the language of the law. *Linguistics and the Human Sciences* 14(1–2): 151–174. https://doi.org/10.1558/lhs.37190

Zaśko-Zielińska, M. (2022) The linguistic analysis of suicide notes. In Guillén-Nieto, V. and Stein, D. (eds.), *Language as Evidence: Doing Forensic Linguistics*. Cham: Springer, pp. 373–417.

Zozula, D. (2019) Features of the language of law: A comparative study of Polish, English and Indonesian legal texts. *International Journal of Legal Discourse* 4(1): 69–86. https://doi.org/10.1515/ijld-2019-2013

4 Positioning and responsibility in the opening statements of the Grenfell Tower Inquiry

Introduction

At around 1 a.m. on 14 June 2017, a fire broke out in the 24-storey Grenfell Tower block of flats in North Kensington, West London. The fire started in Flat 16 on the fourth floor after a fridge-freezer caught fire. Ninety minutes later, the fire had ripped through the entire block, spreading across the eastern and north face of the tower, climbing up the external cladding of the building, a combination of aluminium and plastic, that had been added as part of a refurbishment of the building the year before. Tragically, 72 people died as a result of the fire, making it the deadliest structural fire in the United Kingdom since 1988. The next day, the then Prime Minister of the United Kingdom, Theresa May, announced that there would be a Public Inquiry into the disaster, and it would be chaired by retired judge Sir Martin Moore-Bick. The Inquiry is in two parts. The first part started on 14 September 2017 with Sir Moore-Bick's opening statement, and hearings were held between June and December 2018. On 30 October 2019, Sir Moore-Bick published the Phrase 1 report, totalling 856 pages. Phase 2 commenced in January 2020 and ended in July 2022. The Phase 2 report, totalling some 1,700 pages, was published in September 2024. This chapter focuses only on the opening statements during Phase 1 of the Inquiry. Both reports are available for download from the Grenfell Tower Inquiry website (https://www.grenfelltowerinquiry.org.uk/).

Public inquiries are major investigations – convened by a government minister – that can be gifted special powers to compel testimony and the release of other forms of evidence (Institute for Government 2018). Inquiries cannot determine criminal or civil guilt, but criminal investigations and trials running alongside inquiries will often involve many of the same witnesses, and the findings of public inquiries can lead to separate legal proceedings. The Terms of Reference for Phase 1 of the Inquiry are worth presenting here in their entirety as they are relevant to the analysis in this chapter:

DOI: 10.4324/9781003017301-4

[E]xamine the circumstances surrounding the fire at Grenfell Tower on 14 June 2017, including

a the immediate cause or causes of the fire and the means by which it spread to the whole of the building;
b the design and construction of the building and the decisions relating to its modification, refurbishment and management;
c the scope and adequacy of building regulations, fire regulations and other legislation, guidance and industry practice relating to the design, construction, equipping and management of high-rise residential buildings;
d whether such regulations, legislation, guidance and industry practice were complied with in the case of Grenfell Tower and the fire safety measures adopted in relation to it;
e the arrangements made by the local authority or other responsible bodies for receiving and acting upon information either obtained from local residents or available from other sources (including information derived from fires in other buildings) relating to the risk of fire at Grenfell Tower, and the action taken in response to such information;
f the fire prevention and fire safety measures in place at Grenfell Tower on 14 June 2017;
g the response of the London Fire Brigade to the fire; and
h the response of central and local government in the days immediately following the fire

(Grenfell Tower Inquiry 2021)

This chapter takes a corpus-assisted approach to analysing the ways in which responsibility is mitigated, shifted and allocated in the opening statements that were heard during the evidential hearings in Phase 1 of the Inquiry. After providing details of the corpus, the chapter summarises relevant literature in law and linguistics that has focused on the function and language of opening statements. The analysis presented here draws on the theory of positioning (Davies and Harré 1990), which is described in relation to opening statements, before the analysis sets out the foundations of a model for analysing the discursive allocation of responsibility.

The Grenfell Tower Inquiry Opening Statement Corpus

There are two types of 'opening statement' in Phase 1 of the Grenfell Inquiry. On the one hand, there are opening statements that are written and are submitted to the Inquiry as evidence; on the other hand, there are opening statements that are presented orally by the relevant legal teams during the hearings themselves. The analysis in this chapter focuses on the latter – those that are presented as part of the hearings. In total, there were

22 such opening statements made before the Inquiry, and they were all heard between the 4th and the 7th of June 2018 during the first week of evidential hearings in Phase 1. The exception to this is the first of the 22, which is Sir Moore-Bick's opening statement that he delivered at the formal opening of the Inquiry on 14 September 2017. By far the longest opening statement given during the evidential hearings was that of the Counsel to the Inquiry on 4 June 2018. The remaining 19 were given by 'Core Participants' in the Inquiry. Core Participants have a number of important roles in the Inquiry: they receive and can review relevant evidence in advance of the Inquiry, they can suggest lines of questioning that should be pursued and, with permission, they can ask questions through their legal representatives of other witnesses (Grenfell Tower Inquiry 2019). Core Participants included survivors of the fire at Grenfell Tower, individuals who were residents of the tower at the time of the fire and the families of those who died or were injured as a result of the fire and are unable to participate. In addition, the Chairman granted Core Participant status to others, including individuals or groups who may have played a direct and significant role in relation to the Inquiry's Terms of Reference or who could be subject to explicit or significant criticism in the Inquiry's proceedings or report (Grenfell Tower Inquiry 2019). In Phase 1 of the Inquiry, 504 individuals, 18 organisations, eight public bodies and two trade unions were granted Core Participant status.

Table 4.1 shows the details of the Opening Statement Corpus, which comprises a total of 105,307 tokens across the 22 statements. Here it is worth providing more detail about the different participants, their involvement in the Inquiry and the opening statements themselves. Counsel to the Inquiry are the lawyers appointed by the Chairman to act as the legal representatives of the Inquiry itself. The Counsel to the Inquiry in fact included three senior counsel and some 42 junior counsel, and the opening statement was delivered by Lead Counsel to the Inquiry Richard Millet KC. There are four different groups of Bereaved, Survivors and Residents (often shortened to 'BSRs' in Inquiry proceedings and documents) in the opening statements: group 'G3', 'G4' and 'G10' and the group represented by Imran Khan KC and partners. Each of the groups G3, G4 and G10 has two opening statements delivered by different lawyers representing them. There are opening statements from five public bodies: (1) the Royal Borough of Kensington and Chelsea as the borough of London in which Grenfell Tower is located and the council which owns the tower itself, (2) the Kensington and Chelsea Tenant Management Organisation, (3) the Ministry of Housing, Communities and Local Government and (4) the Metropolitan Police Service and (5) London Fire Brigade as the emergency services that responded to the fire. In addition, there are opening statements on behalf of three commercial organisations.

Table 4.1 Breakdown of the Grenfell Tower Inquiry Opening Statement Corpus

Participant(s)	*Date*	*Tokens*
Sir Martin Moore-Bick, Chairman of the Inquiry	17 Sept 2017	6,880
Counsel to the Inquiry	4 June 2018	16,076
Metropolitan Police Service	5 June 2018	1,059
Bereaved, Survivors and Residents (G4) (Danny Friedman KC)	5 June 2018	4,137
Bereaved, Survivors and Residents (G4) (Stephanie Barwise KC)	5 June 2018	5,693
Bereaved, Survivors and Residents (G4) (Danny Friedman KC)	5 June 2018	2,727
Bereaved, Survivors and Residents (G3) (Sam Stein KC)	5 June 2018	7,208
Bereaved, Survivors and Residents (G3) (Pete Weatherby KC)	5 June 2018	8,739
Bereaved, Survivors and Residents (Imran Khan KC)	5 June 2018	7,583
Mr Behailu Kebede	6 June 2018	3,522
Bereaved, Survivors and Residents (G10) (Leslie Thomas KC)	6 June 2018	5,936
Bereaved, Survivors and Residents (G10) (Michael Mansfield KC)	6 June 2018	9,648
Royal Borough of Kensington and Chelsea	6 June 2018	3,943
Tenant Management Organisation	6 June 2018	2,385
Arconic Architectural Products SAS	6 June 2018	1,662
CS Stokes & Associates Limited	6 June 2018	3,143
Celotex	6 June 2018	396
Ministry of Housing, Communities & Local Government	6 June 2018	989
Mayor of London	6 June 2018	1,459
Fire Brigades Union	7 June 2018	3,901
Fire Officers Association	7 June 2018	1,486
London Fire Brigade	7 June 2018	6,735
	Total	**105,307**

First, there is Arconic Architectural Products SAS, an American industrial company specialising in engineering and manufacturing which installed and approved external cladding to Grenfell Tower. Second, there is CS Stokes & Associates Limited, the company which worked as fire risk assessors for Kensington & Chelsea Tenant Management Organisation prior to the fire. Third is Celotex, a company that manufactures polyisocyanurate insulation that was used in the Grenfell tower cladding system. There are also opening statements from two trade unions – Fire Brigades Union and Fire Officers Association – both representing the fire services. Finally, there are opening statements heard from two individuals: Sadiq Khan, the mayor of London at the time of the Grenfell Tower Fire, and Behailu Kebede, who lived in flat 16 of the tower where the fire first broke out.

All of the opening statements are delivered by lawyers representing the participant in question, and while the mean average statement is 4,787 words, there is substantial variation in the length of the statements for the different participants. The longest statement is the opening by the Counsel to the Inquiry (16,076 words) which is unsurprising given their job of outlining the undisputed facts of the case, what is to be investigated, how it will be done and reiterating the Terms of Reference of the Inquiry. In terms of Core Participants (as opposed to Counsel to the Inquiry), the opening statement of BSR (G10) is the largest at 9,648 tokens, and the shortest is the 369-word statement delivered on behalf of Celotex, some 43 times shorter than that of BSR (G10). Despite the varying sizes of the opening statements, they have shared functions in the Inquiry and play an important role in positioning the Core Participants and providing a lens for the subsequent evidence.

Opening statements as a prologue to the evidence

In the forensic and legal linguistics literature, there has been a relatively small amount of work that has focused on opening statements. The work that has is almost exclusively in the context of a criminal trial and usually gives way to the allure of analysing hostile cross-examination. Nevertheless, the critical importance of the opening statement is well reported, and the work in a criminal law context can be adopted and used to inform the analysis of opening statements in a Public Inquiry context.

In an adversarial criminal trial, characterized by the presence of both a prosecution and defence, the chronology of opening statements being presented before the evidence in a trial is integral to their narrative power. They offer the advocates representing the prosecution (e.g. in England and Wales) or the prosecution *and* defence (e.g. in the United States) the only opportunity to offer their uninterrupted and undisturbed version of events, their 'master narrative' (Heffer 2005: 75), 'macro-narrative' (Cotterill 2003) or 'core narrative' (Gibbons 2003: 157) to the jury. The adjectives 'uninterrupted' and 'undisturbed' used here reflect the uniqueness of the opening statement in the trial. During the examination of witnesses, the main business of both criminal trials and public inquiries, the witnesses being questioned most often bring only a portion of the overall story – the part in which they are implicated. In addition, witnesses are examined by both prosecution and defence, and each works to deconstruct the narrative being developed through the witness by the opposing side. The opening statements, therefore, are the 'clearest instance of the narrative mode in a trial' (Harris 2005: 220) and offer a space in which legal counsel provide a monologic 'roadmap' (Cotterill 2003: 63), over which they have complete control of the narrative and evidence they are going to put to the jury.

Gibbons (2003: 157) describes the intention of the opening statement in an adversarial trial context as being to 'expose the judge (and jury) to a summary of the master narrative' and to 'provide a skeleton for the more detailed evidence that will emerge'.

Opening statements do not have only an introductory purpose; rather, as Gibbons (2003: 157) expands, they play an important role in 'persuading the judge (and jury) to view the evidence in a particular way'. This aligns with Cotterill's (2003: 63) argument that an opening statement 'does not simply serve as an initial orientation to jurors [...] but also functions as a *conceptual* orientation to the trial participants and trial narrative' (original emphasis). This is echoed by Heffer (2021: 199), who describes opening statement narratives as constructing 'a cognitive filter through which jurors will then view subsequent evidence' and by Reinard (2012: 335), who characterizes the opening statement as serving to 'prime the pump' as jurors' assessments of witnesses and evidence tend to follow the agenda set by the opening. Pyszczynski et al. (1981: 435) propose that opening statements create 'thematic frameworks' or 'cognitive schemata' that 'influence jurors' processing and interpretation of testimony and evidence presented throughout the trial' such that 'depending on the framework developed early in the trial, jurors may respond to a given bit of evidence in a variety of ways'. A very similar description is offered by Melilli (2006: 527), who states that 'the opening statement is likely to influence the construct of a framework in the minds of jurors for receiving and interpreting the evidence to follow'. Melilli (2006: 527) describes the perceptions constructed in the minds of jurors by the opening statement as constituting a '"belief system" that colors the processing of the evidence received at trial' and which, to some degree, should be expected to 'cause jurors to perceive, or possibly misperceive, the evidence in certain ways'. The (contrastive) relationship between the narrative(s) presented in opening statements and those elicited from witnesses in evidence, and the reception of those narratives by jurors, is rather eloquently encapsulated by Melilli (2006: 528):

> Evidence is presented to jurors at trial in a disjointed and unfamiliar format, much like the commonly used metaphor of pieces of a jigsaw puzzle. Although it is not a part of the puzzle itself, the picture on the cover of the puzzle box is a welcome assistant to the puzzle solver and undoubtedly influences the behavior during the puzzle solving. So too the opening statement, while not evidence, potentially influences the behavior of the jurors by creating a picture of what the jurors should expect to see after they have received all the pieces of evidence and knitted them together in a unified fabric.

The power, strength and resilience of the conceptual orientation, thematic framework, cognitive schemata/filter or belief system created and instilled by the opening statement are demonstrated by the fact that whichever party is permitted to deliver their opening statement first is most likely to have the greater influence over the jury. This is a long-established phenomenon in legal research. Linz and Penrod (1984: 8), for example, report that the first impressions made on the jury during opening statements become the lasting impressions and so can often make the difference in the outcome of the case. Hans and Sweigart (1993: 1303) refer to this as a 'primacy effect', in which 'information that is presented first has stronger impact'. This effect was demonstrated in an experimental study by Wells et al. (1985), who compared the influence of the timing of the defence opening statement. They found that when the defence opening statement preceded that of the prosecution, mock jurors perceived eyewitness testimony more favourably for the defence than if the prosecution delivered their opening first. This is also noted by Shirkey (2011: 598), who emphasises that the primacy effect of initial opening statements is so strong that 'jurors have been proven to overlook the lack of any evidence later at trial to support opening statements' claims'. Overall, opening statements and their persuasive power can be important determinants of final verdicts (Pyszczynski and Wrightsman 1981: 309), and some research has found that as many as '90% of all jurors reach their final verdict during or immediately after opening statements' (Vinson 1986: 171).

The language of opening statements

Research in both law and linguistics has examined the linguistic and rhetorical mechanisms at work in opening statements which combine to produce the persuasive effects outlined above. Legal research, particularly from the U.S., has tended to focus on the structure and properties of 'storytelling' in opening statements. Snedaker (1991) describes the 'communicative features' of statements and draws particular emphasis to features which 'engage the audience' with the story that is being told such as 'powerful verbs, carefully chosen adjectives and the use of the active voice' (Snedaker 1991: 136). In her analysis of two opening statements in the Chicago Anarchists trial of 1886, she demonstrates the effect that repetition has on reinforcing key phrases central to the master narrative while developing the chronology of the story. At the same time, she shows how features which she refers to as 'imagery' and 'metaphor' are used to add emotion to a story and to create vivid mental representations of the characters and actions of the story. Powell (2001: 96) also advocates for the inclusion of detail which 'creates in the listener a vivid mental image of the events and occurrences' as being 'the very essence of good storytelling'. He goes on to identify a range of storytelling techniques, including choosing simple, straightforward and 'charged' words and the present tense as means by which to create images in the jurors' minds. In addition, he provides advice on how paralinguistic, non-verbal communicative techniques, such as pauses, pace, volume, eye-contact and gesture, can enhance image-creation. Johnson (2011: 43) also implores advocates in the U.S. to 'use impact words and phrases in opening statement' because 'they provide a word picture and evoke images in the minds of the jurors'. He elaborates on this point, arguing that carefully selected words and phrases can be 'attention grabbing' and go 'right to the hearts, minds, and viscera of the jurors' with 'lasting effect' (Johnson 2011: 43). For example, he compares 'accident' and 'crushed' as being appropriate for defence lawyers, with 'impact words' such as 'collision' and 'mangled' being preferred for plaintiff's lawyers. Other recent legal research such as Stolk (2018) has analysed opening statements in terms of broader discursive strategies, focusing mainly on how such strategies are combined by prosecutors to construct 'the paradoxical "ideal" perpetrator stereotype of the sophisticated beast' (Stolk 2018: 701). Drawing on examples from 17 cases across four international criminal courts, Stolk shows how opening statements are used to represent a perpetrator(s) as 'both a sophisticated manipulator as well as an inhuman beast' who is 'not only smart – hence, having accountable parts of humanity – but also thoughtless savages – hence, inhumane and hardly part of humanity' (Stolk 2018: 684).

Just as legal research on opening statements has focused on storytelling, (forensic and legal) linguistics has often approached them from a narrative perspective, primarily their structural patterns, drawing on Labov's (1972) model of oral narrative. Heffer (2005: 75), for example, demonstrates how an opening statement in a drink-driving case in England and Wales exhibits the elements of Labov's model (*orientation*, *complication action*, *evaluation* and *resolution*) as it sets out a temporal sequence of events for the jury. Heffer (2005: 76) notes some elements of the opening statement narrative which distinguish it as a trial narrative in particular, such as the overspecification of orientational detail and the gradual and cumulative building of evaluation as the narrative unfolds, both of which serve to reinforce the crime story in the minds of the jury and therefore strengthen the prosecution's case. Similarly, Harris (2005: 221) analyses an opening statement using a 'modified version' of Labov's narrative structure, comprising the elements of *orientation*, *core narrative*, *elaboration* and *point* (Harris 2001: 60, 2005: 219). In her analysis, Harris (2005: 224) draws particular attention to the 'historical-present' tense, or 'the use of the present tense to refer to past events' (Schiffrin 1981: 45), such as in the extracts 'but he grabs her and throws her onto the bed' and 'as she realizes what is going on, she says stop it hurts'. Such use of the historical present, Harris finds, is restricted to the *core narrative* element (the closest equivalent to Labov's *complicating action*) and the 'heightened sense of drama' it creates in the opening statement is intended and strategic (Harris 2005: 224). In her analysis of the prosecution and defence opening speeches in the O.J. Simpson case, Cotterill (2003: 65) uses a corpus linguistic approach to demonstrate the discursive practice that she calls 'strategic lexicalisation'. This relates to the semantic prosodies and 'connotational loading' of the lexical items chosen by prosecution and defence attorneys in their opening speeches in their depiction of Simpson, the murder victims Nicole Brown Simpson and Ron Goldman and the events that unfolded. Cotterill explicates how the prosecution use terms to construct Simpson as a violent man, capable of murdering his wife. She draws particular attention to terms such as *control*, *encounter* and *cycle*, which are not obvious (what lawyers might call) 'impact' words but are subtle words which have negative semantic prosodies and contribute to the negative representation of Simpson. Cotterill draws on evidence from general corpora to show how these words generally have negative connotations which are then attributed to Simpson in the opening statement. At the same time, Cotterill's analysis of the defence statement shows how they aim to minimise and neutralise these negative prosodies and representations evoked by the prosecution. One way in which this is attempted is through the relexicalisation of alleged assaults as *incidents*, *discussions* and *disputes*, all of which have a more neutral (or at least less negative) semantic prosody and serve to present Simpson as non-violent. Matoesian and Gilbert (2018: 147) present a multimodal analysis of the defence opening statement in the William Kennedy Smith trial and demonstrate how the multimodal combination of speech, gesture and the material artefact of an exhibit reconstruct space, path and motion and 'generate ideological fields that shape inconsistency, credibility and evidence in taken-for-granted ways'.

In terms of precise linguistic features in opening statements, Lipovsky (2017) examines a prosecution opening in a murder case heard in the Supreme Court of New South Wales in Sydney, Australia. Taking a Hallidayan Systemic Functional Linguistic approach, she analyses a number of different features, highlighting 'the ways in which the prosecutor's linguistic and discursive choices contribute to making his opening statement persuasive' (Lipovsky 2017: 88). Her analysis of rhetorical organisation as manifest in clause relations, for example, shows that the statement follows a linear story, with different series of events succeeding each other in chronological order, as this is thought to be more persuasive to the jury. Meanwhile, spatial and temporal 'circumstance' elements were found to be very frequent in the data, reflecting the emphasis on orientation information in these monologues. A transitivity analysis found that agency and responsibility are assigned to the accused, while quotations from the accused are used in a damaging way and as a means of highlighting discrepancies in the accused previous evidence. In terms of verbal processes, Lipovsky also found that quotes from the accused were used to re-enact crucial events of the crime story in such a way that engages. Finally, the strategic use of naming of the defendant was argued to reflect distance between the accused and the jury. A number of these linguistic perspectives and analyses on opening statements are also found in many works by Krisda Chaemsaithong. For example, Chaemsaithong (2018a, 2019a, 2023) analyses the use of naming, 'referential practices' and 'membership categorization' strategies by lawyers in their opening statements and the role they play in the identity construction of participants, particularly victims and defendants, in high-profile trials from the U.S. Elsewhere, Chaemsaithong (2019b, 2021) and Chaemsaithong and Kim (2018) combine transitivity analysis and social actor analysis in examining how representational choices in referential strategies and event description serve to construct versions of people (e.g. defendant, victims) and events that align with and benefit their ideologies, narratives and communicative goals (i.e. prosecution or defence). It is through transitivity choices and their polarization of social actors, Chaemsaithong (2021: 221) argues, that the opening statement is transformed from being informative to argumentative and evaluative. Chaemsaithong (2017a, 2018b) focuses on 'speech reporting' or the 'use of voices' in opening statements. Though essentially monologic, the analyses reveal that opening statements are in fact highly 'heteroglossic' and 'polyphonous' in nature, with the intertextual inclusion of many different voices serving many different functions, including to provide important context, highlight claims, underline shared understanding, as well as serving functions of legitimation, narrative and discourse organisation, all of which can help lawyers improve the credibility and reliability of their arguments (Chaemsaithong 2017a: 12). Lawyers have also been found to enhance the propositional content of their opening statements and boost their credibility by using a range of metapragmatic expressions, which also guide the jurors' comprehension and reception of the statements (Chaemsaithong and Simuang 2023: 14).

In other work, Chaemsaithong examines a group of features that he characterises as being 'dialogic' or audience 'orientation' or 'engagement' devices such as: personal pronouns, directives, questions, asides and markers of shared knowledge to establish authority, solidarity and in-groupness with the jury. The use of such features and their roles in relational work and impression management between lawyer and jury, in particular how they can lead to the latter making certain inferences, have been demonstrated in both the contemporary and historical courtroom (Chaemsaithong 2015a, 2018c). In an earlier paper focusing on the early modern English courtroom (Chaemsaithong 2014), these engagement features were considered alongside markers of speaker attitude, or stance, such as hedges and boosters (cf. Hyland 2005). Such expressions of stance, Chaemsaithong (2014: 360) argues, present certain pieces of evidence as especially worthy of consideration and thus guide the jury's interpretation of that evidence. In a later paper (Chaemsaithong 2017b), stance takes centre stage as the prosecution and defence opening statements in five high-profile U.S. trials are analysed in terms of boosters, hedges, personal pronouns and attitude markers. It is argued that such stance markers 'subtly make the discourse essentially *argumentative*' (Chaemsaithong 2017b: 129, my emphasis) rather than strictly informative as opening statements should be (in theory, at least). Using stance markers in this way, it is argued, allows lawyers to not only 'subtly bypass the legal constraints that prohibit explicit display of personal opinions' but also 'produce a voice that is able to acknowledge, engage with or disalign itself with respect to other positions' and participants, including opposing lawyers, jurors and the general public (Chaemsaithong 2017b: 103, 128).

This chapter contributes to the forensic and legal linguistics literature on opening statements, with the benefit of having 22 different master narratives about the same event. Unlike the majority of other studies detailed here, this analysis does not isolate one linguistic feature (or a set of linguistic features) for analysis. Rather, the opening statements here will be analysed by adopting the perspective of *positioning* to develop a new framework for analysing the allocation of responsibility. While bringing new insights to this type of discourse, positioning theory can provide challenges for corpus approaches.

Positioning and opening statements

In this chapter, the 22 opening statements of the Grenfell Inquiry Phase 1 will be analysed from the perspective of *positioning*. In proposing and explicating the notion of positioning, Davies and Harré (1990: 48) define it as

> The discursive process whereby selves are located in conversations as observably and subjectively coherent participants in jointly produced storylines. There can be interactive positioning in which what one person says positions another. And there can be reflexive positioning in which one positions oneself.

Van Langenhove and Harré (1999: 15–6) describe the theory of positioning in terms of a metaphorical spacial and temporal grid in which social acts and forms of discursive practice such as conversation, institutional practices and societal rhetorics constitute the matter of social reality. Within this grid, positioning refers to the assignment of 'fluid "parts" or "roles" to speakers in the discursive construction of personal stories that make a person's actions intelligible and relatively determinate as social acts'. Van Langenhove and Harré (1999: 24–8) expand on the idea of interactive and reflexive positioning and set out a range of related and overlapping 'modes of positioning'. They describe the different types of *intentional* positioning:

Deliberate self-positioning which 'occurs in every conversation where one wants to express his/her personal identity' through means such as stressing one's agency, referring to one's unique point of view and by referring to events in one's biography.

Forced self-positioning differs only from deliberate self-positioning in that 'the initiative now lies with someone else rather than the person involved'. The example that they provide of a mild 'force' is someone asking 'how have you been lately?' to which a response is demanded.

Deliberate positioning of others is when a speaker deliberately positions someone else in their storyline, a position which may or may not be taken up by the person being positioned.

Forced positioning of others refers to instances in which a speaker is demanded by another speaker to position a third party, who may or may not be present. The example provided is one in which a mother tells her husband to remonstrate their son.

Furthermore, positioning can be *first order* or *second order*. First-order positioning refers to the ways in which speakers position themselves and others, whereas second-order positioning occurs when the first-order position is not taken up and is questioned or negotiated (van Langenhove and Harré 1999: 20). Given the origins and interactional focus of the theory, positioning in discourse studies is traditionally drawn on in the analysis and interpretation of (multi-participant) conversations, such as to 'convey the key set of expectations participants have on where to place the other in a given interaction' (Riberio 2006: 72). However, the key ideas and principles of positioning can be applied also to monologic discourse, specifically opening statements. In their opening statements, as in opening statements in criminal trials, the Core Participants are tasked with *self-positioning* in the story of the Grenfell Tower fire. In doing so, as we will see, they position themselves in relation to other Core Participants, thus also intentionally *positioning others*. Furthermore, if we consider the broader context of these opening statements as being a key element of a public inquiry, this positioning is in some ways *forced*. As a statutory inquiry, the Grenfell Tower Inquiry can compel Core Participants to be part of proceedings and give written or oral evidence or both. Of course, BSRs have been forced into their positions. Therefore, this represents a sort of *forced self-positioning* (and, by extension, *forced positioning of others*) as Core Participants are required to appear and thus required to give opening statements.

Not only can opening statements be analysed from a positioning perspective, but an argument can be made that they are particularly well suited to such an analysis. The reference of 'storylines' in the definition and description of positioning aligns with the narrative properties and characteristics of opening statements as discussed by Harris (2005) and others outlined above. Furthermore, in his proposal of the 'Narrative Navigation' model as a means by which to examine complex narrativity and embedded narrative practices in the adversarial trial, Heffer (2012) identifies 'character navigation' as one of the elements of the model. Character navigation, Heffer (2012: 273) explains, is the 'ongoing ascription and maintenance of a story agent's identity'. Drawing on Bamberg's (2011) concept of identity navigation, Heffer's character navigation relates to the ways in which speakers construct their identities in relation to three points: *agency*, *sameness/difference* from others, and *constancy/change* across time. Heffer describes this character construction in terms of how lawyers 'position' witnesses in forensic narratives, both their own witnesses and those of the opposing side. This concept of character navigation is clearly related to (and seemingly at least partially reliant on) the theory of positioning, providing support for the utility of the theory when analysing the (quasi-legal) narratives in the Inquiry opening statements.

A final consideration relates to the existence of overarching cultural narratives that have developed in public, political and media domains prior to (and alongside) the commencement of the Inquiry. Cotterill (2003: 88) notes how, in high-profile criminal cases (the O.J. Simpson trial in her analysis), the jurors do not approach the trail 'as blank slates' but instead bring with them their own opinions of the defendant. As Cotterill (2003: 89) points out, in this situation, the challenge faced by legal counsel is to deconstruct prevailing images of actors and reconstruct new ones which better serve their master narrative. Furthermore, Harris (2005: 73) notes how criminal trial narratives both reflect and construct wider socio-cultural narratives infused with preconceived stereotypes, prejudices and ideologies which can be exploited by lawyers and can influence jurors' perception of evidence. Because the Grenfell Tower fire received such a huge amount of coverage in the mainstream media and was the subject of considerable commentary on social media, members of the media and the public had already made up their minds as to who was to blame for the fire and the response to it. In other words, characters involved in the story of Grenfell Tower had already been positioned, with their identities being ascribed and determined. In addition, the Grenfell Tower fire and its aftermath are inexplicably intertwined with macro socio-cultural narratives and realities relating to race, power and economic inequalities. The task of the legal counsel for the Core Participants is therefore not only to position their clients and other Core Participants but to do so in light of pre-existing positions that have already been ascribed. As we will see, in some opening statements, this is done quite explicitly.

Positioning is attempted and achieved in discourse using any and all of the interactional resources available to speakers. That is, the 'discursive process(es)' (Davies and Harré 1990: 48) through which positions are negotiated are not a predictable, consistent and finite set of linguistic features. This poses a challenge for corpus methods which rely, at least in the first stages, on (frequently occurring) lexico-grammatical items which emerge and are observed through a quantitative analysis. The approach taken in this analysis is to use lexical items which Core Participants – or legal counsel thereof – use to refer to themselves as entry points into instances of discursive positioning. This is similar to the approach taken by Chaemsaithong (2014, 2015b), who uses first-person pronouns, so-called 'self-mentions', as a means by which to analyse stance in opening statements. In this analysis, self-mentions emerged as statistically salient in a keyword analysis, in which each of the 22 opening statements was compared with the 11-million-word Spoken BNC 2014 (Love et al. 2017). The resultant keyword lists showed that, within the top 15 keywords of each opening statement (and often within the top 5), there are words that reflect the legal counsel for the Core Participants referring directly to their clients (Table 4.2). Of course, this fairly blunt approach may not identify all of the ways in which the Core Participants position themselves, but it does isolate those instances where the discursive practice employed relies at least in part on lexically

Table 4.2 Self-reference keywords in the Grenfell Tower Inquiry Opening Statement Corpus (generated using log likelihood and ranked using log ratio)

Core Participant	*Self-referring keywords*
Arconic	*company* (12th keyword)
Behailu Kebede	*(mr) kebede* (1st)
BSRs (all groups)	*residents* (15th)
Celotex	*celotex* (1st)
Counsel to the Inquiry	*I* (1st) *inquiry* (4th)
CS Stokes Ltd	*stokes* (1st)
Fire Bridge Union	*fbu* (2nd)
Fire Officers Association	*foa* (4th)
London Fire Brigade	*lfb* (2nd)
Mayor of London	none
Metropolitan Police	*metropolitan* (6th), *police* (9th)
MHCLG	*department* (4th)
Sir Martin Moore-Bick	*I* (1st), *inquiry* (2nd)
Tenant Management Association	*tmo* (1st)
Royal Borough Kensington & Chelsea	*borough* (7th), *council* (11th), *kensington* (12th)

observable self-reference. It is worth noting that the first-person singular pronoun *I* was also key for a number of Core Participants. However, unlike Chaemsaithong (2014, 2015b), this analysis is not concerned with the way in which the lawyers position themselves in the opening statements, only how they position the Core Participants, and so the first-person personal pronoun is not included as a self-referring keyword here. There are two exceptions to this: the Counsel to the Inquiry and Sir Moore-Bick as the chairman of the Inquiry. That is because these two speakers represent not a Core Participant but the inquiry itself.

A new model for responsibility allocation

The analysis here took an inductive approach to analysing every concordance line of the self-referring keywords in Table 4.2 in their context within the opening statements. In the process, patterns were identified in how legal counsels positioned their clients, and other participants, with regard to responsibility for various elements of the Grenfell Tower story. These patterns have been grouped together below in a proposed model for analysing the discursive construction of responsibility in this context and others.

The linguistics of blame in the context of Public Inquiries is addressed by Murphy (2019) in his analysis of a series of recent Inquiries in the U.K. (not including The Grenfell Tower Inquiry) as he analyses the language of blame avoidance and the (non-)assignment of blame. The focus of this analysis is different from that of Murphy; much of his analysis focuses on the questioning of participants rather than opening statements, and his approach is primarily focused on the lexical manifestation of blame. The main difference, perhaps, is that while Murphy focus on *blame*, this analysis prefers the discussion of *responsibility*. Nevertheless, Murphy's (2019: 199) definition of blame as 'the assignment of responsibility for a negative action' shows the inexplicable link between the two.

The analysis of the types of positioning discursively enacted by the legal counsel for the Core Participants in their opening statements has given rise to a model of responsibility allocation that comprises four different but related strategies, each of which is discussed below by the presentation of representative examples from the data:

- Impression management
- Pre-emptive allocation
- Delineating involvement and responsibility assignment
- Positive action

Please note, in the discussion below, interpretations of responsibility of any Core Participants are not the opinion of the author. Rather, they are interpretations of the language in the opening statements being analysed. In the Phase 2 report, the panel of the Inquiry was critical of manufacturers of the cladding products, companies involved in the refurbishment of the tower and local and national government (Moore-Bick et al. 2024).

Impression management

Impression management is a well-established concept in corporate discourse and provides a framework for responsibility management in and of itself (e.g. Dunne et al. 2020). Here, the term 'impression management' is used to describe a recurring type of positioning in which Core Participants position themselves as being helpful contributors to the Inquiry. In terms of the structure of the overall statements, positioning of this kind was invariably found at the start and/or the end of the opening statements. Helpfulness is constructed through an openness and transparency to the Inquiry, welcoming the Inquiry's search for objectivity and truth and making commitments to assisting the Inquiry in doing so:

1 I would like to underline, particularly having regard to all that has been said and that I've heard today, **Celotex**'s continued commitment to full, objective and transparent engagement with this inquiry. (Celotex, 6 June 2018)
2 **CS Stokes** is committed to assisting this inquiry as best it can, and particularly in relation to the fire safety order and fire risk assessments carried out under that order, not only in relation to how matters were and remain, but how they might be improved for the future. (CS Stokes, 6 June 2018)
3 In line with the report's recommendations, the **council** reaffirmed its commitment to be open, transparent and fully co-operative with the public inquiry into the Grenfell Tower fire, and to assist the search for the truth. That remains the council's approach to this inquiry. (Royal Borough of Kensington and Chelsea, 6 June 2018)

On face value, it may be obvious that the Core Participants are committed to helping the Inquiry because they are there, giving evidence and making meaningful contributions to the hearings. Nevertheless, explicitly positioning themselves as being co-operative and welcoming to the Inquiry can serve an important rhetorical goal. The Core Participants can be sure that the Inquiry will scrutinise each of their roles in relation to the tower, their involvement in its refurbishment and/or their response to the fire both on the night itself and since. By positioning themselves in this way, the participants are constructing themselves as 'having nothing to hide'. Indeed, one would presumably be reluctant to welcome an Inquiry that was going to publicly and officially point the finger of blame in one's direction. In some ways, the participants are *forced* to position themselves as committed and co-operative, as doing anything else would risk tarnishing their reputation and the Inquiry's and public's perception of them, particularly in terms of responsibility. To this end, then, this positioning is a form of impression management (Goffman 1959), a positive self-presentation motivated by the desire to have the Inquiry and the public perceive them positively. Such impression management can thus be viewed as a persuasion strategy by legal counsel, in an attempt to enhance their clients' credibility, trustworthiness and believability (cf. Hobbs 2003). Ultimately, the hope is that in the eyes of the Inquiry and the public more widely, the roles being constructed here of helpful, transparent and co-operative characters are incompatible with character roles of responsibility, culpability and wrongdoing. Therefore, the Core Participants are using their opening statements not only to provide a conceptual frame for the forthcoming evidence to be heard but also to provide a perceptual frame of themselves; if they are able to make a good first impression, this may protect them against damaging evidence or revelations later in the hearings.

Pre-emptive allocation

The Inquiry, or at least the role of the Inquiry, is also positioned by Core Participants. More specifically, the participants place impositions and demands of various kinds on the Inquiry, responsibilising and making explicit its purpose and process (at least insofar as they see them) in terms of revealing the objective truth. This is a strategy employed particularly productively by the legal counsel of Behailu Kebede towards the end of their opening statement:

4 Mr Kebede hopes that the inquiry, having heard all the evidence, will deliver real justice for the 72 who died, their families and those who survived the fire, and real accountability. He hopes that, despite being prohibited from determining criminal or civil liability, the inquiry will nevertheless make decisive findings and recommendations that will allow others to infer such liability; decisive findings as to which corporate and governmental core participants were responsible for those aspects of the refurbishment that transformed Grenfell Tower into what has been properly characterised by others as a highly combustible deathtrap; decisive findings as to which corporate and governmental core participants caused or contributed to an entirely foreseeable and preventable catastrophe in which a fire confined to a single compartment within the building was able to spread so easily and so quickly in multiple directions inside and outside the building with such devastating consequences.

> On a more personal note, sir, Mr Kebede hopes that, having heard all the evidence, the inquiry will make a clear and unequivocal statement that Mr Kebede was absolutely blameless for the outbreak of the fire, its spread and its fatal consequences. This is vitally important. If the inquiry does not explicitly exonerate Mr Kebede, all the sleazy accusations and hurtful innuendo, all the racism, assumptions and ignorance about Mr Kebede that currently prevail will continue unabated. (Behailu Kebede, 6 June 2018)

In this extract, counsel express how their client 'hopes' that the Inquiry achieves certain aims. That is, using the stance-marking verb *hope*, they set out what the aims of the Inquiry should be from their perspective. In instances such as this, legal counsel go further than framing or pre-empting the evidence that is to be heard – as is generally the key function of opening statements – but in fact make at least a symbolic attempt at influencing the direction of the Inquiry and *shaping* the evidence. In this extract, there are two basic *hopes* expressed: that the Inquiry will deliver real justice for those who lost their lives in the fire and that the Inquiry will find Mr Kebede himself blameless for the fire.[1] Both of these are clear enough, but a further unpacking highlights the multi-layered and multi-functional effects of positioning the Inquiry in this way. First, in the first part of the extract, we have not only an expressed desire for 'real justice' but also an explanation of what this justice looks like. Namely, this would be that the Inquiry delivers decisive findings. In turn, these finds would 'others' to infer that the parties responsible for the disaster are 'corporate and governmental core participants' that were involved in the refurbishment of the building, which rendered Grenfell Tower as a 'highly combustible deathtrap'. Here, counsel for Mr Kebede directly and explicitly assigns the responsibility directly to these Core Participants, ultimately positioning them as the culpable characters in the story of the fire. This positioning is immediately followed by a contrastive positioning of Mr Kebede himself as 'absolutely blameless'. Prior to the Inquiry, Mr Kebede had been subject to substantial attention by the British press which his counsel elsewhere in their opening describes as 'intrusion' and 'harassment'. They make particular reference to an article in the *Daily Mail* 'that seemed to scapegoat Mr Kebede for the fire itself'. Therefore, the positioning of Mr Kebede in the opening statement is *second-order* positioning, in van Langenhove and Harré's terms, in that it is first-order positioning of Mr Kebede that has 'occurred in another discursive practice than the current one' (van Langenhove and Harré's 1999: 23) (i.e. the media). The positioning of Mr Kebede as blameless is presented against a media narrative in which Mr Kebede had already been positioned as to blame. Through positioning, therefore, the extract in (4) discursively shifts responsibility away from Mr Kebede and towards the corporate and governmental parties. It is worth remembering, though, that this is not achieved as a direct statement of fact or presentation of opinion by Mr Kebede's legal counsel. Rather, it is packaged within a positioning of the Inquiry itself and what it may reveal.

This positioning of the Inquiry does not occur only in the opening statement for Mr Kebede. A similar strategy is used by the Fire Brigade's Union (FBU) on a number of occasions. Here, too, we see a shifting and an allocation of responsibility but in far less direct terms than in Mr Kebede's statement:

5 The **FBU** invites the inquiry to consider whether there was in the recent refurbishments a complete failure of the fire safety regime at each stage of the design, planning, building control, building works and supervision of works. (FBU, 7 June 2018)
6 The **FBU** asks the inquiry to consider whether there was a lack of planning for the scale of risk so that it should not have been left to firefighters to develop a strategy on the fire ground in the face of a breach of compartmentation. (FBU, 7 June 2018)

In these examples, the legal counsel for the FBU pre-emptively allocates responsibility. As opposed to explicitly 'hoping' for certain evidence and findings, the FBU instead 'ask' and 'invite' the Inquiry to consider certain things – whether the refurbishment of the Tower represented a 'complete failure' of the fire safety regime and whether a 'lack of planning' resulted in an ineffective evacuation strategy. In combination with these nominalisations, the FBU stop short of referring to corporate and government parties, but the implication is clear: as far as the FBU are concerned, those who were responsible for the refurbishment and the fire safety strategy are responsible for the spread of the fire and the potentially preventable loss of life. Of course, while responsibility is being implied here, it is being shifted away from the fire service whom the FBU represent and instead emphasises the difficult job they had. Therefore, although this is a less direct strategy employed by the legal counsel of the FBU than we saw in the opening for Mr Kebede, they share a motivation: to position their client(s) as blameless and, in doing so, position others as culpable. What has been observed here, however, is that this is achieved by positioning the Inquiry itself and making demands of its process and its findings as a vehicle for allocating responsibility, pre-empting the evidence to be heard in the inquiry.

Delineating involvement and responsibility assignment

Across the opening statements, the finger of blame is rarely, if ever, pointed as explicitly as it is in the opening statement of Mr Kebede. Far more common is the positioning of Core Participants as *blameless* by their legal counsel, a discursive attempt at what Murphy (2019: 199) calls 'blame avoidance'. For Murphy (2019: 139), 'blame and responsibility for an action are intrinsically linked', and he shows how participants in the Leveson Inquiry engaged in blame avoidance strategies in answers to their questions. In the Opening Statements of Phase 1 of the Grenfell Inquiry, there emerges a recurring strategy for shifting responsibility, which involves a two-stage process. First, the legal counsel provides details of what their client *was* (or *were*) responsible for, in a process I call *delineating involvement*. In this stage, the Core Participant is positioned as being liable for the action(s) being described. Second, the legal counsel then introduce an element, factor or character that is culpable for some negative action or outcome in relation to the Grenfell Tower fire and make it clear that this falls *outside* of the involvement or responsibility of their client that has previously been established or delineated. I call this second stage *responsibility assignment*. In this stage, the Core Participant is positioned away from or distant from this agent or action of blame and, in turn, is positioned as blameless. Stage 2 of this process need not immediately follow stage 1 and can occur at some point much later in the Opening Statement. A clear example of this process in action can be seen in the Opening Statement of Arconic:

7 My second point concerns the supply of cladding. As everyone now knows, the **company** was requested to supply a quantity of cladding panels made of what is known as ACM PE, some or all of which were to be fitted to the tower. The panels were of a kind which, among others, the **company** regularly manufactured and supplied. They consisted of two sheets of aluminium with a polyethylene core. The core itself was obviously combustible. The manufacture and supply of these panels was the only part which the **company** played in the events leading up to the fire.

[...]

As regards the cladding system, we have to emphasise that the insulation selected for the project appears to have been the first combustible component in the cladding system which became subject to fire and which had a significant impact on fire spread. The **company** was not in any way responsible for the selection or installation of the insulation material. (Arconic, 6 June 2018)

Before the commencement of the Inquiry, much attention had been focused on the external cladding affixed to the outside of Grenfell Tower in a recent refurbishment. Arconic, then, are in a vulnerable position insofar as their culpability for the rate at which the fire spread, and their legal counsel is tasked with positioning them against this pre-existing backdrop. In doing so, they make use of the two-part strategy outlined above. In the first part of this extract, the legal counsel are clear and unequivocal in their statement that their client Arconic was involved only in the manufacture and supply of the cladding panels that were affixed to the outside of Grenfell Tower in the refurbishment. Given that it had been alleged that these cladding panels were responsible for the rapid spread of the fire, this statement of involvement could be damaging. However, in the second part of the extract, much later in the statement, legal counsel introduces the point that it was the *insulation* used in the panels that was the first combustible element and was the cause of the fire spread. In other words, it was the insulation, rather than the panelling, that was at fault. Following the introduction of the insulation as being to blame, counsel make clear that Arconic had no involvement at all in the selection or installation of this insulation material. Therefore, Arconic are distanced from the insulation which was to blame and are therefore positioned as blameless or, at least, positioned as having reduced responsibility. To summarise, Arconic were responsible for the manufacture and supply of the panels (*delineating involvement*), but it was the insulation, not the panelling, that was responsible for the fire spread (*responsibility assignment*). Therefore, Arconic are not responsible (*positioning as blameless/reduced blame*).

A version of this positioning can also be observed in the opening statement of CS Stokes & Associates Ltd:

8 In written submissions seen in advance, at least one of the BSR core participants suggests that the external walls are within the scope of the fire safety order. As you know, sir, the fire safety order is one of the key pieces of legislation in this area. All of **CS Stokes'** fire risk assessments on Grenfell Tower were carried out pursuant to the fire safety order.

[…]

CS Stokes' position is that the external walls of the tower do not form part of the common parts of the building for the purposes of the fire safety order. Further submissions as to the reasoning behind that will follow, sir, at your invitation. (CS Stokes & Associates Ltd, 6 June 2018)

Here, the legal counsel for CS Stokes & Associates first makes clear that the company was responsible for conducting fire risk assessments at Grenfell Tower. This is a responsibility that is discussed at length throughout the opening. The significant point here is that the company conducted these fire risk assessments in accordance with the fire safety order (*delineating involvement*). Then, in the second part of the extract, the lawyer makes clear that the external walls are not covered by the fire safety order. Therefore, the external walls and combustible cladding that were seemingly responsible for the rapid spread of the fire (*responsibility assignment*) are outside of CS Stokes' remit of responsibility and so they are not culpable for the role that the external of the building played in the fire.

By extension, therefore, CS Stokes & Associates are positioned as blameless in relation to the key factor that caused the fire to spread in the deadly way that it did. CS Stokes & Associates and their relationship with the external cladding are revisited below.

A complex example of this positioning can be seen in the discursive and rhetorical gymnastics executed by the legal counsel for the Royal Borough of Kensington and Chelsea council (RBKC) and the Tenant Management Organisation (TMO). Before these are examined in detail, it is worth noting that RBKC, possibly more so than any other Core Participant, had to engage in second-order positioning in their opening statement. This is mentioned explicitly in the early part of the statement itself:

> 9 There can be no doubt from the coverage in both the mainstream media and social media that **the council** is seen as the public face of those assumed to be responsible for the Grenfell Tower disaster.
>
> [...]
>
> That **the council** should be seen as the public face of the disaster is entirely understandable. The residents were tenants and leaseholders of **the council**. **The council** is and always has been the owner of Grenfell Tower. The residents lived in the borough. They voted in local elections for councillors to represent them in **the council**. So **the council** recognises that it is seen as the public face of the disaster and understands why this is so. (RBKC, 6 June 2018)

RBKC directly address that they have already been positioned as responsible for the fire by the public prior to the Inquiry. Importantly, this is not directly contradicted by RBKC at this precise moment. On the contrary, they acknowledge this position and recognise why this is the case. The decision by the legal counsel to bring this perception of culpability to the foreground could be an appeal to impression management, presenting the council as reasonable and alert to the public's concerns, as a means by which to cultivate a favourable view later in the evidence. Alternatively, and perhaps in the same vein, this could be a strategic acknowledgement by RBKC that they cannot be absolved of all blame, regardless of the discursive measures that they take in an attempt to mitigate it (cf. Murphy 2019: 119). In any case, the tasks for the legal counsel of RBKC in the remainder of the opening statement are to challenge and reverse this positioning of the council being to blame. As we have already seen with other Core Participants, the first stage in this process for RBKC is that they *delineate involvement*; specifically, they state that they funded the refurbishment. At the same time, they make clear that, although they funded the project, a 'huge number of organisations' were involved in the refurbishment:

10 Mr Chairman, although you've only recently started hearing evidence, your investigation has been running full-time for over nine months. You will therefore already appreciate that, whilst **the council** funded the refurbishment of the tower, which was completed shortly before the fire, a huge number of organisations with different specialisms were involved in a variety of ways in that project. This is a theme that I will return to. (RBKC, 6 June 2018)

Here, legal counsel for RBKC not only delineates the client's responsibility but immediately implicates others. As the refurbishment was widely regarded to have rendered Grenfell Tower unsafe, introducing other organisations involved in that refurbishment introduces other potential sources of responsibility and blame. Therefore, we have the beginnings of *blame allocation*. Then, 57 lines later in the opening, as promised, the counsel return to and elaborate on these other organisations. In doing so, they emphasise that it is ordinary, and in fact legally required by the Construction (Design and Management) Regulations, that there be many parties involved in any construction project. Once that has been established, RBKC distance themselves from these other parties and from the refurbishment as a whole by positioning themselves as 'not a relevant organisation'. Thus, when it comes to undertaking the refurbishment project, according to this opening statement, it falls outside of the delineated remit of their responsibility; they only funded it. Then, once RBKC has described themselves as not a relevant organisation, they expand on this by detailing a number of key actions that they *did not* do and that they *were not* responsible for – namely that they did not enter into contracts with commercial organisations that undertook the work in the refurbishment:

11 In this country, construction projects are generally subject to the Construction (Design and Management) Regulations. The Grenfell Tower refurbishment project was no exception. The Construction (Design and Management) Regulations, as the name suggests, regulate the many different organisations typically involved in a construction project. Where did **the council** fit into that framework?

The answer is that, for the purposes of the regulations, **the council** was not a relevant organisation. It did not enter into the contract with Rydon, the principal contractor. It was the Tenant Management Organisation, the TMO, whose role I will return to later, that entered into that contract and became the employer in the language of the contract. While **the council** was the owner, it was the TMO who were the client for the purposes of the regulations.

The council did not enter into contracts with the other organisations involved in the refurbishment project, many of whom are core

> participants in this inquiry. Those commercial organisations were either contractors or subcontractors of the TMO or contractors or subcontractors of Rydon. (RBKC, 6 June 2018)

As can be seen in this extract, not only do RBKC repeatedly position themselves as not responsible, they also explicitly shift responsibility for employing and engaging the contractors to the TMO. Therefore, we have a clear example of delineation of involvement followed by responsibility allocation. Here, unlike some of the other examples, there is another Core Participant that is explicitly responsibilised. In the RBKC's opinion, it would appear that because the TMO signed the contracts with, and employed, the contractors who undertook the refurbishment that rendered the building unsafe and contributed to the deadly spread of the fire, the responsibility is with them. That is not the end of the story in the RBKC's opening statement, however. Once the TMO has been identified as being responsible for the refurbishment, the legal counsel for RBKC distances the council from the TMO:

> 12 I hope that I've also dispelled some misunderstandings about **the council's** role by saying something about the involvement of the many commercial organisations involved in the project whose involvement was understandably more hidden from view.
>
> [...]
>
> Sir, you will of course be aware of this, but some of those following the inquiry may not be, so it is worth repeating. The TMO was at all relevant times a separate legal entity to **the council**, although they worked closely together.
>
> [...]
>
> At the time it was established, the creation of a tenant management organisation and the delegation of functions to it was considered to be a positive and progressive move. It was set up to be independent of **the council**, and it was independent of **the council**. (RBKC, 6 June 2018)

The lawyer clearly describes the separation between their client and the TMO. Because they had positioned the TMO as the responsible party earlier in the statement, distancing the council from the TMO serves to further reduce and mitigate the responsibility of the RBKC. Thus, the attempt at second-order positioning – that is, unpicking the pre-determined perception of the counsel being the 'public face of those responsible for the Grenfell Tower disaster' – has involved implicating a wide range of other, more responsible parties and, most aggressively, positioning themselves as not responsible for the refurbishment beyond funding it. Instead, the TMO is positioned as the responsible agent, and the TMO is quite a separate entity from the counsel. This attempt at second-order positioning is alluded to at the start of this extract; the belief that the counsel is responsible and to blame for the fire is referred to as 'misunderstandings'.

Finally, in this section, it is worth noting how the legal counsel for the TMO, whose opening statement immediately followed that of RBKC, used the same two-part process to delineate their involvement and allocate responsibility. We saw how the RBKC positioned the TMO as 'client', a role that, in their view, rendered the TMO as directly responsible for the refurbishment project. In the TMO opening statement, they too position themselves as client but make clear that, as client, they are not expected to be plan, manage or carry out any of the project themselves. In other words, they are delineating their involvement; whereas for the RBKC 'client' was a culpable position, for the TMO it is not:

> 13 Sir, while TMO is a specialist in the management of social housing stock, it is not a specialist design or construction company and had no in-house expertise in these areas. […] TMO's role in relation to the refurbishment project was that of client, and Mr Maxwell-Scott has mentioned the regulations. But, sir, this was the role it occupied pursuant to the legislation that governs large-scale construction projects such as this one, and these are the Construction (Design and Management) Regulations 2007, which are known as CDM.
>
> Sir, while this is an important role and if I may say, TMO does not seek to underplay the importance of its role – the regulations envisage that clients may not be specialists in design or construction and, therefore, clients are not required to plan, manage or carry out projects themselves. (TMO, 6 June 2018)

The implication here is that the parties who *were* required to plan, manage and carry out projects are those responsible This implication is replaced by explicit positioning some 51 lines later in the opening, in which the legal counsel for the TMO directly refer to Rydon (who were the main contractor for the refurbishment) and Manse Masterdor (who manufactured the fire doors), and implicate CS Stokes and the London Fire Brigade, who advised on fire safety and risk assessments over the course of the refurbishment:

> 14 TMO appointed Rydon as principal contractor, which again is a designation under the CDM regulations, following its successful tender. This was a design and build contract and Rydon was required to carry out the design, construction and completion of both the proposed recladding and installation of windows.
>
> Prior to and during the refurbishment project, TMO engaged the services of the fire safety consultant CS Stokes & Associates Limited, which advised on fire safety matters and completed fire risk

> assessments at Grenfell Tower. TMO also had bimonthly fire safety meetings with the London Fire Brigade throughout the course of the refurbishment.
>
> [...]
>
> One of the topics is fire doors, and it has been widely reported and is referred to in your expert reports that fire doors installed on the flats in 2011 may not have performed to the standard suggested by their fire rating. This will plainly be a matter to be investigated, but it's right to say that TMO procured these doors from a company, Masterdor, who fitted them and held them out as being compliant with prevailing fire standards. (TMO, 6 June 2018)

Here, following the establishment of the TMO as the client in the refurbishment, the opening statement shifts responsibility to these individual contractors with whom the TMO engaged. In doing so, the TMO may be exercising what Murphy (2019: 140) refers to as the 'delegation of responsibility', in which they mitigate their own personal involvement. The process of positioning the contractors as ultimately responsible is completed at the very end of the opening statement:

> 15 Sir, TMO supports the inquiry's thorough investigation into how these materials came to be used by contractors at Grenfell Tower and so widely throughout the housing sector, and how the current systems of building regulations and fire safety, which Dame Judith Hackitt found to be not fit for purpose, were not reviewed prior to this date.
>
> Finally, sir, and importantly, TMO supports a thorough investigation into the nature and implementation of the stay-put policy in relation to high-rise buildings and, crucially for Phase 1, on the instructions residents were given by LFB and dispatchers as events unfolded on the night of 14 June 2017. (TMO, 6 June 2018)

In these closing remarks, the TMO position themselves in alignment with the Inquiry as the discoverers of truth. This also has the effect of impression management detailed above; by positioning themselves in this way, the TMO is constructing a credible, trustworthy and non-culpable role. Meanwhile, the contractors at Grenfell Tower are coded as the direct agents of using the flammable materials, and the London Fire Brigade are presented as responsible for the instructions given to residents during the fire. This way, it is these parties who are discursively positioned as being responsible, not the TMO.

Positive action

The final strategy in this proposed model involves emphasising the *positive* actions that Core Participants were responsible for in relation to the tower and the fire. This is a slightly more offensive strategy of allocating responsibility. It does not involve mitigating any responsibility for negative actions that the participant may have, nor does it involve shifting the responsibility elsewhere. Rather, it sees legal counsel construct a positive representation of their client to the Inquiry and the public. In Dunne et al.'s (2020: 13) terms, legal counsel are creating the impression of their client that 'their work was good' or 'their intentions were good' as a means of managing perceptions of them. In terms of positioning, the legal counsel create a positive character role for their client. Not only are they not to blame, but they should be thanked or praised for the actions that they took. For the first clear example of this, we return to the opening statement for Mr Kebede:

16 In short, Behailu **Kebede** did exactly what Grenfell Tower residents who discovered a fire in their flat were told to do by the fire action notice posted outside the lifts: he telephoned the Fire Brigade on 999 and informed the operator that there was a fire at flat 16, Grenfell Tower, London, W11 1TG; he left his flat promptly, shutting the door behind him; and he used the stairs to go down and exit the building. Indeed, Mr **Kebede** went further than the fire action notice instructed. To his enormous credit, he also made sure that everybody else on the fourth floor had been warned about the fire, and only when he believed that nobody else was left on the floor did he himself leave and make his way downstairs. (Behailu Kebede, 6 June 2018)

We saw earlier that the legal counsel for Mr Kebede urged the Inquiry to find his client blameless for the outbreak and did so in a context in which the media had already portrayed Mr Kebede in a very negative way. In (16), we can see that this is combined with positive representation of Mr Kebede's actions in a clear and direct form of chronological narrative, detailing his actions when the fire started. Most salient here is the statement that not only did Mr Kebede do what Grenfell residents were told to do, he *went further* than what was expected or required of him. Importantly, he is represented here as having gone above and beyond in the interests of his neighbours' safety. In the same way as was argued in the analysis of impression management above, the positioning of Mr Kebede as a caring resident who put himself at risk to warn others is not compatible with an alternative positioning of him where he would act in such a way to put others at risk. Not only does this distance Mr Kebede further away from any responsibility for the fire, it also directly addresses, through second-order positioning, the image of him that had been portrayed in parts of the British press.

The positioning of a Core Participant as going 'above and beyond' in their positive actions in the interests of safety is also observed in the Opening Statement of CS Stokes & Associates:

> 17 Following the fire risk assessment, in accordance with the fire safety order, the record of significant findings and action plan also dated 17 October 2014 was produced by <u>**CS Stokes**</u>. In addition to the proposed cladding being noted in the first row of significant findings, the last significant findings item identified the following as a risk with a high priority for resolution, and I quote: 'The external face of this building is to be overclad. The piece of cladding fixed to the external wall at the moment is on timber batons.'
>
> [...]
>
> Even though, therefore, outside the scope of the fire safety order, by identifying the proposed overcladding as a risk or hazard, and in accordance with the Local Government Association guidance, <u>CS Stokes</u> invited particular attention to the proposed cladding system and thus promoted active consideration of the safety of the cladding system and fire safety issues. (CS Stokes, 6 June 2018).

Throughout the narrative presented by CS Stokes & Associates' counsel, they are positioned as undertaking their job effectively and responsibly. Most importantly here, particular attention is drawn to the warnings and recommendations that they made regarding the external cladding which, at this point, had not been fixed to the external of the building, but a sample had been made available for them to inspect. In the second part of this extract, the legal counsel emphasise that CS Stokes raised concerns and misgivings about the fire safety of the proposed cladding. This is despite the fact that the cladding actually falls outside of his remit as per the fire safety order. In this version of the story, then, CS Stokes & Associates are positioned not only as non-culpable but as actually taking steps to try to prevent fire risks being introduced into or onto the tower. Again, legal counsel position them as not to be blamed or held responsible for any negative action but rather they are to be praised for going 'above and beyond' and predicting the potential safety risks posed by the proposed cladding.

The final example in this chapter returns for the last time to the opening statement of RBKC. By this point (both in the chapter and in the Inquiry), serious concerns had been raised about the fire safety of the materials used in the refurbishment of Grenfell Tower. Furthermore, as we have seen, the RBKC were considered the public face of responsibility for this refurbishment, and in their opening statement, we have observed the steps they take to mitigate that responsibility and their involvement in the refurbishment project. In the Opening Statement, we see the legal counsel seemingly remind the Inquiry and the public that the refurbishment was intended to be a *good* thing, to benefit the residents, and lists a number of 'upgrades' that it included:

18 It is, for all too obvious reasons, easy to forget that the whole point of the refurbishment project was to benefit the residents of Grenfell Tower and the local community by, amongst other things, upgrading the communal heating system – which served approximately 650 properties, including all the flats in the tower – installing new windows in the tower and improving external thermal efficiency and weathertightness in the tower. **The council** provided the funding for the refurbishment project. (RBKC, 6 June 2018)

Following the representation of the refurbishment as a good thing, a positive action (or set of actions), this is followed by a repetition of the fact that the council funded the project. Here, as with Mr Kebede and CS Stokes & Associates, we see the client being positioned as the agent of a positive action. The implication is, therefore, that because the refurbishment was a well-intended project, designed to benefit the residents, the counsel should be viewed positively for providing the money to fund it. Thus, the RBKC are positioned positively, as wanting only good for their residents. This is an identity incongruent with a character that would deliberately take any action to endanger the safety of the residents.

Conclusion

Opening statements, both in a criminal trial and a Public Inquiry, provide legal counsel an opportunity to present their overarching macro-narratives to the audience, in this case, the Inquiry Chair, the panel and the general public. Much of the research on opening statements in both law and linguistics has focused on how lawyers present a certain version of the story and a certain identity for their clients during these opening statements. This chapter has had the benefit of analysing a number of opening statements in relation to the same 'case' – that of the Grenfell Tower disaster. In other words, it has been able to analyse a number of different versions of the story as told from a number of different perspectives. The analysis here adopted the discourse-analytic theory of positioning as a means by which to interpret how legal representatives in the Grenfell Tower Inquiry create character roles, or positions, for their clients in the story of Grenfell. In particular, the focus here has been on how Core Participants are positioned in relation to responsibility. The identification of strategies of positioning has given rise to a suggested four-part model for the allocation of responsibility which comprises *impression management*; *pre-emptive allocation*; *delineating involvement and responsibility assignment* and *positive action*. These elements are related but ultimately discrete from one another. In this context, impression management relates specifically to explicit expressions of Core Participants' commitment to the

Inquiry and its aims. Here, it has been argued that such expressions of commitment serve, in some cases, to create a favourable image for the participant. Pre-emptive allocation also involves positioning in relation to the Inquiry itself and in particular attempts to not only frame the forthcoming evidence but also influence and shape the direction of it, specifically in terms of the identification of those responsible and absolving those not. Delineating involvement and responsibility assignment is itself a two-step process, which starts by counsel clearly setting out the extent of their clients' involvement with Grenfell Tower. This is followed by the identification of some agent or action that was responsible (at least in part) for the disaster by the counsel, before distancing and positioning their client away from this responsible agent or action. Finally, positive action involves legal counsel foregrounding and emphasising the good intentions and good work of their clients, as a means by which to positively represent them.

Positioning is attempted and achieved through a wide variety of discursive processes and so does not immediately and readily lend itself to corpus analysis which relies initially on repeated lexical or grammatical patterns. The decision taken here to focus on keywords that were in some way self-referring has offered one way in which to identify and isolate positioning strategies. Of course, there are different ways in which positioning is manifest, and there is more work that could be done in this direction. What is presented here, however, is an attempt to systematically apply the theory of positioning to opening statements as they are well suited to this type of discourse and its aims. It has been argued here that positioning theory allows us to interpret the strategies employed by lawyers in opening statements to discursively allocate responsibility to and away from characters in the tragic story of the Grenfell Tower disaster.

Note

1 In his report of Phase 1 of the Inquiry, Sir Martin Moore-Bick (2019) concluded that 'Mr Kebede in particular bears no blame for what occurred in his flat, much less for the catastrophic events that followed'.

References

Bamberg, M. (2011) Narrative practice and identity navigation. In J. A. Holstein and J. F. Gubrium (eds.), *Varieties of Narrative Analysis*. London: Sage, pp. 99–124.

Chaemsaithong, K. (2014) Interactive patterns of the opening statement in criminal trials: A historical perspective. *Discourse Studies* 16(3): 347–364. https://doi.org/10.1177/1461445613508900

Chaemsaithong, K. (2015a) Communicating with silent addressees: Engagement features in legal opening statements. *Language and Communication* 43: 35–46. https://doi.org/10.1016/j.langcom.2015.04.004

Chaemsaithong, K. (2015b) Positioning self and others in the courtroom: Person markers in the opening statement. *Poznań Studies in Contemporary Linguistics* 51(1): 1–25. https://doi.org/10.1515/psicl-2015-0001

Chaemsaithong, K. (2017a) Speech reporting in courtroom opening statements. *Journal of Pragmatics* 119: 1–14. https://doi.org/10.1016/j.pragma.2017.08.003

Chaemsaithong, K. (2017b) Evaluative stancetaking in courtroom opening statements. *Folia Linguistica* 51(1): 103–132. https://doi.org/10.1515/flin-2017-0003

Chaemsaithong, K. (2018a) Referential practice and contested identities in legal narratives. *Lingua* 212: 44–59. https://doi.org/10.1016/j.lingua.2018.06.001

Chaemsaithong, K. (2018b) Use of voices in legal opening statements. *Social Semiotics* 28(1): 90–107. https://doi.org/10.1080/10350330.2017.1278913

Chaemsaithong, K. (2018c). Dialogic features and interpersonal management in the early courtroom action game: The case of the opening statement. *Language and Dialogue* 8(3): 341–362. https://doi.org/10.1075/ld.00021.cha

Chaemsaithong, K. (2019a) Names and identities in courtroom narratives. *Names* 67(4): 185–198. https://doi.org/10.1080/00277738.2018.1490515

Chaemsaithong, K. (2019b) Deconstructing competing courtroom narratives: Representation of social actors. *Social Semiotics* 29(2): 240–260. https://doi.org/10.1080/10350330.2018.1434978

Chaemsaithong, K. (2021) Agency, responsibility, and actor positioning in courtroom narratives. *Manusya: Journal of Humanities* 24(2): 204–226. https://doi.org/10.1163/26659077-24020002

Chaemsaithong, K. (2023) Membership categorization devices in courtroom opening and closing speeches. *Social Semiotics*, 1–25. https://doi.org/10.1080/10350330.2023.2184683

Chaemsaithong, K. and Kim, Y. (2018) 'It was him': Representational strategies, identity, and legitimization in the Boston Marathon bombing trial narratives. *Language and Literature* 27(4): 286–310. https://doi.org/10.1177/0963947018794095

Chaemsaithong, K. and Simuang, K. (2023) Lawyers' metapragmatic expressions in the opening speech of Anglo-American criminal trials. *Lingua* 289: 1–16. https://doi.org/10.1016/j.lingua.2023.103536

Cotterill, J. (2003) *Language and Power in Court: A Linguistic Analysis of the O.J. Simpson Trial*. Basingstoke: Palgrave.

Davies, B. and Harré, R. (1990) Positioning: The discursive production of selves. *Journal for the Theory of Social Behaviour* 20(1): 43–63. https://doi.org/10.1111/j.1468-5914.1990.tb00174.x

Dunne, N. J., Brennan, N. M. and Kirwan, C. E. (2020) Impression management and Big Four auditors: Scrutiny at a public inquiry. *Accounting, Organizations and Society* 88. https://doi.org/10.1016/j.aos.2020.101170

Gibbons, J. (2003) *Forensic Linguistics: An Introduction to Language in the Criminal Justice System*. London: Blackwell.

Goffman, I. (1959) *The Presentation of Self in Everyday Life*. London: Penguin.

Grenfell Tower Inquiry (2019) Updated list of core participants. (online). Available from: https://www.grenfelltowerinquiry.org.uk/news/updated-list-core-participants-4 [Last accessed 04 March 2021].

Grenfell Tower Inquiry (2021) Terms of Reference. (online). Available from: https://www.grenfelltowerinquiry.org.uk/about/terms-of-reference [Last accessed 18 March 2021].

Hans, V. and Sweigart. K. (1993) Jurors' views of civil lawyers: Implications for courtroom communication. *Indiana Law Journal* 68: 1297–1332.

Harris, S. (2001) Fragmented narratives and multiple tellers: Witness and defendant accounts in trials. *Discourse Studies* 3(1): 53–74. https://doi.org/10.1177/1461445601003001003

Harris, S. (2005) Telling stories and giving evidence: The hybridisation of narrative and non-narrative modes of discourse in a sexual assault trial. In J. Thornborrow and J. Coates (eds.), *Sociolinguistics of Narrative*. Amsterdam/Philadelphia: John Benjamins, pp. 215–237.

Heffer, C. (2005) *The Language of Jury Trial: A Corpus-Aided Analysis of Legal-Lay Discourse*. Basingstoke: Palgrave.

Heffer, C. (2012) Narrative navigation: Narrative practices in forensic discourse. *Narrative Inquiry* 22(2): 267–286. https://doi.org/10.1075/ni.22.2.04hef

Heffer, C. (2021) Narrative in the trial: Constructing crime stories in court. In M. Coulthard, A. May and R. Sousa-Silva (eds.), *The Routledge Handbook of Forensic Linguistics* (2nd ed.). London: Routledge, pp. 192–210.

Hobbs, P. (2003) 'Is that what we're here about?': A lawyer's use of impression management in a closing argument at trial. *Discourse & Society* 14(3): 273–290. https://doi.org/10.1177/09579265030143002

Hyland K. (2005) Stance and engagement: A model of interaction in academic discourse. *Discourse Studies* 7(2): 173–192. https://doi.org/10.1177/1461445605050365

Institute for Government. (2018) Public Inquiries. (online) Available from: https://www.instituteforgovernment.org.uk/explainers/public-inquiries [Last accessed 14 October 2021].

Johnson, J. A. (2011) Persuasion in opening statement - generating interest in a convincing manner. *Michigan Bar Journal* 90(1): 42–45.

Labov, W. (1972) *Sociolinguistic Patterns*. Philadelphia: University of Pennsylvania Press.

Linz, D. G. and Penrod, S. (1984) Increasing attorney persuasiveness in the courtroom. *Law and Psychology Review* 8(1): 1–48.

Lipovsky, C. (2017) Storytelling in legal settings: A case study from a Crown Prosecutor's opening statement. *Australian Review of Applied Linguistics* 40(1): 71–91. https://doi.org/10.1075/aral.40.1.05lip

Love, R., Dembry, C., Hardie, A., Brezina, V. and McEnery, T. (2017) The Spoken BNC2014: Designing and building a spoken corpus of everyday conversations. *International Journal of Corpus Linguistics* 22(3): 319–344. https://doi.org/10.1075/ijcl.22.3.02lov

Matoesian, G. and Gilbert, K. E. (2018) 'She does not flee the house': A multimodal poetics of space, path and motion in opening statements. *International Journal of Speech, Language and the Law* 25(2): 123–149. https://doi.org/10.1558/ijsll.35619

Melilli, K. J. (2006) Succeeding in the opening statement. *American Journal of Trial Advocacy* 29(3): 525–562.

Moore-Bick, M. (2019) Grenfell Tower Inquiry: Phase 1 Report. Report of the Public Inquiry into the Fire at Grenfell Tower on 14 June 2017 (Volume 4). (online) Available at: https://assets.grenfelltowerinquiry.org.uk/GTI%20-%20Phase%201%20full%20report%20-%20volume%204.pdf [Last accessed April 2024].

Moore-Bick, M., Akbor, A. and Istephan, T. (2024) Grenfell Tower Inquiry: Phase 2 Report overview. Report of the Public Inquiry into the Fire at Grenfell Tower on 14 June 2017. (online) Available at: https://www.grenfelltowerinquiry.org.uk/sites/default/files/CCS0923434692-004_GTI%20Phase%202_Report%20Overview_E-Laying_0.pdf [Last accessed September 2024].

Murphy, J. (2019) *The Discursive Construction of Blame: The Language of Public Inquiries*. Basingstoke: Palgrave.

Powell, G. (2001). Opening statements: The art of storytelling. *Stetson Law Review* 31(1): 89–104.

Pyszczynski, T., Greenberg, J., Mack, D. and Wrightsman, L. S. (1981) Opening statements in a jury trial: The effect of promising more than the evidence can show. *Journal of Applied Social Psychology* 11(5): 434–444.

Pyszczynski, T. and Wrightsman, L. S. (1981) The effects of opening statements on mock jurors' verdicts in a simulated criminal trial. *Journal of Applied Social Psychology* 11(4): 301–313.

Reinard, J. C. (2012) Persuasion in the legal setting. In J. P. Dillard and L. Shen (eds.), *The SAGE Handbook of Persuasion: Developments in Theory and Practice* (2nd ed). London: SAGE, pp. 331–353.

Riberio, B. T. (2006) Footing, positioning, voice. Are we talking about the same things? In A. De Fina, D. Schiffrin and M. Bamberg (eds.), *Discourse and Identity*. Cambridge, UK: Cambridge University Press, pp. 48–82.

Schiffrin, D. (1981) Tense variation in narrative. *Language* 57(1): 45– 62. https://doi.org/10.1353/lan.1981.0011

Shirkey, H. (2011) Last attorney to the jury box is rotten egg: Overcoming psychological hurdles in the order of presentation at trial. *Ohio State Journal of Criminal Law* 8(2): 581–604.

Snedaker, K. H. (1991) Storytelling in opening statements: Framing the argument of the trial. In D. R. Papke (ed.), *Narrative and the Legal Discourse*. Liverpool: Deborah Charles Publications, pp. 132–157.

Stolk, S. (2018) A sophisticated beast? On the construction of an 'ideal' perpetrator in the opening statements of international criminal trials. *European Journal of International Law* 29(3): 677–701. https://doi.org/10.1093/ejil/chy041

van Langenhove, L. and Harré, R. (1999) Introducing positioning theory. In R. Harré and L. van Langenhove (eds.), *Positioning Theory. Moral Contexts of Intentional Action*. Oxford: Blackwell, pp. 14–31.

Vinson, D. E. (1986) *Jury Trials: The Psychology of Winning Strategy*. Charlottesville, VA: Michie Company.

Wells, G. L., Wrightsman, L. S. and Miene, P. K. (1985) The timing of the defence opening statement: Don't wait until the evidence is in. *Journal of Applied Social Psychology* 15(8): 758–772. https://doi.org/10.1111/j.1559-1816.1985.tb02272.x

5 Stance-taking by advocates and judges in the Brexit Hearings

Introduction

This chapter analyses the ways in which advocates and judges discursively enact stance in the unique contexts of the High Court of England and Wales and the United Kingdom Supreme Court. The data for this analysis is taken from one of the most significant cases of constitutional law in British history: 'the Brexit case'. The U.K.'s decision to withdraw from the European Union (EU) in 2016 sparked a legal challenge over whether the government had the power to trigger Article 50 of the Lisbon Treaty without parliamentary approval. The case involved some of the most experienced advocates and the most senior judges in the country.

Although there has been a limited amount of linguistic work undertaken on the Brexit hearings (e.g. Wright et al. 2022), there have been, to date, no analyses of hearings from the higher courts of the U.K. from a stance perspective. The lack of research in this context is explained by the scarcity of data; the production of official transcripts is not the norm, and an exception was made for the Brexit case. Therefore, this data provides a unique opportunity to bring new linguistic insights into the U.K.'s highest courts. The importance of being able to examine discourse in this space has been emphasised by those who have analysed appeal court data in the United States. The value of analysing the 'largely inaccessible legal register' (Finegan and Lee 2021: 55) of (appeal) court discourse is that it is unlike the talk that occurs in most other legal arenas because it can improve our understanding of how 'the law is built and changed' through discourse (Tracy and Parks 2012: 21). More broadly still, judicial review hearings (High Court) and appeal court hearings (Supreme Court) such as those analysed in this chapter provide a window into 'the public face of the law' and 'the only place where members of a society get to see their judges thinking, talking, and moving toward decisions that have major policy implications' (Tracy 2011: 83). As the analysis will show, the unique parameters of the High Court and Supreme Court give rise to distinctive ways of stance-taking

DOI: 10.4324/9781003017301-5

which respond to, and are reflective of, the power dynamics between participants, the relative institutional roles of speakers and the rules of engagement with which all participants must adhere. The discursive strategies that emerge from such a context provide a richer understanding of the ways in which speakers in legal contexts mark stance.

Background to the 'Brexit case'

On 23 June 2016, the U.K. held a referendum on its membership of the EU. The result of that referendum was announced on 24 June 2016, with 51.9% of the voters preferring to leave the EU. In order to start the process of withdrawing from the EU, a member state must notify the European Council of its intention to withdraw by 'triggering' Article 50 of the Lisbon Treaty, a short paragraph which sets out the steps a country needs to go through to withdraw from its treaty obligations (Institute for Government 2016). In the days, weeks and months following the result of the referendum, there was controversy and disagreement over the path that should be taken to triggering Article 50. In brief, the government's view was that it (i.e. the Cabinet or 'Executive') could trigger Article 50 by itself, in accordance with the 'Royal prerogative' over foreign affairs. Legal experts, however, argued that because the withdrawal from the EU would affect the rights of citizens in the U.K., the decision to trigger Article 50 must be approved by a parliamentary vote and primary legislation (i.e. an Act of Parliament). To that effect, British business owner Gina Miller, along with a group of other clients, privately engaged London law firm Mishcon de Reya to take legal steps to ensure that the government would not trigger Article 50 and withdraw from the EU without an Act of Parliament (Mishcon de Reya 2016).

The subsequent legal proceedings took two parts. First, a Judicial Review was commenced in the Administrative Court, Queen's Bench Division of the High Court of Justice (hereafter 'High Court'),[1] and hearings were held on the 13, 17 and 18 October 2016. The High Court ruled that the government could not use Royal prerogative to trigger Article 50. Following this ruling, the government appealed the High Court's decision at the Supreme Court of the United Kingdom (hereafter 'Supreme Court'), the final court of appeal in the U.K. The appeal was heard between 5 and 8 December 2016, and following the hearings, the Supreme Court upheld the High Court's ruling and dismissed the government's appeal by a majority of 8 to 3 (R v Secretary of State for Exiting the European Union [2017] UKSC 5). As a result, the government were forced to introduce to parliament a bill entitled the European Union (Notification of Withdrawal) Act 2017 in January 2017. In February that year, the bill was passed unamended by parliament; in March, it received Royal Assent. On 29 March 2017, the U.K. invoked Article 50, and, almost three years later, on 31 January 2020, the U.K. withdrew from the EU.

The Brexit Hearings Corpus

Given the societal, cultural and political importance of the Brexit case, it endured enormous public and media scrutiny. To ensure transparency and reflect the exceptional public interest in the hearings, verbatim transcripts of all hearings in both the High and Supreme courts were released, and it is these transcripts that comprise the data for this chapter (Table 5.1). There are some elements of the corpus which warrant some explanation before moving on. There were many more lawyers involved in this case than those who submitted oral evidence during the hearings and who therefore appear in the transcripts. For instance, the judgement document from the Supreme Court appeal lists no fewer than 29 legal representatives. The table also shows that, in the High Court, advocates for Gina Miller speak more than their government counterparts, while the reverse is true in the Supreme Court. This can be explained by their alternating roles in the High Court and Supreme Court. In the former, legal counsel for Miller were acting on behalf of the applicant and therefore bore the burden of persuading the court to rule against the government. In the Supreme Court, it was the government as appellant who bore the burden of persuading the court to overturn the High Court decision. Table 5.1 also reflects the fact that Sir James Eadie KC is the primary advocate for the government and Lord Pannick KC is the primary advocate for Miller as they speak by far the most across the hearings.[2] These two advocates were responsible for opening the case and setting out their arguments to which the opposing side responded, with more minor contributions from the others. Although the advocates are organised here as representing the 'Government' or 'Miller', this is somewhat of an oversimplification for those who represent the devolved nations of Scotland and Northern Ireland. The Advocate General for Scotland (who, at the time, was Lord Richard Keen KC) advises the U.K. government on Scottish law. Meanwhile, Lord Advocate (James Wolffe KC at the time) is the chief legal adviser to the Scottish government, and the Attorney General for Northern Ireland (John Larkin QC at the time) is the chief legal advisor to the Northern Ireland Executive. The role of these lawyers is not to represent the U.K. government *per se*; rather, they are there to discuss matters relating to their respective nations. Finally, as the table shows, the Judicial Review in the High Court was heard by three judges, while the Supreme Court appeal was heard by eleven – the maximum number possible. This comes hand-in-hand with a greater amount of judicial intervention in the latter and accounts for the difference in the number of words spoken by the judges in the two hearings.

Given that the analysis here focuses on stance, a note should be made of the nature of the official transcripts that were used as data. The aim of the transcripts is to accurately reflect the ongoing talk. Therefore, they are verbatim orthographic transcripts of the hearings, demarcated for turns by individual speaker. However, save for the marking of interruptions (by a double dash), there is no indication of extralinguistic features of the talk, such as vocalised sounds (e.g. *uh*), pauses, intonation or other more fine-grained elements which one would expect of a more specialised transcript produced for conversation analysis purposes, for example. Therefore, although stance in courtroom contexts can be analysed from a multimodal perspective (e.g. Matoesian 2005), the analysis here is focused only on lexico-grammatical features.[3]

Table 5.1 A breakdown of the Brexit Hearings Corpus

	High Court		*Supreme Court*	
	Speaker	*Tokens*	*Speaker*	*Tokens*
Government	James Eadie KC	22,919	Sir James Eadie KC	54,031
	Attorney General	9,613	Advocate General, Scotland	11,708
	Jason Coppell KC	6,168	Richard Gordon KC	8,312
			Lord Advocate	6,610
			Attorney General, N.I.	4,370
			Attorney General	2,938
	Sub-total	*38,700*	*Sub-total*	*87,969*
Miller	Lord Pannick KC	42,105	Lord Pannick KC	19,905
	Dominic Chambers KC	11,722	Dominic Chambers KC	9,682
	Helen Mountfield KC	11,452	Helen Mountfield KC	8,309
	Patrick Green KC	6,069	David Scoffield KC	4,261
	Manjit Gill KC	4,460	Manjit Gill KC	2,991
			Patrick Green KC	2,650
			Ronan Lavery KC	2,116
	Sub-total	*75,808*	*Sub-total*	*49,914*
Judges	Lord Chief Justice	10,061	Lord Neuberger	7,494
	Lord Justice Sales	4,733	Lord Mance	5,967
	Master of the Rolls	2,923	Lord Carnwath	4,013
			Lord Sumption	3,012
			Lord Reed	2,614
			Lady Hale	1,176
			Lord Kerr	1,169
			Lord Wilson	882
			Lord Clarke	816
			Lord Hodge	649
			Lord Hughes	397
	Sub-total	*17,717*	*Sub-total*	*28,189*
	Total	**132,225**	**Total**	**166,072**

Stance and stance-taking

An influential definition of stance which flavours much of the early work in this area is that by Biber and Finegan (1989: 93): 'the lexical and grammatical expression of attitudes, feelings, judgments, or commitment concerning the propositional content of a message'. Most definitions since have remained close to this, echoing some or most of its scope. Hyland (2005: 176), for example, defines stance as 'the ways writers present themselves and convey their judgements, opinions, and commitments', while for Jaffe (2009: 3) 'stance-taking' involves 'taking up a position with respect to the form or the content of one's utterance'. Researchers have also operationalised different 'types' of stance or stance-taking. For Biber and Finegan (1989: 94), stance comprises *evidentiality* and *affect*; evidentiality refers to the speaker's expressed attitudes towards knowledge, and affect refers to the expression of personal attitudes. Later, Biber et al. (1999) and Conrad and Biber (2000: 57) expanded this into a tripartite distinction of *epistemic*, *attitudinal* and *style* stances. Epistemic and attitudinal correspond to the earlier evidentiality and affect respectively, with the former now framed in terms of certainty/doubt, reliability and limitations of knowledge. Meanwhile, style stance relates to the manner in which information is being presented. Englebretson (2007: 16) divides stance into *evaluation* (value judgments, assessments and attitudes), *affect* (personal feelings) and *epistemicity* ('commitment'). Here, Englebretson's choice of *evaluation* reflects the closeness of the concepts of 'stance' and 'evaluation'. For Thompson and Hunston (2000: 5), 'evaluation' is a broad cover term for a speaker or writer's expression of 'attitude or stance towards, viewpoint, or feelings about the entities or propositions that he or she is talking about', which includes attitudes of obligation and certainty.

Despite these classifications, the distinctions between different 'types' of stance are not clear-cut. It is acknowledged that 'discrete categories inevitably conceal the fact that forms often perform more than one function at once' (Hyland 2005: 176). Myers (2010a: 99) argues that stance category systems quickly become blurred in practice given, for example, that 'an affective response can lead us to a moral judgement'. Du Bois (2007) addresses this blurriness directly in proposing a new theory of stance. He argues for a shift of focus away from stance 'types' to stance 'acts' which can simultaneously express many different kinds of stance. This alternative approach

> recognizes a more complex picture of the stance act, seen as encompassing multiple facets at once. Building a more unified understanding of stance has the advantage of avoiding a limitless proliferation of stance types. Such an approach would seek to interpret the diversity of stances not as distinct types of stance, but simply as different facets of a single unified stance act.
>
> (Du Bois 2007: 145)

This unified understanding of stance takes account of the fact that a single utterance can perform a variety of different stance functions. That is, an utterance can be analysed as at once expressing a speaker's commitment to what they are saying, an expression of affective feeling and an expression of evaluation. This broader approach to stance and stance-taking is the one adopted in this chapter. Rather than homing in on specific types of stance from the outset, the analysis focuses on recurrent linguistic patterns in the discourse as stance acts and, as will be seen below, draws on relevant and particular types or categories of stance as and when they appear in the data.

Stance and corpus linguistics

The identification of stance in discourse is not unproblematic, but the general view is that there are certain sets of linguistic features which can be leveraged for pin-pointing acts of stance-taking. Because stance is 'an emergent property of interaction', it is often 'not transparent in either the linguistic or the sociolinguistic' (Jaffe 2009: 4). A speaker or writer's full linguistic repertoire can be drawn on to express stance, and the lexico-grammatical choices that can be used to express evaluation is endless (Bednarek 2006: 8); indeed, it has been argued that evaluation is intrinsic to *all* language (Pounds 2015: 2). At the same time, however, stance may be marked not by words at all but instead by absence or by alternative means that are opaque to the analyst (Hyland 2005: 177). Nevertheless, many studies of stance have isolated and analysed particular linguistic features – mainly lexico-grammatical features – as being 'stance-markers' or 'resources for stance-taking' (e.g. Biber and Finegan 1989; Hyland 2005; Thompson and Hunston 2000). Myers (2010a: 100), for example, offers a 'grammar of stance-taking', comprising a set of stance-taking devices at the sentence, clause and word level.

These discrete lexico-grammatical stance-markers lend themselves to the use of corpus approaches to analysing stance. Despite 'limits on our knowledge concerning the inventory of stance features in English', Biber and Finegan (1989: 97) sourced 'lexical and grammatical markers of affect and evidentiality' from grammars, dictionaries and thesauruses in order to identify clusters in a corpus of 24 genres on the basis of their relative frequencies of these stance-markers. Hyland (2005) also used English reference works as well as previous literature on stance (which did not yet exist when Biber and Finegan began their work) to derive a list of 320 potentially productive markers of stance (and engagement) which were then used as search terms in a concordance analysis of a 1.4 million–word corpus of academic texts. Myers (2010b) took a more 'bottom-up' approach to identifying stance markers in his corpus of blogs and comments and identified stance-markers emerging from a keyword analysis. Charles (2006) takes a corpus approach in the analysis of stance construction in finite reporting clauses with *that*- complementation focusing on recurring grammatical patterns. Hunston (2007: 36) reflects on the use of corpora in investigating stance and notes that while the quantitative elements of corpus methods are useful in quantifying markers of stance, this should be a *starting point* for the close, qualitative examination of these markers in context. This is because the type of evaluative meaning involved in stance-taking 'does not occur in discrete items but can be identified across whole phrases, or units of meaning' (Hunston 2007: 39). Nevertheless, Hunston (2007: 27–8) argues that corpora are useful in identifying recurring (and thus easily quantifiable) stance-making forms and allowing analysts to examine these forms closely in context. Furthermore, a corpus can help identify and examine forms which, though not carrying stance themselves, often co-occur with stance items. This is the approach taken in this chapter, in which it is argued that stance resides in the collocates of a particular stance-related keyword (the first-person pronoun *I*) and permeates beyond its immediate context across full utterances in their dialogic context.

Stance in the courtroom

The courtroom is a fertile ground for stance-taking. The adversarial courtroom which sees two 'sides' pitted against each other are 'inevitably associated with conflict, disagreement and the often irreconcilable goals of the primary participants' (Harris 2011: 86). Therefore, this renders the courtroom a 'stance-rich environment' (Du Bois 2007: 151). Similar to Hyland's (2005: 176) characterisation of academic writers, lawyers and judges share a professional context in which they are pursuing their personal and occupational goals and are located in a community 'whose members are likely to recognize only certain forms of argument as valid and effective'. Lawyers are what Myers (2010a: 115) would call 'professionals who make facts their business' and therefore have 'developed elaborate codes' for expressing their stance.

Adversarial legal discourse in a trial or hearing is characterised by two main elements that Du Bois (2007: 140) argues constitute stance: it is dialogic and intersubjective. In a courtroom context, a stance-taker's words derive from and engage with the words of those who have spoken before (or will speak later) in the trial or hearing, whether that is a witness being examined, an opposing advocate or a judge. That is, it is dialogic. At the same time, in a courtroom context, a stance-taker's subjectivity is relative and responsive to the subjectivity (or stance) of other parties involved in the trial or hearing such as opposing counsel, the witness or the jury. That is, it is intersubjective. It is well established that stance and acts of stance-taking are inextricably linked to the context in which they are taking place.

The particular parameters of the context shape and constrain the degree and nature of stance expression: 'conventional, socially and culturally embedded practices, roles, and expectations are the backdrop against which stancetaking occurs' (Jaffe 2009: 12). This includes the professional standards of courtesy and the relative status of courtroom speakers. One critical element in this regard is that the Code of Conduct to which advocates in England and Wales must adhere when fulfilling their duties in court states that they 'must not put forward to the court a personal opinion of the facts or the law' unless they are invited or required to do so by the court or by law (Bar Standards Board Handbook 2020). Therefore, in this context, there are important institutional and professional restrictions on the expression of stance, particularly the prohibition of overt affective and evaluative stance-taking.

Whereas quite a sizeable literature has examined stance and evaluation in judicial opinions and written decisions (e.g. Goźdź-Roszkowski 2024; and see Chapter 3), a relatively small but concentrated number of studies have analysed stance in the spoken interaction of the courtroom. In the context of same-sex marriage cases in U.S. state supreme courts, Karen Tracy has shown that the ways in which questions are asked by judges reflect their personal style, political-legal leaning and their stances toward gay marriage (Tracy 2009). Similarly, Tracy and Parks (2012) found that judges tended to engage in 'tougher questioning' with the attorneys they ultimately voted against and argued that the 'tougher questioning of one party than the other [...] functioned as a stance indicator of ideology' (Tracy and Parks 2012: 20). Taking a different approach to analysing oral arguments in cases of same-sex marriage, Tracy (2011) found that the naming strategies used by judges and attorneys to refer to different parties in the cases revealed important aspects of speaker stance. Gales (2021) conducts an appraisal analysis (Martin and White 2005) on unsuccessful parole board hearings in the US. The analysis revealed 'prosodic patterns of manifested stance' and demonstrated the way in which such an approach to legal discourse provides 'a rich methodological resource for uncovering such nuanced stances in these challenging contexts' (Gales 2021: 691).

Magdalena Szczyrbak has adopted a corpus approach to analysing stance in courtrooms in both the U.S. and England and Wales, though in criminal and civil proceedings. Much of Szczyrbak's work takes a corpus-based approach to focusing on a specific set of quantifiable stance-marking verbs used by courtroom participants in the *David Irving v Deborah Lipstadt/ Penguin Books Ltd* libel trial in England and Wales, in which the claimant Irving was a self-representing litigant-in-person. For example, mental verbs *I think* and *I am thinking/wondering/hoping* are reported to convey subjective positioning, certainty and politeness by courtroom speakers in this case (Szczyrbak 2013, 2021a, 2021b). In a similar way, Szczyrbak (2016, 2018) has concentrated on the use of communicative verbs in the Irving trial, primarily verbs of speaking (e.g. *say*, *talk*, *tell* and *speak*), and argues that these verbs are used to lay claim to epistemic priority, shifting and bolstering speakers' own standpoints while challenging those of others. Szczyrbak (2019a) applies this approach to another type of verb, the perception verb *see*, and in particular constructions including *you* + *see*, concluding that they are used frequently in the Irving libel trial as courtroom speakers attempt to challenge opposing stances and to establish legitimacy for their own position (Szczyrbak 2019a: 34). Elsewhere, Szczyrbak (2014) has analysed the use of modal verbs of certainty (e.g. *certainly*, *obviously*, *necessarily* and *admittedly*), comparing their use in the Irving trial with that in the oral arguments from the U.S. Supreme Court and the written opinions from the U.S. supreme court and the Advocates General at the European Court of Justice. On the basis of this cross-genre analysis, Szczyrbak (2014: 98) argues that these modal verbs express politeness, solidarity, power and authority consistently across the different discourse types. In other work, Szczyrbak has demonstrated the use of these stance-taking verbs in trials besides the Irving trial. For example, Szczyrbak (2020) examines the use of *I think* by lawyers, witnesses and judges in the murder trial involving Boston Marathon bomber Dzhokhar Tsarnaev and identifies a range of pragmatic roles that it fulfils, including hedging and boosting claims and as a face-saving device. Szczyrbak (2019b) compares the use of mental and communication verbs by different participants in the confirmation hearing of Judge Brett Kavanaugh to the U.S. Supreme Court. The analysis found that while Kavanaugh as the nominee to the Supreme Court here tended to rely on communication verbs to reassert claims (e.g. *I said*, *I told this committee*, *I'm telling you*), Christine B. Ford (who had brought accusations of sexual assault to Kavanaugh) more frequently used mental verbs (*I think/I thought*, *I believe (so)*) when recounting spatially and temporally remote events. The influences of Szczyrbak's work and the approach she takes on the analysis in this chapter will become clear, particularly given the stance-taking features that are identified from the corpus results.

Other research has focused on stance expressed in different sub-genres of the criminal trial. Mortensen and Mortensen (2017), for example, quantitatively and qualitatively analyse the epistemic stance-taking strategies of three different participants in the witness examination phase of a Danish criminal trial: the defendant, the alleged victim and an eyewitness. On the basis of an analysis centred on modal verbs, epistemic/evidential adverbials and adjectives and cognition and perception verbs, their results show that different participants adopt different 'epistemic stance styles' in relation to the certainty that they attach to their testimony and demonstrate how this style can fluctuate at key points in their evidence. Gales and Solan (2017) analyse three cross-examinations in three different trials and offences:

sexual assault by a male on a female, non-sexual assault by a male on a female, and non-sexual assault by a male on a male. Their analysis identifies the different ways in which witnesses and their honesty, character, competence and capacity are attacked through different stance-marking and judgement strategies in cross-examination. Chaemsaithong (2017) analyses the prosecution and defence opening statements from five high-profile cases in the US. Drawing on Hyland's (2005) components of stance (hedges, boosters, attitude markers and self-mentions), he argues that by using these markers of stance, 'lawyers appear in the text with a considerable degree of visibility', to the extent that the opening statement essentially 'embodies the lawyer's view of "factual" events leading to the trial, displaying different degrees of certainty, and involvement, and affect' (Chaemsaithong 2017: 126). Potts and Weare (2018) analyse 17 sentencing remarks delivered by judges in crown courts of England and Wales in cases where a female defendant was convicted of murder or manslaughter. Through an analysis of referential strategies used by judges when delivering their sentencing remarks in these cases, the authors argue that 'the judiciary invoke patriarchal values and gender stereotypes' when constructing identities and narratives for female offenders and that these naming strategies 'systematically create dichotomous narratives of degraded victims or dehumanised monsters' (Potts and Weare 2018: 21).

There is, therefore, a reasonable understanding of how courtroom participants express stance in courtroom interaction. However, despite previous research finding similarities in stance-taking across cases, courts and courtroom genres, 'the courtroom' is not a monolithic discourse space. What the analysis in this chapter will demonstrate is that the unique institutional configuration, expectations and speaker roles in the higher courts in the U.K. create a context for stance-making quite different from those previously analysed. Therefore, the patterns of stance-taking that emerge from the data are distinctive from that previously identified in the literature.

I collocates and stance-markers

As was emphasised above, 'stance and evaluation emerge in myriad intangible ways' (Szczyrbak 2018: 255) and this can cause difficulties for corpus approaches. One element of the data here that helped in the identification of stance-taking in the Brexit hearings is that the first-person singular pronoun *I* is the top keyword for the corpus when compared against the Spoken BNC2014 (n = 3719, LogL = 27877, LogR = 18.22). To ensure that this did not reflect an over-representation of one set of speakers, separate keyword lists were produced for the advocates and the judges across the two hearings, and *I* returned as the top keyword for both sets of speakers (advocates: n = 3051, LogL = 23883, LogR = 18.18; judges: n = 668,

LogL = 7461, LogR = 18.42). The prominent role of *I* in the data not only reflects the dialogic nature of the interaction but also indicates that the interaction may be characterised by frequent and explicit stance-taking. Self-mention using first-person pronouns is a key element of stance-taking (Hyland 2005: 181) and is used by speakers to index themselves as taking both affective and epistemic stances (Du Bois 2007: 143). Research has consistently found *I*-oriented clauses to contain expressions of stance in English (e.g. Kärkkäinen 2003; Brinton 2008) and courtroom interaction specifically (Szczyrbak 2013, 2016, 2021a, 2021b; Chaemsaithong 2017). Although *I* does not carry stance itself, it frequently co-occurs with stance items such that stance can be identified across phrases and longer units of discourse (Hunston 2007). Therefore, here the keyword *I* is used as a 'smoking gun' of stance expression, an entry point to moments in the interaction where advocates and judges are expressing attitudes, evaluations, knowledge, commitment and certainty in relation to the issues being discussed and to each other. In order to explore this, the strongest R1 collocates of *I* were identified for the advocates and judges separately (Tables 5.2 and 5.3).

Table 5.2 Top lexical R1 collocates of *I* for advocates (ranked by MI³)

	Collocate	*MI³*	*Speakers*	*Freq*		*Collocate*	*MI³*	*Speakers*	*Freq*
1	think	20.46	16	154	26	come	11.82	7	20
2	say	20.21	17	227	27	know	11.59	6	18
3	will	19.47	21	206	28	said	11.57	6	22
4	hope	17.54	17	52	29	entirely	11.47	4	14
5	can	17.21	21	113	30	need	11.41	6	18
6	would	16.28	18	94	31	suppose	10.99	4	7
7	want	16.13	12	48	32	submit	10.98	7	21
8	may	15.89	14	70	33	rely	10.97	4	11
9	invite	15.59	11	37	34	turn	10.95	7	13
10	just	14.71	13	49	35	wish	10.94	7	11
11	accept	14.66	8	34	36	fully	10.47	3	7
12	respectfully	14.36	8	39	37	appear	10.47	8	8
13	wanted	13.93	7	21	38	start	10.46	6	9
14	understand	13.87	11	22	39	move	10.42	5	8
15	won't	13.73	6	16	40	made	10.42	4	17
16	believe	13.30	10	13	41	ask	10.38	7	11
17	apologise	13.05	7	11	42	gave	10.37	4	8
18	emphasise	12.99	7	14	43	identify	10.33	3	7
19	should	12.98	13	30	44	represent	10.32	3	6
20	mean	12.83	7	17	45	agree	10.29	6	10
21	take	12.79	7	32	46	suspect	10.05	3	4
22	quote	12.75	7	14	47	took	9.85	6	8
23	make	12.68	11	30	48	put	9.76	8	14
24	could	12.55	13	30	49	adopt	9.66	7	7
25	can't	12.01	8	13	50	gratefully	9.56	3	4

Table 5.3 Top lexical R1 collocates of *I* for judges (ranked by MI³)

	Collocate	*MI³*	*Speakers*	*Freq*		*Collocate*	*MI³*	*Speakers*	*Freq*
1	think	19.84	13	131	18	asked	9.16	2	5
2	understand	16.20	8	43	19	can	8.80	6	11
3	just	14.73	9	39	20	should	8.77	5	6
4	thought	14.48	7	22	21	fully	8.05	2	3
5	suppose	14.09	8	18	22	remember	7.10	2	2
6	mean	14.02	8	22	23	wondered	6.78	2	2
7	see	13.42	5	21	24	stop	6.52	2	2
8	know	10.86	4	12	25	right	5.96	3	5
9	understood	10.83	3	7	26	put	5.10	2	3
10	wonder	10.75	3	5	27	want	4.95	2	3
11	follow	10.71	2	8	28	agree	4.86	2	2
12	ask	10.55	7	10	29	will	4.81	3	4
13	assume	10.05	2	6	30	said	4.65	3	3
14	would	9.93	6	15	31	may	4.61	3	3
15	beg	9.78	3	4	32	can't	4.06	2	2
16	wanted	9.54	3	6	33	take	3.27	2	2
17	appreciate	9.49	3	5	34	now	2.82	2	2

Almost all of the *I* collocates for both advocates and judges can be classified as belonging to one of five lexico-grammatical categories, all of which have the potential to express stance. First, there are verbs, such as *think*, *understand*, *hope*, *want* and *believe*, which I refer to collectively here as 'mental' verbs. Previous research has identified verbs such as these as being important stance-taking devices for speakers in terms of marking certainty, commitment and evaluation of propositions across a range of contexts (e.g. Kärkkäinen 2003; Kaltenböck 2013; Fetzer 2014; Szczyrbak 2020, 2021a, 2021b). Second, there are verbs, including *say*, *ask*, *invite*, *apologise* and *quote*, which are referred to here as 'speaking' verbs and are also known to mark stance (e.g. Du Bois 2007: 144; Brinton 2008; Szczyrbak 2016, 2018). Third, there are modal verbs such as *will*, *can*, *would*, *may* and *should* which are widely regarded to be among the most explicit stance-markers (e.g. Biber and Finegan 1989; Myers 2010a). Fourth, there is a set of verbs which serve to organise the discourse, such as *take*, *come*, *turn*, *start* and *move*. Verbs such as these, which I refer to as 'metadiscourse', serve as interactive and interactional resources which guide audiences through spoken and written texts and which serve to engage and position readers and listeners in relation to the stance(s) being expressed in the discourse (Hyland and Tse 2004; Hyland 2005). Finally, there are a small number of adverbs – *just*, *fully*, *respectfully*, *entirely* and *gratefully* – which are regularly used to perform stance functions in both legal and non-legal discourse (Biber and Finegan 1989; Mortensen and Mortensen 2017; Finegan and Lee 2021).

In collocation with *I*, these categories and the verbs they comprise, at least part of the time, act as 'stance bundles' (Biber et al. 2004) employed by the advocates when making their oral arguments and by the judges when asking questions of the advocates. The five categories identified in the collocate lists are shared by both sets of speakers. In fact, 20 of the verbs are top collocates of *I* for both advocates and judges. However, their patterns of distribution and relative frequencies are quite different when the advocates and judges are compared (Figure 5.1). Judges have a clear preference for *I* + mental verb collocates, with these verbs collocating with almost half of all instances of *I* in the judge's data. In contrast, modal verbs are the most preferred by advocates, followed by verbs of speaking, and mental verbs account for a much smaller proportion of *I* instances than is the case of the judges. Meanwhile, adverbs are comparatively rare in both sets of data, and metadiscursive verbs are used only by advocates, somewhat unsurprisingly given that they are the parties submitting lengthy oral arguments which need markers of rhetorical organisation. The analysis below focuses on the stance-taking functions of the three most frequent collocate types: mental verbs, speaking verbs and modal verbs. The analysis will show the various ways in which speakers in court hearings express stance in ways that are inextricably linked to their distinctive roles in the dialogue and the broader parameters and expectations of courtroom procedures and expectations.

Modal verbs – I will

Modal verbs as collocates of *I* are far more prevalently used by advocates than by the judges in the hearings, and the most common modal verb

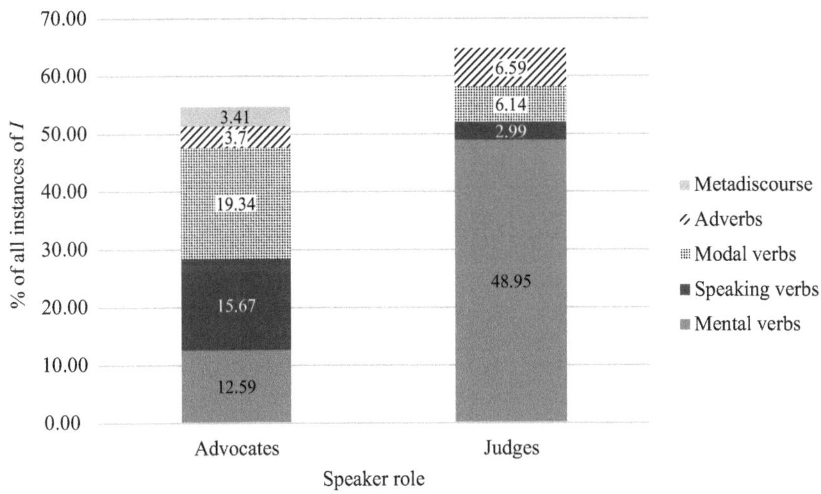

Figure 5.1 Distribution of different collocate types across advocates and judges.

collocate is *will* (Table 5.4). In terms of stance, predictive verbs have long been considered a marker of evidentiality or epistemic commitment, indicating different degrees of certainty (Biber and Finegan 1989: 98), with *will* indicating high certainty. As well as relating to assessments of likelihood, *will* serves the function of expressing speaker volition or intention (Biber et al. 2021: 483).

In the hearings, *I will* has a rhetorical, metadiscursive function for advocates as they use it predominantly to scaffold, signpost and navigate their oral argument. More specifically, advocates use *I will* to commit to doing or saying something later in their submission. A manual coding of concordance lines for *I will* by advocates across both hearings found that 141/206 (68.45%) instances of this collocation were used for this purpose. The most frequent R1 collocates of *I will* show precisely what the advocates are committing to do doing in their arguments: *address*, *come (back)*, *deal*, *develop*, *say*, *seek*, *show*, *submit* and *take*, a sample of concordances for which are shown in Figure 5.2.

Exploring a selection of these instances in more depth demonstrates the different ways in which *I will* is used by advocates in the unfolding of their oral submissions. One type of usage sees advocates using *I will* to foreshadow and signpost something that will come later in their submission:

1 <u>I will submit</u> that these reservations are fatal to reliance on the devolution legislation as giving rise to any necessary implication, or indeed any other indication that the Government cannot exercise its foreign affairs and treaty prerogative in the ordinary way. (Advocate General for Scotland, Supreme Court, 6 December 2016)
2 And then three consequential submissions are that consequently for a minister of the Crown to take a step that will make these rights

Table 5.4 *I* + R1 modal verb collocates in advocate and judge data

Advocates				*Judges*			
Collocate	*MI3*	*Freq*	*% of I*	*Collocate*	*MI3*	*Freq*	*% of I*
will	19.47	206	6.75	*would*	9.93	15	2.25
can	17.21	113	3.70	*can*	8.80	11	1.65
would	16.28	94	3.08	*should*	8.77	6	0.90
may	15.89	70	2.29	*will*	4.81	4	0.60
won't	13.73	16	0.52	*may*	4.61	3	0.45
should	12.98	30	0.98	*can't*	4.06	2	0.30
could	12.55	30	0.98				
can't	12.01	13	0.43				
need	11.41	18	0.59				
	Total	**590**	**19.34**		**Total**	**41**	**6.14**

ım ent, if it had left, for example, a – and	I will	come back to this point -- but if it had left, for
ion 2. From time to time exist. So again,	I will	come back to the point, but the direct answe
ıg sensible about the prerogative. Well,	I will	come back to it when we get to it but the ans
r the law or create a new source of law,	I will	come back to that, but -- and then say: and tl
s 25 we go along. Of course. Of course.	I will	deal with those -- I will do my best to answeı
hips with a copy of that case. My Lords,	I will	deal with that at the appropriate time in the
Bill and we don't need to worry about it,	I will	deal with that. My submission to your Lordsł
extremely difficult for them. For reasons	I will	develop, they have a great deal of difficulty e
um mary on that prim ary argum ent, and	I will	develop these steps if I may, but my subm is
cannot be given on a conditional basis.	I will	say something about that, if I have the time,
ıent – And the legislative consent What	I will	say, my Lord, is there is plenty of evidence, i
pieces of legislation relating to the EU.	I will	say it is entirely consistent with the United Ki
contrary in their skeleton argum ent. 17	I will	seek to deal with their argum ents in reply. Bı
gislative competence is strictly defined.	I will	show your Lordships how that legislative co
contrary to the Bill of 9 Rights 1688, and	I will	show you two authorities on that 10 proposi
ɔnt on an exercise of prerogative power.	I will	submit that Professor Finnis upon whose vi
petence of the devolved legislatures. 7	I will	submit that these reservations are fatal to 8
ɔr to Lord Pannick, there are in addition,	I will	submit, a number of features of the present
l expressed in the various acts to which	I will	take your Lordships, and preempting any de
So my Lords, at something of a canter,	I will	take your Lordships briefly, if I may, to the aı
ıis is clear from a variety of sources but	I will	take the court to two, if I may. The first is Pro
ned friend the Lord Advocate said: well,	I will	take any proposed bill in its narrowest terms

Figure 5.2 Sample concordance lines for *I will* in the advocates' data.

> unavailable without prior parliamentary authority dispenses with the law or the execution of the law and is contrary to the Bill of Rights 1688, and **I will show** you two authorities on that proposition. (Helen Mounfield, High Court, 13 October, 2016).

In judicial contexts, *submit* as seen in (1) refers to the introduction or presentation of an argument or evidence. When used in this way, *will* is being used as an engagement marker (Hyland 2005: 176), focusing the court's attention to particular points in the upcoming discourse. More precisely, *I will* is working as a kind of metadiscursive frame marker (Hyland and Tse 2004: 169), referring to discourse acts or stages still to come in the argument. In Hyland and Tse's (2004: 169) terms, we see *I will* being used as an interactive resource, helping to guide the judges through the argument, priming them to hear certain elements of the submission. In doing so, the advocates are indicating their stance towards these elements of the submission – namely that they consider them to be key aspects of their overall argument, worthy of signposting in this way. Meanwhile, in (2), Helen Mountfield commits to providing ' two authorities' to support her argument. That is, she not only harnesses the power of *will* to signal her intention to presenting a core component of her submission but also exploits its potential in terms of evidentiality, committing to indexing epistemic authority in support of that submission.

In places during the hearings, advocates signpost future points in their argument that are directed towards challenging the opposing side. In such cases, a point or submission made by the other side is accompanied by a commitment to offer a counterpoint in response. Some examples of this include

3 Fourthly, and finally by way of stages in answer to Lord Pannick, there are in addition, **I will submit**, a number of features of the present case and the present context which tend further against existing statutory rights operating as a restriction upon the prerogative to withdraw from these EU treaties. (James Eadie, High Court, 17 October 2016)
4 As far as Mr Pigney is concerned, first of all, the submissions of Ms Mountfield fell into two areas which **I will deal with** in turn: loss of EU citizenship rights and the additional impact of the devolution statutes on the argument. (Jason Coppell, High Court, 18 October 2016)

In these instances, not only is an intention stated to cover a particular element of the advocates' argument but that is framed as a direct challenge to the opposing argument. This brings into focus Du Bois's (2007) emphasis on stance being intersubjective; in the construction of their own stance, the advocates are explicitly inserting into the discourse the 'stance object' (Du Bois 2007: 147), namely the stance to which they are responding. This is a reminder that, in this context, stance-taking is enveloped in, and used to achieve, the main aim of (appellate) court discourse, which is to present the most persuasive argument. This is also observed throughout the hearings where *I will* is used by advocates in their responses to judges' questions. This has the effect of simultaneously deferring an immediate answer to the question and a commit to answering it at a later point:

5 LORD MANCE: How do you get this into the Northern Ireland Act?
MR SCOFFIELD: **I will come to that** in a moment, my Lord; two reasons, perhaps three reasons. (Supreme Court, 6 December 2016)

This commitment in response to judicial questioning serves two purposes. First, it aims to satisfy judges that answers to their questions are coming later in the submission. Second, and much more practical, is that it allows the advocate to negotiate judicial questioning while maintaining the structure and flow of the submission and argument. That is, the desire or need to cover particular elements of the argument at particular times is so strong is that judicial intervention can be temporarily resisted so that the precise order of points in the submission can be retained. A final point to be noted here is that the same approach is taken when advocates are not simply responding to judges but disagreeing with them:

6 THE LORD CHIEF JUSTICE: But that can always be re-enacted as part of UK law.

LORD PANNICK: Yes, but when I come to –

THE LORD CHIEF JUSTICE: It obviously can be, because there would be no reason why it couldn't do that, why Parliament can't do that.

LORD PANNICK: But I have given your Lordship, and **I will develop these arguments**, examples, we say, where Parliament couldn't re-enact. But in any event, I say with great respect, that is not the right question and it is not the right question because if the defendant is going to start a process by notification, which will remove fundamental rights from domestic law, it is nothing to the point, in my submission, and **I will develop this point**, it is nothing to the point that Parliament might be able to put them back. I say that the defendant simply has no power to take them away. (High Court, 13 October 2016)

Here, in an exchange with the Lord Chief Justice, Lord Pannick uses *I will develop* twice in quick succession. In doing so, Pannick is going beyond a straightforward disagreement with the judge and is committing to developing the argument against the point being put to him later in his submission. In turn, this allows him to continue to submit his argument, delay responding to the judge's question and at the same time play a face-saving role insofar as reassuring the judge that an answer is forthcoming and that he is not disregarding the question altogether.

Studies of stance in courtroom discourse have not yet considered the role of *will* as a marker of epistemic commitment by counsel submitting arguments. The examples here show that it is used primarily for rhetorical purposes, particularly managing the overall structure of the submission. At the same time, it can be used to foreshadow particularly pertinent elements of the argument, to direct counter-arguments to the opposing side, to defer answers to judicial questions and to support disagreements with judges. In each of these uses, advocates are marking their stance towards the propositional content of their talk (i.e. the importance of their points) and the talk of others (be that opposing counsel or judges). Ultimately, and in all cases, advocates are sharing their knowledge of what is to come in the oral argument and committing to saying certain things at a future point in the dialogue.

Mental verbs – I think

Mental verbs are very common as R1 collocates of *I* and, unlike modal verbs, are used frequently by advocates *and* judges (Table 5.5). Mental verbs account for a much larger proportion of *I* instances for judges than they do for advocates, perhaps reflecting the different linguistic rights in court. In particular, this may be accounted for by the prohibition of advocates expressing their personal opinions in court, a rule that is less stringently applied to judges. Mental verbs (sometimes referred to as 'cognitive' verbs) are well established in the literature as being means by which to signal opinion and express degrees of epistemic certainty (Aijmer 1997; Myers 2010a: 101; Kaltenböck 2010; Fetzer 2014: 74). Following previous research of mental verbs in the courtroom (Szczyrbak 2013, 2019b, 2020), *think* is by far the most common mental verb for both sets of speakers and so this analysis will focus on this verb. It will start with the advocates' use of *I think* before moving on to compare their use with that of the judges.

In a courtroom context, *I think* can be used as a hedge, marking a speaker's non-commitment and lack of certainty, by both those asking questions (Szczyrbak 2019b: 78) and those answering them (Mortensen and Mortensen 2017: 422; Szczyrbak 2020: 127). In court hearings where the main aim of advocates is to be persuasive, it is unsurprising that *I think* is rarely used to indicate a lack of certainty in the propositional content of what is being said. On rare occasions, it is used to mark uncertainty about the availability of documents to the court and when referring particular parts of that material:

7 The EEA regulations, which I hope were attached to my speaking notes, if they weren't we can ensure copies, but **I think** they were. (Majit Gill, High Court, 18 October 2016)

8 **I think** it is paragraph 12. I will just check that. Paragraph 12 we quote in the annex. (James Eadie, Supreme Court, 5 December 2016)

Far more common in the hearings is the use of *I think* by advocates not to mark a lack of certainty, but to display a certain stance orientation to what they are saying and to frame an upcoming opinion sequence (cf. Kärkkäinen 2003: 115; Szczyrbak 2020: 128). One area in particular where advocates use *I think* to mark their stance is where they are presenting points that they consider to be uncontroversial or agreed-upon:

9 So these are, and I don't want to provide too much of a categoric hierarchy but **I think** one can see if you have a change to the forestry or agricultural provisions of schedule 7, that is no doubt an important change in many instances, but it is not seismic, but what is seismic is taking out the EU component. (Richard Gordon, Supreme Court, 8 December 2016).

10 Your Lordships and your Ladyship will be well aware that there was in 1972 a debate, which we hear much less of nowadays, as to whether

Table 5.5 *I* + R1 mental verb collocates in advocate and judge data

Advocates				*Judges*			
Collocate	*MI3*	*Freq*	*% of I*	*Collocate*	*MI3*	*Freq*	*% of I*
think	20.46	154	5.05	think	19.84	131	19.61
hope	17.54	52	1.70	understand	16.20	43	6.44
want	16.13	48	1.57	thought	14.48	22	3.29
wanted	13.93	21	0.69	suppose	14.09	18	2.69
understand	13.87	22	0.72	mean	14.02	22	3.29
believe	13.30	13	0.43	see	13.42	21	3.14
mean	12.83	17	0.56	know	10.86	12	1.80
know	11.59	18	0.59	understood	10.83	7	1.05
suppose	10.99	7	0.23	wonder	10.75	5	0.75
wish	10.94	11	0.36	follow	10.71	8	1.20
agree	10.29	10	0.33	assume	10.05	6	0.90
suspect	10.05	4	0.13	wanted	9.54	6	0.90
adopt	9.66	7	0.23	appreciate	9.49	5	0.75
				remember	7.10	2	0.30
				wondered	6.78	2	0.30
				right	5.96	5	0.75
				want	4.95	3	0.45
				agree	4.86	2	0.30
				take	3.27	2	0.30
	Total	**384**	**12.59**		**Total**	**327**	**48.95**

> Parliament itself could have revoked the 1972 Act. **I think** we all now accept that, of course, Parliament, by reason of parliamentary sovereignty, can do what it likes, but the idea that ministers could revoke this fundamental change to our constitutional order, in my submission, is inherently unlikely. (Lord Pannick, Supreme Court, 6 December 2016)

Here, the advocates are signalling points that they are making which they assume to be taken-for-granted and obvious to the court. They are taking the liberty to assume what the judges (and opposing counsel) *see* and *accept*. In this way, *I think* is used as a device for efficiently dealing with unproblematic elements of their talk, explicitly marking to their audience that they do not consider these points to be reasonably contestable. Of course, the assumption that something is obvious is itself an expression of opinion by the advocate, albeit indirectly. However, the advocates here are simultaneously relying on the hedging quality of *I think* to soften an assertion which may otherwise be too blunt (Aijmer 1997: 22). In other words, one function of *I think* when used in the courtroom may be to camouflage opinions in such a way that allows advocates to smuggle in their standpoint while remaining safe from sanction by the court.

There is similar use of *I think* in which advocates increase the epistemic distance from their utterance and imbue their talk with a level of tentativeness when they are negotiating potentially troublesome elements of the interaction. One such context is in cases where advocates are offering their interpretation of a point that is being put against them. Note the extended length of the extract here, necessary to capture the relevant preceding talk:

11 LORD MANCE: Is there a slight curiosity here, in that when we signed up to the EEC [European Economic Community], we recognised that there were two types of legislative process, one rather less imperative than the other; that is the process of EU or EC [European Commission] legislation by directives, which, as my Lady pointed out, has led to a large body of law in this country which you accept will remain effective after withdrawal. And yet the directly effective rights under the treaties and non-discrimination and all the regulations which are directly effective, are conditional, you say, on membership. So that one body of legislation under the treaty is not conditional, but another body is conditional; is there an oddity there?

MR EADIE: True that it is, but, as it were, that is because of the way in which the directive side of things is transposed, but what will go when we go is the obligation to comply with the directives.

LORD SUMPTION: That will, I suppose, effect a legal alteration, even to the extent that rules have been transposed. The alteration will be that whereas before they were entrenched by the fact that they could not validly be amended or repealed without – inconsistently with the treaties.

MR EADIE: Now they can be.

LORD SUMPTION: That will change, they now can be so they will be less secure rights.

MR EADIE: That is true, my Lord. We don't quibble with that. That is another consequence. **I think** the point my Lord, Lord Mance was putting to me is doesn't it all feel a bit adventitious, because you have one body of rights which are already domestically implemented in that way and will stay, as it were. But the key point is that when we go, the obligation to continue to comply, to continue to achieve as a result will also go. (Supreme Court, 6 December 2016)

In this example, *I think* is doing a great deal of discursive work, as we see James Eadie using it to preface a paraphrase of Lord Mance's question a few turns earlier. Eadie responded to this question directly when it was first asked, but after partially agreeing, he challenged Lord Mance's point, indicated by *true that it is*, **but**. At this point, it would seem that this point had been dealt with. However, following Lord Sumption's intervention,

Eadie again reinserts and indirectly quotes Lord Mance in his response, again challenging his point with a *but*-prefaced clause. The motivation, it seems, for brining Lord Mance's point back to the fore is to emphasise to Lord Sumption that his question relates to something different (and uncontested) to the matter currently at hand in the talk. Using *I think* in this way to (re)visit a question asked earlier in a stretch of talk has been identified by Kärkkäinen (2003: 126) as a way to mark a transition in the discourse, with *I think* acting as 'a point from which the final answer is formulated'. This function seems to be in action here, as Eadie quickly resolves Lord Sumption's immediate question and then returns to Lord Mance's, reiterating his response and thus guiding the flow of the argument back on track. In this way, then, *I think* serves a discourse-organisational function, reorienting the talk towards the progression of the advocate's argument. However, there is a more pragmatic role being played by *I think* in Eadie's answer. It allows him not only to paraphrase Lord Mance's question but to 'reformulate' it, before proceeding to address the new version of the question. Reformulation of this kind is well established as a tool of narrative transformation in court, as speakers 'summarize or gloss the gist of a previous discourse by changing the lexical items, but by maintaining some degree of semantic equivalence' (Cavalieri 2009: 210). Usually reserved for use by lawyers when questioning witnesses, reformulations allow the lawyer to substitute the witness in the role of storyteller and produce a self-serving version of the story and making the witness agree with it (Cavalieri 2009: 211). Such reformulation is demonstrated in (11) by the fact that the point is paraphrased by the advocate immediately after *I think*. The ability to paraphrase an argument or point being made (in this case, by a judge) is a powerful rhetorical tool insofar as it allows the speaker to control the discourse and identify the elements of that argument that they can (or want to) address. At the same time, the hedging effect of *I think* serves as 'protective envelope' (Szczyrbak 2020: 128) which decreases the advocate's commitment to this reiteration of the point. Given the power dynamics in court as well as the professional standards that advocates are expected to display, they do not want to be perceived by the court as wilfully misrepresenting the words of a judge. Therefore, the use of *I think* allows them to avoid this charge and present their version of another's words under the veil of indirectness and tentativeness.

Kärkkäinen (2003: 130–5) shows how, in everyday interactions, *I think* is used by speakers in second pair parts to introduce a slightly new or different slant in an answer and to preface a disaligning opinion sequence. Both of these functions are observed in use by the advocates:

12 LORD MANCE: [...] But **I thought** that your case was a separate case, namely to say that even if the 1972 Act didn't – will allow the

use of the prerogative in the way that Mr Eadie submits, nonetheless the devolution legislation makes it impossible; that is also part of your case, is it?

MR GORDON: It is part of it, but **I think** the most important part of it is this: that the Advocate General for Scotland seeks to knock out our case by saying, if Mr Eadie is right on the construction of the 1972 Act, the dominoes fall and we must lose. (Supreme Court, 8 December 2016)

13 LORD JUSTICE SALES: If the royal prerogative in its material respect has been abrogated by the 1972 Act, I hadn't understood that it was the Crown's argument that it was somehow restored by the 2008 Act.

MR EADIE: Well, **I think** the Crown's argument is that it wasn't abrogated by either. (High Court, 17 October 2016)

In these examples, the advocates make use of *I think* to conduct some redressive action on a point put to them by the judges. While in (12) Richard Gordon uses it to refocus Lord Mance's attention to what he considers to the 'most important part' of the argument being discussed, in (13) James Eadie uses it to correct an apparent misunderstanding in Lord Justice Sales' previous turn. Both of these are potentially problematic and difficult efforts to undertake by the advocates, as they are essentially a form of disagreement with a more powerful participant in this context. In such cases, one interpretation of the use of *I think* is as a face-saving device (Szczyrbak 2020: 130) weakening the bluntness of the reply and mitigating any potential face-threat perceived by the judge. However, Fetzer (2014: 80) discusses the clusters *but I think* and *well I think* in political talk and proposes that, in such configurations, *I think* has the effect of 'boosting' the force of second argument. In this case, the second argument is the corrective action undertaken by Gordon and Eadie. In any case, whether *I think* is used as a face-saving mitigation device or an argumentative booster (or indeed a deliberately vague combination of the two), it serves an important rhetorical function for advocates as they navigate interaction with judges.

Example (12) is noteworthy for not only Richard Gordon's use of *I think* but also Lord Mance's use of the past tense form *I thought*. The picture that emerges from the Brexit hearing data is that, like advocates, judges use *I think* for a range of interactional purposes. In fact, they use it more frequently than advocates. Staying with *I thought* for now, the judges use *I thought* to signal the status of their knowledge regarding a particular point at hand, such as in (12) above and here:

14 THE LORD CHIEF JUSTICE: What you are saying is that in paragraph 1 of Article 50, is where it says 'any member state may decide to

withdraw from the Union, in accordance with its own constitutional arrangements', you can't say; well, the executive can give notice, but Parliament has to approve the terms. It can't give that sort of notice.

LORD PANNICK: That is my case. My case is –

THE LORD CHIEF JUSTICE: No, **I thought** it was your case. But it is a matter of some importance.

LORD PANNICK: It is of vital importance. It is of vital importance to our case that the agreement or otherwise of Parliament is irrelevant. It is simply irrelevant. (High Court, 13 October 2016)

In the same way as *I think*, *I thought* is a clear marker of epistemic (un) certainty and is the third most common cognitive verb collocate of *I* for judges while not appearing in the advocates' data at all. The presupposition underlying the judges' use of *I thought* in this context is that the advocate will solve this uncertainty. Therefore, not only is it a marker of epistemic stance, it is also an (indirect) indication to the advocate that they need to do more to provide clarity. As is seen in both (12) and (14), this clarification does come from both Richard Gordon and Lord Pannick. The product of these exchanges is that the argument is *co-constructed* by the advocates and the judges, with the latter's probing of the argument being put them resulting in accepted and agreed-upon points. *I thought* is also used by the judges in a similar, albeit more combative way, when uncertainty is targeted towards something specific the advocate has said:

15 THE LORD ADVOCATE: It is perhaps not an entirely incidental point that when the United Kingdom was founded in 1707, it was to Parliament and not to the Crown that the power to change the laws in use in Scotland was given. That is Article 18 of the Act of –

LORD HODGE: Exclusively given?

THE LORD ADVOCATE: Well, the power was given in terms of the Acts of Union.

LORD HODGE: **I thought** you said only by the British Parliament.

THE LORD ADVOCATE: It certainly was not given to the Crown. (Supreme Court, 07 December 2016)

16 LORD PANNICK: If I am unable to persuade your Lordships of two things, first that the relevant legal principle is essentially that stated by Lord Oliver, and that its application in the circumstances of this case is in my favour, because the notification does remove statutory rights, if I can't persuade your Lordships of both of those elements, we lose.

LORD JUSTICE SALES: **I thought** you were maintaining an alternative submission that even if it is not a common law limitation, there is implied abrogation of the prerogative power.

LORD PANNICK: Yes, your Lordship is absolutely right. (High Court, 13 October 2016)

Both of these examples see the judges expressing uncertainty over something that the advocates have previously said. The combination of *I thought* with verbs of speaking in declarative question turns such as these serves as 'confirmation-seeking questions and they suggest the preferred response drawing on earlier testimony' (Szczyrbak 2020: 129). Here, we see the nature of interaction between judge and advocate mirroring that of lawyer and witnesses during cross-examination in the criminal courtroom where confirmation-seeking questions of this kind are common and very powerful tools of discursive control which lawyers use to restrict the possible answers that witnesses can give, namely 'yes' answers. Indeed, these questions have this very effect in both (15) and (16), where the Lord Advocate is forced to soften his claim and Lord Pannick concedes and agrees with Lord Justice Sales. Therefore, in the same way that has been well documented in cross-examination, the relative roles and status of speakers in the High Court and Supreme Court underlie the communicative rights and obligations of those speakers.

Returning to the present form *I think*, this verb accounts for as much as 19.61% of judges' *I* instances, compared with only 5.05% for advocates, meaning that *I think* is far more characteristic of judicial talk than it is of advocates' talk. Like *I thought*, the present form is also used by judges to place an imposition on advocates to provide additional detail or clarification:

17 **I think**, at some stage, I want to understand what is the scope of the executive's power under Article 50. But come to it when you want to. And whether there is a difference between the giving of the notice and the conclusion of the agreement, and whether the conclusion of the agreement has to be expressly authorised by Parliament. **I think** we need clarity. **I think** that has to be clarified, because the construction, you know, the approach to Article 50 must depend on what the Crown is entitled to do. (Lord Chief Justice, High Court, 17 October 2016)

The Lord Chief Justice uses *I think* three times in quick succession in this extract to repeatedly make the point to the advocate (in this case, James Eadie) that they must clarify an important point. In this case, *I think* appears to be primarily serving its politeness function, somewhat mitigating the imposition. This is supported by other face-saving strategies employed by the judge. Notably, the Lord Chief Justice does not directly mention Eadie, preferring instead to focus on himself (*I want to understand*), the court collectively (*we need clarity*) and use the passive voice (*that has to be clarified*). This shows that even in this rigidly hierarchical speech situation, there are still face-saving displays of courtesy from the judiciary to the advocates, mandated by the professional standards of the court. The Lord Chief Justice's use of *I think* can be contrasted with Lady Hale's in the Supreme Court:

18 LADY HALE: Do you also say that 'with regard to' means something different from 'relate to'?

THE LORD ADVOCATE: It is certainly a different phrase, my Lady, and I did make the point yesterday that this phrase doesn't use the language used elsewhere in the Act; it points back to the language used in the – originally in the memorandum of understanding, and which I say in turn is explicated by the practice which I have set out in my –

LADY HALE: You have to say it means something different from 'relate to', **I think**, don't you? Because this court has given 'relate to' – when considering whether the Scottish Parliament has acted within its powers, it has given 'relate to' a very specific meaning. You have to say it means something different. (Supreme Court, 8 December 2016)

Despite its typically epistemic designation and its ability to mark tentativeness as in (17), *I think* can also be used to express authoritativeness and conviction (Brinton 2008: 219). So-called 'deliberative' *I think* signals 'careful deliberation, objectivity and so, perhaps, authority' (Preisler 1986: 107) and this deliberative function, often appearing in medial or final position as is the case here, 'seems to be an effect of the speaker's planning' and 'adds weight to the assertions being made' (Aijmer 1997: 22–24). Therefore, while from the perspective of politeness Lady Hale's use of *I think* may be softening the blunt assertion made directly before it, there is also an interpretation that its placement here is not so much concerned with mitigating a face-threat as it is with explicating and emphasising her thought process as the authoritative party in this exchange. This interpretation would seem to be supported by other elements of the turn, namely the restrictive confirmation-seeking tag question and the unmitigated repetition of the assertion at the end of the turn. The interpretation of *I think* being used by judges as a marker of authority is not entirely independent of its more typical epistemic function insofar as it expresses knowledge. Indeed, as is observed in (19) and (20), the judges' legal and case knowledge is a source of authority:

19 THE LORD CHIEF JUSTICE: If you are right about the Referendum Act, the 2015 Act, ie that that hasn't somehow conferred authority on government, and **I think** it is more an authority argument rather than

anything else, probably; your argument logically follows that if there is no authority from that, Parliament has to take the decision. It is no part of your case to say: well, Parliament, you know, can decide in any particular way. It is just it goes to Parliament for Parliament to deal with.
LORD PANNICK: Yes. (High Court, 18 October 2016)

20 LORD JUSTICE SALES: I am not sure this helps us very much, because **I think** the passage that you are particularly focusing on is the concession.
LORD PANNICK: Yes. (High Court, 13 October 2016)

In both of these examples from the High Court, the judges are robustly challenging the submission of Lord Pannick and are doing so in such a way that relies on their knowledge of the nature of legal argument (in 19) and their knowledge of a passage being discussed (in 20). *I think* is used to engage this knowledge in marking their stance towards Lord Pannick's submission and prefaces their assessment and evaluative opinion of what is being argued. Given the superior status of the judges in this interaction, and their professional expertise and experience, the expression of this knowledge is imbued with a quality of authority which, in this context, is difficult for Lord Pannick to challenge. Indeed, in both of these examples, he agrees with the judges.

The final analysis of *I think* as used by the judges relates closely to something observed above in the advocates data, namely to reformulate a point being put to them:

21 THE LORD CHIEF JUSTICE: **I think** what you are saying is, essentially, if legislation is needed, that then confers a mandate to use agency and then it is absolutely up to Parliament, not a matter for us, the terms of the mandate.
LORD PANNICK: Yes. (High Court, 13 October 2016)

It was argued above that when advocates use *I think* in offering their interpretation of a question being put to them, they do so to produce a preferred version of another's words that they can then address and answer. We see something similar here from the Lord Chief Justice as he paraphrases (indicated by the adverb *essentially*) and reformulates the point that Lord Pannick is making. Summary, repetition and reformulation such as demonstrated here not only are found in witness examination but also have been identified as a discursive strategy used in police interviews, whereby interviewing officers select the most institutionally important elements of the suspect's talk and thus produce a transformed, agreed-upon and 'fixed' version of the evidence (Kozin 2008; Johnson 2015, 2020; May et al. 2021). The same effect is at work in (21), where the Lord Chief Justice summarises and reformulates Lord Pannick's point – a summary and reformulation which Pannick accepts – and thus this version is settled on as the submission being made and is carried forward through the proceedings. Such attempts at a judge's reformulation in seeking an established and fixed version of the submission are not always as successful, however:

22 LORD SUMPTION: But we cannot decide, **I think** you accept, that any of the issues before us, on the assumption that by the time that the withdrawal actually occurs, the European Communities Act would have been repealed or significantly modified; that may well be a practical possibility, but it is not something that we can assume in point of law.

MR EADIE: You cannot assume that, because it may not happen, apart from anything else.

LORD CARNWATH: But we cannot assume that it will not happen. For my part I am not – having seen (Inaudible) for myself, I am not accepting the suggestion that it is completely irrelevant.

MR EADIE: And I am not accepting that and I am not sure –

LORD CARNWATH: **I think** he probably was.

MR EADIE: If that was the impression given, I am not. But it is – I am perfectly content –

LORD SUMPTION: You seem to have given two diametrically opposed answers in the last five minutes to the same question, but we will obviously have to work out which answer we accept.

LORD CARNWATH: We will have the transcript. (Supreme Court, 6 December 2016)

In the first instance, Lord Sumption uses *I think* in an attempt to summarise and fix a version of James Eadie's submission that he 'accepts'. However, rather than confirming this, Eadie challenges the assertion made by the judge and disagrees with his reformulation. In turn, Lord Carnwath also attempts to establish Eadie's acceptance, in a hedged and indirect way (*I think* he probably *was*). Following this, Eadie continues to insist that he is not accepting the point and creates for the judges some excuse for thinking that he does (*if that was the impression given*). The result of Eadie's disagreement with the judges is Lord Sumption pointing out Eadie's seemingly contradictory answers, emphasising that it is 'obvious' that an agreed version of the submission needs to be established before the interaction can continue along its original course. Indeed, the discussion on this point continues for a further fifty lines in the transcript, before the President of the

Supreme Court tells Eadie: 'we had better let you proceed with your argument as you had planned to'. The important point here is that if the advocates do not accept or agree with the reformulated version of their submission offered by the judges, then this can be damaging for them, not only in terms of perceptions of their credibility and consistency to the court but also in more practical terms, such as the time lost and deviations away from their argument in order to rectify the apparent misunderstanding.

This analysis has identified advocates and judges exploiting the full range of stance-marking potential offered by *I think*. It has been argued that, rather than predominantly being used to mark uncertainty, *I think* instead fulfils a range of more nuanced stance-related rhetorical and interactional purposes. For advocates, *I think* offers a means by which to smuggle their personal evaluations of the issues at hand into a context in which the explicit expression of such opinion is prohibited. It has also been shown that advocates use *I think* to reformulate judges' questions and remain in control of their submissions as well as allowing advocates to soften assertions and operate in a face-saving way. For judges, *I thought* is a main way in which they challenge or probe an advocate's submission, whereas *I think* is used as a tool to mark authority and 'fix' a reformulated version of advocates' arguments into the fabric of the discourse – a right reserved for the more institutionally powerful speakers.

Speaking verbs – I say

The role of speaking verbs (often alternatively referred to as 'reporting verbs' or 'communication verbs') in court has been the focus of a good deal of attention. In particular, the reporting or quoting the words of others in the courtroom has been found to be an effective means by which lawyers cast doubt on the testimony of witnesses, embed police interviews into courtroom interaction, demonstrate the defendant's criminal liability and re-contextualize historical speech that can damage a witness (Matoesian 2000; Johnson 2013; May et al. 2021: 26). Similarly, in terms of speaking verbs as stance-markers, analysis of *you*-oriented reported speech has found lawyers disaligning and challenging the opposing party's standpoints and initiating disagreements, such as through 'are you saying', 'is that what you are telling us' and 'did you say?' questions (Szczyrbak 2016, 2018). In the same way, verbs of speaking are a frequent resource drawn on by legal participants in the Brexit hearings (Table 5.6). Three things are obvious in Table 5.6. First is that we are not dealing with the advocates reporting the speech of *others*; these are all R1 collocates of *I*, indicating that the advocates are reporting *their own* speech. Second is that advocates are far more frequent users of speaking verbs than are judges, for whom these verbs rarely occur. Third, *say* is by far the most frequent verb,

Table 5.6 I + R1 speaking verb collocates in advocate and judge data

Advocates				*Judges*			
Collocate	*MI3*	*Freq*	*% of I*	*Collocate*	*MI3*	*Freq*	*% of I*
say	20.21	227	7.44	*ask*	10.55	10	1.50
invite	15.59	37	1.21	*beg*	9.78	4	0.60
accept	14.66	34	1.11	*put*	5.11	3	0.45
apologise	13.05	11	0.36	*said*	4.65	3	0.45
emphasise	12.99	14	0.46				
quote	12.75	14	0.46				
make	12.68	30	0.98				
said	11.57	22	0.72				
submit	10.98	21	0.69				
rely	10.97	11	0.36				
made	10.42	17	0.56				
ask	10.38	11	0.36				
gave	10.37	8	0.26				
identify	10.33	7	0.23				
put	9.76	14	0.46				
	Total	**478**	**15.67**		**Total**	**20**	**2.99**

accounting for almost half of all of the speaking verbs (227/478 = 47.49%). Therefore, this analysis will focus on *I say* as used by the advocates.

I-oriented speaking verbs have been analysed in the literature as markers of stance in court. Modalised 'I would say', 'I have to say' and the polite form 'if I may say so' have all been observed in courtroom talk, and 'what I said' is used as a discourse-structuring device and to return to previous testimony (Szczyrbak 2016). Meanwhile, the present progressive 'I am (not) saying' has been identified as a useful means by which speakers in court can position themselves and others and negotiate respective viewpoints, with 'what I am saying' fulfilling an emphatic function (Szczyrbak 2018). Chaemsaithong (2017: 115) has also observed that lawyers use reporting verbs with first-person pronouns, such as 'I will paraphrase' and 'I quote' for evidential purposes, supporting their statements with external sources. However, the prevalence of *I say* in the advocates data here is somewhat of an anomaly against the backdrop of this literature. What makes this verb all the more interesting is the peculiarity of its use; it is generally used by advocates to preface an argument, point or submission that they are making:

23 <u>I say</u> that the correct approach to answering that question is not to ignore the entire legislative scheme and come at it on the basis that there is an a priori constitutional principle in play. (James Eadie, Supreme Court, 8 December 2016)

24 <u>I say</u> a child of six could understand this point, because if you tell a child it cannot go out and play in the garden but it can play in the

house, it has no power, the analogue, to going out in the garden. (Richard Gordon, Supreme Court, 8 December 2016)

25 It is significant, I say, that the words 'from time to time' come under the rights et cetera which flow from the treaties and not the treaties; it is the rights from time to time, not the treaties from time to time. (Helen Mountfield, Supreme Court, 8 December 2016)

The advocates are making explicit the act of saying. They could say all of these things without the inclusion of this explicit signal and retain the original meaning. Therefore, it can be inferred that *I say* in this context has a stance-marking role, operating as an epistemic parenthetical comment clause similar in structure and function to *I think*. Structurally, it shares a number of features with *I think* (see Kärkkäinen 2003; Kaltenböck 2013). As we can see in (23)–(25), it can occur in initial and medial position, with or without the *that*- complementizer (46/227 instances occur with *that* = 20.26%) and has scope over clausal host constructions. In addition, as we will see, *I say* occurs in longer clusters that are often associated with *I think*. Functionally, *I say* displays the speaker's stance towards the content of the proposition within its scope. Indeed, in every example above, *I say* could be replaced with *I think* and the meaning of the submission would remain the same.

The analysis of *(I) say* as a comment clause in and of itself is not a new idea. After commenting that 'it comes as no surprise that verbs of communication can function parenthetically as comment clauses, comparable to the functioning of mental verbs as "epistemic parentheticals"', Brinton (2008: 73–78) identifies six different functions of *(I) say* in present-day English. However, none of these functions matches the stance-marking role we see in the advocates' talk. The reporting of one's own speech has been interpreted as a means by which to index stance, but primarily in relation to epistemic authority (Clift 2006). However, *I say* is being used here to express evaluative or perhaps even affective stance insofar as it introduces the advocates' opinion. As has been emphasized throughout this chapter, advocates are prohibited from expressing their personal opinion in court. This accounts for why the advocates would use *I say* to fulfil the role of what, in almost every other interactional context, would be played by *I think*. This is where a key distinction between *I say* and *I think* (and between speaking and mental verbs generally) is operationalized by advocates. Whereas mental verbs depict the 'internal reality' still in the private domain, verbs of speaking refer to the same reality made public (i.e. externally manifested) (Shinzato 2004: 862). This point is reiterated by Fetzer (2008: 387), who emphasises that 'cognitive verbs indicate that subjectively qualified information is made explicit' and that *I think* reflects 'the speaker's subjective domain, assigning it the status of personal opinion' whereas *I say* 'extends the validity of the proposition to the public domain'. Szczyrbak (2019b: 85) notes the difference between courtroom participants whose responses to questions are characterised by mental verbs and those who prefer communication verbs. The former, it is argued, foreground their own mental operations (e.g. 'I think/thought/believe'), whereas the latter prefer external domains of reference and thus avoid references to their inner thoughts and feelings. Therefore, in using *I say* on occasions such as those above, advocates adhere to the rules of engagement by backgrounding their subjective opinions in a way that *I think* would foreground. Of course, one can *say* something without necessarily *thinking* it or believing it to be true. Therefore, *I say* may be considered a quasi-stance-marker. The court has some indication as to the advocates' basic stance towards the arguments they are submitting by virtue of the fact that they are submitting them at all. However, by introducing these arguments with *I say* rather than *I think*, the advocates' personal opinions remain implicit and obscured.

Carrying forward an understanding of the stance-marking function of *I say*, a number of the most frequently occurring clusters in which occurs can be examined, and a sample of this is shown in Figure 5.3.

f the United Kingdom under Article 50, and	I say	that it is of the nature of conventions that tr
l obtained. I say that if that were the law, and	I say	it is not the law for other reasons, then that
ɔnal procedures of the European Union; and	I say	that the hypothetical bill withdrawing us fror
e plain that the convention is engaged, and	I say	that it cannot matter as a matter of substai
thing to do with this case, in particular, and	I say	it very respectfully, but in particular the Refi
are currently conferred via the 1972 Act. As	I say,	the basic point that we make at this stage
ɔligations or renegotiate the agreement. As	I say,	the broader point that I make, and it is a li
liament. Yes. Yes. The general principle as	I say	in our dualist system requires the interven
e courts into the political arena. My Lord, as	I say,	I have accepted that it is part of the court's
y around those; the problem with those, as	I say,	is that you come back to that being precis
nmon law, the prerogative can be used, as	I say,	without any recourse to Parliament, to driv
d and convention rights are concerned? As	I say,	your Lordship points correctly to the defini
There was the 1975 Referendum Act but as	I say,	the wording is materially identical to the 2
consequentially authorising the notice. But	I say	that within that proposition are a whole sei
ole of the United Kingdom Parliament, but,	I say,	of all the representative legislatives of the
vith CRAG, if I may. It will be 17 a treaty, but	I say	likely to fall within the procedures 18 withir
skeleton argument in a footnote. But what	I say	is that the European Communities Act say
ce. I will elaborate on that and explain what	I say	the position is. But, ultimately, I say that the
do with the Northern Irish assembly. What	I say	is that if a bill were presented to the UK Pa
ue it or consider that it confers rights. What	I say	is that all those cases are entirely consist
hat. I have set out in my case in detail what	I say	is the practice in relation to the scope and
ne Crown. I say that is consistent with what	I say	is the limiting rule of constitutional law, tha
in charge in this area Indeed, that is what	I say.	Parliament as the source? Indeed. I am

Figure 5.3 Sample concordance lines for *I say* in the advocates' data.

The sample here shows four recurring patterns in which *I say* appears, which combined account for almost one third of all *I say* instances in the data of the advocates (73/227 = 32.16%): *and I say*, *as I say*, *but I say* and *what I say*. *I say* is preceded by the coordinating conjunctions *and* and *but* a total of 38 times. For example:

26 **I say** that I can sustain my argument simply on the basis that Parliament, in 1972, has conferred statutory rights and it has also done so in other legislation, which I will show your Lordships. **And I say** that the effect of notification is to defeat those statutory rights. **And I say** it is sufficient for my purposes that the defendant cannot use prerogative powers so as to defeat rights which have been conferred by Parliament. (Lord Pannick, 13 October 2016)

27 LORD MANCE: Now, that might lead to a breach at the international level and trouble with the Commission and others but that is the –

LORD PANNICK: I recognise the limits of the submission, **but I say** it is at least consistent with my submission that Parliament regards itself as in charge in this area. (Supreme Court, 6 December 2016)

The co-occurrence of *I say* with *and* corresponds with what Fetzer (2008, 2014) found to be a salient discourse pattern with *I think* in political talk. Her interpretation of *and I think* can be mapped onto *and I say* in this data. That is, *and I say* has the function of connecting two arguments, and the second strengthens the first and thus *and I say* acts as a booster, intensifying the speaker's epistemic certainty and commitment towards the validity of their claim (Fetzer 2014: 80). In (26), *and I say* immediately follows a previous, unprefaced *I say*-initial claim. This supports the interpretation of *I say* serving a function of strengthening and intensifying the argument being put by Pannick. It might be argued in these cases that *I say* carries a stronger stance-marking force than *I think*; in this exchange, Lord Pannick is 'epistemically robust' (Clift 2006: 572) in what he is saying, with no markers of uncertainty or mitigation that undermine the authority with which he is making his submission. Less common, though still present, is the cluster *but I say* (e.g. in 27). This pattern was also identified in *but I think* by Fetzer (2014: 80), who notes that the presence of *but* indicates that the second argument is going to differ or contrast in some way from the first. This is the case here with *but I say*, in which Lord Pannick simultaneously performs two actions. On the one hand, *but I think* rectifies or lessens the impact of the concession that he makes immediately prior in which he acknowledges a weakness in his submission. Here, *but I say* is used to indicate that this weakness is not fatal to his argument. On the other hand, *but I say* also counters a challenge made by Lord Mance, demonstrating the utility of this cluster in negotiating discursive conflict between advocate and judge.

Finally, attention shifts to two additional patterns, *as I say* (n = 27) and *what I say* (n = 13), in which *I say* appears to retain stance-marking function but also has a quoting function, with advocates referring (back) to something they have previously said. Whereas it is clear that *as I say* indicates a repetition of prior speech, that is less clear with *what I say* (at least less clear than it would be in the past tense *what I said*). Nevertheless, in terms of stance, both of these clusters emphasise the importance of the point being made while marking continuity of standpoint (cf. Szczyrbak 2016: 155, 161):

28 It is possible. Again, one can't exclude it. That is why I chose the wording so carefully, because that theoretical possibility exists. **As I say**, the government's view at the moment is it is very likely that any such agreement would be subject to ratification, and therefore fall within the provisions of this Act. (James Eadie, High Court, 18 October 2016).

29 […] but I do say it is significant that what these judges assumed was consistent with **what I say** was the orthodox position; I do say it is significant that are no dicta to the contrary. (Helen Mountfield, Supreme Court, 8 December 2016)

The interpretation of *I say* as a stance-marking feature, and more specifically one that effectively plays the role of *I think*, is not one that has been suggested before, at least in the context of courtroom interaction. It would appear as though *I say* signalling the speaker's orientation towards the content of what they are saying is a product of the unique contextual demands of the (appeal) court, where advocates are expected to robustly and persuasively submit their arguments while refraining from making explicit expressions of personal opinion. In such a context, *I say* offers advocates a useful alternative to *I think*. Adopting that view allows for the interpretation of longer clusters, such as *and/but I say* and *as I say*, as behaving like their *I think* counterparts, as boosting, emphasising and marking consistency of stance.

Conclusion

The courtroom is a stance-rich environment. This is particularly true in England and Wales and other adversarial systems in which two 'sides' discursively compete to produce the most persuasive version of the facts. In the High Court and Supreme Court, advocates' stance is enacted in relation to and alongside the stance-taking of judges, who are the more powerful and superior participants in this context. This chapter has observed the ways in which the power dynamics at play, the relative roles of advocates and judges, and the broader contextual demands of the court influence the marking of stance in interaction by legal speakers.

The strongest collocates of *I* – the top keyword in the corpus – all provided some indication as to the nature and breadth of stance-taking in the Brexit hearings. Focusing on three categories of collocates (modal verbs, mental verbs and speaking verbs), this chapter has identified resources for stance-taking which, until now, had not been observed as operating in this way. The first important point to emerge was that advocates and judges appeared to mark stance in different ways; whereas advocates preferred modal and speaking verbs, judges preferred mental verbs. Taking the most common of these verbs in turn, the precise functions to which speakers put *I will*, *I think* and *I say* revealed some patterns of use distinctive to this context. *I will* has previously not been examined in great depth as a stance-marker in court, yet here it was found to have typically epistemic and discourse-organisational qualities that advocates rely on when structuring their submission and navigating judicial intervention. In contrast, *I think* has frequently been the focus of stance studies in court, and in the same way as previous studies, this mental verb proved to be a valuable resource for advocates. However, what seems to differentiate its use in this context is the way in which it is used to reformulate judges' questions as well as serving its tried-and-tested function of mitigating potential face threats and softening the bluntness of assertions. All of these, however, can be interpreted as being a response to the rules of engagement in court, where questions are to be answered but opinions are not to be expressed and participants are to uphold the highest levels of professional courtesy. In comparison with advocates, much less had previously been known about judges' use of *I think/thought*. This analysis has found that it offers a means by which judges can challenge the submissions of advocates, mark their authority and 'fix' a version of advocates' argument in place before resuming the interaction. As was shown, this is not always without the advocate being dealt a damaging blow. In some ways, the interactions between judge and lawyer have been shown to mirror those of lawyer and witnesses, underlining the influence of speaker status in court. Finally, it has been argued that *I say* holds a special role in court discourse, replacing *I think* as the predominant marker of stance, behaving structurally and functionally in the same way as its mental verb counterpart, all the while making a necessary distinction between expressing opinion and making submissions to the court.

Much work remains to be undertaken on the courtroom discourse in the U.K. and on the Brexit hearings. What this chapter has highlighted, though, is that stance is enacted in distinctive and institutionalised ways in this context, giving rise to new insights into how speakers can navigate their position in the high-stakes discourse at hand.

Notes

1 This is now called the 'King's Bench Division' following the death of Queen Elizabeth II in September 2022 and the accession of King Charles III to the throne.

2 Post-nominal initials 'KC' signify 'King's Counsel' status, which is a recognition of excellence and one of the highest honours a solicitor can attain. At the time of the hearings, these lawyers were referred to with title 'QC', meaning 'Queen's Counsel'. The general rule is that this title is ambulatory, meaning that a lawyer ought to be referred to by their present title, rather than adjusting for the past (Granet 2022).

3 Such a multimodal analysis is possible, however, at least for the Supreme Court hearings, with video recordings of proceedings available at https://www.supremecourt.uk/cases/uksc-2019-0192.html.

References

Aijmer, K. (1997) I think - an English modal particle. In T. Swan and O. J. Westvik (eds.), *Modality in Germanic Languages: Historical and Comparative Perspectives*. Berlin: Mouton de Gruyter, pp. 1–48.

Bar Standards Board Handbook (2020). Part 2C: The Conduct Rules, C1 You and the court. Rule C7.4 - Not abusing your role as an advocate (online). Available from: https://www.barstandardsboard.org.uk/the-bsb-handbook.html [Last Accessed 20 January 2022].

Bednarek, M. (2006) *Evaluation in Media Discourse: Analysis of a Newspaper Corpus*. London: Bloomsbury.

Biber, D. and Finegan, E. (1989) Styles of stance in English: Lexical and grammatical marking of evidentiality and affect. *Text & Talk* 9(1): 93–124. https://doi.org/10.1515/text.1.1989.9.1.93

Biber, D., Johansson, S., Leech, G., Conrad, S. and Finegan, E. (1999) *Longman Grammar of Spoken and Written English*. Harlow: Pearson Education Limited.

Biber, D., Conrad, S. And Cortes, V. (2004) If you look at...: Lexical bundles in university teaching and textbooks. *Applied Linguistics* 25(3): 371–405. https://doi.org/10.1093/applin/25.3.371

Biber, D., Johansson, S., Leech, G., Conrad, S. and Finegan, E. (2021) *Grammar of Spoken and Written English*. Amsterdam/Philadelphia: Benjamins.

Brinton, L. J. (2008) *The Comment Clause: Syntactic Origins and Pragmatic Development*. Cambridge, UK: Cambridge University Press.

Cavalieri, S. (2009) Reformulation and conflict in the witness examination: The case of public inquiries. *International Journal for the Semiotics of Law* 22: 209–221. https://doi.org/10.1007/s11196-009-9103-y

Chaemsaithong, K. (2017) Evaluative stancetaking in courtroom opening statements. *Folia Linguistica* 51(1): 103–132. https://doi.org/10.1515/flin-2017-0003

Charles, M. (2006) The construction of stance in reporting clauses: A cross-disciplinary study of theses. *Applied Linguistics* 27(3): 492–518. https://doi.org/10.1093/applin/aml021

Clift, R. (2006) Indexing stance: Reported speech as an interactional evidential. *Journal of Sociolinguistics* 10(5): 569–595. https://doi.org/10.1111/j.1467-9841.2006.00296.x

Conrad, S. and Biber, D. (2000) Adverbial marking of stance in speech and writing. In S. Hunston and G. Thompson (eds.), *Evaluation in Text: Authorial Stance and the Construction of Discourse*. Oxford: Oxford University Press, pp. 56–73.

Du Bois, J. W. (2007) The stance triangle. In R. Englebretson (ed.), *Stancetaking in Discourse: Subjectivity, Evaluation, Interaction*. Amsterdam/Philadelphia: Benjamins, pp. 140–182.

Englebretson, R. (2007) Stancetaking in discourse: An introduction. In R. Englebretson (ed.), *Stancetaking in Discourse: Subjectivity, Evaluation, Interaction*. Amsterdam/Philadelphia: Benjamins, pp. 1–25.

Fetzer, A. (2008) 'And I think that is a very straight forward way of dealing with it.': The communicative function of cognitive verbs in political discourse. *Journal of Language and Social Psychology* 27(4): 384–396. https://doi.org/10.1177/0261927X08322481

Fetzer, A. (2014) I think, I mean and I believe in political discourse: Collocates, functions and distribution. *Functions of Language* 21(1): 67–94. https://doi.org/10.1075/fol.21.1.05fet

Finegan, E. and Lee, B. T. (2021) Legal writing: Attitude and emphasis. Corpus linguistic approaches to 'legal language': Adverbial expression of attitude and emphasis in supreme court opinions. In M. Coulthard, A. May and R. Sousa-Silva (eds.), *The Routledge Handbook of Forensic Linguistics* (2nd ed) London: Routledge, pp. 48–63.

Gales, T. (2021) 'Prison has been a proper punishment': Investigating stance in forensic and legal contexts. In M. Coulthard, A. May and R. Sousa-Silva (eds.), *The Routledge Handbook of Forensic Linguistics* (2nd ed). London: Routledge, pp. 675–693.

Gales, T. and Solan, L. M. (2017) Witness cross- examinations in non- stranger assault crimes: An appraisal analysis. *Language and Law/Linguagem e Direito* 4(2): 108– 139.

Goźdź-Roszkowski, S. (2024) *Language and Legal Judgments: Evaluation and Argument in Judicial Discourse*. London: Routledge.

Granet, E. (2022) Navigating past titles. *Notes on the Style of the Law* (online). Available at: https://www.legalstyle.co.uk/2022/11/navigating-past-titles.html?m=1 [Last accessed 03 September 2024]

Harris, S. (2011) The limits of politeness re-visited: Courtroom discourse as a case in point. In Linguistic Politeness Research Group (ed.), *Discursive Approaches to Politeness*. Berlin & New York: Mouton de Gruyter, pp. 85–108.

Hunston, S. (2007) Using a corpus to investigate stance quantitatively and qualitatively. In R. Englebretson (ed.), *Stancetaking in Discourse: Subjectivity, Evaluation, Interaction*. Amsterdam/Philadelphia: Benjamins, pp. 27–48.

Hyland, K. (2005). Stance and engagement: A model of interaction in academic discourse. *Discourse Studies* 7(2): 173–192. https://doi.org/10.1177/1461445605050365

Hyland, K. and Tse, P. (2004) Metadiscourse in academic writing: A reappraisal. *Applied Linguistics* 25(2): 156–177. https://doi.org/10.1093/applin/25.2.156

Institute for Government (2016) Brexit Brief: Article 50 (online). Available from: https://www.instituteforgovernment.org.uk/brexit/brexit-brief-article-50 [Last Accessed 13 January 2022].

Jaffe, A. (2009) Introduction: The sociolinguistics of stance. In A. Jaffe (ed.), *Stance: Sociolinguistic Perspectives*. Oxford: Oxford University Press, pp. 3–28.

Johnson, A. (2013) Embedding police interviews in the prosecution case in the Shipman trial. In C. Heffer, F. Rock and J. Conley (eds.), *Legal-Lay Communication: Textual Travels in the Law*. Oxford: Oxford University Press, pp. 147–167.

Johnson, A. (2015) Haunting evidence: Quoting the prisoner in 19th Century Old Bailey trial discourse. The defences of Cooper (1842) and McNaughten (1843).

In J. Arendholz, W. Bublitz and M. Kirner-Ludwig (eds.), *The Pragmatics of Quoting Now and Then*. Berlin: Mouton de Gruyter, pp. 369–400.

Johnson, A. J. (2020) 'Are you saying you were stabbed...?' Multimodality, embodied action, and dramatised formulations in "fixing" the facts in police interviews with suspects. In M. Mason and F. Rock (eds.), *The Discourse of Police Interviews*. Chicago: Chicago University Press, pp. 268–298.

Kaltenböck, G. (2010) Pragmatic functions of parenthetical 'I think'. In G. Kaltenböck, W. Mihatsch and S. Schneider (eds.), *New Approaches to Hedging*. Bingley: Emerald, pp. 243–272.

Kaltenböck, G. (2013) The development of comment clauses. In B. Aarts, J. Close, G. Leech and S. Wallis (eds.), *The Verb Phrase in English. Investigating Recent Language Change with Corpora*. Cambridge, UK: Cambridge University Press, pp. 286–317.

Kärkkäinen, E. (2003) *Epistemic Stance in English Conversation: A Description of its Interactional Functions, with a Focus on I think*. Amsterdam/Philadelphia: John Benjamins.

Kozin, A. V. (2008) Unsettled facts: On the transformational dynamism of evidence in legal discourse. *Text & Talk* 28(2): 219–238. https://www.degruyter.com/journal/key/text/html

Martin, J. R. and White, P. R. R. (2005) *The Language of Evaluation: Appraisal in English*. Basingstoke: Palgrave.

Matoesian, G. M. (2000) Intertextual authority in reported speech: Production media in the Kennedy Smith Rape trial. *Journal of Pragmatics* 32: 879–914. https://doi.org/10.1016/S0378-2166(99)00080-6

Matoesian, G. M. (2005) Struck by speech revisited: Embodied stance in jurisdicational discourse. *Journal of Sociolinguistics* 9(2): 167–193. https://doi.org/10.1111/j.1360-6441.2005.00289.x

May, A., Holt, E., Al Saeed, N. and Ahmad Sani, N. (2021) Legal talk: Socio- pragmatic aspects of legal questioning: Police interviews, prosecutorial discourse and trial discourse. In M. Coulthard, A. May and R. Sousa-Silva (eds.), *The Routledge Handbook of Forensic Linguistics* (2nd ed). London: Routledge, pp. 13–31.

Mishcon de Reya (2016) Article 50 process on Brexit faces legal challenge to ensure parliamentary involvement. 3 July 2016 (online). Available from: https://www.mishcon.com/news/article-50-process-on-brexit-faces-legal-challenge-to-ensure-parliamentary-involvement-07-2016 [Last accessed 13 January 2022].

Mortensen, S.S. and Mortensen, J. (2017) Epistemic stance in courtroom interaction. In: F. Poggi and A. Capone (eds.), *Pragmatics and Law: Practical and Theoretical Perspectives*. Cham: Springer, pp. 401–438.

Myers, G. (2010a) *The Discourse of Blogs and Wiki*. London: Bloomsbury.

Myers, G. (2010b) Stance-taking and public discussion in blogs. *Critical Discourse Studies* 7(4): 263–275. https://doi.org/10.1080/17405904.2010.511832

Potts, A. and Weare, S. (2018) Mother, Monster, Mrs, I: A critical evaluation of gendered naming strategies in English sentencing remarks of women who kill. *International Journal of the Semiotics of Law* 31(1): 21–52. https://doi.org/10.1007/s11196-017-9523-z

Pounds, G. (2015) Evaluative language. In K. Tracy (ed.), *International Encyclopedia of Language and Social Interaction*. London: Wiley. https://doi.org/10.1002/9781118611463.wbielsi063

Preisler, B. (1986) *Linguistic Sex Roles in Conversation: Social Variation in the Expression of Tentativeness in English*. Berlin: Mouton de Gruyter.

R v Secretary of State for Exiting the European Union [2017] UKSC 5 (online) available from: https://www.supremecourt.uk/cases/uksc-2016-0196.html

Shinzato, R. (2004) Some observations concerning mental verbs and speech act verbs. *Journal of Pragmatics* 36: 861–882. https://doi.org/10.1016/S0378-2166(03)00002-X

Szczyrbak, M. (2013). “I think my own view is that...” On the linguistic construction of evidence in courtroom discourse. *Topics in Linguistics* 12: 65–74.

Szczyrbak, M. (2014) Of course, indeed or clearly? The interactional potential of modal adverbs in legal genres. *SKASE Journal of Theoretical Linguistics* 11(2): 90–102.

Szczyrbak, M. (2016) Say and stancetaking in courtroom talk: A corpus-assisted study. *Corpora* 11(2): 143–168. https://doi.org/10.3366/cor.2016.0090

Szczyrbak, M. (2018). Verba dicendi in courtroom interaction: Patterns with the progressive. In S. Goźdź-Roszkowski and G. Pontrandolfo (eds.), *Phraseology in Legal and Institutional Settings: A Corpus-based Interdisciplinary Perspective.* London: Routledge, pp. 240–257.

Szczyrbak, M. (2019a) But, you see, the problem is: Perception verbs in courtroom talk: Focus on ‘you see’. *Topics in Linguistics* 20(1): 24–40. https://doi.org/10.2478/topling-2019-0002

Szczyrbak, M. (2019b) Epistemic stance in the Kavanaugh confirmation hearing: Focus on mental and communication verbs. *Discourse and Interaction* 12(2): 72–94. https://doi.org/10.5817/DI2019-2-72

Szczyrbak, M. (2020) Verb patterns in trial discourse: The case of ‘I think’. *Discourse and Interaction* 13(2): 119–135. https://doi.org/10.5817/DI2020-2-119

Szczyrbak, M. (2021a) I’m thinking and you’re saying: Speaker stance and the progressive of mental verbs in courtroom interaction. *Text & Talk* 41(2): 239–260. https://doi.org/10.1515/text-2019-0145

Szczyrbak, M. (2021b) Evidentiality in US Supreme Court opinions: Focus on passive structures with *say* and *tell*. In S. Gozdz Roszkowski and G. Pontrandolfo (eds.), *Law, Language and the Courtroom: Legal Linguistics and the Discourse of Judges*. London: Routledge, pp. 27–38.

Thompson, G. and Hunston, S. (2000) Evaluation: An introduction. In S. Hunston and G. Thompson (eds.), *Evaluation in Text: Authorial Stance and the Construction of Discourse*. Oxford: Oxford University Press, pp. 1–27.

Tracy, K. (2009) How questioning constructs appellate judge identities: The case of a hearing about same-sex marriage. *Discourse Studies* 11(2): 199–221. https://doi.org/10.1177/1461445608100944

Tracy, K. (2011) What’s in a name? Stance markers in oral argument about marriage laws. *Discourse and Communication* 5(1): 65–88. https://doi.org/10.1177/1750481310390167

Tracy, K. and Parks, R. M. (2012) ‘Tough questioning’ as enactment of ideology in judicial conduct: Marriage law appeals in seven US courts. *The International Journal of Speech Language and the Law* 19(1): 1–25. https://doi.org/10.1558/ijsll.v19i1.1

Wright, D., Robson, J., Murray-Edwards, H. and Braber, N. (2022) The pragmatic functions of ‘respect’ in lawyers’ courtroom discourse: A case study of Brexit hearings. *Journal of Pragmatics* 187: 1–12. https://doi.org/10.1016/j.pragma.2021.10.028

6 Online discourses of sexual consent and resistance

Content warning

The literature review, analysis and examples below contain references to, details of and discussions about sexual violence against women and girls. Readers therefore are urged to exercise caution and discretion before continuing.

Discourse, consent and 'utmost resistance'

'Judge who asked woman why she couldn't keep knees together resigns'. So read a CNN headline on 10 March 2017 (Grinberg 2017) following the resignation of Canadian federal judge Robin Camp in the wake of comments he made as a provincial court judge during a rape case over which he presided in 2014. Camp made a series of interjections throughout the complainant's cross-examination by the defence lawyer to ask the complainant questions directly. One section which garnered criticism unfolded as follows:

Justice Camp: But when – when he was using – when he was trying to insert his penis, your bottom was down in the basin. Or am I wrong?
Complainant: My – my vagina was not in the bowl of the basin when he was having intercourse with me
Q: All right. Which then leads me to the question: Why not – why didn't you just sink your bottom down into the basin so he couldn't penetrate you?
A: I was drunk
Q: And when your ankles were held together by your jeans, your skinny jeans, why couldn't you just keep your knees together?
A: (no verbal response)
Q: You're shaking your head
A: I don't know

DOI: 10.4324/9781003017301-6

This was during the trial of 29-year-old Alexander Wagar for the rape of a 19-year-old girl, in which Camp acquitted Wagar. On review of the trial and Camp's decision, the Court of Appeal of Alberta quashed Camp's verdict and ordered a retrial, which eventually took place in January 2017 and after which Wagar was, once again, acquitted. It was during this retrial when Camp's comments came to light, and he was forced to resign from his post following the Canadian Judicial Council's recommendation that he be removed from the bench.[1]

Camp's questions to the complainant in the extract above rely on victim-blaming and rape myths; the implicit (defence) argument is that the complainant could have done more to prevent the rape (i.e. 'just keep her knees together') and the fact that she did not do this means that she was essentially giving consent and therefore no rape has occurred. Many (if not most) cases of rape and sexual assault that make it to trial hinge not on whether sex took place but on whether or not that sex was consensual. 'Consent' is a state of mind rather than an explicit speech act; people can consent without expressly stating 'I consent' (Tiersma 2007: 91). Consent, therefore, is determined by interpretations and inferences of a person's behaviour, and 'the inferences that people draw are dependent on their beliefs about how people act or should act in specific situations' (Tiersma 2007: 95). One such belief, and that which can be seen in Judge Camp's questioning above, relates to the link between consent and resistance; did the rape complainant resist *enough* to prevent an assault or to communicate her dissent to her attacker? Ehrlich (2001: 67), in her seminal work on courtroom discourse in rape cases, notes that

> the 'utmost resistance standard' is the primary ideological frame through which the events in question and, in particular, the complainants' actions are understood and evaluated. This (re)framing functions to characterize the women as not 'resisting to the utmost' and ultimately (re)constructs the events as consensual sex, thus protecting the interests of the defendant.

The 'utmost resistance' standard, Ehrlich (2001: 65) explains, was a statutory requirement in cases of rape in the United States until the 1950s and 1960s. The standard held that if a woman did not resist a man's sexual advances to the utmost, then rape did not occur. Ehrlich (2001: 92) argues that the utmost resistance standard, though no longer legislatively mandated, still circulates within the criminal justice process for rape cases. In particular, the stressful cross-examination of rape complainants is characterised by questions which presuppose their behaviour to be lacking in appropriate resistance, framing the alleged victims as 'ineffectual agents' who 'consented' to sex by failing to resist (Ehrlich 2001: 92). The cross-examiner's ultimate aim in such reframing and representation of the complainant, of course, is to have the effect of calling into questions their allegations (Ehrlich 2012). Ehrlich (2001) provides numerous examples of this in action during witness examination, including cases in which the defence attorney suggests that a rape complainant could have done more during an attack to let other people in the vicinity know she was being assaulted; that a complainant knew she was in a place where she could have gone to avoid an attack; that a woman saying that she did not want to sleep with a man being insufficient to communicate a lack of consent; and that a woman could have 'sat up' during an attack and tried to reason with the assailant. Ehrlich (2013, 2016) also highlights cases where an agreement to have sex is not a signal of consent but rather a means by which to avoid further, escalated and intensified physical aggression from their attacker that they may be subjected to if they continued to physically resist.

Beliefs and misconceptions about consent and resistance infiltrate the legal system long before cross-examination in court. MacLeod (2010: 190) and MacLeod (2016) analyse police interviews with women who reported rape and found that they anticipate assumptions by the police officer (or any future audience) that they might have been expected to take some 'other' and 'more' action in resisting the rape (MacLeod, 2016: 106). This manifests in excuses such as 'I think I was in too much shock to do anything', 'I was that drunk I couldn't lift my body up' and 'he was too strong so I just gave up'. Ideological assumptions around sexual consent and resistance are so prevalent that MacLeod (2010: 194) argues that

> rather than merely responding to the content of interviewers' questions, interviewees support their answers with excuses for levels of resistance which might potentially be construed as insufficient or ineffective. These certainly appear to be more easily categorisable as excuses rather than justifications, in that they appear to display an awareness of a 'correct' way to behave which differs to the course of (in)action the interviewees actually took.

Ideological assumptions and expectations about resistant behaviour have also been found to shape rape suspects' perceptions of sex. In her analysis of a police interview with a rape suspect, Haworth (2017) finds that a rape suspect inadvertently makes clear that his assumptions of what rape entails are wrong. For example, he believes the fact that the victim wasn't screaming helps his case (Haworth, 2017: 201–203). He also emphasises that he had no reason to believe that she wasn't consenting because 'nothing was said' (Haworth, 2017: 207). The suspect therefore relies on normative assumptions about how (much) women should resist if they want to communicate a lack of consent.

The discursive construction of resistance and consent, therefore, has been well studied by forensic and legal linguists. Understandably, the focus to date has been on this construction at various points in the criminal justice process. An area that has received very little coverage by comparison is how the interlinking notions of sexual resistance and consent are constructed in discourse *outside* the legal system and in society at large. This chapter therefore aims to do this and particularly explore how discourses of resistance and consent emerge and are navigated within a very particular community of practice: the pick-up artist (PUA) community. PUAs are a community of 'self-designated or aspiring seduction experts' (Dayter and Rüdiger 2019: 13). As we will see, the ideologies and actions of members operating in the PUA community are, at the least, 'rather unsavoury from a moral point of view' (Dayter and Rüdiger 2019: 18), particularly in relation sex, consent and women's resistance. Although for many the PUA community may appear to be an extreme group on the fringes of society, O'Neill (2018) insists that the community should be taken seriously rather than simply caricatured. On the basis of her ethnographic research with the seduction industry and its members, O'Neill (2015: 10) challenges the cultural narrative in which the seduction community are considered 'pathetic, pathological or perverse – an army of sleazebags, saddos and weirdos', arguing that the PUA community is 'not so much a deviation or departure from current social conventions as an extension and acceleration of existing cultural norms'. The online PUA community therefore represents a useful space in which to investigate discourses and societal ideologies of consent and resistance. Following an introduction to PUAs, an overview of existing research into the PUA community, and a description of the 26 million–word corpus, the analysis focuses on the community-specific term 'LMR' ('last-minute resistance') as a means by which PUAs construct, negotiate and represent women's consent and resistance to sex.

The pick-up artist community

Wikipedia (2018) defines PUAs as 'self-identified seduction community' and describes the seduction or pick-up community as 'a movement of men whose goal is seduction and sexual success'. The so-called 'speed seduction movement' gained prominence and popularity, especially within North America, during the mid-2000s, accelerated by Neill Strauss's bestselling book *The Game: Penetrating the Secret Society of Pick-up Artists* (Strauss 2005) and subsequent cable TV shows. Today, pick-up artistry can be a lucrative business for some of the most high-profile individuals or 'instructors'; a 7-day training programme with one U.K.-based PUA is currently priced at £17,000.[2] As Hall and Canterberry (2011: 840) highlight, the popularity of such books, TV shows and courses demonstrates that 'young men are seeking information about how to seduce women aggressively and successfully'.

Central to the PUA's seduction of women is a series of routines, techniques and 'scripts' that men are to follow to achieve sexual success with a woman. Such techniques are multifaceted and varied but tend to originate with the three-stage model of human courtship as outlined by Erik von Markovic (also known as 'Mystery') in his book *The Mystery Method: How to Get Beautiful Women into Bed* (Mystery 2007), the phases of which are now well established within the PUA community: (i) attraction, (ii) comfort and trust, (iii) seduction. The systematicity of the routines and scripts advocated by PUAs is imbued within the community with a sense of methodical 'scientificness', which is manifest in the 'scientified perception of PUA activities and the employment of pseudo-scientific discourse by community members' (Dayter and Rüdiger 2016: 343). Interviews with members of the PUA community reveal that young men do not enter the community solely to aggressively pursue sexual relations with women but instead report being motivated by self-reflection and self-improvement, in response to expectations and cultural beliefs about masculinity (e.g. Schuurmans and Monaghan 2015). However, PUAs and the community have received substantial criticism. In the popular media, PUAs and their practices are regularly labelled as sexist and misogynistic (e.g. Steadman 2014; Bess 2018; Hall 2019). On occasion, some high-profile PUAs make headline news. For example, in 2014, American PUA Julian Blanc was rejected a British visa to enter the country following a 150,000-signature online petition and amid accusations that he promotes sexual assault (Travis 2014). Similarly, a Glasgow-based PUA was convicted and given a two-year prison sentence for charges of threatening and abusive behaviour after he featured in a hidden-camera BBC documentary called "The Seduction Game" (Bonnar 2019).[3] In her analysis of *The Mystery Method* (Mystery 2007), Denes (2011: 418) argues that PUAs misappropriate science and scientific language and that the system proposed by Mystery (2007) moves 'from a seduction script, focused on conversation and comfort, to a more aggressive and coercive approach reflecting characteristics of rape script'. O'Neill (2018: 152) characterises seduction of the type advocated by PUAs as 'cynical, calculating' disingenuous', a process in which 'trust is conjured rather than cultivated' and involves the 'reduction of sexual pleasure to little more than the mechanical pursuit or procurement of orgasm'. To be against seduction of this kind, O'Neill (2018: 152) argues, is

> [T]o be against sex that serves as a means to enhance or affirm oneself over and at the expense of others. It is to categorically refuse any form of sexual coercion, whether through premeditated emotional manoeuvrings or the carefully calculated weight of expectation. It is

to absolutely oppose sexual violence in the myriad forms this sadly but predictably takes.

The language of pick-up artists

There is a growing body of linguistics research into the PUA community. An early example of such work is Hambling-Jones and Merrison (2012), who analyse the face-to-face interactions between PUAs and previously unacquainted women. In their paper, Hambling-Jones and Merrison (2012) use as data surreptitiously audio-recorded interactions between women and male PUAs (retrospective consent was obtained) and analyse the interactions through a pragmatic-(im)politeness lens. As the researchers point out, the *interaction* is given primacy by PUAs as a means by which to attract women (rather than physical attraction or social status *per se*), and they aim to demonstrate the ways in which PUAs go about the activity of playing the 'game'. Although PUAs and members of the community do meet face-to-face, such as at the type of workshop or 'bootcamps' mentioned above, most of the interaction between members of this community of practice now takes place online, with 'individual bloggers, dating coaches and relationship experts, all providing niche services and products on how to seduce women' (King 2018: 300). One online space in which PUAs and members of the community regularly interact with each other is in online discussion forums, and data from such online forums have been subject to linguistic analysis. Dayter and Rüdiger (2016) analyse the reconstruction of experience through narrative in PUA forum posts. Employing a corpus analysis of 37 forum postings (totalling 24,000 tokens) collected from publicly accessible Anglophone PUA forums, they identified three hierarchical frames in PUAs 'field reports' posted online, which are 'narrative constructions of encounters between the PUAs and women' (Dayter and Rüdiger 2016: 337). Their analysis demonstrated how the field reports comprise the frame of 'PUA training' in which posters index their membership through specialised scientified PUA terminology, 'personal narrative' in which posters include appropriate details in order for their report to be ratified as authentic by fellow members, and 'success' in which almost any outcome or response from women in the encounter is constructed as being successful and as the PUA achieving their goal. Meanwhile, Dayter and Rüdiger (2019) explore in greater depth the nature and functions of PUA vocabulary in their 37-post corpus. They find that PUA terms used in the posts consist of (i) pseudoscientific terminology, particularly from the domains of military, business and science; (ii) numerals and quantification in the form of performance statistics, rating of women, age of women, ratio of women to men and date/time details; (iii) abbreviations and acronyms; and (iv) word-formation processes of compounding and conversion. It is argued by Dayter and Rüdiger (2019: 14) that such vocabulary is used with the aims of creating a sense of 'scientificness' or 'expertness' around the community and its techniques, in a way that its usage can signal group membership and can be persuasive to members and would-be members that such technical language is representative of a unique set of skills and expertise that makes them different from non-PUA counterparts.

In later work, Rüdiger and Dayter (2020) identified three types of self-praise in the interactions between PUAs: *bragging*, which involved making positive statements about themselves; *evidential*, in which members reported events and behaviours recognised as laudable by other members; and *proxy*, whereby posters quote someone else's alleged positive assessment of them. Rüdiger and Dayter (2020: 25) found that, contrary to the generally negative perception of bragging and boasting in society, self-praise is not only 'a completely acceptable discursive move within the PUA community' but a central component to the community values of confidence-building and mutual support. Elsewhere, Dayter and Rüdiger (2020) focus on the ways in which the PUA community refer to women across a range of online spaces, including blogs, PUA websites, forums, Twitter and YouTube. Their analysis revealed, perhaps counterintuitively given the ideological basis of the PUA community, that explicitly derogatory terms were relatively rare. Instead, PUAs were found to regularly infantilise women (through the use of *girl*, *babe*, *baby* and *child*) and refer to women using PUA-specific vocabulary which both signals group membership and 'indexes the position of women in the PUA ecology' (through references such as *target*, *HB [hot babe]*, *obstacle*, *option* and *rotation*) (Dayter and Rüdiger 2020: 81). This aligns with the findings of Krendel's (2020) exploration of three anti-feminist *Reddit* sub-communities, one of which comprised mainly PUAs. An analysis of the discursive patterns associated with the terms *woman/women* and *girl*(s) in these communities demonstrated the ways in which women and girls were constructed as immoral, deceptive, irrational and unhappy as well as being dehumanised and objectified.

Many studies have analysed online PUA discourse with a view to identifying the construction and negotiation of masculinities in such spaces. Cosma and Gurevich (2018) perform a qualitative discourse analysis on a series of extracts taken from PUA websites with the aim of identifying how notions and ideals of masculinity are discursively created in PUA advice. They find that PUAs endorse a narrowly defined hegemonic masculinity while rejecting alternative masculinities and that PUA leaders position themselves as 'authoritative voices' on self-improvement in pursuit of this idealised masculinity (Cosma and Gurevich 2018: 95). Elsewhere, Cosma and Gurevich (2020) find that masculinity is constructed in relation to women's bodies. They find that the relentless pursuit of obtaining sex with multiple women is framed as a means by which men must defend their masculinity that is under attack, that the amassing of casual sexual partners is a method for men to (re)gain control over women and themselves, and that attaining consent from women is central to the 'achievement' of masculinity. Ging (2019) also examines masculinities across 38 online communities, including PUA forums alongside sub-reddits, 4chan boards, religiously conservative groups and men's rights websites. Through a critical discourse analytic approach, she finds that, although the manosphere is not a homogenous monolithic ideological block (the ideologies in some areas of the manosphere may not be present in other areas), seemingly contradictory types of masculinity – alpha, beta, jock, geek, straight, gay, Christian and atheist – 'can coalesce when the common goal is to defeat feminism or keep women out of the space' (Ging 2019: 653). This coalescence, Ging (2019: 653) continues, hinges on a 'common preoccupation with male hegemony as it relates to heterosexual – not homosexual – gender relations'.

Finally, some studies have used quantitative methods from Natural Language Processing to identify discourses in online PUA language. Mountford (2018), for example, focuses specifically on one blog, *Return of Kings* (*RoK*), written by 'Roosh V', formerly one of the world's most famous PUA and prominent figures in the manosphere. A topic modelling procedure conducted on a corpus of over two million tokens found thirteen lexically derived topics. Mountford (2018: 7) identified two main topics of these thirteen. The first, appearing in 46% of all documents, is 'Goals and Growth', which 'underlines the deep link of self-improvement content and prescriptive masculinity' and is made up of lexical items, including *life*, *time*, *get*, *mindset* and *strive*. The second, found in 35% of documents, 'Pickup', 'is focused on prescriptive dating advice and recounting encounters with women' and is typified by words referring to women, such as *bitch*, *blonde* and *brunette*. These two main topics, Mountford (2018: 10) argues, are supplemented by others such as 'Personal Relationships and Political', 'Prescriptive Society', 'International Society Comparison' and 'Learning and Teaching'. On the basis of such findings, *RoK* can be 'seen as prescribing a new form of masculinity that is consciously constructed in reaction to feminist and societal shifts' (Mountford 2018: 1). Schmitz and Kazyak (2016), meanwhile, analyse twelve prominent men's rights–affiliated websites and found two divergent ideological discourses, both of which 'promoted men's entitlement to social power' (Schmitz and Kazyak 2016: 1). On the one hand, some of the sites created hyper-masculine content that used themes of explicit aggression towards women, espousing the evils of feminism and reducing women to sexual commodities. On the other hand, some sites embraced a more socio-political stance to combatting perceived institutional misandry.

The analysis in this chapter contributes to this growing literature on the discourse of PUA communities online and focuses specifically on the discursive representation of resistance to sex. One of the main aims (if not *the* aim) of the PUA community is to share structured scripts, routines and techniques for achieving sexual success with women and providing advice, support and self-praise for doing so. For that reason, online discussions between PUA members offer a unique communicative space to analyse discursive constructions resistance particularly in the 'field reports' shared by aspirational and practicing PUAs and posted to forums. Dayter and Rüdiger (2022: 183) suggest that the analysis of PUA discourse would benefit from the perspectives of forensic linguistics, given that the movement 'poses a threat to women's online and offline safety'. An attempt to provide such a perspective has been made previously (Wright 2020, 2021; Wright 2024), and these attempts are expanded here. Specifically, the analysis below represents a significant expansion of the exploration of the Seduction Forum Corpus (SFC) in Wright (2020).

The Seduction Forum Corpus

The corpus used for this analysis is a purpose-built specialised corpus comprising posts and threads from a popular and (at the time of collection) publicly accessible PUA online discussion forum. The forum has all the hallmark generic conventions of discussion forums that have remained largely stable since the earliest internet message boards of the 1990s (Dayter and Rüdiger 2016: 338). The forum is based on an individual making an initial 'post' on the topic of their choosing and a subject heading to reflect that, which may or may not elicit responses from other forum members. The post and any subsequent replies constitute a 'thread'. Each post on the forum (whether an initial post or a reply to another) is accompanied by the date and time of the post, the author/member name, their location, an avatar, when they first joined the forum, the number of posts that member has made overall and their reputation. With every post, members can choose to 'like' or reply directly to the initial post or to another member's reply. The posts to the forum are varied; some explicitly ask the community for seduction advice, some explicitly give such advice, and notwithstanding a series of posts about travel, fitness, entertainment and current affairs, the majority of posts are 'field reports' in which members provide narrative accounts of their encounters with women. These reports are a tool for members to reflect 'on their interactions and discussing – often dialogically – what did or did not work for them' (Hambling-Jones and Merrison 2012: 1116) in which PUAs describe their experiences with women and invite comments, feedback, advice and praise from other community members (Dayter and Rüdiger 2020: 70). The extent to which these reports and accounts are grounded in truth is unknowable. The forum itself has a list of rules and is policed both by the members themselves via the berating of poor-quality posts and by forum administration, as members can be banned.

The data were collected from the forum using GNU wget web-scraping scripts, and the posts and threads themselves were downloaded with all of their accompanying metadata. The dataset was pre-processed, which involved removing all of the web-associated HTML tags and removing duplicate text in instances where a reply had 'quoted' chunks of the original or another post, and the files were stored as .txt and .json files.[4] Following the pre-processing and data clean-up, the final corpus consists of 8,988 threads, comprising 25,788 individual posts and totalling 26,527,412 tokens. A discussion of the ethical considerations made when collecting and presenting this data appears in Chapter 2.

Consent and resistance in the Seduction Forum Corpus

The focus of the analysis in this chapter is on the ways in which the inextricably linked notions of *consent* and *resistance* are discursively constructed in the SFC. For this reason, and on the basis that *consent* and *resistance* are the legally relevant words, the SFC was probed for frequencies of the lexemes *consen** and *resis** directly. To say that overt posts about consent and resistance were the main topics of conversation in the forum would misrepresent the data. At the same time, however, explicit mentions of consent and resistance are by no means rare or exceptional (Table 6.1).

What is immediately clear is that *resistance*, *resistant* and the act of *resist(ing)* are far more commonly part of the discourse of the forum than are explicit mentions of *consent(ing)* and *consensual*. One possible explanation of this is that in a law-abiding community *consent* is an assumed

Table 6.1 Frequency of *consen** and *resist** in SFC

Word	*Freq.*	*Word*	*Freq.*
consent	417	*resistance*	1,337
consensual	108	*resist*	444
consenting	34	*resistant*	133
consented	15	*resisted*	105
consents	10	*resisting*	100
consensually	5	*resists*	66
consensuality	1	*resistances*	4
consenty	1	*resistive*	3
		resistants	2
		resistible	1
Total	**591**	**Total**	**2,196**

element of sexual intercourse and therefore obtaining of consent is less likely to be explicitly discussed. However, this is not entirely the case in the corpus in question; for example, we see group members discussing how they ensure(d) they obtain(ed) consent from women before having sex:

1 I made her **consent** to sex by text message to make sure I wouldn't drive hours for nothing.
2 I would bang the girl but first I would print a contract in which she gives me **consent**. I'd probably record it too in case she regrets it the next day.
3 I just talk sexy to girls and they give their verbal **consent** back.

The focus of this analysis will be on the *resist** by virtue of its much higher frequency. Tokens derived from *resist** appear with a frequency of 0.08 per 1,000 words in the corpus as a whole. However, the next analytical step in identifying the ways in which *resist** is represented in collocation patterns, reveals that uses of such words are not monolithic or homogenous throughout the corpus (Table 6.2). There are some entries in the top 20 most frequent collocates of *resist** that warrant particular attention in the context of this analysis. First, two of the collocates in the list relate to amounts; *no* and *some* are the 8th and 19th most frequent collocates of *resist**. As shown in the following examples from the data, the collocation

Table 6.2 Top 20 collocates of *resist** words in SFC (L5 > R5)

N	*Word*	*With*	*Texts*	*Total*	*Total left*	*Total right*
1	THE	resistance	12	337	197	140
2	AND	resistance	12	304	140	164
3	OF	resistance	12	285	240	45
4	TO	resist	12	230	155	75
5	I	resistance	11	216	90	126
6	A	resistance	12	211	120	91
7	HER	resistance	12	171	83	88
8	**NO**	**resistance**	**11**	**169**	**156**	**13**
9	SHE	resistance	11	160	100	60
10	UP	resistance	12	157	126	31
11	**MINUTE**	**resistance**	**11**	**156**	**152**	**4**
12	**LAST**	**resistance**	**11**	**149**	**147**	**2**
13	YOU	resistance	11	141	73	68
14	THE	resist	12	141	24	117
15	WITH	resistance	12	123	89	34
16	IS	resistance	12	118	44	74
17	BUT	resistance	11	114	39	75
18	THAT	resistance	11	110	49	61
19	**SOME**	**resistance**	**12**	**108**	**100**	**8**
20	I	resist	12	107	84	23

pattern of *no/some + resistance* appears in members posting field reports of their (alleged) sexual encounters with women:

4 She put up almost no resistance. I was fucking her within minutes.
5 I didn't expect it to happen so fast. There was no resistance, therefore we banged.
6 With no resistance, as soon as she gets back to my place she takes her clothes off and we fucked.

In contrast to these examples where the forum posters remark about the lack of resistance they allegedly received from their sexual partners, there are also many cases where posters report experiencing *some* resistance or provide advice on what to do in the face of *some* resistance:

7 When she gave me some resistance to meeting with me or hanging out I laughed and started ignoring her messages.
8 I then suggested we take shots at my car. She obliges with some resistance.
9 then she warmed up a bit and after some resistance I ended up banging her.
10 She agreed and I went to her place. There was some resistance but I eventually sealed the deal.
11 Went to the hotel, overcame some minor resistance and smashed her, fell asleep, smashed her again then we had breakfast.

Whereas some instances of *some resistance* referred to a woman's resistance to some prior step or escalation in the pick-up encounter (e.g. 7 and 8 above), others do relate directly to a woman's resistance to sex (9–11). Resistance is obviously something that members of the forum are conscious of and sensitive to. They consider it necessary to explicitly give information about resistance whether there was some or not. From this we might infer that experiencing *no resistance* or experiencing and subsequently overcoming *some resistance* are both victories for those using PUA techniques. In examples (9)–(11), the posters report experiencing some resistance from women with whom they eventually have sex. That is, despite the resistance the women put up, the men report having sex with them anyway. This discourse is brought into even sharper focus by two other collocates of *resist** in Table 6.2: *last* and *minute*. These collocates occur 152 and 147 times respectively to the left of *resistance*, and almost all of these occur together; the phrase *last-minute resistance* appears 139 times in the SFC. For example:

12 Your need to think about taking her somewhere, get her tipsy or high and alone, and then hammer through any last-minute resistance.

13 Got her upstairs fine, but had a lot of **last-minute resistance**. I hadn't had this much **last-minute resistance** for a while, it was at least half an hour.
14 If it takes hardly any game to get her in bed, and she puts up no **last-minute resistance** (LMR) when you go to take her clothes off then the chances are she's had a lot of dick.

The last example here provides the accompanying acronym *LMR*, which is far more commonly used in the corpus in place of the phrase *last-minute resistance* itself. Whereas the full phrase appears 139 times, the acronym *LMR* occurs with a frequency of 1,348 – almost ten times as frequently and more frequent than the word *resistance* itself. LMR is semantically distinct from *resistance* more generally as it is more temporally salient; it specifies that the resistance was timed *immediately* before the sexual act is to, or did, take place. Definitions of LMR from PUA websites include the following:

> Basically it's when a girl you're hitting on puts up a barrier and stops things from going any further (i.e. the bedroom for sex) because she doesn't want to be seen as a slut by you or her friends. So she gets defensive and blurts out standard lines to throw you off the scent and to let you know that she needs more work before you get her in the sack.
>
> (PUA Training 2020)

> Last Minute Resistance is where a girl will prevent a man from escalating beyond a certain point in the bedroom. Often these moments of LMR occur when things are heating up towards sex, such as when you attempt to remove clothes, or attempt any sexual moves beyond kissing. This resistance can occur for several reasons; she feels things are moving too quickly, she is nervous, she doesn't want to feel slutty by giving it up too easily, etc.
>
> (PUAmore 2016a)

> Last-minute resistances (LMR) are tactics, strategies, or inborn and involuntary responses with which women delay or postpone sex once a man starts escalating towards sex.
>
> (The Power Moves 2021)

These definitions all offer some 'explanation' for why a woman may put up so-called 'last-minute resistance'. In the first two, it is claimed that women resist sex because they do not want to be seen as promiscuous, easy or 'like a slut'. Similarly, the third definition considers LMR to be tactical and strategic while being 'involuntary' and outside of the woman's conscious control. All of these notions are returned to in the analysis below.

It is not surprising that the members of the SFC and the PUA community more widely have produced an acronym as shorthand for *last-minute resistance*, nor that the acronym is far more commonly used than the full phrase. Dayter and Rüdiger (2019: 16) argue that the use of acronyms by the PUA community is a signal of its being a specialised discourse community, distancing the layperson and the uninitiated. The concept of LMR has also been discussed in the academic literature on PUAs. O'Neill (2018) identifies LMR as one of the most well-established and commonly referenced concepts in the community. It represents the belief that women only give the impression of resistance prior to having sex as a way to preserve their reputation and is one of the most central tenets of seduction theory and practice 'because it epitomises the idea that the affective and relational dynamics that typically precipitate heterosexual sex can be wilfully produced by one party over another' (O'Neill, 2018: 98). Similarly, Cosma and Gurevich (2020: 55) argue that, in the PUA community, breaking a woman's LMR is a way for a man to 'establish control and display his resolve – confirming his authenticity as a man who is not weak or willing to change his mind'.

The definitions of LMR, notwithstanding the very existence and use of a phrase and acronym relating to women showing resistance to sexual advances, provide an insight into the group members' ideological perspectives towards resistance; it is viewed as a 'problem' that needs to be handled and dealt with, and steps are advocated to break down this resistance. The remainder of the analysis in this chapter, using a collocation analysis of the acronym *LMR* as a starting point, further explores the ideologically fuelled discourses surrounding resistance to sex in the SFC and will demonstrate the ways in which the discursive constructions of LMR blur the lines between resistance and consent in this online PUA community.

Discourse prosodies of last-minute resistance

The identification of discourse prosody depends on the analysis of collocates, as frequent use of particular semantically related collocates may result in 'particular meaning attributes' being associated with a term across a corpus (Gabrielatos and Baker 2008: 12). Discourse prosodies are 'open ended and typically have great lexical variability' (Stubbs 2001: 88), and collocates need not be directly adjacent to the node for their meaning to influence that of the node (Baker et al. 2008: 278). Discourse prosodies capture more than just negative or positive semantic prosodies of a word instead offering more nuanced and specific meanings (Baker et al. 2008: 286; see also Baker et al. 2013). More specifically, discourse prosodies are attributive or evaluative, in the sense that they 'express speaker attitude' (Stubbs 2001: 65). Partington (2014: 283) prefers the term *evaluative* prosody, as it relates to words or terms 'whose evaluative potential becomes apparent when interacting with other items in discourse'. Most usefully for the current analysis is that the discourse prosody/prosodies that a term has can open 'a window on values and attitudes present throughout a discourse community' (Mautner 2016: 170). That is, the prevalence of certain discourse prosodies reflects not simply the spread of a particular use of language, or even shared associative meanings, but also 'a shared reality of the respective discourse community' and indicates 'the subtle ideological foundations of habitual ways of thinking and writing' in that community (Rheindorf 2019: 46).

This analysis therefore aims to identify the discourse prosodies of *LMR* in the PUA community in the SFC. The first step required the identification of collocates of the term. For the collocation analysis, the association measure of choice was MI^3. The collocates within an L5–R5 span of *LMR* were ranked by their MI^3 score, and the top 100 collocates were included in the analysis. The next step was to group semantically similar collocates on the basis of analysis of all the concordance lines. From the top 100 collocates, six categories of collocates emerged, in total accounting for 49 of these collocates (Table 6.3).

As can be seen, most of these collocates are lexical collocates, predominantly verbs (e.g. *battle*, *break*, *plow*, *encounter*) and adjectives (e.g. *heavy*, *fierce*, *shit*). However, function words characterise some of the categories, such as determiners (e.g. *any*, *much*, *(a) lot*) and prepositions (e.g. *after*, *past*, *through*). From these six collocate categories, four distinct but interrelated discourse prosodies emerge which will form the structure of the qualitative analysis that follows. These prosodies each relate to some ideological perspective on women's resistance to sex and provide an insight into the beliefs and motivations expressed by members of this particular PUA community of practice. They are (i) resistance as something to be

Table 6.3 L5–R5 collocates of LMR by MI^3 (frequency in brackets)

Category	*Collocate of 'LMR'*
Tackling resistance	*battle* (16), *battled* (3), *battling* (3), *break* (17), *breaking* (10), *busting* (7), *comfort* (13), *deal* (23), *defeating* (4), *overcome* (32), *overcoming* (20), *past* (20), *plow* (6), *push* (21), *tactics* (11), *through* (72)
High resistance	*anti* (9), *crazy* (13), *extreme* (12), *fierce* (5), *heavy* (26), *hour(s)* (23), *lot* (33), *massive* (11), *more* (43), *strong* (15)
Low resistance	*any* (38), *bit* (21), *much* (35), *no* (137), *some* (87), *whatsoever* (10), *zero* (34)
Fake resistance	*asd* (20), *shit* (36), *tests* (17) *token* (14)
Experience	*encounter(ed)* (17), *gave* (26), *getting* (29), *giving* (30), *got* (50)
Post-resistance	*But* (75), *after* (45), *bang* (42), *sex* (27)

overcome, (ii) resistance as insincere, (iii) resistance as remarkable, and (iv) resistance as temporary.

Resistance as something to be overcome

The first discourse prosody for discussion is one in which LMR from women and girls is represented by forum members as something that is to be defeated, battled or overcome by men. This prosody is most plainly represented by the collocates in the 'tackling resistance' category in Table 6.3. Some field reports by forum members detail the ways in which they experienced LMR from their targets but persevered nonetheless:

15 She drove almost an hour to come over tonight, I had to <u>**push through**</u> a lot of LMR – she kept saying no sex but that didn't stop me.
16 We leave to a high-class hotel in town and after going up to our room she puts on a robe and we get at it. Have some LMR but <u>**plow through**</u> and fuck the shit out of her.
17 But I had to put up with her shitty screams and <u>**get past**</u> LMR. The sex was poor.
18 Gave me a load of LMR but I <u>**pushed through**</u>. But she gave the worst blowjob I've ever had. She used too much teeth and I had to hit her on the head and give her directions.

In these examples, the forum members recount experiences in which they report to plainly persist in their sexual advances despite resistance by women. The resistance was clear enough for them to mention it here, so the possible argument that the resistance was not communicated clearly enough does not apply (e.g. Ehrlich 2015). On the contrary, the posters of these field reports appear to take some pride in having persevered through LMR which, according to these reports, is manifest in 'she kept saying no' and 'shitty screams'. In (17) and (18), other recurring interlinking discourses are apparent. In both of these examples, the forum posters negatively evaluate the sexual activity after having been made to 'get past' or 'deal with' LMR, while in (18), there is an expression of physical violence in 'hit her on the head'. It may be inferred from these cases that a woman's LMR may be met with degradation and physical abuse, even after sex. The notion of a woman's resistance to sexual activity as being something to be overcome, as demonstrated in (15)–(18), is also explicitly signalled by the collocate *overcome/overcoming* itself:

19 I knew we were interested in each other when we first met. There was a lot of LMR but that was <u>**overcome**</u> by effort, logic or bulldozing.

20 How forceful is everyone when trying to **overcome** LMR? Is it just on a case by case basis? Last week I had a date and the girl came back to my place and she ended up leaving in a huff because I let my hand wander after she had already said we weren't having sex. [...] I need to get better at dealing with this silliness.

The transitive sense of the verb 'overcome' is defined as 'to get the better of, defeat, overpower, prevail over (an enemy, person or thing opposing one, etc.)' (Oxford English Dictionary 2024). This meaning is borne out in collocation patterns, as the top 25 collocates of *overcome* in COCA (Davies 2019) include *obstacles*, *barriers*, *adversity*, *fear*, *problems*, *challenges*, *poverty*, *difficulties*, *evil*, *opposition* and *addiction*. Therefore, framing a woman's resistance to sex as something to be *overcome* represents such resistance as a problem and an adversarial enemy and in turn demonstrates the community's attitude towards women's sexual resistance. A solution to such a problem is expressed in (19) in terms of 'bulldozing' which aligns with the persistence, perseverance and pressure discussed in the examples above of 'ploughing' and 'pushing' through LMR, to achieve the aim of having sex with a woman, despite a clear lack of consent. The post in (20) is different from the others in that it is requesting advice from the community about overcoming LMR. Notably, their question is how 'forceful' to be when trying to have sex with someone who is resisting, indicating that force is an inherent factor in overcoming LMR. Various other elements of extract (20) are worthy of note. One is the dehumanising reference to (sexual) encounters with women as 'cases', which reflects the misogynistic ideologies underlying much of these posts and/or may be interpreted as an attempt to frame PUA discourses as being 'scientific'. In addition, there is further evaluation of the LMR reported in (20) which provides an insight into the community's views on sexual resistance. The user recounts a situation in which he attempted to overcome LMR and the girl left 'in a huff', before ending the post by lamenting the 'silliness', as they see it, of LMR. Such descriptions of resistance frame it as being childish and trivial, which serves to diminish and delegitimise the resistive actions of the woman as not to be taken seriously. This supports Dayter and Rüdiger's (2020) point that PUAs infantilise women. An interpretation of this may be that, by viewing LMR as trivial, members of the PUA community are more easily able to morally navigate disregarding resistance and 'bulldozing' through it. This suppression and delegitimisation of LMR as not serious reemerge later in the analysis.

Further contributing to the community's construction of resistance from a position of adversarial opposition are posters' accounts of *battling* and *defeating* LMR using *tactics*:

21 I get annoyed by LMR every time. If I win the **battle**, I'll still be angry because she rejected me first, but if I lose the **battle**, I'll also be annoyed. So I always push through LMR as far as possible, unless she leaves.

22 Once you got them back to your place, it's about escalating and **defeating** LMR.

23 She gave some token resistance but also its also a cultural thing. Was no match for my **LMR beating tactics**.

All three of these LMR collocates that are categorised as 'tackling resistance' in Table 6.3 draw on military and war metaphors, representing the pursuit of sexual satisfaction as a fight with winners and losers. This is clearest in (21) and (22) in which LMR is 'battle(d)' and 'defeated' respectively. The use of military metaphor in this way within the PUA community was also found by Dayter and Rüdiger (2016: 339), who argue that forum members use terminology related to the military domain in such a way as to reframe a romantic encounter as another type of activity which is 'not as firmly predicated on a man's self-worth as a deserving partner or a good human being' and therefore 'removes the insecurities associated with it'. In other words, in the same way that trivialising a woman's resistance makes it easier to ignore it, so too might recasting of the sexual encounter as something entirely different. In their later study, Dayter and Rüdiger (2019: 15) identified terms from the military domain, such as *engage* and *target*, to portray women as 'adversaries who are either to be hunted or defeated'. Similarly, they argue that the military domain is appealing to PUAs as it implies being 'a real man' is a military-typical attribute 'such as power, physical strength and grit'. In the same way, the use of 'tactics' in (23) represents the man's actions as carefully planned, strategic and methodical and imbues them with some sort of intellectual currency. By describing persisting with sexual advances in the face of clear resistance from a woman in this way allows the forum poster to portray themselves as having positive, cerebral qualities rather than predatory, aggressive ones.

It is not difficult to infer from these forum discussions of 'overcoming', 'battling', 'pushing through' that what these posts may represent are narratives of rape and sexual assault. It appears, if these field reports are taken on face value, that they detail instances where a man has ignored a woman's resistance to their sexual advances and has engaged in sexual activity with the women without consent. It is not the case in these instances that a lack of consent was not clear or explicit and that any non-consensual sexual activity was a result of 'miscommunication'. Rather, these posters not only were clear on the lack of consent shown by their targets but are proud and boastful that they were able to persevere *anyway*. Regardless of what women do and what clear signals of resistance they communicate, men (at least as represented by this particular corner of the PUA community) will persevere with their sexual advances until they have gotten what they wanted. Within their ideological framework, their status as an alpha-male, a successful proponent of PUA 'methods' and a victor on the sexual battlefield depends on it. The victims and their sexual resistance are nothing more than an inconvenient obstacle to overcome in pursuit of this perceived status and success. This reflects the belief that, within the PUA community, 'sex with women is framed as an obstacle one must "work through" to become the true, ideal self' (Cosma and Gurevich 2018: 95). What we see in these field reports is a manifestation of Cosma and Gurevich's (2020: 54) observation that in this community consent is framed as an obstacle to overcome and to do so is a source of praise and respect. The ways in which some members of the PUA community morally legitimise their behaviour is situated within a misogynistic, hegemonic masculine ideological framework, in which the sexual encounter is recast as another type of activity entirely, and a woman's resistive actions are downplayed and trivialised and considered a mere impediment to men achieving control. Additional interwoven threads of this ideology are displayed as the three remaining LMR discourse prosodies.

Resistance as insincere

Ehrlich (2001: 127) writes:

> A woman may say 'no' with sincerity to a man's sexual advances, but the 'no' gets filtered through a series of cultural beliefs and attitudes that transform the woman's direct negative into an indirect affirmative, for example, 'she is playing hard to get, but of course she really means yes'.

Evidence of the 'cultural beliefs and attitudes' to which Ehrlich refers here abounds in the SFC. One of the major discourse prosodies surrounding LMR as revealed by the collocate analysis of the term is 'fake resistance' – the representation of women's resistance as being false, inauthentic and insincere (Table 6.3). The main way in which LMR is framed as being insincere in the SFC is through the description of the resistance as being *token*:

24 On our first date I took her back to my place, got her in bed and she even gave me **token** LMR as if we were still teenagers, which was nice.
25 And I would think it through and decide if she was having doubts that it would be wrong for something to happen. When really it was the most **token** of LMR – she was probably just frustrated that I hadn't taken off her underwear off yet.
26 I gave her many orgasms, and I know pushing through her **token** LMR really turned her on.

Token is used here in such a way that indicates that the LMR expressed by the women in question is symbolic, performed for the sake of appearances. In the PUA community, 'with token resistance, we are in the realm of the "no means yes", and she will actually be (very) disappointed if you stop' (The Power Moves 2021). In short, 'token resistance' is when a 'woman says no to sex even when they mean yes' (Muehlenhard and Hollabaugh 1988: 872). The examples of *token LMR* in (24)–(26) reveal a lot about how the PUA community view such resistance. In the simplest terms, the resistance is not considered genuine. In (24), there is a similar strategy to that used above (extract 20) where non-genuine 'token' resistance is associated with juvenility and sexual immaturity on the part of the woman, whose expression of resistance is considered the behaviour of a 'teenager'. The male poster appears to take pleasure in her resistance, disregarding it and condescendingly describing it as 'nice'. In (25), not only is the resistance not considered genuine, it is framed by the poster as signalling the exact opposite of resistance; he reports that likely what the woman was really trying to communicate was that she could not resist any longer and could not wait for him to take off her underwear. Note in this instance the poster does take a moment to consider whether or not the woman does actually want to have sex with him, but then quickly resolves that 'in reality', of course, she does. A similar recasting of LMR is seen in (26). Here, the forum member is certain that 'pushing through' the woman's 'token' LMR, rather than being a cause for concern for the woman and her safety, was in fact the source of sexual arousal for her. These examples speak to Ehrlich's (2001: 127) point above; men acknowledge that there was some resistance from the women, but both consider it to be 'token' rather than real, and as sign of encouragement or enjoyment from the women, transforming the resistance into a signal of consent.

Denes (2011: 416) writes about 'token resistance' as it is described in Mystery's (2007) early PUA book which reflects and shapes much of the PUA community. According to Denes (2011: 416), in an attempt to convince his readers that no women can resist his seduction methods, any and all resistance men might encounter is 'never to be taken as legitimate, but rather, as token resistance (saying no to sex when meaning yes)'. Denes (2011: 416) quotes Mystery as he describes 'token LMR' as an attempt by women to have sex without appearing promiscuous, as a woman 'wants things to happen, but she wants it to feel right and she doesn't want it to be her fault' (Mystery 2007: 148). Part of this non-appearance of promiscuity is a woman's 'anti-slut defence' ('ASD') so-called in the PUA community. ASD is a well-established concept in the community and is defined as 'a method used by a girl to abstain herself from responsibility during a situation where there is a likelihood of sex/intimacy' (*PUAmore* 2016b). Appropriately, in the SFC, discourses of LMR and ASD overlap, as the latter is a common collocate of the former:

27 I encountered levels of **ASD** and LMR that were not apparent on the first date – I'm still fairly new to this, and my poor attempts to overcome the unexpected LMR backfired.
28 It takes game to disable **ASD** and LMR after you get her back to your place.
29 You could have (should have) fucked her on that first date. She was asking for it she just needed you to plow through her very weak LMR/**ASD**.

The first thing to note in all of these examples is that LMR and ASD appear to be considered one and the same or at least very closely related. In other words, for these forum members, a woman's resistance to sexual activity is actually a manifestation of ASD. By this logic, then, rather genuinely expressing resistance and lack of consent to any further sexual contact, these women actually *do* want to have sex but are showing resistance only so as to not appear a 'slut' to themselves or anyone else. Conceptualising resistance as an insincere self-protective measure used by women to save their own reputation rather than an actual lack of consent serves to diminish the legitimacy of the resistance and in turn makes it an easier moral decision for men to continue with sexual advances; women really do want to have sex, regardless of what they say or do. That is, resistance is 'routinely expected to arise rather than read as a signal to stop' (Cosma and Gurevich 2020: 54). For Dayter and Rüdiger (2019: 16), phrases such as 'anti-slut defence' demonstrate how women's behaviour is represented 'as a defence mechanism that needs to be overcome by the attacking force, i.e. the pick-up artist'. This analysis can be applied to (27)–(29) as they all express a desire to 'overcome', 'disable' and 'plow through' ASD. 'Disable' is particularly noteworthy here, as it draws specifically on the idea of ASD as a 'mechanism' that can be activated and deactivated by the man. ASD is given the same short-shrift treatment as LMR in (29), and again the two things are conflated. Resistance is considered a (very weak) self-defence mechanism through which the man in question should have plowed. Moreover, rather than being treated as signals that the woman did not consent to escalated sexual activity, ASD and LMR are instead thought to be signs that 'she was asking for it'.

The final collocates for discussion in this section are *shit* and *test*. These words are both returned as collocates of LMR (Table 6.3) but in fact almost always appear together; of the 36 times *shit* appears as a collocate of LMR, 32 are in the phrase *shit test*. *Shit tests*, like *token resistance* and *ASD*, are community-based register-specific 'technical' terms. They are defined as 'often unconscious (and sometimes conscious) tests that women throw at men in order to quickly determine their social status' and occur 'when a woman gives a guy a hard time, usually for the purpose of seeing how he will react' (*PUA Lingo* 2008). As with the definitions of many other PUA terms, the extent to which women are in conscious control of their actions is questioned. Presumably, if a woman's behaviour is believed to be sub-conscious, then it is easier to dismiss any signs of non-consent as being 'accidental' rather than real. At the same time, the behaviour of a woman is framed from the ego-centric position that it is designed to evaluate how *men* react. *Shit tests* of this kind are bundled together with LMR in various ways in SFC:

30 SO much LMR. She said she wasn't ready like 10 times, I but I plowed through that. The language reminded me of some of the LMR and **shit-tests** I've heard here. It was funny.
31 15 minutes later we were making out – but every time I reached for her pussy I got heavy LMR, **shit testing** me all evening.
32 What's a good response when she says 'not on the first date' type of LMR? I failed that **shit test** but the prospect of a second date is strong.

Framing LMR together with shit-tests creates the sense of battle or competition between the men and women in pick-up encounters. It implies that resistance is a 'test' that the woman is setting for the man, and he will either pass or 'fail' (as in 32) depending on whether or not they end up having sex. This way, LMR and shit-tests are conceptualised as deceptive and manipulative strategies used by women to counteract the pick-up strategies employed by men. A potential sexual encounter therefore becomes an adversarial battle of tactics, with a winner and a loser, rather than a moment of consensual intimacy. Considering resistance in this way and repositioning the event as adversarial 'game' re-contextualise the attempts at sexual activity and ultimately make it easier for men to ignore resistance; passing a shit-test and/or overcoming LMR is an alpha-status-affirming victory for the PUA.

There is an obvious danger in the ideological assumption reflected here that LMR is 'token' resistance, the product of some self-protective 'anti-slut defence' or a deceptive shit-test set by women to challenge men. Such assumptions reinforce the belief that women will eventually succumb to the sexual advances of men. Token resistance can 'encourage men to ignore women's refusals', and previous encounters of token resistance can strengthen a man's belief that 'women's refusals are not to be taken seriously' (Muehlenhard and Hollabaugh 1988: 878). Viewing resistance in such a way makes it 'difficult to envisage any situation in which a woman's "no" would legitimately be heard as such' (O'Neill 2018: 101). This belief can lead to sexual assault. Accounts by convicted rapists of their crimes demonstrate the ways in which their (mis)understanding of consent is based on notions of token resistance as they describe that their victims said no but that they didn't think that they meant it (Scully and Marolla 1984: 534; Pemberton 2012: 130). In the posts analysed here, discourses of resistance are framed within ideological frames of 'anti-slut defence', 'shit-tests' and 'token resistance' as the *norm*. In turn, this undermines the legitimacy and sincerity of a women's resistance and demonstrates and exemplifies Denes's (2011: 417) warning that the PUA community 'may be perpetuating false beliefs about the prevalence of token resistance and inadvertently contributing to sexual aggression'.

Resistance as remarkable

The fact that some level of resistance is routine and expected by PUAs is reflected in how noteworthy they consider it to be when they do not face resistance. *No* and *zero* are the second- and third-highest ranking in terms of MI^3 scores in the corpus. Both of these collocates signal the lack of resistance reported by posters:

33 When I asked her about it afterwards (since there was absolutely **no** LMR and she jumped on my dick moments after we kissed) she said that she wasn't worried.
34 By that point she was laying down – **zero** LMR. I took her clothes off easily and we banged.

We have seen in the sections above that a woman's resistance to sex is no deterrent to PUAs, who see such resistance as a deceptive test of their masculinity which they must overcome. Here, focus shifts to field reports in which PUAs describe *not* being able to overcome LMR. Such posts share collocates of LMR that were categorised as 'High resistance' (Table 6.3). In instances such as this, the remarkable or surprising nature of resistance is emphasised by PUAs:

35 Pulled a girl in a club last night, but couldn't overcome **heavy** LMR. Not usually an obstacle for me.
36 The last few times I did this it resulted in two lays and 1 heavy make out. Could've easily been all three if not for a strange case of **strong** LMR.
37 Got a second date with a girl but got **severe** LMR and never got the bang. So this seems a bit unusual.
38 My last 3 pulls have all put up **massive** LMR. I only banged one of them and that was after a whole night of trying [...] normally I consider pushing through LMR to be a strength of mine, so I'm a bit confused and attempting to diagnose the problem.

In these instances, the LMR reported by forum members is so *heavy*, *massive*, *strong* and *severe* that they are unable to 'overcome' it and are not successful in having sex with the women in question. When they are forced to post field reports of encounters such as these where they are not able to escalate to sex, the steadfastness of the woman's resistance is emphasised by these evaluative adjectives as being remarkable or unusual. Moreover, such instances are described as 'strange' (36) or 'unusual' (37) and are a source of confusion (38). A woman's resistance to the sexual advances of man can only be considered strange, unusual or confusing when viewed from a particular ideological perspective. In a belief system that considers consent to be tacitly presumed (Cosma and Gurevich 2020: 54), experiences where consent is *not* given need to be accounted for by PUAs. Such an ideology is characterised by patriarchal beliefs related to male sexual entitlement and female sexual compliance. The brand of masculinity which underlies 'The Red Pill' philosophy and online spaces such as those occupied by PUAs is 'orientated to achieve the traditional hegemonic aims of sexual conquest, social dominance, and self-improvement using misogynistic philosophy' (Mountford 2018: 2). This belief is situated within a wider patriarchal world-view which includes the belief that men are entitled to sex and that 'men have strong, and often uncontrollable, sexual needs that must be fulfilled and that women must serve that purpose' (Bouffard 2010: 871). Therefore, when individuals with this perspective encounter a woman's resistance to the extent where they do not eventually have sex, their reaction is one of confusion that such resistance is unusually and puzzlingly high. Such is the unexpectedness of effective resistance from women that it is framed as a 'problem' which needs to be 'diagnosed' (38). Indeed, there is further evidence of forum members trying to account for the *extreme* or *severe* LMR that they counter:

39 She invited me to her place and I thought I was going to get the bang but she put up <u>extreme</u> LMR twice. My analysis is the same as yours: she was recently a "victim" of a dumping and is trying to get a man to sign up to a relationship before putting out.

40 There's also the advantage that if she turns out to be looney or starts giving you <u>severe</u> LMR then you're free to walk away without having to worry about how you're going to get this weird chick to move out.

Here, the commenters resolve that there must be something wrong with the women in question that explains the amount of resistance that they put up. Rather than legitimately not consenting to sex , the women either must be reeling from a recent bad relationship (39) or are 'loony' and 'weird' (40). When the misogynistic patriarchal ideals underlying the PUA ideology hold the traditional sexual script 'in which women's role is to act resistant to sex and men's role is to persist in their sexual advances despite women's resistance' (Muehlenhard and Hollabaugh, 1988: 872), there needs to be some explanation when this does not come to pass. To put it another way, there must be something unusual at play when a woman's resistance to sex is revealed to be genuine rather than 'token'. As is demonstrated by these examples, this is regarded as being the fault of the woman, again undermining any genuine resistance and serving to diminish women's agency in consensual sex.

Posts in the corpus also show that PUAs weigh up the trade-off between overcoming unusually high levels of LMR and their subsequent levels of satisfaction:

41 I got a girl to my place and we kissed but the bitch was teasing me with **crazy** LMR and saying she don't have sex without love. She wasn't hot enough to be worth it so I kicked her out.

42 The date is usually boring, **heavy** LMR, and even if do you have sex with her the sex is bad. Then you find yourself asking, was that worth it?

43 Today I had a date with tall girl but she gave me **crazy** LMR. I could barely get her top off but no chance with the pants. I pulled my dick out and she gave me a rubbish handjob. I also noticed her freakishly large feet.

In (41), the poster determined that the woman in question was not worth battling 'crazy' LMR so he kicked her out. However, as (42) and (43) show, even if they do have sex, the men are resentful of the initial resistance and insult the woman or her sexual performance. Research into sexual coercion (e.g. Baumeister et al. 2002; Bouffard, 2010) has argued that some men may interpret a woman's resistance to their sexual advances as a personal insult and a denial of their freedom and entitlement to gain sexual gratification and therefore may react angrily. One manifestation of this anger in this PUA community is to degrade and demean any woman who has the audacity to show them resistance, regardless of whether or not they eventually had sex.

Resistance as temporary

In most of the examples of posts analysed to this point, the LMR experienced by forum members was temporary. That is, despite there being resistance, the men report eventually having sex with the women. The final discourse prosody to be addressed here emerging from the collocates of LMR will focus on this temporariness of LMR and how it is constructed in the forum. There are two main collocate types which form the basis of this analysis: the analysis of *but* and the analysis of temporally salient collocate *hour(s)*.

But is the tenth strongest collocate of LMR in the corpus, reflecting its frequent and important role in the discourse of resistance in this context. The ideational function of *but* is to 'mark an upcoming unit as a contrast with a prior unit' (Schiffrin 1987: 176), and it is interesting with regard to 'LMR' given that 71 of its 75 instances appear *after* 'LMR'. There are two main patterns in which LMR is followed by *but*. The first, and less prevalent of the two, are posts in which authors report how they pushed through some LMR, or thought about it, *but* in the end relented in their advances:

44 I call her on it and said "oh you're pulling that card already". I push through some more LMR <u>but</u> couldn't get through it. I whipped out my dick but it didn't help.

45 Looking back I did everything I could try to overcome the LMR <u>but</u> she just wasn't having any of it.

46 She was tipsy and didn't want to do anything more that night. There was a little bit of LMR <u>but</u> I didn't want to push past that since she was tipsy. That's where things can go bad.

47 I was wise to not go full blast trying to push through LMR, <u>but</u> pulled back at the right time and almost started feeling guilty.

Two different scenarios are represented in these examples. In (44) and (45), the situation did not escalate to sexual intercourse despite the man's best efforts. They chose to halt their sexual advances because they 'couldn't get through' the resistance or because the woman 'wasn't having any of it'. However, in (46) and (47), the men report deciding to cease in their attempts to push through LMR. Interestingly, both of these posts strike a reflective tone of a sort we have not yet seen in the data. In (46), the forum member reports that they didn't want to push through resistance because the girl was drunk and states that 'that's where things can go bad'. It might be inferred from this that 'goes bad' refers to possible ramifications for the poster if he persisted in having sex with a girl who was intoxicated, presumably given the implications of consent in such circumstances. Whether or not he would have continued to challenge resistance had she not been drunk is unknown. In (47), the poster recounts 'pulling back' and not pushing through LMR and reports feelings of guilt, signalling that this poster (at least) acknowledges the seriousness of pushing through resistance.

In stark contrast to these examples, the most prevalent pattern emerging from *but* collocates is one in which forum members report experiencing LMR but continuing sexual escalation and eventually having sex:

48 She told me "just to let you know we are not going to have sex today". She meant it. I couldn't overcome her LMR <u>but</u> put her hand on my dick and she started rubbing.

49 Last night a girl gave me tons of verbal LMR **but** her body was screaming yes so I just pushed on.
50 There was a bit of LMR **but** there was real attraction so things went through after some simple back and forth.
51 There was LMR **but** the bang was inevitable. I slept over at hers and we banged in the morning too.

These examples represent a pattern similar to many of those that have already been analysed. However, each of them gives new and a slightly different insight into the community's perception of resistance and how or why it is overcome. In (48), the poster reports using a strategy when faced with resistance of forcing the woman to initiate sexual contact by grabbing her hand and placing it on his genitals. While a different form of coercion to 'pushing through' a woman's resistance, forcing her to touch a penis against her consent is coercion nonetheless and is a common behaviour reported in this corpus (Wright 2021). In (49), we see the man disregarding a woman's explicit verbal resistance in favour of an interpretation that her 'body was screaming yes'. Although this poster does not elaborate on what precise physical behaviour led him to this interpretation, Denes (2011: 417) emphasises that central to the pick-up script is the belief that unless physical force is used to stop the sexual behaviour, the woman is consenting to the activity and verbal resistance can be ignored. In (50), the poster describes how he ignored LMR and continued to make sexual advances but in doing so removes entirely any mention of sex. Instead, he describes what is presumably the ensuing sexual intercourse as 'things went through'. In some ways, this serves to mitigate, or at least make implicit, the potential sexual aggression involved in such a way that posters perceive their responsibility to be diminished (as was noted earlier in the analysis) and instead framing persistence against resistance as almost transactional, thus removing any moral agency from the behaviour. Finally, in (51), we see the expression of the sentiment which essentially underlies all of these previous examples; there was some LMR but sex 'was inevitable'. In one sentence, this encapsulates many of the ideologies around resistance that this chapter has identified.

These examples all demonstrate the ways in which members of the forum report ignoring verbal resistance from women and persist in their sexual advances. However, this persistence is brought into even sharper focus by the final LMR collocate to be examined in this analysis – *hour(s)*:

52 We hung out in her room again. I spent about 6 **hours** with her battling LMR (I feel like it was a mistake to spend that long with her). [...] I managed to get her down to her panties but it was very late so eventually I gave up and left.

53 On saturday a virgin girl came over, got the bang after load of LMR and "she wasn't ready" but I managed to get it after like 3 **hours** of LMR haha.

54 Same epic LMR but few **hours** later it was done. The walls are broken, her castle of resistance is in ruin after a 3 **hour** siege.

These examples emphasise the perseverance of some forum members in attempting to overcome LMR; they report spending hours persisting and insisting on sexual escalation in the face of resistance. Again, all three of the examples here demonstrate the men essentially ignoring resistance and continuing in their pursuit of sexual gratification. This is clear in (52), where the poster reports spending as long as six hours 'battling' LMR. The poster laments that it was maybe a 'mistake' spending so long 'battling' this girl's LMR presumably not because she was resisting but because it was ultimately a fruitless endeavour for him. The story is different in (53), however, where a forum member reports experiencing LMR and imitates the woman explicitly saying that 'she wasn't ready' to have sex. He claims to have persisted for three hours before he eventually 'managed to get it'. Earlier in the analysis, we saw the military metaphor being used to recast the persistence against resistance being recast as a 'battle'. No clearer is this metaphor than in (54), in which various elements of the metaphor are invoked; the LMR was 'epic', and the woman's resistance is represented as her 'castle of resistance'. The repeated sexual advances over three hours is said to have left her resistance 'in ruin'. The continuation of this metaphor reveals a telling and recurrent ideology within this particular PUA community – a man who can persevere through a woman's resistance is glorified as victorious while she is the defeated loser. In legal contexts, women are expected to meet the standard of 'utmost resistance' in order to demonstrate that they did not consent to sex. These examples reflect the fact that women may face *utmost persistence* from men, sometimes over the course of several hours.

Conclusion

Existing research in forensic linguistics which examines the discursive relationship between notions of consent and resistance has done so mainly in the context of police interviews and courtroom cross-examination. The analysis in this chapter has shifted the focus away from the legal space into an online PUA community, whose primary goal is to achieve sexual gratification from women. The findings here add a new dimension to the discursive relationship between resistance and consent. Ehrlich (2012: 401) argues that the utmost resistance standard invoked by the defence lawyers in rape and sexual assault cases is problematic because it 'downplays and obscures the unequal power dynamics that often characterize male/female sexual relations'. The analysis here has revealed first-hand accounts of these unequal power dynamics. The discourse prosodies revealed by the analysis have shown that resistance is considered to be an obstacle that must be pushed through or a problem that must be solved. It is recast by men as a fight or competition with winners and losers or a test set by deceptive and manipulative women. Women's agency in consensual sex is trivialised, diminished and delegitimised, and beliefs about resistance and consent are fuelled by ideals of male entitlement and female compliance. Although some PUA definitions expressly state that men should 'under no circumstances make the girl feel pressured' (*PUAmore* 2016a), what ultimately has emerged from this analysis is that women's resistance to sex is routinely ignored. The examples analysed here provide a crucial insight into the force, persistence, and aggression that women can face from men – all the while being held accountable for the violence they face if they are deemed to not have resisted 'enough'.

Finally, the online context and nature of this communication cannot be overlooked or underestimated. The relationship between online activity and offline behaviour is becoming increasingly clear, with research finding that the communities and communications in which individuals are involved online affect their actions offline. Sillence (2010), for example, found that in a healthcare context, forum members use advice from fellow members to support and reinforce their offline clinical decision-making, such as their interactions with doctors. At the same time, it is now thought that the vast amount of radicalisation and violent extremism occurs in online spaces (Edwards and Gribbon 2013). Online discussion forums are places where like-minded people with similar values and norms seek each other out to collectively reinforce their beliefs and rationalise their actions. This effect often can be exacerbated when the ideologies they share are widely stigmatised by 'outsiders'. Bloch (2016) analyses this phenomenon in an anti-immigrant forum in which members reject the opposing view that they are racist and within the forum share accounts with each other that construct positive identities and affirm and legitimise one another's emotions and beliefs (Bloch 2016: 265). In a PUA context, ideologies not only are affirmed but are celebrated, as members are vying for each other's approval in a quest to construct the ideologically constructed hypermasculine alpha-male identity so revered in the community (Schuurmans and Monaghan 2015). Therefore, in a situation in which dangerous ideologies about women's resistance to sex are being shared and reinforced, and tales of sexual victory after pushing through or overcoming sexual resistance are proudly told, this may increase the risk of forum members committing violent sexual crimes offline. Indeed, recent research has found that individuals who hold problematic beliefs about sex, such as a perspective that sex is a game in which men must emerge victorious, are especially likely to use the kinds of techniques promoted by the PUA community to manipulate potential sexual partners (Klement et al. 2019). Ultimately, therefore, online communities and discussion spaces such as that analysed in this chapter have the potential to become the source of cyber-enabled violence against women and girls. Some of the posts that have been presented here may constitute incitement – or admission – of such violence.

Notes

1 Camp was reinstated into the Law Society of Alberta in 2018.
2 johnnycassell.com.
3 The PUA in question later had his conviction quashed on the basis of a legal challenge to the cross-examination conducted in the original trial.
4 I owe an enormous debt of thanks to Dr Ikechukwu Ekene Onyenwe for his work on the collection and preparation of this data.

References

Baker, P., Gabrielatos, C., KhosraviNik, M., Krzyżanowski, M., McEnery, T. and Wodak, R. (2008) A useful methodological synergy? Combining critical discourse analysis and corpus linguistics to examine discourses of refugees and asylum seekers in the UK press. *Discourse & Society* 19(3): 273–306. https://doi.org/10.1177/0957926508088962

Baker, P., Gabrielatos, C. and McEnery, T. (2013) Sketching Muslims: A corpus driven analysis of representations around the word 'Muslim' in the British press 1998–2009, *Applied Linguistics* 34(3): 255–278, https://doi.org/10.1093/applin/ams048

Baumeister, R. F., Catanese, K. R., and Wallace, H. M. (2002) Conquest by force: A narcissistic reactance theory of rape and sexual coercion. *Review of General Psychology* 6(1): 92–135. https://doi.org/10.1037/1089-2680.6.1.92

Bess, G. (2018) What it's like to be hit on by a pick-up artist. *Vice*. (online). 19 January 2018. Available from: https://www.vice.com/en_us/article/bjy3q4/playing-the-game-the-game-a-haunting-pick-up-artistdating-sim-angela-washko [Last accessed 19 October 2021].

Bloch, K. R. (2016) "It is just SICKENING": Emotions and discourse in an anti-immigrant discussion forum. *Sociological Focus* 49(4): 257–270. https://doi.org/10.1080/00380237.2016.1169901

Bonnar, M. (2019) The seduction game. *BBC* (online). 7 October 2019. Available from: https://www.bbc.co.uk/news/extra/tmZeuc7TX0/the-seduction-game. [Last accessed April 2020].

Bouffard, L. A. (2010) Exploring the utility of entitlement in understanding sexual aggression. *Journal of Criminal Justice* 38(5): 870–879. https://doi.org/10.1016/j.jcrimjus.2010.06.002

Cosma, S. and Gurevich, M. (2018) (Re)producing the 'natural man' in men's online advice media: Achieving masculinity through embodied and mental mastery. *Psychology & Sexuality* 9(1): 86–97. https://doi.org/10.1080/19419899.2018.1434230

Cosma, S. and Gurevich, M. (2020) Securing sex: Embattled masculinity and the pressured pursuit of women's bodies in men's online sex advice. *Feminism & Psychology* 30(1): 42–62. https://doi.org/10.1177/0959353519857754
Davies, M.· (2019) The Corpus of Contemporary American English (COCA). Available from: https://www.english-corpora.org/coca/
Dayter, D. and Rüdiger, S. (2016) Reporting from the field: The narrative reconstruction of experience in pick-up artist online communities. *Open Linguistics* 2(1): 337–351. https://doi.org/10.1515/opli-2016-0016
Dayter, D. and Rüdiger, S. (2019) In other words: 'the language of attraction' used by pick-up artists. *English Today* 35(2): 13–19. https://doi.org/10.1017/S026607841800007X
Dayter, D. and Rüdiger, S. (2020) Talking about women: Elicitation, manual tagging, and semantic tagging in a study of pick-up artists' referential strategies. In: S. Rüdiger and D. Dayter (eds.), *Corpus Approaches to Social Media*. Amsterdam/Philadelphia: Benjamins, pp. 63–86.
Dayter, D. and Rüdiger, S. (2022) *The Language of Pick-Up Artists: Online Discourses of the Seduction Industry*. London: Routledge.
Denes, A. (2011) Biology as consent: Problematizing the scientific approach to seducing women's bodies. *Women's Studies International Forum* 34(5): 411–419. https://doi.org/10.1016/j.wsif.2011.05.002
Edwards, Cand Gribbon, L. (2013) Pathways to violent extremism in the digital era. *The RUSI Journal* 158(5): 40–47. https://doi.org/10.1080/03071847.2013.847714
Ehrlich, S. (2001) *Representing Rape: Language and Consensual Sex*. London: Routledge.
Ehrlich, S. (2012) Perpetuating – and resisting – rape myths in trial discourse. In E. Sheehy (ed.), *Sexual Assault Law, Practice and Activism in a Post-Jane Doe Era*. Ottawa: University of Ottawa Press, pp. 389–408.
Ehrlich, S. (2013) Post-penetration rape and the decontextualization of witness testimony. In J. Conley, C. Heffer and F. Rock (eds.), *Legal-Lay Communication: Textual Travels in the Law*. Oxford: Oxford University Press, pp. 189–205.
Ehrlich, S. (2015) 'Inferring' consent in the context of rape and sexual assault. In L. Solan, J. Ainsworth and R. Shuy (eds.), *Speaking of Language and Law: Conversations on the Work of Peter Tiersma*. Oxford: Oxford University Press, pp. 141–144.
Ehrlich, S. (2016) Post-penetration rape: Coercion or freely given consent. In S. Ehrlich, D. Eades, and J. Ainsworth (eds.), *Discursive Constructions of Consent in the Legal Process*. Oxford: Oxford University Press, pp. 47–70.
Gabrielatos, C. and Baker, P. (2008) Fleeing, sneaking, flooding: A corpus analysis of discursive constructions of refugees and asylum seekers in the UK press, 1996-2005. *Journal of English Linguistics* 36(1): 5–38. https://doi.org/10.1177/0075424207311247
Ging, D. (2019) Alphas, betas, and incels: Theorizing the masculinities of the manosphere. *Men and Masculinities* 22(4): 638–657. https://doi.org/10.1177/1097184X17706401
Grinberg, E. (2017) Judge who asked woman why she couldn't keep knees together resigns. *CNN* (online). 10 March 2017. Available from: https://edition.cnn.com/2017/03/09/world/robin-camp-rape-comments-judge-resigns-trnd/index.html [Last accessed 26 October 2021].
Hall, H. (2019) Sleazy pick-up artists are thriving – and they're exploiting men's insecurities over #MeToo to do it. *The Independent* (online). 8 October 2019.

Available from: https://www.independent.co.uk/voices/seduction-boot-camp-panorama-pick-up-artists-metoo-misogyny-a9148041.html [Last accessed 19 October 2021]

Hall, J. A. and Canterberry, M. (2011) Sexism and assertive courtship strategies. *Sex Roles* 65(11–12): 840–853. https://doi.org/10.1007/s11199-011-0045-y

Hambling-Jones, O., and Merrison, A. J. (2012) Inequity in the pursuit of intimacy: An analysis of British pick-up artist interactions. *Journal of Pragmatics* 44: 1115–1127. https://doi.org/10.1016/j.pragma.2012.04.008

Haworth, K. (2017) The discursive construction of evidence in police interviews: Case study of a rape suspect. *Applied Linguistics* 38(2): 194–214.

King, A. S. (2018) Feminism's flip side: A cultural history of the pickup artist. *Sexuality & Culture* 22(1): 299–315. https://doi.org/10.1093/applin/amv009

Klement, K. R., Xoxakos, P., Nazario, M., Erickson, J. M., Salley, S., Pieterick, M., DeLaFuente, J. L., Hemmerling, T. R., Martin, K. and Sagarin, B. J. (2019) Winning the game: How sexual narcissism relates to adversarial sexual beliefs and pick-up techniques. *Sexuality & Culture* 23(4): 1283–1300. https://doi.org/10.1007/s12119-019-09618-2

Krendel, A. (2020) The men and women, guys and girls of the 'manosphere': A corpus-assisted discourse approach. *Discourse & Society* 31(6): 607–630. https://doi.org/10.1177/0957926520939690

MacLeod, N. (2010) *Police Interviews with Women Reporting Rape: A Critical Discourse Analysis*. Unpublished PhD dissertation, Aston University.

MacLeod, N. (2016) 'I thought I'd be safe there': Pre-empting blame in the talk of women reporting rape. *Journal of Pragmatics* 96: 96–109. https://doi.org/10.1016/j.pragma.2016.03.008

Mautner, G. (2016) Checks and balances: How corpus linguistics can contribute to CDA. In R. Wodak and M. Meyer (eds.), *Methods of Critical Discourse Analysis* (3rd ed.). London: Sage, pp. 154–179.

Mountford, J. B. (2018) Topic modelling The Red Pill. *Social Sciences* 7(3). https://doi.org/10.3390/socsci7030042

Muehlenhard, C. L. and Hollabaugh, L. C. (1988) Do women sometimes say no when they mean yes? The prevalence and correlates of women's token resistance to sex. *Journal of Personality and Social Psychology* 54(5): 872–879. https://doi.org/10.1037//0022-3514.54.5.872

Mystery. (2007) The *Mystery Method: How to Get Beautiful Women into Bed*. New York: St. Martin's Press.

O'Neill, R. (2015) The work of seduction: Intimacy and subjectivity in the London 'seduction community'. *Sociological Research Online* 20(4): 172–185. https://doi.org/10.5153%2Fsro.3744

O'Neill, R. (2018) *Seduction – Men, Masculinity and Mediated Intimacy*. Cambridge, UK: Polity.

Oxford English Dictionary (2024) overcome, v. OED Online September 2024. Oxford: Oxford University Press. Available from: www.oed.com/view/Entry/134418 [Last accessed 22 October 2024].

Partington A. (2014) Evaluative prosody. In K. Aijmer and C. Rühlemann (eds.), Corpus *Pragmatics: A Handbook*. Cambridge, UK: Cambridge University Press, pp. 279–303.

Pemberton, S. L. (2012) *Talking about Rape: A Discursive Study of Convicted Adult Rapists' Accounts of Rape*. PhD dissertation, Nottingham Trent University. Available from: https://irep.ntu.ac.uk/id/eprint/19/

PUA Lingo (2008) Shit Test. (online) Available from: https://www.pualingo.com/shit-test/ [Last accessed 27 October 2021].

PUA Training (2020) *Last Minute Resistance guide: 5 things women say before sex*. (online). Available from: https://www.puatraining.com/blog/last-minute-objections-anti-slut-defence [Last accessed 21 October 2021].

PUAmore (2016a) *Last Minute Resistance*. (online) Available from: https://puamore.com/wiki/lmr-last-minute-resistance/ [Last accessed 21 October 2021].

PUAmore (2016b) *Anti-Slut Defense*. Available from: https://puamore.com/wiki/lmr-last-minute-resistance [Last accessed 27 October 2021].

Rheindorf, M. (2019) *Revisiting the Toolbox of Discourse Studies: New Trajectories in Methodology, Open Data, and Visualization*. Basingstoke: Palgrave.

Rüdiger, S. and Dayter, D. (2020) Manbragging online: Self-praise on Pick-up Artists' forums. *Journal of Pragmatics* 161: 16–27. https://doi.org/10.1016/j.pragma.2020.02.012

Schiffrin, D. (1987) *Discourse Markers*. Cambridge, UK: Cambridge University Press.

Schmitz, R. M. and Kazyak, E. (2016) Masculinities in cyberspace: An analysis of portrayals of manhood in men's rights activist websites. *Social Sciences* 5(2). https://doi.org/10.3390/socsci5020018

Schuurmans, J. and Monaghan, L. (2015) The Casanova-myth: Legend and anxiety in the seduction community. *Sociological Research Online* 20(1) (Online). https://doi.org/10.5153/sro.3535

Scully, D. and Marolla, J. (1984) Convicted rapists' vocabulary of motive: Excuses and justifications. *Social Problems* 31(5): 530–544. https://doi.org/10.1525/sp.1984.31.5.03a00050

Sillence, E. (2010) Seeking out very like-minded others: Exploring trust and advice issues in an online health support group. *International Journal of Web Based Communities* 6(4): 376–394. https://doi.org/10.1504/IJWBC.2010.035840

Steadman, I. (2014) The sexist pseudoscience of pick-up artists: The dangers of "alpha male" thinking. *New Statesman*. (online). 4 June 2014. Available from: https://www.newstatesman.com/future-proof/2014/06/sexist-pseudoscience-pick-artists-dangers-alpha-male-thinking [Last accessed 26 October 2021].

Strauss, N. (2005) *The Game: Penetrating the Secret Society of Pickup Artists*. New York: HarperCollins.

Stubbs, M. (2001) *Words and Phrases: Corpus Studies of Lexical Semantics*. London: Blackwell.

The Power Moves. (2021) *10 Ways to Overcome Any Last Minute Resistance*. (online). Available from https://thepowermoves.com/last-minute-resistance/ [Last accessed 21 October 2021].

Tiersma, P. M. (2007) The language of consent in rape law. In J. Cotterill (ed.), *The Language of Sexual Crime*. Basingstoke: Palgrave, pp. 83–103.

Travis, A. (2014) Julien Blanc barred from entering UK. *The Guardian*. (online). 19 November 2014. Available from: https://www.theguardian.com/lifeandstyle/2014/nov/19/julien-blanc-barred-entering-uk-pick-up-artist [Last accessed 26 October 2021].

Wikipedia. (2018) *Pickup artist*. (online). Available from: https://en.wikipedia.org/wiki/Pickup_artist [Last accessed 26 October 2021].

Wright, D. (2020) The discursive construction of resistance to sex in an online community. *Discourse, Context & Media* 36: 1–9, https://doi.org/10.1016/j.dcm.2020.100402

Wright, D. (2021) Corpus approaches to forensic linguistics. In M. Coulthard, A. Johnson and R. Sousa-Silva (eds.), *The Routledge Handbook of Forensic Linguistics* (2nd ed.) London: Routledge, pp. 611–627.
Wright, D. (2024) The importance of context in analysing the incitement of violence: A case study of an online community. In S. Rüdiger and D. Dayter (eds.), *Manipulation, Influence and Deception: The Changing Landscape of Persuasive Language*. Cambridge, UK: Cambridge University Press, pp. 157–176.

7 The reporting of new laws in the British national press

Introduction

Public confidence in the criminal justice system is a priority for the Ministry of Justice in the U.K. Ensuring that the public believe that the law is fair and effective is 'important for the efficient functioning of the system, for example in securing cooperation from victims and witnesses' (Jansson 2015: 1). However, for those who do not have personal experience with the legal system and for whom the law and legal processes are absent from ordinary everyday lived experiences, there is 'ample opportunity for the media to act as a proxy for personal contact with the legal system' (Gies 2007: 3) which can 'ultimately prove corrosive of law's authority and autonomy' and severely compromise people's confidence in the legal system (Gies 2007: 1–2).

The media can have a considerable effect on people's understanding of the law and legal system, or what Trubek (1984: 592) refers to as their 'legal consciousness': 'that aspect of consciousness of any society which explains and helps justify its legal institutions'. The media has the power to integrate 'law's there and then with daily life's here and now', and whether it is portrayed as 'menacing, reassuring or simply irrelevant', the media gives the law 'a visceral presence in the here and now of the lifeworld' (Gies 2007: 31). Although it is possible for the media to have a positive impact on people's understanding of the law and contribute to a healthy public debate on issues of justice (Gies 2003: 23), the contribution of the media to the public's legal consciousness is generally considered to be negative. Gies (2007: 1–2) describes the 'mass media's iron grip on the popular legal imagination' as a 'persistent stream of distorted and sensationalised media portrayals' which 'act as a poor proxy for a proper understanding of what law is about'.

Persuasion is one of the main functions of newspaper discourse, aiming at 'regulation of the addressee's behaviour and thinking' (Smirnova 2009: 79). This may be particularly true of newspaper reporting on the

DOI: 10.4324/9781003017301-7

law; the very nature of the law and its application leaves 'considerable scope for widely differing and conflicting interpretations' which casts 'serious doubt on the possibility of an unbiased or undistorted portrayal of law' (Gies 2005: 171). News media are able to produce ideologically skewed representations of the law to serve their political aims, be that in support of a given law(s) or in opposition. These representations can shape public opinion about particular legislative proposals, which in turn can place pressure or scrutiny on political or legal actors and shape beliefs on fundamental issues such as justice, fairness and morality. At the same time, the media can influence discourses around crimes and offences themselves, emphasising some offences more than others and constructing stereotyped, 'ideal' images of offenders and victims.

This chapter explores the ways in which new laws and new legislation are reported in British national newspapers. In particular, it takes the view that newspapers report on new laws not purely to inform but to persuade or encourage their readers to support or oppose particular legislative proposals. For this reason, the chapter takes a corpus-assisted approach to analysing implicit argumentation within newspaper coverage of new laws, whether they are being proposed, debated, passed or enforced. Rather than focusing on any one new law or issue, as has tended to be the tradition in the literature, this chapter focuses on how 'new law(s)' or 'new legislation' has been represented *generally* in the first two decades of the twenty-first century. In order to do this, it proposes a new method of identifying and analysing arguments using corpus-assisted methods, combining collocation analysis with an established model of analysing argument patterns.

Legislation and media influence

New laws or legislative changes can feature in the news media at different points in the law-making process. They can be reported on when they are first mentioned or mooted by (usually) those involved in law-making, while they are being formally proposed and debated by governments and law-makers and then, if/when they are passed, enacted and come into force. Smith et al. (2016: 58–9) remind us that the relationship between media and policy is bidirectional and mutually enforcing and that while 'organizations, lobbyists and specialized interests may be using the media as one level of influence on policy', legal decision-makers themselves are critical consumers of media messages as well as active agents who shape its content. There is a good amount of evidence in the literature on media and law that demonstrates the effect that media coverage can have on both the perception and understanding of the law (or, more specifically, particular pieces of legislation) and how this coverage can influence the law-making process.

The power of the media is such that it can be the very driving force behind the introduction of new legislation or policy changes. For example, a campaign by the now-defunct British Sunday tabloid newspaper *The News of the World* in 2000 was integral in helping 'to create conditions conducive to extraordinary measures the government was already contemplating' in respect of the laws surrounding child sex offences in the U.K. following the murder of nine-year-old Sarah Payne (Critcher 2002: 526). Media coverage of offences have been found to shape official regulation, legislative agendas and even the terminology of the laws themselves. Meyer (2010) shows how representations in the press of paedophiles as evil, organised and cunning individuals who obtain jobs involving children or groom children by befriending them have informed and influenced employment vetting regulations in the U.K. and the Sexual Offences Act 2003. Shelby and Hatch (2014) also found that in the legislative documents associated with 'Megan's Law'[1] in the United States, highly publicised and sensationalised cases of children victimised by a stranger sexual predator 'are relied on to construct a singular image of sexual violence' which 'obscures other types of sexual assault and might discourage victims of less well-publicized but more widespread forms of sexual violence' (Shelby and Hatch 2014: 403, 415). As well as supporting and shaping new legislation, the media can play a central role in blocking a proposed law. For example, Bauder (2008) shows how German media presented immigration as a dangerous threat to the country by creating a discursive link between immigration and terrorism that stemmed legislative change that was intended to attract skilled migrants.

Most legislative debates played out in the media see both supportive and oppositional coverage of the proposed changes, which generally reflect the views of different stakeholders involved. This has been demonstrated in studies of media coverage related to the introduction of a soft drinks levy in the U.K. (Hilton et al. 2019), increasing the age for the legal sale of tobacco in the U.S. (Hrywna et al. 2022) and proposed pension reforms in Lithuania (Juska 2021). Such commentaries about the law in the media, though ideologically fuelled and subject to influence and input from parties with vested interests, can bring to light important details about law for the public and can help mediate public understanding (if not support) of the current and proposed state of legislation in relation to the issue at hand. Brubacher et al. (2015: 233), for example, argued that the balanced coverage of the Motor Vehicle Act in British Colombia, Canada between 2010 and 2015 played an important role in 'generating public awareness of the legislative changes and helped mediate the changes in drinking and driving behavior brought about by the new laws'. Likewise, McGinty et al. (2016: 12) found that the reporting for and against the legalisation of marijuana in the U.S. has, perhaps inadvertently, provided the public with the best available evidence in relation to the costs and benefits of the policy itself. In a similar way, Pallin et al.'s (2021) content analysis of U.S. newspaper coverage of extreme risk protection order laws in 2018 following the Parkland school shooting 'appeared to facilitate discussion of various strategies for preventing gun violence' and 'may help counter the conventional narrative about gun violence as extreme and unchangeable' (Pallin et al. 2021: 9, 11).

However, in cases where the media debate is more polarised (and polarising), there is a risk that instead of illuminating the public on issues of law and policy, the media can obscure and obfuscate the details, motivations and relative costs/benefits of proposed legislation. For example, Schindel and Given (2013) show how in the media debate around a Canadian law that permitted pharmacists the authority to independently prescribe medicines, pharmacists were simultaneously represented as qualified *and* unqualified to prescribe medicine and both responsible *and* not responsible for diagnosis. The change itself was portrayed as both an improvement in access to healthcare *and* a risk to patient safety. The presentation of these contradictory positions, Schindel and Given (2013: 392) argue, provides an unclear message which does not serve the public interest. Similarly, analyses of news coverage of the Human Rights Act (1998) in the U.K. have shown how the media routinely oversimplify complex human rights cases, depicting it as 'The Looney Law' (Mooney 2002: 395) and a 'villains' charter' (Gies 2010), implying that the law serves to protect those who do not deserve protection and ignores those who do. Paterson and Coffey-Glover (2018) and Turner et al. (2018) found that the polarised newspaper coverage of the debate around the Marriage (Same-Sex Couples) Bill in the U.K. reduced the complexities of the debate to the semantics of 'marriage' (Paterson and Coffey-Glover 2018: 200) and presented the debate as an oppositional conflict which always had a victim (marriage itself, people of faith, the church) and which squeezed out any neutral ground in the debate (Turner et al. 2018: 194).

Finally, in some cases, the media coverage of a proposed legislative change does not reflect a 'debate'. Domke (2006) found that, with respect to the anti-terror U.S. Patriot Act which was introduced, debated and enacted between 11 September 2001 and 25 October 2001, the media reporting across 18 leading print and television news outlets across the country essentially 'echoed' the political messaging of the George W. Bush Administration at the time. In this way, Domke et al. (2006: 209) argue, the news media pressured Congress to pass the legislation in a time of crisis, actively encouraging political actors and the public to rally behind the president and the proposed legislation, while silencing any potential dissident voices. Similarly, Bossio's (2011) detailed account of the reporting of changes to Australian anti-terror laws in the immediate aftermath of 9/11 in two mainstream newspapers shows that even when there is substantial opposition to particular laws, newspapers amplify official governmental discourses, admiring the state actors' determination in implementing the laws and attacking those opposed to them (including other newspapers).

It is clear from the existing literature that 'the news media has the capacity to both set and change policy agendas through mobilisation of the public and public opinion' (Ducat et al. 2009: 164). With some exceptions (e.g. Paterson and Coffey-Glover 2018, Turner et al. 2018), the majority of the studies outlined here are not linguistic but originate from media and journalism, politics or law. At the same time, one thing that binds these studies together is that they all focus on specific individual laws. Doing this allows these studies to provide contextually rich thematic or content analyses of media coverage against a detailed and thorough social, cultural and legislative history around the law(s) being analysed. Therefore, although we know much about the relationship between the media and the law and how this manifests in specific cases at specific times and in specific countries, we know much less about the media representation of legal and legislative changes *en masse*. It is that gap which the analysis in this chapter seeks to address.

The New Laws in the News Corpus

The corpus used in this chapter was designed to capture as much U.K. national news coverage about the introduction of new laws as possible over a substantial period of time. To this end, a search was performed in the Nexis UK newspaper database for the phrase 'new law' or 'new laws' or 'new legislation' to appear anywhere in the articles of all British national newspapers between 1 January 2000 and 1 March 2020. The cut-off date of 1 March 2020 was chosen because later in the month the restrictions that were put in place by the U.K. government to tackle the spread of COVID-19 prompted a huge legislative response and the introduction of a quite unprecedented number of emergency laws in a short timeframe (Cormacain 2020). Therefore, the analysis here aims to identify trends in the media discourse during more 'ordinary' times of lawmaking. After duplicate articles were removed, the corpus comprised 75,563 articles and 59,582,160 words (Table 7.1). The newspapers included in the corpus, including their daily, Sunday and online versions, are *Daily Mail*, *Daily Star*, *Daily Telegraph*, *Express*, *Guardian*, *Independent*, *Metro*, *Mirror*, *People*, *Sun* and *Times*. After 2011, there is a marked increase in the number of articles and words in the corpus. This does not necessarily indicate an increased interest in new laws at that time but rather is due to the availability of articles published online (in addition to those originally in print) via Nexis after this point. The corpus is also imbalanced in favour of newspapers considered 'right-wing' or at least 'right-leaning' (cf. Wright and Brookes 2019), with 53,523

Table 7.1 Breakdown of the New Legislation Corpus by year

Year	*Articles*	*Words*
2000	1,421	953,816
2001	1,653	1,049,916
2002	1,736	1,096,870
2003	2,019	1,206,529
2004	2,187	1,375,040
2005	3,068	1,984,929
2006	2,990	1,914,384
2007	2,739	1,779,965
2008	2,252	1,369,368
2009	2,309	1,522,135
2010	2,526	1,556,226
2011	2,812	1,835,358
2012	5,422	4,273,839
2013	5,880	4,106,453
2014	6,055	4,715,227
2015	5,309	4,736,707
2016	5,859	6,694,510
2017	5,067	4,178,968
2018	5,885	5,114,018
2019	6,928	6,975,385
2020	860	781,415
Total	74,977	59,221,058

(70.75%) of all articles in the corpus coming from the *Daily Mail*, *Daily Star*, *Daily Telegraph*, *Express*, *Sun* and *Times*. Meanwhile, the left-leaning newspapers in the corpus are *Guardian*, *Independent*, *Metro*, *Mirror* and *People*. Again, rather than necessarily reflecting a disproportionate pre-occupation with new laws in the right-wing press, this instead reflects the reality of a British newspaper media dominated by such outlets (Smith 2017). The corpus included a range of newspaper sub-genres, such as news, opinion pieces, columns and letters to the editor. Later in the analysis, the newspapers are compared on the basis of their 'broadsheet' and 'tabloid' status. The tabloid newspapers in the corpus are the *Express*, *Daily Mail*, *Daily Star*, *Metro*, *Mirror*, *People* and the *Sun*. The broadsheet newspapers are the *Telegraph*, *Guardian*, *Independent* and the *Times*.

Using corpus techniques to analyse argumentation

Before describing the two defining elements of the approach to analysing arguments in this chapter, it is perhaps worth clarifying why such an analysis is appropriate here. Based on the overview of the literature on media representation of the law, it is clear that it is a type of discourse that is well suited to an argument-oriented analysis (cf. Reisigl and Wodak 2016: 27).

First, given its concern with law-making, this type of news reporting is situated at the interface of political, legal and media fields of action and is specifically aimed at the formation of public opinion. Second, it is socially *constituted* as well as socially *constitutive* insofar as its ability not only to evaluate the law-making process but to affect it. Finally, it relates to a macro-topic (usually a particular issue or proposed legislative change in relation to that issue) which involves social actors with different perspectives. At least one of the main purposes of the media coverage of legal changes is to *persuade* its readership, 'either in the sense of convincing by sound arguments or in the sense of influencing somebody suggestively and manipulatively by fallacies' (Reisigl 2014: 70). Therefore, to approach the analysis of these texts from an argumentative perspective seems fitting. The method applied here was designed and implemented in order to maximise transparency in relation to two main elements of the analysis, based on recommendations in previous work, namely Žagar (2010), Reisigl (2014) and Rheindorf (2019): (i) the identification of lexical clues to argumentation and (ii) the reconstruction of the arguments.

Identifying arguments

Approaches to analysing argumentation in (critical) discourse studies, particularly those adopting the Discourse Historical Approach, have typically drawn on the concept of *topoi* or 'content-related warrants or "conclusion rules" that connect the argument or arguments with the conclusion' (Reisigl and Wodak 2001: 75). For the most part, the specific issues that topoi have been used to understand are exclusionary and discriminatory discourse(s) relating to immigration, racism, ethnicism and nationalism (e.g. Reisigl and Wodak 2001, 2016; Richardson 2004; Hart 2010; Wright and Brookes 2019). Generally speaking, the way in which topoi are operationalised as a means of conducting critical discourse analysis (CDA) is that the analysis is carried out against a background of pre-determined lists of topoi (based on previous writing and knowledge on the topic), and content in the data that relate to these topoi is identified. In this way, the analysis of topoi might be considered 'top-down'. By contrast, instead of taking this top-down approach, the method employed in this chapter used corpus techniques to, as Žagar (2010: 25) proposes, 'mine' the data to bring its own arguments to the surface. This bottom-up approach relied on a collocation analysis of the search terms *new law(s)* and *new legislation* to identify 'semantic indicators' of specific arguments (Reisigl 2014: 93). All L1 and R1 lexical collocates of these terms with an MI^3 score of over 11 were included in the analysis. The application of this threshold follows Brezina et al. (2015) and is stricter than the lower thresholds of 3 or 6 used in some studies as representing 'genuine' collocations (e.g. Hunston 2002; Durrant and Doherty 2010).

The analysis also extended, as an exception, to R2 collocates in the infinitive form with an intervening *to* (e.g. 'new laws to curb'). Given that *to* was the most frequent collocate overall (n = 7135) and had the highest MI^3 score (MI3 = 28.30), the decision was taken to include these verbs in the analysis. The collocate span was restricted to a narrow span of collocates – L1 and R1 – to focus the analysis on those adjectives and verbs which immediately preceded and followed the search term, with the added benefit of returning a manageable number of collocates to deal with in the analysis.

Once all of the L1 and R1 collates which satisfied the MI^3 threshold were identified and isolated, they were manually categorised on the basis of their meaning(s)-in-use as being indicative or suggestive of particular arguments. This was an iterative process of grouping semantically similar collocates together first based on close reading of concordance lines, without determining the name or scope of the arguments that they may be related to; following Reisigl's (2014: 93) advice, the aim was to 'avoiding being too specific and too arbitrary'. Taking a quantitative approach to identifying the lexical anatomy of arguments in this way has the benefit of ensuring that the emergent arguments reflect *patterns* in the data, in the sense that they recur and are more representative of the discourse as a whole than low-frequency but eye-catching instances (cf. Rheindorf 2019: 334). As Rheindorf (2019: 344) notes, however, lexical items on their own, such as the collocates used here, are limited as a means by which to analyse argumentation. Therefore, a second stage of the method was followed to identify the scope, nature and nuances of the arguments being made in the data.

Reconstructing arguments

Generally speaking, in news discourse, the producers of text do not make explicit the argument that they are making; 'the conclusion is not spelled out. It is implicit in the argument. An initial, explicit or inferable, premise presupposes a particular conclusion' (Hart 2010: 66). However, even though this is the case, it has been argued that studies in (critical) discourse analysis which analyse arguments in discourse need to do more to reconstruct the arguments themselves, rather than simply referring to topoi or evoking them, and should explicate how the topoi being proposed or observed link arguments to conclusions (Žagar 2010: 11; Reisigl 2014: 86). Following recommendations by Žagar (2010: 22) and Reisigl (2014: 74), Toulmin's (2003 [1958]) model for analysing the pattern of arguments was used to reconstruct the arguments identified in the corpus. In Toulmin's model, topoi, to which he gives the more general label 'WARRANT', are considered within their wider argumentation scheme. Figure 7.1 outlines the six elements of Toulmin's (2003: 89–105) model for the form of arguments and gives a brief description of each element.

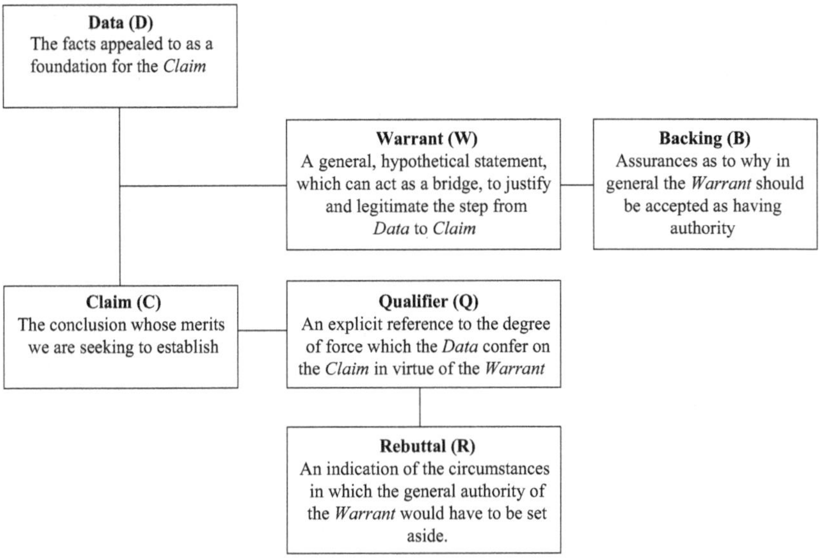

Figure 7.1 A diagram explaining Toulmin's (2003 [1958]) model for analysing patterns of arguments.

According to Toulmin's model, the CLAIM is the main assertion or point of the argument in question, which needs to be supported and justified, and the DATA is the explicit information or evidence on which the CLAIM is based, that would be provided should the argument be challenged along the lines of 'What have you got to go on?' By contrast, a challenge of 'How do you get there' requires not more data but instead is required to show that the step from the DATA to the CLAIM is an appropriate and legitimate one. This requires a WARRANT or a proposition that bridges the step from DATA to CLAIM in the form of a general or hypothetical statement (i.e. 'if *D* then *C*'). Toulmin's WARRANT roughly equates to 'topos' in the sense it creates the link between argument and conclusion (cf. Reisigl 2014: 75). Importantly, the WARRANT is implicit as opposed to explicit in way that DATA are. This three-part structure of DATA–WARRANT–CLAIM reflects that which is often cited by those in CDA, usually via Kienpointner (1992, 1996), of 'argument'–'topoi'–'conclusion'. For Toulmin, however, the pattern of argument is more complex than this and must account for different types of challenge. For instance, whereas some WARRANTS 'authorise us to accept a CLAIM unequivocally', others require us 'to make the step from data to conclusion either tentatively, or else subject to conditions, exceptions, or qualifications' (Toulmin 2003: 93). Therefore, in this model, the BACKING stands behind a WARRANT in support of its authority and helps to prove the general acceptability of the link between DATA and CLAIM; that is, it helps answer the question, 'Why should this warrant be accepted?' Indeed, there are some instances in which the authority of a WARRANT cannot be accepted and therefore it becomes impossible to bridge the step between DATA and CLAIM. These circumstances are represented in statements or propositions called REBUTTALS. The existence of valid rebuttals to an argument are acknowledged within this model by QUALIFIERS, such as 'probably' or 'usually', which make the CLAIM more tentatively. To demonstrate the model in use in full, Toulmin (2003: 97) provides the following example,[2] which is gradually built up over the course of his explanation (emphasis is mine):

> [I]n support of the CLAIM (**C**) that Harry is a British subject, we appeal to the DATA (**D**) that he was born in Bermuda, and the WARRANT (**W**) can then be stated in the form, 'A man born in Bermuda may be taken to be a British subject': since, however, questions of nationality are always subject to qualifications and conditions, we shall have to insert a QUALIFYING 'presumably' (**Q**) in front of the conclusion, and note the possibility that our conclusion may be REBUTTED (**R**) in case it turns out that both his parents were aliens or he has since become a naturalised American. Finally, in case the WARRANT itself is challenged, its BACKING (**B**) can be put in: this will record the terms and the dates of enactment of the Acts of Parliament and other legal provisions governing the nationality of persons born in the British colonies.

In sum, the argument in simple form would follow:

> Harry was born in Bermuda (**D**), and a man born in Bermuda will generally be a British subject (**W**) on account of statutes and other legal provisions (**B**). So, presumably (**Q**), unless both of his parents are aliens or he has become a naturalised American (**R**) Harry is a British subject (**C**).

The application of this model cannot rely on the quantification and identification of collocates alone (Rheindorf 2019: 134) but instead requires the careful reading of concordance lines for each collocate and qualitative analysis of the co-text surrounding given concordance lines. Using Toulmin's model in this way allows the analyst to make explicit the arguments being made even when (or especially when) they are not explicit in the original articles. In doing so, it goes some way to providing methodological transparency in identifying arguments in discourse and provides clarity when presenting the results of the analysis.

Analysis

This analysis will present and explicate the main patterns that emerge from the reporting of new laws and legislation over a 20-year period from 2000 to 2020. A total of eight themes or 'argument schemes' make up the analysis: PROHIBITION, PERMISSION, IMPOSITION, TOUGHNESS, NECESSITY, PROTECTION, CONTROVERSY and SCOPE. The names of these argument schemes are primarily based on the shared meanings of the collocates on which they are based, while reflecting the general theme of the argument itself. Drawing on Aristotelian terminology, these argument schemes can be considered as 'spaces', 'locations', or '"empty places" where concrete arguments, for different purposes, can be found' (Žagar 2010: 14). That is, a particular newspaper when reporting about a particular law or legislative change can invoke any of these schemes to present an argument either for or against that law or legislative change. In this way, these eight schemes are placeholders, elements of scaffolding that the newspapers can fill to construct their own argument to serve their own purposes. In the analysis below, each argument scheme will first be stated in full, the collocates which serve as lexical indicators to the argument are presented and then the composition of the argument is explicated with representative examples from the corpus.

Prohibition

The full argument scheme in relation to PROHIBITION is

> The new laws on *x* are prohibitive (**D**) and laws which are prohibitive should be supported (**W**) because they prevent things that should be prevented and increase protection for citizens and society (**B**). So, usually (**Q**), unless they make people's lives harder, have negative consequences or protect people who do not 'deserve' to be protected, (**R**) the new laws on *x* should be supported (**C**).

There are 88 collocates of *new law(s)/new legislation* which present laws as prohibiting, forbidding or restricting some action(s) or behaviour(s) – the largest number of collocates contributing to any of the argument schemes (Table 7.2).

Starting with the CLAIM, the overall (implicit) assertion of this argument is that the new laws in question should be supported. The DATA on which this argument is based and that is made explicit by these mainly verb collocates is that the laws are prohibitive in some way, preventing or outlawing certain practices and behaviours. Therefore, the implicit WARRANT at the heart of this argument scheme, linking the DATA and CLAIM, is that prohibitive laws should be supported. Of course, there needs to be some BACKING to support the authority of this WARRANT and convince readers that the WARRANT is valid and should be accepted; in other words, the reason *why* they should support prohibitive laws. Toulmin (2003: 96) states that the kind of BACKING that must be provided for establishing the authority of a WARRANT 'will change greatly as we move from one field of

Table 7.2 Collocates of new law(s)/legislation related to PROHIBITION

Position	*Collocate (frequency)*
L1 adjectives	*restrictive* (24), *repressive* (16)
R1 verbs	*banning* (753), *restricting* (125), *outlawing* (110), *preventing* (91), *criminalising* (78), *limiting* (77), *bans* (67), *cracking (down)* (52), *prohibiting* (44), *threatens* (37), *punishing* (38), *clamping* (38), *blocking* (34), *tightening* (27), *barring* (26), *curbing* (22), *prohibits* (21), *stops* (21), *threaten* (20), *forbidding* (19), *violates* (17), *prevents* (14), *removes* (14), *penalising* (12), *toughening* (11), *criminalises* (10), *restricts* (8), *curtailing* (7), *revoking* (7), *abolishes* (6), *interferes* (6), *tightens* (6), *dampens* (2), *threatens* (2)
R1 *to* +	*stop* (559), *tackle* (550), *prevent* (354), *ban* (319), *curb* (257), *crack* (240), *regulate* (230), *combat* (198), *deal* (156), *end* (148), *clamp* (111), *block* (106), *limit* (90), *control* (88), *outlaw* (76), *cut* (71), *punish* (69), *reduce* (68), *restrict* (66), *prosecute* (64), *jail* (61), *fight* (59), *tighten* (56), *criminalise* (55), *stamp* (46), *cap* (34), *halt* (28), *lock* (24), *deter* (23), *avoid* (19), *bar* (14), *penalise* (14), *boot* (13), *crackdown* (13), *shackle* (13), *shut* (13), *confiscate* (10), *stifle* (10), *curtail* (9), *fix* (9), *muzzle* (9), *stem* (9), *trap* (9), *prohibit* (8), *toughen* (8), *detain* (7), *discourage* (6), *imprison* (6), *constrain* (5), *deny* (5), *silence* (5)

argument to another'. This means that we can expect the BACKING offered for different WARRANTS within the different argument schemes to take different shapes. The BACKING offered in this particular argument scheme is that such prohibitive laws outlaw things that deserve to be outlawed. For example:

1 Upskirting has now become a crime and as of April 12, 2019, police can arrest under the new offence. Offenders are facing up to two years in jail and being placed on the sex offenders register. The **new law banning** the invasive practice will come into force across England and Wales. (*The Express*, 12 April 2019)

2 THE END OF PUPPY FARMING; ANOTHER MIRROR VICTORY. **New law bans** third-party pet sales to stop callous commercial breeders. (*Daily Mirror*, 22 August 2018)

3 Calls for **new law banning** adults sending sexual messages to children; There is no specific offence making online grooming illegal. (*The Independent*, 24 October 2014)

4 Prime Minister Theresa May called the attacks in east London 'horrific' as reports last night suggested **new laws restricting** the sale of acid could be proposed within days. (*The Express*, 15 July 2017)

These examples reflect the predominant pattern in the data; the things being prohibited are deserving of being prohibited – upskirting, puppy farming, grooming, violence and the sale of acid. These laws are presented as outlawing invasive and misogynistic practices (example 1), criminalizing those behaving in dangerous or irresponsible ways (2), filling a gap in the current legislation protecting children (3) and as a response to events and preventing them happening again (4). In other words, prohibitive laws (would/will) improve the legislative status quo in such a way that they improve the protection of citizens and society. The strength of the BACKING, and therefore the authority of the WARRANT, relies on a consensus among the newspapers' readerships that these are things that *should* be stopped, restricted or prevented. That is, they appeal to 'commonsense knowledge' (Wodak 2012: 529) or 'the common-sense reasoning typical for specific issues' (van Dijk 2000: 98).

However, there are also laws that are represented in such a way that their prohibitive nature is *not* beneficial to citizens and society in the same way:

5 A game of blind man's bluff. A **new law banning** poison will make it even harder to outwit moles, says Jonny Beardsall. (*Daily Telegraph*, 12 November 2005)
6 They warn that **new legislation banning** the display of cigarettes in Britain's shops from next year could fuel the illegal trade in tobacco and play into terrorists' hands. (*The Express*, 25 July 2010)
7 Satanists, witches and cult members will be protected by controversial **new laws banning** incitement to religious hatred. (*The Independent*, 10 June 2005)

In these cases, the laws are *unnecessarily* prohibitive; they are portrayed as making people's lives harder (5), having perhaps unforeseen negative consequences (6) or protecting people who apparently do not deserve protection (7). Circumstances such as these, in which the WARRANT and therefore the overall CLAIM of the argument cannot be accepted, represent REBUTTALS to the conclusion that prohibitive laws should be supported. The existence of these rebuttals requires the argument scheme to include the QUALIFIER that prohibitive laws should *usually*, but not always, be supported.

Permission

Not all laws are prohibitive in the ways that have been observed above; some laws are permissive. That is, rather than banning or stopping some form of action or behaviour, they allow or permit it. The full argument scheme in relation to PERMISSION is

> The new laws on *x* are permissive (**D**) and laws which are permissive should be supported (**W**) because they improve the rights, freedoms and lives of citizens (**B**). So, usually (**Q**), unless the new laws give permissions to already powerful actors or to 'undeserving' people, (**R**) the new laws on *x* should be supported (**C**).

All of the collocates that contribute towards this argument are verbs that represent the new laws as granting permission in some way, and they are the explicit lexical indicators of the DATA in this argument scheme (Table 7.3). The CLAIM about new laws in this argument scheme is that they should be supported. The implicit WARRANT, therefore, is that permissive laws should be supported. The BACKING that is used to support the validity and acceptability of this WARRANT is in the presentation of these laws granting new permissions, rights and freedoms to (vulnerable) members of society. For example:

8 The **new law allows** employees to take a short amount of time off to deal with specific circumstances involving a dependent, and the illness of a child is specified as such. (*The Independent*, 26 February 2000)
9 The Government yesterday announced **new legislation allowing** householders to use all force necessary to protect themselves or their properties. (*The Sun*, 20 July 2010)
10 Women in their 40s can sue the NHS from today if they are refused free fertility treatment. A **new law allows** patients to take legal action if they are denied health care on the basis of age. (*The Daily Mail*, 1 October 2012)
11 A woman is calling for **new laws to allow** victims of domestic violence to withhold their addresses in court to protect them and their children. (*The Telegraph*, 6 October 2013)

Permissive laws give citizens such as employees (8), householders (9), patients (10) and victims (11) new rights or protections that represent an

Table 7.3 Collocates of new law(s)/legislation related to PERMISSION

Position	*Collocate (frequency)*
R1 verbs	*allowing* (769), *allows* (258), *allow* (68), *permitting* (63), *allowed* (54), *enabling* (52), *granting* (40), *guaranteeing* (38), *lets* (22), *legalising* (22), *permits* (21), *authorising* (19), *facilitating* (10), *empowers* (5), *decriminalizes* (3)
R1 *to* +	*allow* (465), *help* (160), *enable* (55), *let* (44), *legalise* (21), *save* (20), *permit* (14), *assist* (10), *decriminalize* (7), *liberalise* (5)

improvement on the current legislative situation. That is, ultimately, these laws improve people's lives. Again, this BACKING appeals to and relies on a common agreement among the readership that these represent positive changes and changes which should be supported. As was the case with the PROHIBITION argument, permissive laws do not always stand to change things for the better:

12 The **new legislation allows** employers to obscure the fact that they are not paying homecare staff for all their working hours and allows them to pay illegal wages. (*The Mirror*, 15 April 2018)
13 In a speech to the Association of Certified Chartered Accountants Ireland last Friday, Shatter said he was anxious to ensure a **new law allowing** banks to repossess family homes would include 'additional safeguards' for homeowners. (*The Sunday Times*, 3 March 2013)
14 Bain is likely to call for savings of at least £150m and for **new legislation to allow** the government to close fire stations as part of the cutbacks. (*The Sunday Times*, 1 December 2002)
15 A BLUNDERING minister signed off a **new law allowing England yobs** to attend the World Cup. (*Daily Star*, 10 February 2014)

While there are laws that grant members of the public new freedoms and rights, there are also those laws that grant new powers to already powerful groups and authorities within society. The REBUTTAL here is that laws which permit employers to underpay staff (12), allow banks to repossess family homes (13), pave the way for the government to cut back on public services (14) and give undeserving 'yobs' particular freedoms (15) cannot be supported. The WARRANT in this argument scheme therefore seems to hinge on to whom the laws are giving new permissions; some groups should be allowed certain new rights and freedoms, while others should not. In these cases, the WARRANT does not have authority and the CLAIM cannot be accepted and therefore the argument needs to include the QUALIFIER that permissive laws should *usually* (not always) be supported.

Imposition

Another argument pattern that emerges from the data is one which emphasises that laws are imposed on one group by another. The full argument scheme for IMPOSITION is

> The new laws on *x* are imposed upon one group by another (**D**) and laws that are imposed upon one group by another should be supported (**W**) because they force powerful groups to act in different ways to protect the public (**B**). So, usually (**Q**), unless the new laws are imposed on

(vulnerable) citizens or the UK by an external authority (i.e. the European Union) (**R**) the new laws on *x* should be supported (**C**).

This argument comprises 32 collocates of *new law(s)/new legislation* which indicate that the laws (will) force, compel or oblige an imposed-upon group to behave in new or different ways (Table 7.4). In a way, this is somewhat of a misnomer insofar as *all* laws are imposed in one way or another. However, there are clear patterns in the use of this argument in the data. Generally, the CLAIM in this argument is that imposed laws should be supported. The BACKING for the implicit WARRANT that imposed laws should be supported is that these laws will change currently unfavourable or unfair practices and/or are a 'solution' to long-standing or serious social issues. Usually, this is the U.K. government imposing laws which can be seen as taming big, powerful and unwieldy companies and therefore protecting citizens from some sort of current or potentially damaging (mis)behaviour. For example:

16 The Prime Minister will hold meetings early in the new year with retailers and advertisers to 'put a spotlight' on their conduct. If voluntary codes of conduct fail to do enough to protect children, ministers are threatening to legislate and **impose new laws**. (*The Telegraph*, 23 December 2011)

17 In July, Mr Cameron threatened to **impose new laws** on internet giants if they did not blacklist key search terms for such images, as part of a crackdown on online porn. (*The Independent*, 29 March 2014)

18 **New law forces** big firms to come clean on gender pay gap. (*The Times*, 6 April 2017)

19 But now Ministers are being urged to recommend **new laws to require** that photos of innocent members of the public are deleted from the Police National Database. (*Mail on Sunday*, 15 November 2015)

20 Soaring water bills down south are also in Mr Miliband's sights after households were hit with a 3.8 per cent rise, taking the annual charge

Table 7.4 Collocates of *new law(s)/legislation* related to IMPOSITION

Position	*Collocate (frequency)*
L1 verbs	*impose* (48), *enforce* (49), *enforcing* (24)
R1 verbs	*making* (394), *requiring* (380), *forcing* (331), *requires* (157), *makes* (138), *regulating* (68), *make* (63), *imposing* (66), *demanding* (49), *demanded* (42), *compelling* (41), *forces* (40), *mandating* (38), *imposed* (14), *impose* (48), *require* (33), *stating* (25), *obliging* (18), *dictating* (15), *stipulates* (15), *stipulating* (13), *asserting* (7), *designating* (8), *stipulate* (5), *decreeing* (4)
R1 *to* +	*make* (567), *encourage* (46), *require* (38), *compel* (13)

to £388. He plans new laws forcing suppliers to provide special rates for the poorest families. (*The Sun*, 29 September 2013)

These laws target 'retailers and advertisers', 'internet giants', 'big firms', the police and utility suppliers, with the aim of improving the practices and actions of these groups and in doing so increasing the protection of the general public. This is protection from things such as children being exposed to sexualized advertising (16) and online pornography (17), unequal exploitation of women workers (18), unnecessary storage of personal records (19) and poor families from 'soaring' water bills (20). In some cases, such as in (16) and (17), the new laws are weaponised as almost a threat to the agencies involved and are conditional on a change of practices; *if* nothing is done, then new legislation will be introduced. In this way, the government and lawmakers are portrayed as saviours of their citizens. As has been seen with the previous argument schemes, the success of this BACKING and the authority of the WARRANT depend on a consensus that the introduction of these protections is a positive thing. It is quite possible that the subjects of these new laws, the companies and agencies involved, would not be as supportive of these changes.

Imposed laws are not always represented as offering positive change, and this is particularly the case when the new laws are seen to be imposed on the general public, rather than powerful groups, *or* when the laws are being imposed on Britain (or 'us') by an external actor. For example:

21 Labour has long feared Brexit will lead to new laws forcing us to work longer, or curtailing rights. (*MailOnline*, 5 May 2019)
22 A new law compelling immigrants to be able to speak English to join their spouses living in the UK is 'blatantly racially discriminatory', a court has heard. (*The Independent*, 27 July 2011)
23 Downing Street shot down Dr Fox after he opposed a new law forcing us to give away billions more abroad. (*The Sun*, 18 May 2011)
24 The British people should not have new laws imposed from abroad, he will declare, extolling the benefits of leaving the EU's customs union and the single market. (*The Daily Mail*, 13 February 2018)

Any laws that are imposed that have negative effects on individual citizens, be that economic or social (21 and 22 respectively), or that undermine the independence and sovereignty of Britain (23 and 24) should not be supported. In these REBUTTALS, the WARRANT does not hold, and the CLAIM of support cannot be accepted. This, in turn, requires the argument scheme to include the QUALIFIER that imposed laws, at least when being imposed on certain powerful groups, should *usually* be supported.

Toughness

One argument pattern in the data relates to the strictness or toughness of the laws. The full argument scheme for TOUGHNESS is

> The new laws on *x* are tough (**D**) and tough laws should be supported (**W**) because they improve protections and the lives of citizens (**B**). So, usually (**Q**), unless there is evidence that the laws are *too* tough (**R**) the new laws on *x* should be supported (**C**).

There are only five collocates contributing to this argument, and they were all L1 adjectives pre-modifying *new law(s)/new legislation*: *tough* (n = 1931), *strict* (188), *tougher* (78), *harsh* (63) and *stringent* (39). Although this is a much smaller number of collocates than were indicative of the previous argument schemes, *tough* was in fact the most frequent L1 collocate of *new law(s)/new legislation* in the corpus. Overall, the CLAIM of this argument is that the new laws should be supported. The implicit WARRANT that links this CLAIM to the DATA that the laws are tough is therefore that tough laws should be supported. Examples of this argument scheme in the corpus are

25 **TOUGH new laws** to keep kids out of the clutches of evil perverts were announced yesterday. (*The Sun*, 13 January 2000)
26 Terror suspects who skip bail and try to flee Britain could be jailed under **tough new laws** after Jihadi Sid disappeared only to show up in Syria as ISIS's new executioner. (*Daily Mail*, 6 April 2016)
27 Ministers look to impose **tough new legislation** on strikes as thousands of Southern commuters face another day of travel chaos amid mounting anger over the worst rail dispute in a generation. (*Daily Mail*, 14 December 2016)
28 A NEW crackdown on under-aged boozing was welcomed yesterday. Under **tough new legislation** pubs that allow people under 18 to drink could be closed. (*The Sun*, 17 July 2000)

These 'tough' laws will keep children 'out of the clutches of perverts' (25), prevent terror suspects escaping to abroad (26), reduce 'travel chaos' by clamping down on disruptive industrial action (27) and crack down on 'under-age boozing' (28). Again, then, the BACKING supporting the WARRANT in favour of tough laws is that they should be supported because they result in positive change, at least as these newspapers and their readership see it. Their designation as 'tough' indicates an awareness that these laws could be considered problematic by some, however. The law in (25) involves an erosion of people's privacy online, and the law in (26) restricts people's movement overseas. In (27), the legislation in question affects workers' right to industrial action, and the law in (28) could be considered punitive by closing pubs and ruining people's livelihoods. However, the argument here is that the potential benefits outweigh the costs and so the 'toughness' of these laws is justified. With some laws, though, the toughness is not justified, and 'tough' becomes 'strict', 'stringent' and 'harsh':

29 But after a batch of imported squid and shrimp was found to be infected with salmonella four years ago, the EU introduced **stringent new laws** on processing and hygiene. The fishermen preparing the delicacy by traditional methods were unable to comply and the trade died. (*Daily Star*, 12 December 2000)

30 As people are forced outside to have a fag, they claim female drinkers are now being left exposed to violent pill-popping predators. Already a huge number of women each week report the spiking of their drinks. Now care groups fear there will be a huge increase in date rapes because of the **strict new laws**. (*The People*, 4 April 2004)

31 Ministers are set to phase in **harsh new laws** in two stages – despite fears that record numbers of drivers will lose their licenses. Both the RAC and the AA, rapped the move as unnecessary. Britain's accident rate has fallen to the lowest in Europe. (*Daily Star*, 15 February 2001)

In each of these cases, the laws are *too* tough. Although there may be some benefit to these laws, it is their trade-offs that are emphasised. In these examples, these trade-offs are EU laws[3] to reduce the risk of food poisoning resulting in a fishing trade dying (29), no smoking laws resulting in an increased likelihood of women being date raped (30) and road safety laws and punishment being considered punitive given the alleged safety record of British drivers (31). In such cases, the WARRANT that tough laws improve protection for people and make their lives better does not hold – they make people's lives worse. Therefore, the REBUTTAL to this argument is that the benefits do *not* outweigh the costs, and the laws cannot be supported. To take account of this, the argument scheme contains the QUALIFIER that tough new laws should *usually*, not always, be supported.

Necessity

The full argument scheme in relation to NECESSITY is

> The new laws on *x* are necessary (**D**) and necessary laws should be supported (**W**) because they provide new protections for citizens and society that are not provided by current legislation (**B**). So, often (**Q**), unless

current laws are considered to be adequate (**R**) the new laws on *x* should be supported (**C**).

The argument related to the necessity of new legislation is signalled by a total of 19 verb collocates in the corpus (Table 7.5), which represent the DATA in this argument, the presentation of the laws in question as being 'needed' or 'required'. The CLAIM in this pattern is that the new legislation should be supported. The implicit WARRANT is therefore that necessary laws should be supported. The BACKING for this warrant is different in nature from those analysed to this point, insofar as the newspapers rely on expert voices to lend authority and legitimation (van Leeuwen 2008: 102) to the WARRANT. This is achieved by directly or indirectly reporting the words of others who state that new legislation is needed:

32 Steve Goody, director of external affairs at Blue Cross, said: 'The current Dangerous Dogs Act is totally inadequate. We **need new legislation** with tougher measures covering out-of-control dogs wherever they are and whatever the breed, allowing authorities to step in before attacks happen.' (*The Independent*, 17 April 2012)

33 The Justice Secretary Chris Grayling has said we **need new laws** to jail Twitter trolls for two years, four times the current sentence. (*The Independent*, 24 October 2014)

34 'It is fatuous to pretend that elderly laws can cope with modern communications, as Mr Farr convincingly demonstrates. No doubt our intelligence agencies take their legal duties seriously, but the problem is that those legal duties fail to address the 21st century. We **need new laws** to counter new threats, carrying public confidence with them.' (*The Guardian*, 18 June 2014)

35 Home Secretary David Blunkett sensibly **wants new legislation** to ensure that action can be taken against those who incite racism against whites or Moslems. We must endorse his plans, otherwise Britain will

Table 7.5 Collocates of *new law(s)/legislation* related to NECESSITY

Position	*Collocate (frequency)*
L1 verbs	*need* (431), *require* (290), *promised* (187), *wants* (179), *back* (115), *want* (103), *demanded* (93), *support* (85), *demand* (93), *demanding* (69), *backed* (58), *backing* (50), *promising* (36), *requires* (34), *welcomed* (32), *pledged* (40), *recommended* (35), *threatened* (23)
R1 verbs	*needed* (117)

become a breeding ground for the fanaticism which we fear it already harbours. (*The Express*, 1 October 2001)

The BACKING that is offered to support the general authority of this WARRANT is provided by an emphasis on the fact that these laws would or will provide protections for citizens in society that do not currently exist. In (32) a director of an animal welfare charity states that current laws against dangerous dogs are 'totally inadequate' and in (33) the Justice Secretary implores for new laws allowing for more severe sentences, implying current punishments are not enough to deter would-be offenders. Example (34) sees Charles Farr – at the time the director general of the U.K. Office for Security and Counter-Terrorism – and leading military figures emphasise the need for 'new laws as a new response for new threats' (cf. Bossio 2011: 266) in addressing international terrorism. Meanwhile, in (35) the need for new legislation is emphasised by a vision of what would happen if new laws were *not* introduced. Therefore, the laws are necessary because, without them, there is a risk of danger, threat or injustice because there are no (sufficient) laws currently in place.

There is a straightforward REBUTTAL to this argument which undermines the authority of the WARRANT – that the laws are *not* necessary, needed or required. This is a substantial counter-argument in the data; of the 431 instances of *need* as an L1 collocate of *new law(s)/new legislation*, some 125 (29%) are negated with modal verbs such as *didn't, do(es) not/doesn't* and *won't/wouldn't*. Similarly, 67 (21%) of the 290 instances of *require* are negated, for example:

36 But he [Stephen Timms, the School Standards Minister] said: "If someone causes harassment, they can be taken before the courts. We **don't need new legislation**, we just need the will to use the powers that are there". (*The Guardian*, 3 April 2002)

37 The French-born chief executive of the London stock exchange simply wants to see those laws used: 'We **don't need new laws**. It's about serving real sanctions – not a rap on the knuckles – that serve as a warning to the community by using the laws on the statute book.' (*The Times*, 11 August 2014)

38 Broadcasters fear that they are an easy target for campaigners and the Government when compared with Facebook and Google, which also carry advertising for junk food, it added. A pre-watershed ban could be achieved through changes to existing rules **that would not require new laws**. (*The Daily Mail*, 3 March 2019)

As reflected in these examples, new laws are usually considered to be unnecessary when there is a sense that existing laws provide sufficient protection or provision. In that way, the rebutting counter-argument is a reversal of BACKING in the main argument. Either way, the necessity of new legislation appears to be evaluated on the basis of existing law(s). This REBUTTAL is far more frequently observed in the corpus relative to those in the other argument patterns in this analysis, and the QUALIFIER of the CLAIM needs to reflect this. Whereas *usually* has been used to qualify the CLAIM elsewhere, *often* is preferred in this case to signal downgraded authority of the CLAIM in terms of comparative frequencies in this dataset.

Protection

The PROTECTION argument scheme is the only one in this analysis that comprises collocates that are all of the same lemma: *protect* (n = 8), *protecting* (93), *protects* (37) and *to protect* (823). The argument in full is

> The new laws on *x* are protective (**D**) and laws which are protective should be supported (**W**) because they protect people against risk and danger and protect their rights (**B**). So, usually (**Q**), unless the new laws protect people or things who/that do not 'deserve' to be protected (**R**), the new laws on *x* should be supported (**C**).

The CLAIM of this argument is that the new laws should be supported based on the DATA that they are protective, with the implicit WARRANT that laws which are protective should be supported linking the DATA and CLAIM. The BACKING for this warrant relates to *who* is being protected by the laws, with some beneficiaries appearing frequently across the 20 years: *children* (63), *women* (30), *rights* (28), *victims* (19), *workers* (19), *vulnerable (people)* (18), *whistleblowers* (17), *young (people)* and *consumers* (15). New laws are reported as protecting these groups from a range of threats, dangers and injustices, for example:

39 Up to mid-January, the Metropolitan Police had made 129 requests to YouTube to remove videos, of which 102 were taken down. The removal rate has increased sharply since the Government threatened **new laws to protect** children and young people against online harms. (*The Telegraph*, 12 February 2019)

40 It was a good year for **new laws to protect** women. Coercive control was made a criminal action under new legislation that comes into force this week. (*The Telegraph*, 30 December 2015)

41 A MAN committed suicide after running up debts of £130,000 on 22 credit cards, prompting calls from the credit industry for a **new law to protect** vulnerable customers. (*The Telegraph*, 22 January 2005)

As has been seen in other argument schemes, this BACKING relies on a common-sense consensus that these groups *should* be (increasingly) protected from things that cause them harm or risk, such as children from online harm (39), women from coercive partners (40) and vulnerable customers from financial exploitation (41). The positive framing of these new laws is further demonstrated by the evaluation they are afforded. In (39), the new laws are presented as already working in removing potentially harmful content from YouTube, and in (40) the laws are part of a 'good year' for women, while in (41) the new laws are seen as designed to prevent further avoidable suicides due to debt. The argument that these laws are for the common good further strengthens the case that they should be supported, and the BACKING takes the form of emphasising the benefit that the laws will bring.

There are, however, on occasion some people who are *not* deemed deserving of protection, or there are things that, if protected, could lead to negative and unfavourable outcomes. For example:

42 They'll get payouts if attacked by victims; mad **new laws to protect** burglars. (*The Express*, 6 May 2003)

43 Because of its origin, the Act gives rights to individuals against their governments, rather than rights to society against anyone who would undermine it. It is a very potent piece of legislation that **protects the rights of terrorists**, but does nothing to protect us from terrorism. (*The Daily Mail*, 6 October 2007)

44 It is clear that the man was a protester and not a terrorist, so how can these laws have been applicable? We have one of the first examples of how this new legislation will be used to stifle dissent. This legislation was intended to protect the people; in this case it was used to **protect the establishment** against a harmless member of the people. (*The Independent*, 30 September 2005)

In these cases, the implicit argument is that the laws should not be supported because the protection they offer is not of the 'right' things or people, at least in relation to the (assumed) ideological position of the readers to whom they are appealing: burglars, terrorists and 'the establishment'. These then represent examples of REBUTTALS of the WARRANT, and they require the argument to QUALIFY that protective new laws should only *usually* be supported.

Controversy

Throughout the 20-year dataset, a recurring argument is that a new law or new laws are controversial in some way. The CONTROVERSY argument scheme is the only one in which the CLAIM is that the laws should be opposed:

> The new laws on *x* are controversial (**D**) and controversial laws should be opposed (**W**) because they are unfair, erode citizens' rights, or have negative effects on citizens and/or society (**B**). So, usually (**Q**), unless the benefit of those laws can be said to outweigh the costs (**R**) the new laws on *x* should be opposed (**C**).

The collocates that were found to contribute to this argument are all L1 adjectives pre-modifying *new law(s)/new legislation*: *controversial* (n = 524), *radical* (92), *damaging* (28), *contentious* (24) and *daft* (14). The DATA for this argument is that the laws are controversial in some way, and the CLAIM is that the laws should be opposed. The WARRANT which links these is that controversial laws should be opposed. The BACKING for this WARRANT represents the laws as being considered controversial for one of two reasons which can be said to broadly relate to perceptions of 'fairness'. On the one hand, there are those laws that are morally unfair and that, if enacted, would risk taking something from citizens or posing a threat to them. For example:

45 FAMILIES CAN'T STOP DOCTORS TAKING ORGANS; **Controversial new law** on donor cards. (*Daily Mail*, 31 August 2006)
46 A **controversial new law** allowing doctors to use experimental drugs on dying cancer sufferers is set to clear a major Parliamentary hurdle today. (*The Daily Mail*, 3 January 2015)
47 WhatsApp is one of the most popular instant messaging apps in the world, with more than 800 million monthly active users, but **controversial new legislation** could see the app banned in the UK unless the company agrees to give British intelligence agencies access to encrypted communications. (*The Telegraph*, 13 July 2015)

In (45), the new laws on donor cards gave primacy to the deceased's wishes when it comes to donating their organs, with family members losing the right 'to block the removal of organs from loved ones who carried donor cards'. In (46), the law is controversial because opponents claimed that allowing doctors to use experimental drugs to treat cancer did 'not have enough protection for patients'. In (47), the controversy arises from proposed legislation that could see citizens' WhatsApp messages passed to the British government, thus representing a threat to their privacy. All of these examples see citizens apparently being put at risk or having their current rights potentially eroded. The second source of controversy relates to the unfairness of the laws themselves, that they are in some way unjust and not fit for purpose, for example:

48 THE number of roadside speed cameras is likely to double under a **controversial new law** announced yesterday. For the first time, police

chiefs will be given a direct financial interest in trapping as many motorists as possible. (*Daily Mail*, 8 December 2000)

49 Euro judgment day; Murder case couple first to get bail under **controversial new law**. A COUPLE facing a murder charge became the first alleged violent offenders to be freed on bail by a judge under controversial European human rights laws yesterday. (*Daily Mail*, 17 August 2000)

50 SCHOOL chiefs refused to tell an angry mum how her son broke his teeth because of **daft new laws**. Wendy Pearce was told they were restricted by the Freedom of Information Act. (*Daily Star*, 14 September 2005)

51 VIOLENT thugs will receive harsher sentences for assaults on gays than on heterosexuals under **controversial new laws** announced today. (*Daily Mail*, 15 January 2008)

In (48) the new law is presented as being controversial as it is seemingly a mechanism for making money, and in (49) the *Daily Mail* rely on the well-established trope that murderers are not deserving of human rights (Mooney 2002; Gies 2010) and therefore the law is considered controversial. The example in (50) reports a mother who asked to see a copy of the school's accident and injury policy and was told to submit a written request and wait for 20 days as per the Freedom of Information Act. The controversy here seems to be rooted in the belief that this law creates an obstruction for a mother finding out how her son became hurt. Finally, (51) relates to the legislative change in Scotland that saw attacks on gay people become aggravated hate crimes and therefore carry more severe punishments on conviction. The unfairness and controversy here are rooted in the belief, expressed by some politicians at the time, that this would create a 'two-tier' legal system that disadvantaged heterosexual victims. These laws, then, are controversial because they are deemed unfair in some way and are presented as a 'topsy-turvy' version of law and justice that, based on assumed shared beliefs and common-sense understandings, cannot possibly be supported.

That said, the warrant that controversial laws should be opposed does not hold in cases where the perceived or potential negative effects of the laws are outweighed by the benefits that the legislative change will bring. In other words, the 'benefit' is worth the 'cost'. For example:

52 PAEDOPHILES WHO attempt to pick up or 'groom' children on the internet will be jailed under a **controversial new law** to be proposed by the Home Office today. The 'anti-grooming' order is aimed at stopping suspected sex offenders from posing as children or teenagers in chatrooms as a ploy to meet new victims. (*The Independent*, 8 May 2001)

53 THE British government yesterday vowed to push through a <u>**controversial new law**</u> allowing scientists to create embryos mixing human DNA and animal cells. UK's Health Secretary Alan Johnson defended the move saying the embryos could help cure diseases affecting millions of people. (*The Mirror*, 24 March 2008)

54 <u>**Radical new law**</u> making everyone an organ donor unless they opt-out could save 700 per year, the government says. (*The Independent*, 5 August 2018)

In these cases, the controversial nature of these laws is offset (at least to some extent) by the positive changes they could bring and therefore they can be supported. For example, the invasion of privacy involved in monitoring people's internet usage is worth it if it helps to catch paedophiles (52). The same is true of the law that would allow the mix of human and animal cells in (53). Although the article states that some warn that 'mad scientists' are 'mixing animals and humans in Frankenstein-style experiments', readers are told that the change in law could help cure millions of people. Example (54) sees another, more recent, organ donor law hit the news than that in (45) above. This time, the characterisation of the law as 'radical' is quickly followed by the justification that it could save 700 lives per year. Here, then, although these are 'controversial' or 'radical' new laws, there is a justification provided for why one might find the laws legitimate despite their controversial nature. Such examples can be said to offer a REBUTTAL to the WARRANT that controversial laws should be opposed; in some cases, the benefit of the laws outweighs their costs and therefore they can be supported. Ultimately, this requires a QUALIFIER to be added to the argument, that controversial new laws should *usually* be opposed.

Scope

The last of the eight argument schemes to be discussed in this analysis is that relating to SCOPE:

> The new laws on *x* are wide-ranging in their scope (**D**) and laws with a wide-ranging scope should be supported (**W**) because they address a wide range of issues, hold power to account and increase protection of the public (**B**). So, usually (**Q**), unless the new laws go too far in their scope, encroaching on or risking people's rights, freedoms or lives (**R**) the new laws on *x* should be supported (**C**).

The CLAIM of this argument is that the laws should be supported, based on the DATA that they are wide-ranging in scope. The collocates which are the explicit lexical indicators of the DATA relating to the scope of a law are all L1 adjectives: *sweeping* (107), *comprehensive* (33), *ambitious* (18) and *unwieldy* (5). The WARRANT linking the DATA to the CLAIM is that laws which are wide-ranging in scope should be supported. The BACKING that provides support for the authority and acceptability of this WARRANT measures the scope or reach of a law by a range of different means, including the number of issues they intend to address (55), the range of people at whom they are 'targeted' (56), their coverage in relation to a particular issue (57), the number of criminals it affects (58) and the amount of money they will generate (59):

55 TONY Blair yesterday vowed to 'reclaim the streets' from terrorists, thugs and binge drinkers. <u>Sweeping new laws</u> will be introduced to combat everything from alco-pops to al-Qaeda, the PM said. (*The Sun*, 18 May 2005)

56 Hospitals, schools, local authorities and even the police face legal action if they fail to comply with <u>sweeping new laws</u> requiring that all public bodies improve services for the disabled. (*The Times*, 12 December 2006)

57 We are now in touching distance of a <u>comprehensive new law</u> covering every single surveillance power at the disposal of the government – which will have been thoroughly debated in both houses of parliament, including scrutiny of hitherto secret capabilities. (*The Guardian*, 5 November 2015)

58 It prompted Boris Johnson to promise <u>sweeping new laws that</u> will see hundreds of terrorists already in jail locked up for longer. (*Daily Mail*, 5 February 2020)

59 CONSUMERS stand to gain millions of pounds in damages under <u>sweeping new laws</u> designed to crack down on anti-competitive abuses by companies. (*The Times*, 27 March 2002)

As has been observed across the other argument patterns in this analysis, the BACKING for the WARRANT in this argument is provided in the form of explicit detail about the benefits that such laws would bring. In (55), the laws will 'combat' alco-pops and al-Qaeda and everything in between, which is undeniably a broad range of issues that will be addressed. In (56) and (57), the reader is to find solace in the fact that 'even the police' and the government themselves will be subject to new laws, ensuring maximum protection for the public. Example (58) is taken from a news article in the wake of two terrorist attacks in the U.K. in which the attackers had recently been released from prison. The 'sweeping new laws' designed to keep terrorists in prison for longer, then, is presented as a means by which to avoid a similar tragedy in the future. Lastly, in (59), the emphasis is that 'consumers' will be the beneficiaries of the money reclaimed by the new laws. These explicit BACKINGS are provided to support the implicit WARRANT that 'sweeping' or 'comprehensive' new laws provide substantial benefits for society on the basis of their scope.

However, there is evidence in the corpus that the scope of new laws can extend *too far*, at which point the implicit argument is that they cannot be supported. This is usually when they encroach on seemingly unproblematic issues and *deprive* rather than *protect* the public (60), when their extent threatens to set the country off on a so-called legislative 'slippery slope' of increasingly liberal or permissive laws that threaten the lives or rights of citizens (61), or when they are perceived as flagrant power grabs of the government over the public (62):

60 ENJOYING a glass of wine with a picnic could soon be illegal, thanks to **sweeping new laws** being introduced by over-zealous local authorities. (*The Express*, 26 June 2009)
61 The danger now is that a **sweeping new law** on euthanasia and assisted suicide would give the official nod to taking 'any steps which might lead to the death of another citizen'. (*The Times*, 5 February 2008)
62 **SWEEPING new laws** to allow ministers to release the private details of millions of people to a string of public bodies or private firms have been condemned as being 'open sesame to a vast increase in government power'. (*The Independent*, 27 January 2009)

In these cases, the laws are so broad in their scope to the point that they begin to harm rather than protect. The implication is that such laws cannot be supported and therefore circumstances such as these serve as REBUTTALS that mean the WARRANT cannot be accepted. Therefore, the CLAIM must be QUALIFIED, laws wide ranging in scope should *usually*, but not always, be supported.

Summary of argument schemes

The eight argument schemes that have been identified and discussed here are summarised in Table 7.6. Although each argument has been discussed individually in turn here, they are not entirely discrete from one another; for example, laws can be considered controversial because they are imposed, or they can be too tough because their scope spreads too far. One thing that all of these arguments have in common is that the CLAIMS on which they are based all distil down to the new laws should be either supported or opposed. This essentially 'for-or-against' argument may seem crude, but it reflects the largely binary reporting on new laws and legislative changes that has been seen in the previous literature.

The status of these eight arguments as being significant elements of the media discourse around the introduction of new laws in the U.K. is further

Table 7.6 Summary of all eight argument schemes identified

PROHIBITION	The new laws on *x* are prohibitive (D) and laws which are prohibitive should be supported (W) because they prevent things that should be prevented and increase protection for citizens and society (B). So, usually (Q), unless they make people's lives harder, have negative consequences or protect people who do not 'deserve' to be protected, (R) the new laws on *x* should be supported (C).
PERMISSION	The new laws on *x* are permissive (D) and laws which are permissive should be supported (W) because they improve the rights, freedoms and lives of citizens (B). So, usually (Q), unless the new laws give permissions to already powerful actors or to 'undeserving' people, (R) the new laws on *x* should be supported (C).
IMPOSITION	The new laws on *x* are imposed upon one group by another (D) and laws that are imposed upon one group by another should be supported (W) because they force powerful groups to act in different ways to protect the public (B). So, usually (Q), unless the new laws are imposed on (vulnerable) citizens or the UK by an external authority (i.e. the European Union) (R) the new laws on *x* should be supported (C).
TOUGHNESS	The new laws on *x* are tough (D) and tough laws should be supported (W) because they improve protections and the lives of citizens (B). So, usually (Q), unless there is evidence that the laws are *too* tough (R) the new laws on *x* should be supported (C).
NECESSITY	The new laws on *x* are necessary (D) and necessary laws should be supported (W) because they provide new protections for citizens and society that are not provided by current legislation (B). So, often (Q), unless current laws are considered to be adequate (R) the new laws on *x* should be supported (C).
PROTECTION	The new laws on *x* are protective (D) and laws which are protective should be supported (W) because they protect people against risk and danger and protect their rights (B). So, usually (Q), unless the new laws protect people or things who/that do not 'deserve' to be protected (R), the new laws on *x* should be supported (C).
CONTROVERSY	The new laws on *x* are controversial (D) and controversial laws should be opposed (W) because they are unfair, erode citizens' rights, or have negative effects on citizens and/or society (B). So, usually (Q), unless the benefit of those laws can be said to outweigh the costs (R) the new laws on *x* should be opposed (C).
SCOPE	The new laws on *x* are wide-ranging in their scope (D) and laws with a wide-ranging scope should be supported (W) because they address a wide range of issues, hold power to account and increase protection of the public (B). So, usually (Q), unless the new laws go too far in their scope, encroaching on or risking people's rights, freedoms or lives (R) the new laws on *x* should be supported (C).

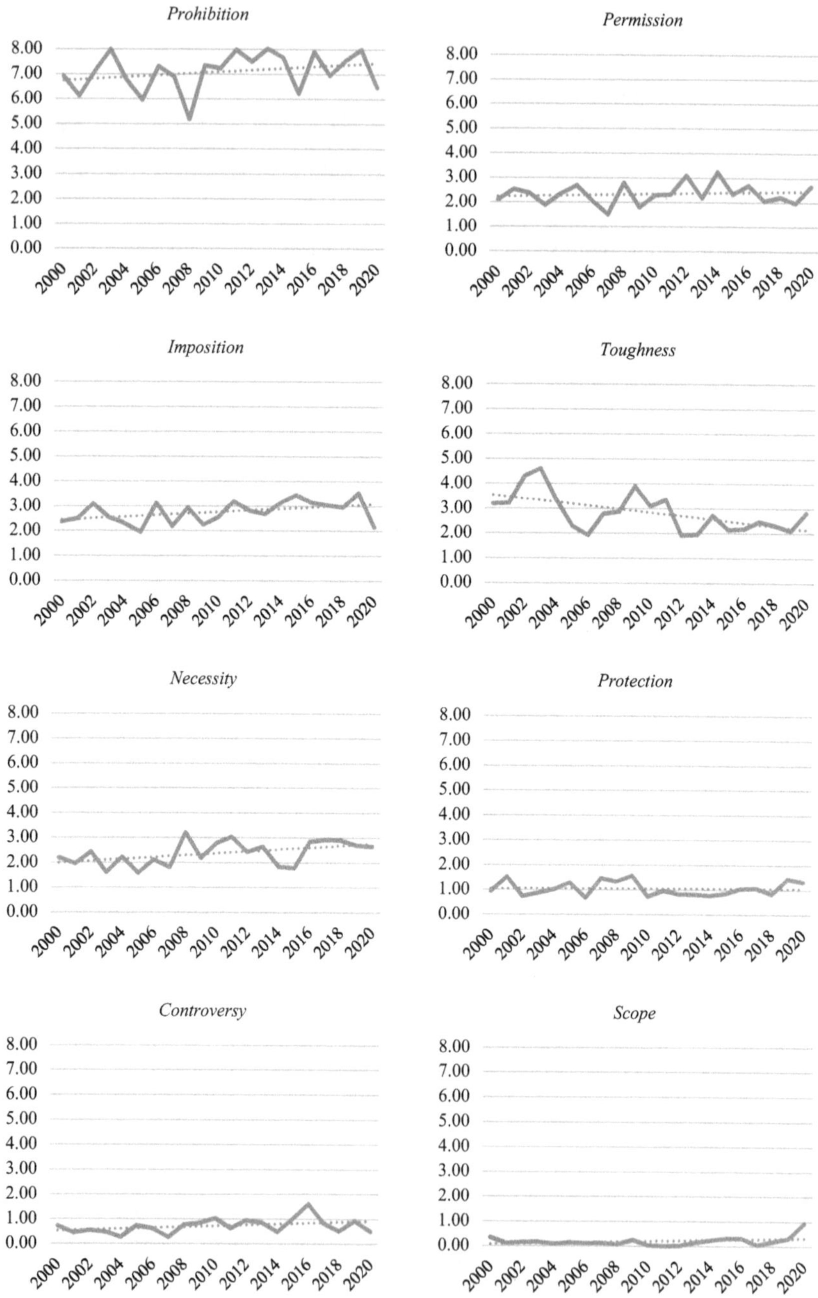

Figure 7.2 The relative frequencies of collocates related to the eight argument types over time as a proportion of all instances of *new law(s)/new legislation*.

supported by three observations relating to their consistency and stability across the corpus. The first is that all eight arguments are present throughout the full 20-year timeframe covered by corpus. Figure 7.2 shows the relative frequency of the collocates related to each of the eight arguments as a proportion of all instances of *new law(s)/new legislation* across the 20 years. Although some are generally more frequent than others (compare, for example, PROHIBITION and SCOPE) and there are fluctuations in frequency from year to year, the trendlines for all eight are relatively flat. Possible exceptions to this are NECESSITY and TOUGHNESS, which see a slight upward and downward trend respectively than the other arguments. This suggests that, over time, new laws are being described more in terms of their necessity and less in terms of their 'toughness' than they once were. The flat trends for the eight arguments suggest that they are stable in their presence in the reporting across the 20 years and have remained relatively consistent fixtures in the British press coverage of new legislation for at least two decades.

Second, it stands to reason that politically right- and left-leaning newspapers will espouse different views about laws on the basis of their different ideological position on the issues at hand (and sometimes even the same law). Despite this, the distribution of the eight arguments is almost identical in the right-learning and left-leaning press. Figure 7.3 shows that when the relative frequency of the sets of collocates associated with each

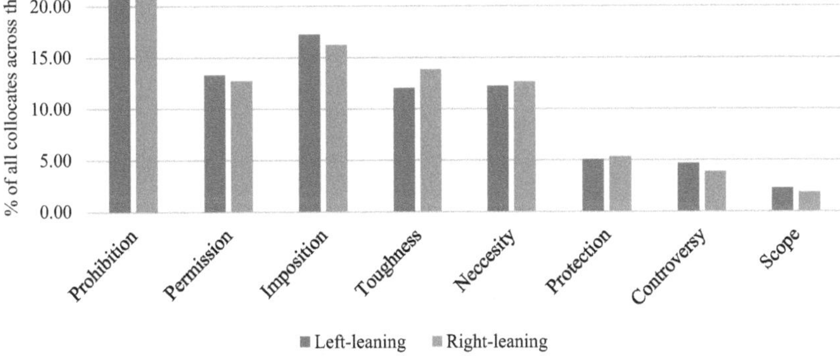

Figure 7.3 Distribution of argument schemes compared across left- and right-leaning newspapers.

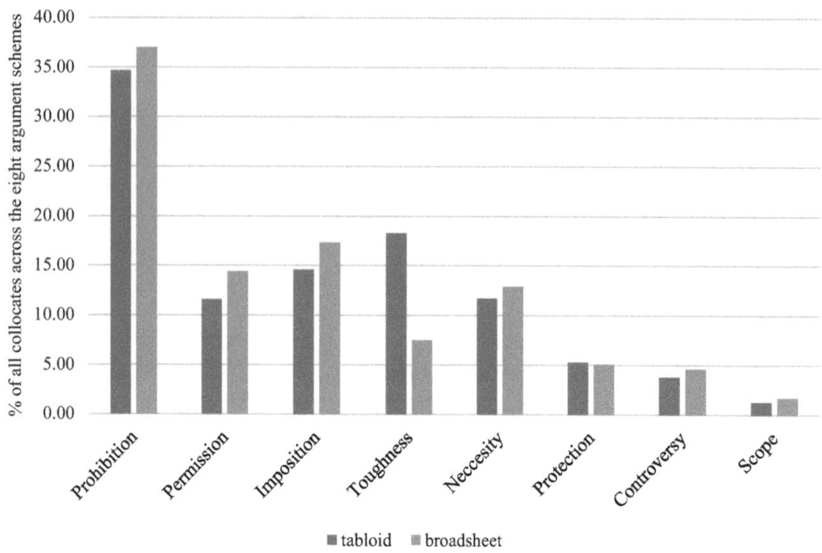

Figure 7.4 Distribution of argument schemes compared across tabloid and broadsheet newspapers.

individual argument scheme is considered as a proportion of *all* collocates for all eight argument schemes, the eight schemes account for almost equal proportions across the right- and left-leaning newspapers. While there might be newspaper-specific differences with regard to particular laws or particular governments of the time, and explorations of that are a ripe area for future research, this indicates that the eight argument patterns explicated here characterise and reflect the national press reporting of new laws *generally*, regardless of the political allegiances or ideological slant of the individual newspapers. Third, the same is true along the tabloid/broadsheet distinction (Figure 7.4). Although the TOUGHNESS argument scheme is more prominent relative to the others in the tabloid newspapers than in the broadsheet ones, the other seven are found in almost equal proportions regardless of newspaper type.

Conclusion

The relationship between law and the media is complex and bidirectional. Media discourse, particularly that in mainstream national newspapers, can influence public support or opposition for new laws and legislative changes proposed or made by the lawmakers of the time. In doing so, newspapers have the power to both reflect and shape readers' beliefs about justice, morality and fairness. The vast majority of previous work concerned with the newspaper coverage of new laws has not been linguistic in focus and has isolated individual laws or legislative proposals related to specific issues and offences and tracked them over time. This chapter aimed to make a corpus linguistic contribution to this space, focusing on the representation of 'new law(s)' and 'new legislation' generally, without a particular interest in certain laws or offences.

The methodological approach taken here has combined collocation analysis with Toulmin's (2003 [1958]) model of argumentation patterns to identify and analyse the ways in which new laws are reported in the British national press. Given the generally persuasive nature of newspaper discourse (cf. Smirnova 2009) and that the media often present legal debates in a binary support-or-oppose way, this chapter has taken the perspective that argumentation is an appropriate way of understanding the discursive representation of legislation in the press. The analysis has found eight overarching 'argument schemes' that British national newspapers have employed when reporting on new laws over the twenty years between 2000 and 2020, which are essentially themes around which their representation hinges: PROHIBITION, PERMISSION, IMPOSITION, TOUGHNESS, NECESSITY, PROTECTION, CONTROVERSY and SCOPE. The corpus was mined (Žagar 2010: 25) to bring markers of content-related arguments to the surface; collocates of *new law(s)/new legislation* were relied on as explicit lexical indicators of potential arguments or patterns of representation. After the eight argument schemes had been identified on the basis of these collocates, Toulmin's model was used in an attempt to reconstruct the arguments in full. The use of Toulmin's model was motivated by the fact that the arguments being made are *implicit*. The model therefore provides a means by which these implicit arguments can be reconstructed by the analyst and made explicit, for the purposes of identifying and analysing (potential) arguments being made regarding new laws. The reconstruction of these arguments by definition relies on a level of analyst subjectivity to make the connections between the different elements of the argument (e.g. DATA, WARRANT, CLAIM), to 'fill the gaps' and make visible the invisible. In this analysis, this subjectivity has been reduced, or delayed, by the use of corpus methods in the first instance. This corpus approach has allowed for the determination of what the 'main' argument is and what the 'rebuttal' to that argument is in each case, based on their relative frequency, which is possible only through a quantitively oriented analysis. The aim here was to provide a range of examples from the corpus for each argument, providing evidence for how they manifest in the reporting.

Every one of the laws that appear in these examples used throughout this chapter could have its own chapter dedicated to it, with a close, nuanced analysis of the supporting and opposing arguments presented over time. However, the aims here were to be broader than that and to find general patterns in the arguments made relating to the new laws and to provide a framework for future linguistic and/or discourse analyses of media representations of the law. It has been found that new laws are discussed on the basis of the behaviours that they prohibit or permit, who are imposing them onto whom, how tough they are perceived as being, how necessary they are in the context of existing legislation, who and what they protect, their scope and reach and the level of controversy they can be considered to bring with them. Depending on the ideological position of a newspaper on a given issue, or the position of the political or stakeholder voices that they represent, arguments can be made to support or oppose a new or proposed piece of legislation. The eight argument schemes outlined here are therefore key spaces in which the debate about new laws takes place across the U.K. press.

A final question remains over the status of this analysis as being 'forensic' or 'legal'. The functional aim of forensic linguistics is to 'improve the delivery of justice through language analysis' (MacLeod and Grant 2017: 173). The analysis presented here has been concerned with understanding the potentially persuasive and ideologically motived mechanisms that are at play when the law is represented in the media. The discourse is argumentative in nature rather than strictly informative, and this has the potential to obstruct or even prevent democratic debate on important social issues. One may argue that deliberately misleading or manipulating the public's perceptions of the law in such a way that they may lose confidence in the justice system, or not have fundamental misunderstandings as to how it works, represents significant barriers to justice, however 'justice' is conceived. The argument schemes outlined in this chapter provide a new way of analysing and understanding the discursive means by which this unfolds in the media.

Notes

1 Megan's Law, enacted in response to the rape and murder of seven-year-old Megan Kanka in New Jersey in 1994, requires law enforcement authorities to make available to the public information on registered sex offenders living in their community. Following a campaign by the parents of Sarah Payne and the media, a similar scheme was established in the U.K. – the Child Sex Offender Disclosure Scheme – referred to as 'Sarah's Law' during the campaign.
2 Some of the language in this example is reflective of the publication date of the first edition of the work in 1958.
3 A full treatment of how EU laws are represented in the British press is a topic best saved for a different book.

References

Bauder, H. (2008) Media discourse and the new German immigration law. *Journal of Ethnic and Migration Studies* 34(1): 95–112. https://doi.org/10.1080/13691830701708783

Bossio, D. (2011) A war about meaning: A case study of media contestation of the Australian anti-terror laws. *Continuum* 25(2): 261–271. https://doi.org/10.1080/10304312.2011.553945

Brezina, V., McEnery, T. and Wattam, S. (2015) Collocations in context: A new perspective on collocation networks. *International Journal of Corpus Linguistics* 20(2): 139–173. https://doi.org/10.1075/ijcl.20.2.01bre

Brubacher, J. R., Desapriya, E., Chan, H., Ranatunga, Y., Harjee, R., Erdelyi, S., Asbridge, M., Purssell, R. and Pike, I. (2015) Media reporting of traffic legislation changes in British Columbia (2010). *Accident Analysis & Prevention* 82: 227–233. https://doi.org/10.1016/j.aap.2015.05.022

Cormacain, R. (2020) Keeping Covid-19 emergency legislation socially distant from ordinary legislation: principles for the structure of emergency legislation. *The Theory and Practice of Legislation* 8(3): 245–265. https://doi.org/10.1080/20508840.2020.1786272

Critcher, C. (2002) Media, government and moral panic: the politics of paedophilia in Britain 2000-1. *Journalism Studies* 3(4): 521–535. https://doi.org/10.1080/14616700220000019182

Domke, D., Graham, E. S., Coe, K., Lockett John, S. and Coopman, T. (2006) Going public as political strategy: the Bush administration, an echoing press, and passage of The Patriot Act. *Political Communication* 23(3): 291–312. https://doi.org/10.1080/10584600600808844

Ducat, L., Thomas, S. and Blood, W. (2009) Sensationalising sex offenders and sexual recidivism: impact of the Serious Sex Offender Monitoring Act 2005 on media reportage. *Australian Psychologist* 44(3): 156–165. https://doi.org/10.1080/00050060903127499

Durrant, P. and Doherty, A. (2010) Are high-frequency collocations psychologically real? Investigating the thesis of collocational priming. *Corpus Linguistics and Linguistic Theory* 6(2): 125–155. https://doi.org/10.1515/cllt.2010.006

Gies L. (2003) Explaining the absence of the media in stories of law and legal consciousness. *Entertainment Law* 2(1): 19–54. https://doi.org/10.16997/eslj.147

Gies, L. (2005) Law as popular culture: cross-disciplinary encounters. *Continuum* 19(2): 165–180. https://doi.org/10.1080/10304310500084376

Gies, L. (2007) *Law and the Media: The Future of an Uneasy Relationship*. London: Routledge.

Gies, L. (2010) The hard sell: promoting human rights. *International Journal for the Semiotics of Law* 24: 405–422. https://doi.org/10.1007/s11196-010-9186-5

Hart, C. (2010) *Critical Discourse Analysis and Cognitive Science: New Perspectives on Immigration Discourse*. Basingstoke: Palgrave Macmillan.

Hilton, S., Buckton, C. H., Patterson, C., Katikireddi, S. V., Lloyd-Williams, F., Hyseni, L., Elliott-Green A. and Capewell, S. (2019) Following in the footsteps of tobacco and alcohol? Stakeholder discourse in UK newspaper coverage of the Soft Drinks Industry Levy. *Public Health Nutrition* 22: 2317–2328. https://doi.org/10.1017/s1368980019000739

Hrywna, M., Singh, B., Wackowski, O. A., Hudson, S. V., Delnevo, C. D. (2022) Can states continue to set the agenda for Tobacco 21? Insights from U.S. News Coverage between 2012–2020. *Nicotine & Tobacco Research* 24(8): 1305–1309. https://doi.org/10.1093/ntr/ntac025

Hunston, S. (2002) *Corpora in Applied Linguistics* (1st ed.). Cambridge, UK: Cambridge University Press.

Jansson, K. (2015) Public confidence in the Criminal Justice System – findings from the Crime Survey for England and Wales (2013/14). Report by the Ministry of Justice. Crown Copyright. Accessible online: https://assets.publishing.service.

gov.uk/government/uploads/system/uploads/attachment_data/file/449444/public-confidence.pdf

Juska, A. (2021) A shift to libertarian paternalism in old-age income security: discourses on pension privatization reforms in Lithuania 2016–2018. *International Social Security Review* 74(2): 3–27. https://doi.org/10.1111/issr.12263

Kienpointner, M. (1992) *Alltagslogik. Struktur und Funktion von Argumentationsmustern*. Stuttgart-Bad Cannstatt: frommann-holzboog.

Kienpointner, M. (1996) *Vernünftig Argumentieren. Regeln und Techniken der Argumentation*. Reinbek bei Hamburg: Rowohlt.

MacLeod, N. and Grant, T. (2017) 'go on cam but dnt be dirty': linguistic levels of identity assumption in undercover online operations against child sex abusers. *Language and Law/ Linguagem e Direito* 4(2): 157–175.

McGinty, E. E., Samples, H., Bandara, S. N., Saloner, B., Bachhuber, M. A. and Barry, C. L. (2016) The emerging public discourse on state legalization of marijuana for recreational use in the US: analysis of news media coverage, 2010-2014. *Preventive Medicine* 90: 114–120. https://doi.org/10.1016/j.ypmed.2016.06.040

Meyer, A. (2010) Evil monsters and cunning perverts: representing and regulating the dangerous paedophile. In M. Deflem (ed.), *Popular Culture, Crime and Social Control*. Bingley: Emerald Publishing, pp. 195–218.

Mooney, A. (2002) Human rights, linguistics and the law: the UK and beyond. *International Journal for the Semiotics of Law* 15: 389–398. https://doi.org/10.1023/A:1021207630059

Pallin, R., Aubel, A. J., Knoepke, C. E., Pear, V. A., Wintemute, G. J., Kravitz-Wirtz, N. (2021) News media coverage of extreme risk protection order policies surrounding the Parkland shooting: a mixed-methods analysis. *BMC Public Health* 21: 1–13. https://doi.org/10.1186/s12889-021-11909-z

Paterson, L. L. and Coffey-Glover, L. (2018) Discourses of marriage in same-sex marriage debates in the UK press 2011-2014. *Journal of Language and Sexuality* 7(2): 175–204. https://doi.org/10.1075/jls.17022.pat

Reisigl, M. (2014) Argumentation analysis and the Discourse-Historical Approach. A methodological framework. In C. Hart and P. Cap (eds.), *Contemporary Critical Discourse Studies*. London: Bloomsbury, pp. 211–236.

Reisigl, M. and Wodak, R. (2001) *Discourse and Discrimination: Rhetorics of Racism and Antisemitism*. London: Routledge.

Reisigl, M. and Wodak, R. (2016) The discourse-historical approach (DHA) In R. Wodak and M. Meyer (eds.), *Methods of Critical Discourse Studies* (3rd ed.). London: SAGE, pp. 23–61.

Rheindorf, M. (2019) *Revisiting the Toolbox of Discourse Studies: New Trajectories in Methodology, Open Data, and Visualization*. Basingstoke: Palgrave.

Richardson, J. (2004) *(Mis)Representing Islam: The Racism and Rhetoric of British Broadsheet Newspapers*. Amsterdam/Philadelphia: Benjamins.

Schindel, T. J. and Given, L. M. (2013) The pharmacist as prescriber: a discourse analysis of newspaper media in Canada. *Research in Social & Administrative Pharmacy* 9(4): 384–395. https://doi.org/10.1016/j.sapharm.2012.05.014

Shelby, R. M. and Hatch, A. R. (2014) Obscuring sexual crime: examining media representations of sexual violence in Megan's law. *Criminal Justice Studies* 27(4): 402–418. https://doi.org/10.1080/1478601X.2014.928459

Smirnova, A. V. (2009) Reported speech as an element of argumentative newspaper discourse. *Discourse & Society* 3(1): 79–103. https://doi.org/10.1177/1750481308098765

Smith, H. M., Smith, J. W., Silka, L., Lindenfeld, L., and Gilbert, C. (2016) Media and policy in a complex adaptive system: insights from wind energy legislation in the United States. *Energy Research & Social Science* 19: 53–60. https://doi.org/10.1016/j.erss.2016.05.016

Smith, M. (2017) How left or right-wing are the UK's newspapers? *The Times*. (online). 06 March 2017. Available from: https://www.thetimes.co.uk/article/how-left-or-right-wing-are-britain-s-newspapers-8vmlr27tm [Last accessed 25 March 2022].

Toulmin, S. E. (2003) *The Uses of Argument*. Cambridge, UK: Cambridge University Press. (1st ed. 1958).

Trubek, D. M. (1984) Where the action is: critical legal studies and empiricism. *Stanford Law Review* 36(1/2): 575–622.

Turner, G., Mills, S., van der Bom, I., Coffey-Glover, L., Paterson, L. L. and Jones, L. (2018) Opposition as victimhood in media debates about same-sex marriage. *Discourse & Society* 29(2): 180–197. https://doi.org/10.1177/0957926517734422

van Dijk, T. A. (2000) "On the analysis of parliamentary debates on immigration". In M. Reisigl and R. Wodak (eds.), *The Semiotics of Racism. Approaches in Critical Discourse Analysis*. Vienna: Passagen Verlag, pp. 65–84.

van Leeuwen, T. (2008) *Discourse and Practice: New Tools for Critical Discourse Analysis*. Oxford: Oxford University Press.

Wodak, R. (2012) Politics as usual. Investigating political discourse in action. In J. P. Gee and M. Handford (eds.), *The Routledge Handbook of Discourse Analysis*. London: Routledge, pp. 525–540.

Wright, D. and Brookes, G. (2019) 'This is England, speak English!': a corpus-assisted critical study of language ideologies in the right-leaning British press. *Critical Discourse Studies* 16(1): 56–83. https://doi.org/10.1080/17405904.2018.1511439

Žagar, I.Ž. (2010) Topoi in critical discourse analysis. *Lodz Papers in Pragmatics* 6(1): 3–27. https://doi.org/10.2478/v10016 010-0002-1

8 Conclusion

This book captures a snapshot of time during a period in which corpora and corpus linguistic methods are becoming increasingly popular and prevalent in forensic and legal linguistics. Even during the time that it has taken to write this book, several articles and chapters have been published that apply corpus linguistics in specific forensic and legal contexts. I have attempted to incorporate as many of these as possible here but will have inevitably missed some, not to mention those that are currently in preparation and will be published as or after this book becomes available. Nevertheless, it is hoped that this book has represented the ways in which corpus linguistics has transformed from being a potentially useful methodological tool for forensic and legal linguists, as proposed by Coulthard (1994), to being one of the most established and widely used methodologies in the discipline. Corpus linguistics is found in every corner of forensic and legal linguistics and, more importantly, at every boundary. It is a driving force in pushing where those boundaries are, whether that is related to increasing and improving the knowledge that we have about discourse in a certain legal or forensic context, overcoming previous limitations or restrictions on access to certain types of data, or producing brand-new areas for research within the scope of forensic and legal linguistics. Corpus approaches are not only sustaining large parts of the discipline; they are allowing them to thrive.

At the same time, corpus linguistics has and will change over time. New tools will become available, and new facilities will be added to existing tools. This will allow forensic and legal linguists to manipulate, analyse and interpret their data in new ways, producing types of analysis that it may not be possible to foresee at the moment. In particular, corpus-assisted discourse studies, as applied in this book, is going through somewhat of a reflective period, with research looking inward and identifying ways in which the methods and processes associated with the approach can be improved, made more reliable or transparent (e.g. Rheindorf 2019; Gillings and Mautner 2024; Bednarek et al. 2024).

DOI: 10.4324/9781003017301-8

Forensic and legal linguists stand to benefit from these reflections and improvements, but they can also play an important role in them. As detailed in Chapter 2, forensic and legal linguists often by necessity have to overcome challenges in data availability, data collection and data ethics that may be particular, or particularly pronounced, in the types of data they work with as specialised corpora. The processes and principles that forensic and legal linguists follow can offer examples of good practice for other corpus linguists dealing with similar data and for those whose area of study is not legal or forensic but nevertheless face similar challenges. At the same time, forensic and legal linguists can lead the way in developing and applying new methods of corpus-assisted discourse analysis to the discourses and contexts that they explore. This has been attempted in this book, with corpus linguistic techniques being combined with or embedded into discourse analytic theories and frameworks of positioning, stance, discourse prosody and argumentation.

Making predictions about the future direction of a discipline or subdiscipline is on the one hand very easy and on the other hand very difficult. It is easy because certain things are predictable; people are going to continue to use corpus methods in forensic and legal contexts, for instance. It is difficult because certain things are difficult or impossible to predict. It is in this context that I make the following three projections.

First, claims of data scarcity in corpus-based forensic and legal linguistics research will (or should) subside. As this book has shown and has presented in its own analysis chapters, corpora and corpus methods are widely and fruitfully applied across the entire field. Therefore, it seems unnecessary to bemoan the lack of data for much longer. This does come with some significant caveats, however. Some areas of institutional discourse, such as police interviews, are likely to remain largely inaccessible and rightly so. Similarly, those working in forensic casework are always going to be bound by the circumstances of the case in terms of how much data or evidence they have access to; in addition, they are not suddenly going to be permitted to release and publish that evidence in academic work. However, some areas of legal discourse for which it has traditionally been difficult to access data are showing signs of becoming more accessible. For example, the recording and broadcasting of sentencing remarks in serious high-profile cases in England and Wales in 2022 was heralded by some as the start of the 'opening up' of the criminal justice system (Daw 2022). If and when criminal courtroom proceedings become more accessible to the public in the interests of open justice and public confidence in the system, this would provide the linguist with new sources of data. At the same time, however, it is the responsibility of the analysts themselves to find a way. That is, time does need to be spent overcoming the challenges involved in accessing certain data types, or as has been advocated and demonstrated in this book, alternative sources of data can be used, whether that be quasi-legal genres (Chapter 4), seizing opportunistic releases of data (Chapter 5), relying on certain forensically relevant parts of the 'clear web' (Chapter 6) or focusing on language data *about* the law, from the outside looking in (Chapter 7).

Second, the benefits of corpus linguistics will become increasingly clear to, and welcomed by, those outside of linguistics and outside of academia. On the one hand, this will result in greater interdisciplinary collaboration in forensic and legal research and practice. This is already happening in some areas, such as research in statutory interpretation where linguists are working with lawyers to develop new methodologies (e.g. Egbert and Lee 2024; Gries et al. 2024), as well as in multidisciplinary projects on witness cross-examination (e.g. Jackson et al. 2024). On the other hand, this will also lead to new opportunities for linguists to collaborate with external partners in law enforcement, (inter)national security and the criminal justice system. Forensic and legal linguists often work in areas that have direct applications to professional practice and can make a significant contribution to addressing serious challenges. Again, this is already happening in some areas, such as in the investigation of online grooming (Grant and MacLeod 2020; Lorenzo-Dus et al. 2023). As the profiles of both corpus and forensic/legal linguistics become more widely known to other academic and scientific disciplines and to those outside of academia, new areas of research and application will emerge.

The third and final prediction is partially an inevitable result of the previous two. It is likely that, over time, the boundaries, scope and remit of 'forensic' and 'legal' linguistics will change. It is probably reasonable to assume that when writing 30 years ago, Malcolm Coulthard (1994) would not have envisaged the rate at which forensic linguistics would grow in subsequent years, the directions that it would take and the topics, tasks and issues that would fall under its purview. There is no reason to suspect that the next 30 years will not see a similar transformation. However, as far as corpus linguistics goes, its methods and processes are far more well known and well established than they were in 1994, when Coulthard was writing. Therefore, it is likely that the rate of change in the next few decades will be quicker and more significant than we have previously seen. As a community, forensic and legal linguists should be prepared to see the scope of the discipline expand and potentially look very different, very soon. Corpus linguistics is sure to be a main character in that story.

References

Bednarek, M., Schweinberger, M. and Lee, K. (2024) Corpus-based discourse analysis: from meta-reflection to accountability. *Corpus Linguistics and Linguistic Theory*. https://doi.org/10.1515/cllt-2023-0104

Coulthard, M. (1994) On the use of corpora in the analysis of forensic texts. *The International Journal of Speech, Language and the Law* 1(1): 27–43. https://doi.org/10.1558/ijsll.v1i1.27

Daw, C. (2022) Allow TV full access to our courtrooms and justice will truly be seen to be done. *The Observer* (online) 31 July 2022. Available at: https://www.theguardian.com/commentisfree/2022/jul/31/allow-tv-full-access-to-our-courtrooms-and-justice-will-truly-be-seen-to-be-done (last accessed April 2024).

Egbert, J. and Lee, T. R. (2024) Prototype-by-component analysis: A corpus-based, intensional approach to ordinary meaning in statutory interpretation. *Applied Corpus Linguistics* 4(1): 1–9. https://doi.org/10.1016/j.acorp.2023.100078

Gillings, M. and Mautner, G. (2024) Concordancing for CADS: practical challenges and theoretical implications. *International Journal of Corpus Linguistics* 29(1): 34–58. https://doi.org/10.1075/ijcl.21168.gil

Grant, T. and MacLeod, N. (2020) *Language and Online Identities: The Undercover Policing of Internet Sexual Crime*. Cambridge, UK: Cambridge University Press.

Gries, S. T., Slocum, B. G. and Tobia, K. (2024) Corpus-linguistic approaches to lexical statutory meaning: extensionalist vs. intensionalist approaches. *Applied Corpus Linguistics* 4(1): 1–14. https://doi.org/10.1016/j.acorp.2023.100079

Jackson, J., Doak, J., Saunders, C., Wright, D. and Cooper, D. (2024) *Mapping the Changing Face of Cross-Examination in Criminal Trials*. Publicly available report for the Nuffield Foundation. https://doi.org/10.17631/rd-2024-0001-drep

Lorenzo-Dus, N., Evans, C. and Mullineux-Morgan, R. (2023) *Online Child Grooming Discourse*. Cambridge, UK: Cambridge University Press.

Rheindorf, M. (2019) *Revisiting the Toolbox of Discourse Studies: New Trajectories in Methodology, Open Data, and Visualization*. Basingstoke: Palgrave.

Index

FSC
www.fsc.org
MIX
Papier | Fördert gute Waldnutzung
FSC® C083411

Kolibri 360 GmbH
Ferdinand-Jühlke-Straße 7
99095 Erfurt, Deutschland
produktsicherheit@kolibri360.de